Hindus

'In this major study of Hindu beliefs and practices, Julius Lipner deliberately adopts an informal style, in order to engage in an exploratory conversation with the reader, and his own fascination with the subject does indeed come over in an infectious manner.'

Dr J. L. Brockington, University of Edinburgh

'*Hindus* provides interesting and unusual information as well as illuminating insights to experts on India. The work is literate and humorous, informed and respectful, well-documented and reliable – in short it makes fascinating reading and admirably covers all the important bases.'

Professor Klaus Klostermaier, University of Manitoba

'The book is a remarkably sophisticated survey of Hindu beliefs and practices . . . *Hindus* succeeds admirably in its task, in conveying the richness, complexity, fluidity and struggles of a vast and vibrant tradition. The author must be congratulated for writing a book of sustained erudition and empathy.'

Professor Arvind Sharma, *Religion*

'*Hindus* is the fruit of personal reflection and extensive study on many aspects of the tradition, and on the ways in which it has been represented in the modern world, both in India and in the West. It is particularly concerned to show the exuberant Hindu love of life.'

Dr Dermot Killingley, *The Journal of the Royal Asiatic Society*

'This is quite simply the best book I have read on Hinduism in a long time. I say this conscious of the weight of all the books on the subject I have gone through . . . over the last four decades. . . . Every topic . . . is treated lucidly, incisively, often wittily. . . . So many facts, concepts, theories are thus brought in to illuminate the main arguments that the book is virtually a small encyclopedia of Hinduism.'

Girish Karnad, *The Book Review*

'Lipner weaves together various themes, ideas and stories so as to lead the reader into an understanding of Hindus in a radial and spiral rather than linear fashion. The result is a fresh and most engaging presentaton of the tradition that communicates well to those of other traditions while it brings new insights to Hindus about their own religion. This book has a permanent place on my shelf.'

Professor Harold Coward, *The Hindu-Christian Studies Bulletin*

'*Hindus* is lucidly written and as readable as it is informative. . . . Throughout the book, the emphasis is on understanding the true spirit of this ancient religion and Lipner succeeds admirably in his endeavour to acquaint the reader with the positive force he calls the "dynamic, living reality" of Hinduism.'

Veena Seshadri, *The Indian Review of Books*

Julius Lipner was born and raised in India, where he experienced and learned about Hinduism first hand. He lectures in Religious Studies in the Faculty of Divinity at the University of Cambridge and is the author of a number of books including *The Face of Truth: A Study of Meaning and Metaphysics in the Vedāntic Theology of Rāmānuja* and *Hindu Ethics: Purity, Abortion and Euthanasia* (co-authored with H. Coward and K. Young).

The Library of Religious Beliefs and Practices
Series editors:
John Hinnells *University of Manchester* and
Ninian Smart *University of California at Santa Barbara*

This series provides pioneering and scholarly introductions to different religions in a readable form. It is concerned with the beliefs and practices of religions in their social, cultural and historical setting. Authors come from a variety of backgrounds and approach the study of religious beliefs and practices from their different points of view. Some focus mainly on questions of history, teachings, customs and ritual practices. Others consider, within the context of a specific region or geographical region, the interrelationships between religions; the interaction of religion and the arts; religion and social organisation; the involvement of religion in political affairs; and, for ancient cultures, the interpretation of archaeological evidence. In this way the series brings out the multi-disciplinary nature of the study of religion. It is intended for students of religion, ideas, social sciences and history, and for the interested lay person.

Other titles in the series include:

Religions of Oceania
Tony Swain and *Garry Trompf*

Theravāda Buddhism
A Social History from Ancient Benares to Modern Colombo
Richard Gombrich

Mahāyāna Buddhism
Paul Williams

Muslims
Their Religious Beliefs and Practices
Vol. 1: The Formative Period
Vol. 2: The Contemporary Period
Andrew Rippin

Religions of South Africa
David Chidester

Hindus

Their religious beliefs and practices

Julius Lipner

ROUTLEDGE
London and New York

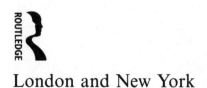

First published 1994
by Routledge
11 New Fetter Lane, London EC4P 4EE

Simultaneously published in the USA and Canada
by Routledge
29 West 35th Street, New York, NY 10001

First published in paperback 1998

Typeset in Times by J&L Composition Ltd, Filey, North Yorkshire
Printed and bound in Great Britain by
Mackays of Chatham PLC, Chatham, Kent

British Library Cataloguing in Publication Data
A catalogue record for this book is available from the British Library

Library of Congress Cataloguing in Publication Data
Lipner, Julius.
Hindus: their religious beliefs and practices/Julius Lipner.
p. cm.
Includes bibliographical references and index.
1. Hinduism. I. Title.
BL1202.L56 1994 93-3813

ISBN 0-415-05181-9 (hbk)
ISBN 0-415-05182-7 (pbk)

This book is dedicated to the memory of my brother in law, Pradeep Kumar Neogy (1950–93), who will be sadly missed.

Life is the roll of a wave, youth's beauty endures but a day,
Wealth takes fancy's form, and pleasure's flow is like monsoon's lightning-flash,
Even love's embrace by loved ones offered does not last.
So fix your minds on Brahman, to reach life's dreadful ocean's further shore.

(From the *Fine Sayings* of Bhartṛhari)

Contents

Preface

It was some years ago, during dinner at a conference in Canada I recall, that John Hinnells asked me if I would 'like to write a book on Hinduism'.

'Perhaps,' I replied warily. 'But I already have a number of things on my plate, so to speak. Anyway, tell me what you have in mind.'

He told me.

'It's for this series we're editing. I want a book to cover Hinduism, but I don't want it to do so chronologically in the usual way. I want it to be different. I want it to deal with essentials of Hindu religion, of course, but not only from the point of view of belief; it's got to tell us how Hindus practise their faith. And it must have a scholarly foundation,' he added, warming to his theme.

I paled at the prospect.

'This book on Hinduism,' he went on remorselessly, 'must be rooted in the historical tradition. It's got to have a historical perspective. Otherwise things hang in the air. And bring in your own experience here and there. Tell us the odd story, anecdote, etc. That makes for interesting reading, you know. Also, try and draw in the religion of ordinary folk in the towns and villages, and what they call the little tradition,' he added. 'Tradition*s*,' he corrected himself. 'And oh! I'd like it done in a couple of years, if possible. Well, what do you say?'

I was horrified. A book on Hinduism – a complex, multi-faceted, intractable phenomenon spanning over three thousand years – fitting this description would be a Herculean task. It would be madness to accept.

I accepted. And I've had second thoughts ever since. But it's been an instructive and salutory experience. I've had a chance to collect my thoughts on a great and marvellous religious phenomenon in mid-career, to appreciate even more its extraordinary richness, the way it encompasses human experience from the sublime to the ridiculous, to realise anew how much I didn't know.

You will have to judge how badly I've succeeded. I have been constrained not only by the magnitude of my task, but inevitably by limitations of space and time. Here I must thank John Hinnells and Heather Gibson at Routledge for fighting valiantly on my part to win me rather more space and time than was originally apportioned.

My approach has been mainly historical and phenomenological but also philosophical; occasionally I've made other kinds of comments (sociological, anthropological) on my material. I have refrained, on the whole, from sustained analysis of philosophical-theological doctrine; there has been too much to do at the level of basic explanation. My approach has also been 'radial'; that is, rather than attempting to have my say on a particular topic (e.g. the status of women) in only one place in the book, I've returned to themes on more than one occasion but from different angles. So on a number of points the effect will be cumulative. I have also tried to give my approach a narrative quality, not only by telling and, hopefully, communicating through stories (an extended example of this can be found in Chapter 8: it is only by leading the reader at some length through the story that my point can be made), but also by trying to do justice to the story of the Hindu phenomenon itself. This story does not lead to some resounding climax; rather, if I've understood its modality correctly, the Hindu narrative, in the complexity of its plots and sub-plots, proceeds radially and spirally, on and on. I hope something of this will emerge from a reading of this book. It is for this reason that my style is on the whole informal. I have found it congenial to engage in an exploratory conversation with the reader, which brings me to readership.

A chief aim of this book is to introduce the serious undergraduate and the reflective layperson to the phenomenon of religious Hinduism. Some of the discussions may be found to be intellectually exacting; but it is hoped that this will stimulate further study. Further, the book is intended to work on several levels. For various reasons, as all teachers of Hindu religion know, it is the nature of such 'introductory' books to be perused no less by scholars and advanced students. I hope I have something of significance to say to these interested parties too. Passages and themes of the book can be taken up for seminar or classroom discussion, for challenging enquiry in the form of essays or research (e.g. the relationship between language and reality in Hindu thought, the status of the female in social and theological contexts, the discipline of visualisation in Hindu worship, the role of canonical texts as authoritative, counter-Vedic modes of striving for salvation). There remains much to pursue; it is impossible to be exhaustive in the writing of such a book.

For reasons given in the book, I have concentrated on the 'Sanskritic tradition',[1] though as requested, I have sought in various places to consider instructively non-Sanskritic or semi-Sanskritic forms of Hinduism. But I have not drawn in those who are still the *populi ignoti*, the unknown peoples, of India at large – the so-called *adivasis* or original tribal inhabitants. Generally they are not regarded as Hindus, though no doubt they may be more or less Hinduised. A word here about what may be perceived as the 'Bengal bias' of the book. First, if there is such, I do not believe it is intrusive; second, I would regard it as a strength rather than as a weakness. Such specificity can help earth the book, and can throw into relief the interplay between similarity and difference in the multi-faceted phenomenon that is 'Hinduism'.

Because the serious reader is interested in seeing how my thoughts no less than the tradition relate to the original language, I have interposed, inevitably arbitrarily to some extent, the relevant Sanskrit terms in the text. I have added a select glossary and a list of abbreviations of titles, etc. mentioned in the text for ready reference. I hope the detailed contents descriptions at the beginning of each chapter will be helpful to the reader in following my train of thought. Realism has prompted me to confine the select bibliography exclusively to material in English. Unless specified to the contrary, all translations are my own. The names of modern people and current places have not been given diacriticals, and are referred to by their conventional spellings. Finally, I wish to record my thanks to the anonymous reader of the typescript, for the nice things said and the many valuable suggestions made. The latter have certainly borne fruit in a better book, though final responsibility for what's been written must remain mine, of course.

For various reasons, not least because of its length, this book was much delayed through publication. Again, many thanks to John Hinnells and Heather Gibson for expedition, encouragement and support. And special thanks to my students, wave after wave of them, for their interest and enthusiasm and questions. That helped greatly. The dedication speaks for itself.

Julius Lipner
Cambridge

Preface to the paperback edition

I am grateful that this book, first published as a hardback four years ago, is now being brought out in a paperback version. I have taken the opportunity to correct a number of typographical and other errors, and, within the strict constraints imposed by the publisher not to increase the length of an already big book, to make small but I hope significant changes to reflect the current position of a particular ongoing debate: that about the origins of the so-called Aryan/Vedic civilisation. Did this culture originate outside the subcontinent or was it essentially indigenous? Both sides of this debate, it seems to me, have more to do to establish their positions and, indeed, to take account of their opponents' points of view. The matter is still to be decided, though I incline to the received view that the early religion of the Vedas was not substantially formulated in the subcontinent. At present the debate is too ideological for comfort; more must be done on a scholarly basis, combining archaeological, textual and other evidence, to make the picture clearer.

The photograph on the cover depicts very well the theme of the 'polycentric' Ancient Banyan of Hinduism that runs through this book.

Abbreviations

AEV:	*Aspects of Early Viṣṇuism* (Gonda 1954)*
AV:	*Atharva* Veda
BAUp:	*Bṛhadāraṇyaka* Upaniṣad
BCE:	Before the Common Era
BCL:	*Banaras: City of Light* (Eck 1983)*
CE:	Of the Common Era
ChāndUp:	Chāndogya Upaniṣad
EA:	*Śiva: The Erotic Ascetic* (O'Flaherty 1981)*
FOT:	*The Face of Truth* (Lipner 1986)*
HIL:	*A History of Indian Literature* (Gonda 1975)*
HML:	*Hindu Monastic Life* (Miller and Wertz 1976)*
HT:	*Hindu Tantrism* (Gupta *et al.* 1979)*
IAA:	'Indo-Aryan and Aryan' (Allchin 1990)*
KathUp:	*Kaṭha* Upaniṣad
KauUp:	Kausītaki Upaniṣad
Mbh:	The Mahābhārata
MaitrīUp:	Maitrī Upaniṣad
Manu:	The *Manu Smṛti* (Doniger with Smith 1991)*
NCW:	*A Net Cast Wide* (Lipner with Killingley 1986)*
OEHM:	*The Origins of Evil in Hindu Mythology* (O'Flaherty 1976/1980)*
PPP:	'The Purāṇas – priestly or popular?' (Brockington 1987)*
RV:	*Ṛg* Veda
SBE:	*Sacred Books of the East* Series, ed. Max Müller
SBR:	*Srī Bhāṣya* of Rāmānujāchārya
SF:	*The Sword and the Flute* (Kinsley 1977)*
SH:	*A Survey of Hinduism* (Klostermaier 1989)*
SSDT:	*The Sants: Studies in a Devotional Tradition of India* (Schomer and McLeod 1987)*

SSV: '*Oṃ*: The sacred syllable in the Veda' (Killingley 1986)*
ST: *The Sacred Thread* (Brockington 1981)*
TADN: *Tattva-artha-dīpa-nibandha* of Vallabha
TSSH: *Textual Sources for the Study of Hinduism* (O'Flaherty 1988)*
TVSS: 'The Tamil Veda of a *Śūdra* Saint' (Hardy 1979)*
VC: 'Varṇa and caste in Hindu apologetic' (Killingley 1991)*
VS: *Vedārthasaṃgraha* of Rāmānuja

* For further details see Bibliography

1 About 'Hindu', Hinduism and this book

'Hinduism': a plural phenomenon, a global reality. Various descriptions of Hinduism. An image of Hinduism. 'Hinduism' – a cluster word; 'Hindu' not necessarily a religious description. Origins of 'Hindu'; not simply an outsider term. The Sanskritic, Brahminic tradition and its place in Hinduism and in this book. Various 'essential' characteristics of Hinduism considered: caste, particular beliefs, specific practices, the Veda. The relationship between 'Hinduism' and other Indian traditions: two illustrations. Ways Hindus describe themselves. Names for India. Our approach.

Here we go again: yet another book on Hinduism! In an apparently saturated market, is there room for more? The answer must be: surely yes. Not necessarily for this particular one of course, but in theory for an endless stream of books. Hinduism – or the plural reality labelled as such – has been a major cultural phenomenon for well over 3,000 years. It has regularly produced men and women down the ages who have made outstanding contributions across the range of the civilised human endeavour that we have come to appreciate in our increasingly cross-cultural world: in religion and philosophy, in the sciences and the fine arts, in physical, technical and literary skills. Outstanding Hindus apart, Hinduism has sustained and oriented every aspect of the lives of countless ordinary people. It has played a crucial part in the rise of at least two other great religions – Buddhism and Sikhism – and in the development of two more, Christianity and Islam, during the many centuries that these two faiths have been present in the Indian subcontinent. All this is reason enough to continue the study of Hinduism indefinitely.

But Hinduism remains a major world force today, its contemporary global influence apparently greater than ever. This century, in one way or another, India has occupied a prominent place in the public eye: as the 'jewel in the crown' of the widespread British empire; in the march to independence with Mahātmā Gandhi so poignantly in the lead; as the scene of some of the most horrific religious and political strife ever recorded; as the theatre for more than one internecine war; as the stage for literary and artistic genius of the calibre of R. K. Narayan, Rabindranath Tagore, Satyajit Ray and Ravi Shankar; as the home of yoga and age-old religious and philosophical wisdom; as exporter to the West of assorted gurus and godmen; as the appropriate context for the work of a Mother Teresa; as a developing country fast acquiring scientific and technological expertise (India has its own space and nuclear capability), economically poor yet justly proud of its rich cultural heritage. And the dominant and dominating context of this kaleidoscopic image has been Hinduism. Hindus comprise about 80 per cent of the subcontinent's population, or over 600 million people.

While Indians have always ventured beyond the shores of the subcontinent for trade and other reasons, it has been in the last 150 years or so that we have witnessed unprecedented Indian emigration to various parts of the world. Today there are appreciable numbers of Indians in Europe (including Britain), North America and Africa, the Middle East and Australasia. And again it is largely in terms of Hinduism that this presence has been felt. Thus, not only numerically but also geographically, Hinduism is a major global phenomenon.[1] All the more reason then for its continued study.

What exactly is Hinduism? Hindus have a tendency to regard certain things as having an inner proper form (*svarūpa*) – hard to know if not unknowable – which may be experienced under different aspects or which manifests itself under different forms (*bahurūpa*). Hinduism itself seems to be something like this. It is experienced as so many things by Hindus and non-Hindus alike that one may well ask if it has a *svarūpa* at all. The issue is complicated by the fact that many otherwise perceptive Hindus – who should know better as adherents of a tradition pervasively suspicious of absolutist claims! – act and talk as if *their* brand of Hinduism is the only thing that matters, or is what Hinduism is all about. To form some idea of the enormous complexity of this multi-faceted reality, here is a sample of what both Hindus and non-Hindus have considered Hinduism, and Hindus, to be:

1 [Hinduism] is both a way of life and a highly organized social and religious system . . . quite free from any dogmatic affirmations concerning the nature of God (p. 1). The Hindus themselves call

their religion the *sanātana dharma*, 'eternal *dharma*' (p. 2) . . . and any writer on Hinduism who accepts [this] definition . . . must choose between producing a catalogue which will give . . . the maximum number of facts . . . or . . . attempt, at his peril, to distil from the whole mass of his material the fine essence that he considers to be the changeless ground from which the proliferating jungle that seems to be Hinduism grows (p. 3).[2]

2 Acceptance of the *Veda* as revealed scripture is certainly the most basic criterion for anyone to declare himself a Hindu (the preferred self-designation of Hinduism in Indian languages is *Vaidik dharma*, the religion of the *Veda*) (p. 16).[3]

3 Within Hinduism, one person's sacred scripture is by no means necessarily someone else's. This individual may assign a minor role to a god whom another individual worships with deep devotion as . . . Lord of the world . . . . Even the doctrine of reincarnation . . . is *not* a universally accepted part of Hindu teaching and faith . . . . As [Indian] government officials see it, every Indian is automatically a Hindu unless he or she specifically claims adherence to another religion (pp. 138–9) . . . [Hinduism is not a religion but] a collection of religions . . . containing elements of shared traditions, and religions that have continually influenced each other down through the ages, and that have jointly contributed to forming the culture of India. (p. 143).[4]

4 The caste system, though closely integrated into the [Hindu] religion, is not essential to it (p. 4). . . . Even the profession of belief in the authority of the Veda is not essential.[5]

5 Caste is the Hindu form of social organization. No man can be a Hindu who is not in caste (p. 214). . . . Here, then, we have the Hindu world-theory in all its permanent essentials: God real, the world worthless; the one God unknowable, the other gods not to be despised; the Brahmans with their Vedas the sole religious authority; caste a divine institution, serving as the chief instrument of reward and punishment; man doomed to repeated birth and death, because all action leads to rebirth; world-flight the only noble cause for the awakened man and the one hope of escape from the entanglements of sense and transmigration (p. 216).[6]

6 Hinduism can be described as many religions . . . and it also pervades Hindu life as lived in the world in every nook and cranny . . . . Despite its all-too-obvious inconsistencies, Hinduism is one whole. Even those features in it which seem to have no connection with religion, as understood today, stem from its basic character as natural offshoots (p. 1). . . . Hinduism differs fundamentally

from Christianity in this, that for its followers it is not an alternative to the world, but primarily the means of supporting and improving their existence in it (p. 9) . . . . Salvation [*mokṣa*] is never the object of the religious observances and worship of the Hindus (p. 10).[7]

7 The three . . . divisions of the Vedānta, the Upaniṣads, the Brahma Sūtra and the Bhagavadgītā . . . form together the absolute standard for the Hindu religion (p. 18) . . . . Mokṣa is spiritual realisation. The Hindu Dharma says, Man . . . lives or must live by his life of spirit. Mokṣa is . . . the fulfilment of the Spirit in us in the heart of the eternal. This is what gives ultimate satisfaction, and all other activities are directed to the realization of this end.[8]

8 The Hindus certainly differ from us in every respect (p. 17) . . . the Hindus believe that there is no country but theirs, no nation like theirs, no kings like theirs, no religion like theirs, no science like theirs (p. 22). . . . As the word of confession, 'There is no god but God, Muhammad is his prophet' is the shibboleth of Islam . . . so metempsychosis is the shibboleth of the Hindu religion. Therefore he who does not believe in it . . . is not reckoned as one of them (p. 50).[9]

9 The Hindu's Hinduness does not depend on any particular religious belief . . . . Neither does the Hindu's Hinduness rest upon considerations of food and drink . . . . The basis of Hinduness, its essence, are the duties of caste and stage of life and the one-centredness directing them . . . . The tendency to one-centred thinking, the seeing into the thinghood of a thing, the experience of ultimate non-difference between Agent and effect, the knowledge of the deceptiveness of multiplicity, comprise the Hindu's Hinduness. We find its beginning in the Veda and its completion in the Vedānta.[10]

The above list represents quite a mixed – at times inconsistent – collection of assertions and emphases. We are told that Hinduism is a way of life; it is a collection of religions. Hindus are not in the least interested in salvation. Hindus direct all their activities to the realisation of salvation. Hinduism begins in the Veda and is consummated in the Vedānta. The Vedānta forms the absolute standard of the Hindu religion; Hinduism is religiously undogmatic. Hinduism is a highly organised social and religious system; it is the eternal dharma; the religion of the Veda. On the other hand, it is a system to which neither caste nor belief in the authority of the Veda is essential. It is a system to which belief in rebirth is essential; a system to which belief in rebirth is *not* essential. Hindus are proud; yet as they are undogmatic they tend to be tolerant. Hinduism is primarily the means for Hindus to support and improve their multifarious existence in the world; on the other hand, realisation of the deceptiveness of the world's multiplicity is part of the essence of Hinduness. And we may ask: Is there a 'fine essence' to the 'changeless ground' of Hinduism? In what sense is Hinduism 'one', yet a 'proliferating jungle'? In any case, every Indian is supposed to be a Hindu unless he or she repudiates this label.

I have not quoted the extracts above in order to criticise them, though in due course we shall have occasion to question some of these statements. The authors of some of the passages go on to make careful distinctions, mindful of the bewildering perplexity of their subject matter. The point is that the phenomenon of Hinduism is both vast and bewildering. One cannot write about it without being selective, without approaching it from one point of view at the expense of others, without committing oneself to this interpretation rather than to that. Hinduism is a way of life, a collection of religions, a complex culture, one yet many. How to do justice to this phenomenon within the pages of one book? The reader must bear with its interpreter and not expect too much. It is by piecing together facts and interpretations gleaned from a variety of sources that more and more of the jigsaw will become visible. So let me propose another image to help us understand this fascinating reality and the scope of this book.

The pride and joy of the Calcutta botanical gardens (located in a western suburb of the city) is a vast, magnificent banyan tree (*ficus benghalensis*). The characteristic of the banyan is well known: from widespread branches it sends down aerial roots, many of which in time grow thick and strong to resemble individual tree-trunks, so that an ancient banyan looks like an interconnected collection of trees and branches in which the same life-sap flows: one yet many. Reputed to be over 200 years old,[11] with a canopy about 4 acres in extent, the Great Banyan of Calcutta is a 'proliferating jungle', organically if attenuatedly one, as vigorous as ever, new branches and roots forever springing up or down as others wither away. The Great Banyan is not a bad symbol of Hinduism. Like the tree, Hinduism is an ancient collection of roots and branches, many indistinguishable one from the other, microcosmically polycentric, macrocosmically one, sharing the same regenerative life-sap, with a temporal foliage which covers most of recorded human history. But unlike the botanical model, the Hindu banyan is not uniform to look at. Rather, it is a network of variety, one distinctive arboreal complex shading into another, the whole forming a marvellous unity-in-diversity. In this book we shall explore some of the more prominent of the roots and branches of the wondrous ancient banyan of Hinduism mainly in its original soil, take account of those that are lesser known, and try to analyse important features of the sap that vitalises the whole, so that we may catch some perspective of the vast phenomenon as it extends in space and time.

What, then, is Hinduism? A provocative response would be to say that there is no such thing. The term itself is a western abstraction of fairly recent coinage, giving the impression that Hinduism is a block reality, a homogeneous system, easily defined, which all Hindus acknowledge in more or less the same way.[12] But as we shall see, this is not the case. Whatever else it may be, Hinduism is not a seamless system of belief in the way that many imagine or expect 'isms' to be. In fact, to use yet another image, Hinduism is an acceptable abbreviation for a *family* of culturally similar traditions. It is a family term. Just as in an extended family there are a number of features distributed among its members, not uniformly but in permutations such that any two or more members (even distant cousins) can be identified as belonging to the same family, so too in Hinduism there are many traditions over which distinctive characteristics are distributed in overlapping ways such that we may identify each of these traditons as belonging to the same cultural family. Some of these traditions may have more of these characteristics in common, making them more strongly Hindu. Others may share fewer traits, yet if these traits are dominant ones they would still allow us to identify the traditions to which they belong as Hindu.

The advantage of defining Hinduism in terms of traditions which share a family resemblance is that it does away with the tendency to look for an 'essentialist' definition of Hinduism. This implies that whatever is being defined has a static essence or core which contains a number of necessary attributes. By listing these attributes you will be able to identify various things as falling under the definition if they match the list. Hinduism is not a reality that succumbs to this process. As we have indicated, it is a kind of unity-in-diversity, a continuum forever adapting to new circumstances. As some roots or branches wither away there is renewal and growth elsewhere. It would be inappropriate to look for a static essence of such a phenomenon.

The family resemblance way of describing Hinduism also allows us to be realistic. The term 'Hinduism' is here to stay; it is no use suggesting that we must discard it because it tends to mislead us in the ways we have noted. It is more helpful to refine our use of the term and use it with discrimination. We have suggested two ways of doing this. Further, our use of Hinduism gives flexibility. When does someone cease to belong to a family? When he or she is disowned by, or disowns, the family? When their relationship by blood becomes too distant? When they no longer have identifiable family resemblances? In other words, when certain decisions are made by the appropriate people. Our way of defining Hinduism allows for this flexibility of decision which, as we shall see, the complexity of the Hindu phenomenon requires. So much then for methodological considerations about defining Hinduism.

Let us now enquire into some facts and characteristics about what it is to be a Hindu. So far I have tried to avoid simply identifying Hinduism with a *religious* way of life. It is not necessary to be religious, namely to believe in some world-transcending reality, personal or otherwise, in terms of which human fulfilment may be attained, to be Hindu. The overwhelming majority of Hindus *are* religious, at least in this minimal sense, and the overwhelming proportion of human endeavour that has gone into the making of historical Hinduism *has* been religious in this way. This is a very important fact about Hinduism. It is for this reason that the major emphasis of this book will be religious. But it is important to note that one may be accepted as a Hindu by Hindus, and describe oneself perfectly validly as a Hindu, without being religious in the sense noted. One may be polytheistic or monotheistic, monistic or pantheistic, even agnostic or atheistic, and still be a Hindu. This is why I have described Hinduism as essentially a cultural phenomenon. Now we shall consider the origins of the word 'Hindu'.

The term derives from what is known today as the Indus river in the north-west of the subcontinent. For nearly 3,000 kms, from its tributaries in the foothills of the Himalayas to its mouths in the Arabian Sea, this mighty river acts as a natural boundary to the bulk of peninsular India for those entering from the western mountain passes. The received wisdom is that towards the beginning of the first millennium BCE, a people known as the Aryans,[13] who came from the west beyond the passes, began to dominate the riverine north-west. Their view of the world was developed in a vast body of sacred utterances called the Vedas. In one of the oldest portions of the Vedas, the Ṛk Saṃhitā (dating to about 1200–1000 BCE), there are references to a river called the *Sindhu* (e.g. RV. 5.53.9; 8.20.24). According to the Vedic Indians, rivers, like other natural forces had a sacred power deriving from a transcendent source. Was *Sindhu* originally the name of some great river with mystical properties in a distant homeland?[14] In the plural, this term was also used to refer to rivers in general, often with emphasis on their fast-flowing, regenerative waters. The Aryans would have been impressed with the swift, bountiful currents of the great river of the north-west or of one of its tributaries, flowing through land that was often naturally arid. It is easy to imagine them investing these powerful waters with the mystical properties attributed to rivers in their folk memory and calling them the 'Sindhu'. In some instances the term by association may have denoted those among the newcomers who had settled on the river's banks. Certainly this settling did not occur in a sudden mass-migration from outside. The so-called newcomers must have dribbled in over generations, their numbers and culture gradually gaining strength. In short, in the Indian context, *sindhu* started out as a geographical word with strong cultural resonances. The name 'Sind', which designates the sub-Punjab area of the Indus today, is derived from this usage.

At least from earliest historical times the inhabitants of the riverine north-west have been in touch with peoples from outside, if not through war then by trade. It was no different with the Aryans as they settled in the region, mingling with the native inhabitants whom they encountered. Towards the middle of the first millennium BCE the Persians, under Darius I, began to conquer Indus territory, referring to its inhabitants as 'Hindus'. This word was both geographical and cultural: it referred to the people around and beyond the Sindhu – to where and how they lived and to what they looked like. No doubt it also had political overtones in so far as these people and their land were envisaged as becoming part of the Persian empire. Clearly the Persian 'Hindu' was derived from 'Sindhu', the word the early Vedic Indians used to describe the great river as well as themselves, also in a geographical-cultural sense. Thus the generally accepted view that 'Hindu' is an outsider term, imposed gratuitously on the peoples of the subcontinent by foreigners, is hardly the case. 'Hindu' is quite faithfully derived from insider usage. The view *is* true to the extent that (a) the Persian use of 'Hindu' was on the whole undiscerning: it tended to lump all those indigenously associated with the great river culturally into one heap; and (b) this usage persisted as the basis of subsequent (usually equally indiscriminate) attempts by foreigners to designate all those who lived on and beyond the river boundary. This was the case despite the fact that the Vedic Indians themselves soon outgrew their original use of the term *sindhu* and began to describe different features of their developing identity in different ways.

In the first quarter of the third century BCE, Alexander of Macedon swept through Darius' empire and invaded the north-west of the subcontinent. Now Greek civilisation became a force to contend with in the region. Taking their cue from the Persians, the Greeks referred to the great river as the *Indos* and to those who dwelt around or beyond it by the vague term *Indikoi* (Latin: *Indus, India*, etc.). It is from these words that we get 'India' and 'Indian'. Similarly, the Arabic word for India was 'al-Hind'. The Muslims, as their contact with the subcontinent increased from very early in their history, tended to refer to those who dwelt in this land, but who were neither of their faith nor Buddhists, as 'Hindus'. Here a religio-cultural sense dominated. This is the sense consistently used by the Muslim observer, al-Biruni, in his famous account of the Hindu way of life, written in about 1030 CE. It is significant that Biruni concentrated on the beliefs and practices of the Brahmins since it was his view that 'the main and most essential point of the Hindu world of thought is that which the Brahmans think and believe, for they are specially trained for preserving and maintaining their religion'.[15]

Is Hinduism then best summed up as the Brahmin way of life? The answer depends on one's perspective. Most Hindus were not and are not Brahmins. Many, especially those in circumstances most vulnerable to the traditional exercise of Brahmin power, understandably resent being represented by or assimilated into Brahminic culture. But it is undeniable that from earliest times Brahminic culture has overshadowed the Hindu way of life. 'Brahminic culture' must be understood in a broad sense as referring to beliefs and practices that are far from homogeneous but which have been propagated or ratified by Brahmin authority. Brahminic culture includes atheism, agnosticism and theism; monism, monotheism and polytheism; traditional caste practices and their rejection or re-interpretation; Vedic ritual and Tantric and *bhakti* religion (see Chapter 12); and widely divergent understandings of Hindu *dharma* (that is, an acceptable way of life socially and religiously). All these things, in innumerable combinations within the vast fabric of Hinduism, have been in some form or other approved, defended, prescribed and standardised by often conflicting or contending sources of Brahmin authority. And the point is that it is undeniable that from the beginning of Hinduism as we know it, Brahmin and non-Brahmin Hindus alike have had to articulate their identity as Hindus in terms of Brahminic culture, whether they have challenged or accepted it, rebelled or acquiesced. It is in this sense then that this book will be concerned with Brahminic culture, though we shall have many opportunities to note not only how nebulous the concept is, but some of the main challenges to the prevailing Brahminic norms.

We may add here that the vehicle *par excellence* of Brahminic culture – its flagship language, so to speak – has been Sanskrit (including Vedic Sanskrit). I think it would be true to say that for all of its history, Brahminic culture in the broad sense intimated above has been propagated either through Sanskrit or by (sometimes notional) reference to what have been regarded as normative Sanskrit texts. This has had interesting repercussions throughout India for the relationship between Sanskrit on the one hand and vernacular and regional languages on the other. It was from the nineteenth century that the custom of transmitting Brahminic culture via the actual use of Sanskrit generally began to wane. However, the process of 'Sanskritisation', viz. the imposition/acceptance of Sanskritic norms into Hindu culture, continued – and continues – in important ways. We shall have more to say about Sanskrit and Sanskritisation later.

So, one may ask, if Hinduism in its generic sense pivots on Brahminic culture, is *caste* an essential feature of the Hindu way of life? Reluctant to appear to prevaricate as I am, the answer must be: Yes and No. For the overwhelming majority of Hindus, *in the history of the subcontinent*, having a caste status of some kind has been probably *the* distinguishing feature of individual Hindu identity. But as in other aspects of the Hindu phenomenon, the matter does not end here. Distinguishing feature from whose point of view: that of the individual (or individual groups) concerned, or of the dominant social/religious/political authority of the community at large? In the nineteenth century, members of a number of reform-minded groups repudiated their former high-caste obligations in no uncertain terms. But they often still regarded themselves as Hindu (indeed, quintessentially Hindu), and were in fact treated as Hindus, outcastes or not, by many Hindus outside those groups. The Lingayats, who have had a recognisable community identity in India for nearly a thousand years and who dominate parts of modern Karnataka State, theoretically at least reject traditional caste divisions and practices. Yet they are regarded as within the caste system by non-Lingayats, Hindu or otherwise.[16] And there are many westernised Hindus in India today who openly live in direct opposition to traditional caste observances but who consider themselves as Hindus and are considered as such by the more 'orthodox'.[17]

In fact, caste has had a significantly ambivalent role in traditional Hindu society. Those who have formally renounced the world (*saṃnyāsins*) are supposed to have transcended caste. No doubt they were born into the system, but as renouncers they are reckoned to be 'dead' to these worldly, distinguishing features. I remember how, many years ago when I was new to the study of Hinduism, I fell into conversation with a Hindu monk and asked about the circumstances which led to his entering the monastery. With a smile he declined to answer my question, saying, 'That individual, with the caste and other associations which people in this world make so much of, has ceased to exist.' This response is in accord with the strictest traditions of Hindu monasticism. Yet, in a sense, renouncers are supposed to symbolise the culmination of Hinduism. What, we may ask, does the transcending of caste in this context signify about its place in the Hindu way of life?

Further, it is well known that for hundreds of years there have been Indian Christians who have either maintained caste and have been acknowledged as such by their Hindu peers, or who have involuntarily been slotted into high or low positions in the caste hierarchy by the power-brokers of Hindu society. In south India in the seventeenth century, many of the high-caste converts of the Italian Jesuit missionary, Roberto de Nobili, were allowed to follow traditional caste observances by the Church without formally repudiating their caste allegiance. This experiment is often thought to have worked in that their non-convert peers did not ostracise them. Can such Christians be called Hindus? In the late nineteenth century Brahmabandhab Upadhyay (see n. 10), an influential Bengali-Brahmin convert to the Roman Catholic faith, devoted much of his life to trying to show that he was both Hindu and Catholic. For him, to be Hindu was to have a certain kind of cultural orientation, not a particular set of religious beliefs. Whether this claim of Upadhyay's was credible at the time to many, Hindus and Christians alike (it was certainly unusual), is not the point. The point is that an increasing number of Indian Christians are making a similar claim today.

Does anything turn on the distinction between 'being *a* Hindu' and 'being Hindu' here, the distinction between being labelled, or affirming a kind of identity on the one hand, and one's allegiance to a way of life on the other?[18] Nothing crucial, I think, in so far as we are talking about Hindu identity and its recognition rather than the quality of one's commitment to Hinduism in some form. 'Being a Hindu' implies the possibility of 'being Hindu', and vice versa. They are potentially mutual implicates.

In the considerable history of Hinduism outside India, the role of caste as potentially determinative of Hindu identity has often been, if not irrelevant, then substantially minimised. This further complicates the issue. Take, for example, the Indian Ocean island of Mauritius where Hinduism has been thriving for about 150 years. There are about half a million Hindus in Mauritius (about half the population). In Mauritius, Hindus can be found among well-to-do as well as poorer strata of society; further, they are influential in all the important dimensions of the country's life, not least in politics, so we are not talking about a backward or poorly represented community. Yet, while in Mauritian Hindu society caste distinctions and affiliations of a kind resembling those of the Indian subcontinent are present (and, it seems, exploited, mainly by politicians), they are fast dissolving or at least mixing in the proverbial melting-pot. For as 'love-marriages' rather than arranged marriages become increasingly popular among Mauritian Hindus, existing caste patterns will break up and become less determinative of identity within and for Hindu society. There is evidence to show that ethnic and other groupings (e.g. Tamils as opposed to others) will supplant caste in this respect. However, there is no reason to suppose that Mauritian Hindus will not continue to value their identity as Hindus or to study the Indian origins of their Hindu culture (not least by sitting school examinations in Hinduism, as at present). One cannot make generalisations then as to *how* and, in important cases, *whether*, caste is constitutive of being a Hindu.

So does one have to believe something specific to be a Hindu? We have given ample indication that one does not. What about belief in the rule of karma and rebirth? For al-Biruni this was the shibboleth or distinctive feature of Hindu religion. To begin with, though it is undeniable that many Hindus, inside and outside India, do follow this belief, it is not specifically Hindu. Thus most Buddhists and Jains and even some Christians believe in some form of karma and rebirth. And some Hindus, especially an increasing number of westernised Hindus, do not accept this belief (see Chapter 9). We have already noted that Hinduism has to do with a way of life, not a definite creed.

Is this way of life equivalent, as one or two interpreters seem to claim in the extracts quoted earlier, to what is known either as *Vaidika dharma* or as *sanātana dharma*, i.e. the code of practice (*dharma*) that is eternal (*sanātana*) or based on the Vedas (*Vaidika*)? Hardly. Many Hindus call themselves sanātanists, i.e. those who follow the eternal *dharma*. But we shall see that it is far from clear what this eternal *dharma* is. We have noted that Hinduism is a dynamic, living reality (or rather, a macro-reality of organically united micro-realities, analogous to an old banyan) whose strength lies in its ability to adapt to circumstances while it maintains strands of continuity with the past. But one cannot trace this continuity in an essentialist manner. It is a continuity of vital elements whose composition varies as a function of the different living centres of Hinduism which are to be found not only in the world at large but, perhaps most importantly, in India itself. These vital elements cannot be isolated as static essences. The elements composing one person's or group's eternal *dharma* may differ significantly from those of another. Yet both are Hindus. And who is to say which perception of eternal *dharma* is normative? Besides, the expression 'eternal (*sanātana*) *dharma*' seems to imply that Hinduism cannot or should not undergo change. But this is a highly contentious implication, to say the least. Where does reformed Hinduism – with which Hindu history is replete – fit in? And the multitude of little and great reformers of Hinduism, often regarded as the glory of Hindu tradition by Hindus and non-Hindus alike? It seems that to say that one is a sanātanist is more prescriptive than descriptive. It is chiefly to say what one believes Hinduism should be rather than what Hinduism is. It is to say that one does not belong to, or rather want to belong to, particular reform movements in Hinduism. (On the other hand, it may be to say that one should belong to this rather than to that reform movement, since the former has captured what the latter has not, i.e. the eternal essence of Hinduism.) It is a declaration of intent, and a rather tendentious if unclear declaration at that.

Similar comments apply to the description of Hinduism as the *Vaidika dharma*, i.e. the way of life which is based on the Vedas. First, this description implies that Hinduism is necessarily religious. We have questioned this; one can be a Hindu without being religious in any obvious sense of the term. To be a Hindu is to be culturally, not necessarily religiously, marked in some way. Second, many Hindus down the centuries have either theoretically or practically repudiated or at least in varying degrees bypassed the Vedas or parts thereof in living their lives. Many Hindus are and have been quite unfamiliar with these sacred utterances. This does not mean that their life's orientation cannot be traced to the Vedas or that it does not, at least in an attenuated sense, derive from them. But it does put the Vedas in perspective.

Having said this, we must acknowledge the immense and pervasive importance of the Vedas in the history of Hinduism. Most Hindus are religious, and a great many religious Hindus at least implicitly acknowledge the authority of the Vedas in orienting their lives, although, as will become clearer in the course of this book, the relationships between their lives and Vedic content are often complex, tortuous and obscure. There is point in saying, as one modern commentator has done, that acceptance of the authority of the Vedas often amounts to 'no more than a declaration that someone considers himself a Hindu'.[19] But, as we have noted, a great many Hindus also challenge the authority of the Vedas and in the process give them a high profile. So, positively or negatively, the Vedas stand out in the history of Hinduism.

In the light of what has been said, let us return to the relationship between 'Hinduism' and other long-standing Indian religions such as Buddhism and Jainism. Today, it is customary to distinguish between the religion(s) of the Hindus (or less accurately, Hinduism) and those of the Buddhists, Jains and Sikhs (or Buddhism, Jainism and Sikhism). There is something in this. Thus for reasons of convenience if not of scholarly propriety, we can say that this is a book on Hinduism and not on Buddhism, Jainism, etc. But this kind of distinction is a fairly recent one, bound up not only with western preconceptions about the nature of religion in general and of religion in India in particular, but also with the political awareness that has arisen in India in the aftermath of westernisation. In fact it was in the nineteenth century, especially in Bengal, the bridgehead between Hindu and British culture, that more or less systematic attempts were made by both British and Hindu writers to articulate what Hinduism or Hinduness (*hindutva* in Sanskrit) was. In the process they helped create a new reality for their readers. And it is no accident that the troubles in the Punjab in the recent past derive from a mix of religion and politics in which, for the first time in the history of the subcontinent, formal barriers are being drawn between Hindu and Sikh. In pre-modern times it was not so: in fact, it could not be so. It is part of the same phenomenon that on a populist level in the country a separatist Hindu identity is being shaped that rests as much (if not more) on political as on religious considerations.

In pre-modern India, people whom we today describe as Hindus tended not to label themselves as such in opposition to those we call Buddhists, Jains, etc. This is because the term 'Hindu', in so far as it had currency, was essentially a racial-cultural expression, and Buddhists, Sikhs, Jains, and those we refer to as Hindus now, all shared the same multi-faceted ethnicity of the subcontinent. They perceived themselves as all belonging to the same extended cultural family. They argued among themselves religiously and doctrinally all the time, but not in terms of ethnocentric distinctions. Vaiṣṇava

Advaitins argued with Vaiṣṇava Dvaitins, and Vaiṣṇavas argued with Śaivites, and Śaivites disputed with Buddhists (or Bauddhas, i.e. the followers of the Buddha), and Buddhists quarrelled with Logicians or Naiyāyikas, and so on, but there was little argument, if any, between Hindus as Hindus and Buddhists or Jains or Sikhs. The arguments were doctrinal, soteriological, religious, not ethnocentric or cultural in this sense. According to the current meaning of the term Hindu, either all or none of these groups were Hindus. The following examples will illustrate this.

The first we take from a story in the Kāśī Khaṇḍa of the *Skanda Purāṇa*, compiled in the main probably by the thirteenth century CE.[20] God Śiva and his wife Pārvatī wanted to take up residence in Benares,[21] beautiful as a lotus, luminous as the sun, foremost city in all the world. The problem was that Śiva himself had agreed to allow a powerful ascetic, Divodāsa, to rule Benares. Without Divodāsa's consent or fall from power, Śiva could not move into the city as ruler. For his part, Divodāsa, by his firm adherence to *dharma*, had established so impregnable a reign that Śiva decided that Divodāsa could only be toppled by a stratagem which exploited some chink in his dharmic armour. So he sent various *devas* (heavenly personages, or gods) and other associates to Benares to spy on Divodāsa, and if possible, detect some dharmic flaw. Many went on this errand – Sūrya, the sun; Lord Brahmā, the fashioner of the world; numerous *yoginīs* (sorceresses) and *gaṇas* (gnomish henchmen) – all to no avail. Indeed, having failed in their task they stayed on in Benares, entranced by the city's charms. Finally Śiva sent Viṣṇu.

Viṣṇu transformed himself into a Buddhist monk; his consort Śrī took the form of a Buddhist nun, and their great bird companion, Garuḍa, assumed the shape of the monk's disciple. The three of them preached the Buddhist way in the city, and the trick worked. Among other things, the 'Buddhists' preached that the world had no maker, that the killing of animals for sacrifice was wrong, even according to the scriptures, and that caste distinctions were unacceptable.

> Hearing these teachings, which were contrary to the *dharma* of castes, the citizens began to go astray . . . . Soon everything was awry; the breakdown of order and of caste had begun. . . . These Buddhists had successfully cracked the perfect *dharma* of the kingdom. Divodāsa's power began to fade and his dissatisfaction with kingship began to increase.[22]

Eventually Divodāsa left Benares, allowing Śiva entry.

What is interesting here from our point of view is that the

Buddhists are cast as the villains of the piece, and that the grounds on which they are distinguished from those who follow the accredited *dharma* are socio-religous. The Buddhists preach a message that overturns traditional caste and sacrificial practices. In short, they do not follow Vedic *dharma*. This is why Buddhists are to be kept at arm's length. The contrast here is between Vedic and *anti*-Vedic *dharma*: it is not drawn on cultural or ethnocentric grounds. It would make no sense to distinguish between Hindus and Buddhists here, since in the *original* ethnocentric sense of the term Hindu (with which the Brahminic redactor of the myth may well have been familiar), those who followed the Buddhist *dharma* and those who followed the Vedic *dharma* were equally Hindus.

Our second example is taken from a later time, in a context where the Muslim threat to traditional religion was predominant. Here, Hindu is used as a distinguishing term. A survey of three Sanskrit and ten Bengali Gauḍīya Vaiṣṇava hagiographic texts ranging from the first half of the sixteenth century to the second half of the eighteenth century shows that the term Hindu is used a handful of times but only in the Bengali texts.[23] Perhaps the authors considered Sanskrit too formal and proper a medium for such foreign words. In any case, Hindu generally occurs in contexts in which Gauḍīya Vaiṣṇava devotees of Kṛṣṇa wished to distinguish themselves (or on occasion, the indigenous population as a whole) from the Muslims, regarded as 'Yavanas'[24] or 'Mlecchas',[25] i.e. foreigners. And it is Muslims who are often depicted as using the term 'Hindu'. What seems to emerge is that Hindu is a separatist term distinguishing 'us' from 'them', originally imposed by foreigners on the local inhabitants and appropriated by these inhabitants in their dealings with the foreigners. The use of the term here exploits ethnocentric, i.e. racial and other cultural connotations, including reference to habits, manners and religious beliefs. Hindu is not used, as O'Connell points out, in an intramural sense; that is, to distinguish between local non-Muslim groups.

But there have always been figures, even in the context of established Muslim rule in India, who have sought to rise above the constraints of religious labels. An outstanding example is Kabīr (fifteenth to sixteenth centuries). Firm data about Kabīr's life are scarce. He seems to have been born in a community of Muslim weavers, but in time he repudiated any formal allegiance to Islam. Kabīr preached an eclectic faith of devotion to God which transcended the religous boundaries of his environment. In this respect the following verses are typical of Kabīr's thought.[26]

'Gorakh! Gorakh!'
cries the Jogī,
'Rām! Rām!'
says the Hindu.
'Allah is One'
proclaims the Muslim.
But, O Kabīr,
My Lord pervades all'.[27]

Again:
'The god of Hindus resides in a temple;
The god of Muslims resides in a mosque.
Who resides there
Where there are no temples
Or mosques?
O Seeker, follow your own path,
Forget the mosque, forget the temple,
Be your own light.
Open your eyes and see
That Rāma and Allāh are One!'
(Kumar 1984: 31)

'Neither a Hindu nor a Muslim am I!' cried Kabīr, 'A mere ensemble of five elements is this body, where the spirit plays its drama of joy and suffering!' (1984: 31). Yet today Kabīr is generally regarded as a Hindu.

As we have indicated, in modern times the word 'Hindu' has been suffused with political connotations not only in India but outside the subcontinent. Further, it has become an acceptable self-description, still with fairly fluid boundaries. Thus we distinguish between Hindus and Buddhists or Sikhs or Muslims, but the expressions Hindu-Christian and Hindu-Catholic, for instance, are also catching on. No definite or necessarily *religious* connotation (in any obvious sense of the term) attaches to the word. Hindu is primarily a cultural, orienting term, its original geographical and racial implications having been minimised if not generally lost with the spread of Hinduism in the world. Thus even western converts to Hindu religions, e.g. members of the Hare Krishna movement, may well be and generally have been called Hindus.[28] In passing, we note that in the modern, makeshift sense of the word, this is a book on Hinduism. More specifically, it is a book on religious Hinduism. In other words we shall not be exploring at the micro-level those centres of the Indian cultural phenomenon which are described today as Buddhist,

Jain, Sikh, etc., for all their interlocking with so-called Hindu centres of the phenomenon.

We will now briefly consider how Hindus have traditionally preferred to identify themselves, notwithstanding modern usage. Individuals were designated in a variety of ways: by a given proper name, by reference to village, to lineage, to family and other personal relationships, to caste status, to religious affiliation, to character or physical traits and/or particular events, acts or circumstances associated with the person being identified. In short, at any one time, a particular individual would be singled out or addressed by one of a range of possible designations, depending on context. Here are some examples with reference to well-known characters in Hindu tradition.

Kṛṣṇa, a very important human *avatāra* or incarnation (more properly, descent) of deity is of course often referred to by his human name 'Kṛṣṇa' (which means 'dark-coloured'). But in his human circumstances he is also referred to as 'Vāsudeva', i.e. son of Vasudeva (his father); on occasion as 'Devakīputra', i.e. son of Devakī (his mother) (see *ChāndUp*. III.17.6); or as 'Vārṣṇeya' (of the Vṛṣṇi tribe). He was also called 'Keśava' (having fine hair), 'Madhusūdana' (slayer of the ogre Madhu, from an episode in his life), and so on. Kṛṣṇa's close friend Arjuna, besides being known by this name, was also called 'Pārtha', i.e. son of Pṛthā (his mother, whose other name was 'Kuntī': hence Arjuna was sometimes called by the metronymic 'Kaunteya'); his patronymic was Pāṇḍava, from Pāṇḍu. On occasion Arjuna was called 'Savyasācī', i.e. the ambidextrous (wielder of the bow), in tribute to his prowess as a warrior, and so on. Bhīma (the terrible), one of Arjuna's brothers, was like his name in character. He was also called 'Vṛkodara' (Wolf-belly) because of his voracious appetite.

Rāma, the hero of the epic, the *Rāmāyaṇa*, and later developed by Vaiṣṇavas as the other great human *avatāra* of the God Viṣṇu, was also addressed by such expressions as 'Rāghava' (Raghu's descendant) and 'Raghunandana' (Scion of Raghu), patronymics derived from his great-grandfather, Raghu; 'Ikṣvākusūta' (descendant of Ikṣvāku, first king in Ayodhya of the solar dynasty); 'Sītāpati' (husband of Sītā who was herself called on occasion 'Jānakī' or daughter of (King) Janaka), and 'Jānakīśa' (Lord of Jānakī); 'Rāvaṇāri' (foe of (the ogre-king) Rāvaṇa) and 'Sugrīvamitra' ('friend of Sugrīva' or 'handsome-neck', a monkey-king), etc. Indeed, Vālmīki, the reputed author of the *Rāmāyaṇa*, acquired his name from the ant-hill (*valmīka*) which is said to have formed about him as he sat absorbed in contemplation for a long time. Scarcely a generation or two ago, a husband would refer or call to his wife, not by her given name, but by the description, 'Mother of N__' (their son or daughter). These examples are not exhaustive, of course, even with respect to the individuals mentioned, but they give an idea of how Hindus referred to each other and addressed one another as individuals. Today most of these modes of address are obsolete, but not all. Thus in Bengali (Hindu) homes, it is still common for the eldest brother's wife to be addressed by more junior members of the family not by her given name but by a relational term, 'Boudi' (elder wife), which functions virtually as a proper name and affirms her position in the extended family.

Groups tended to be referred to by names designating family (e.g. Pāṇḍava), clan (Vṛṣṇi, Kaurava, Rajput), caste/sub-caste/hereditary social stratum (Brāhmaṇa, Caṭṭopādhyāy, Vaiśya, Caṇḍāla), village or occupation, depending on context. Names for religious sects/denominations were also important. Thus Rāmānuja, a leading theologian of the Śrī Vaiṣṇava community, argued vigorously in his works against various (religious) opponents, whom he knew as Prābhākaras, or Sāṃkhyas, or Bhedābhedavādins, or Pāśupatas, or Bauddhas, or Jainas, and so on. Some of these religious designations could be quite colourful. Thus there were Saivite sects called 'Kāpālika' (bearer of the skull, from *kapāla* or skull, the most distinctive of the insignia of the members of this group), 'Kālāmukha' ('black-faced'), and 'Kānphaṭā' (split-ear, from distinctive earrings worn). Many group names carried more than one connotation, i.e. they could refer not only to caste but also to occupation, or to religious affiliation, or to clan-caste – in short, to a combination of two or more of the main designations mentioned above. Among Hindus today modes of group-naming are still similar to the ways of the past. However, in the aftermath of a developing history of communal conflict and division in the subcontinent, even unlettered peasants would now be disposed to identify themselves as basically Hindus in contrast to being Muslims, Christians, Sikhs, etc.

We have already seen how India acquired its name. In Sanskrit however, the traditional name of the country is Bhārata, and it is this name (in one variant or another) which is used today by most Indians, including Hindus, as the most common alternative to India. It appears, in Devanāgarī script, on Indian postage stamps. For many Hindus at least, Bhārata has more than just modern political connotations. It is a word steeped in sacred history. Bhārata is derived from Bharata, the founder of a dynasty whose origin is lost in the mists of ancient legend. His descendants, the Bhāratas, were first thought of as holding sway in the north central regions of the subcontinent; subsequently Bhārata (or in its compound form, Bhāratavarṣa, Land of the Bhāratas) came to stand for the whole land-mass between the Himalayas in the north and the line of the Vindhya range towards the west. Gradually the application of Bhārata was extended to cover more and more of the subcontinent under Brahminic cultural influence. Today, in its precise sense, the word stands for the political entity that is India.

The sense of the more traditional application of the term can be gleaned from that of a word which is more or less synonymous: Āryāvarta, or Land of the Aryans. The Aryans, it may be remembered, were those, possibly immigrants from the north-west, who began to dominate India in the latter half of the second millennium BCE. 'Ārya', which is how these peoples described themselves in distinction from their co-inhabitants, means 'noble, respectable, accredited', and ever since Hindus have described their culture as 'aryan' as distinct from ways of life that are 'mleccha' or barbaric. Thus Āryāvarta is the land where Aryan, in fact Brahminic or Vedic, culture – its sacred language (Sanskrit), its *dharma*, its worship, its norms and social practices – prevails. Most Hindus today would repudiate the culturally and religiously imperialistic implications of the word Bhārata, though the term still retains residual romantic and historical connotations for some.

Bearing in mind what I have said about the meaning of 'Hinduism' and Hindu, let me now conclude this chapter with further comments about the scope of this book. Our study of the Hindu tradition will be largely phenomenological and historical. That is, we shall be analysing the ideas, views and practices of the Hindus from their historical origins to the present day, not only in the role of observers but as far as possible from inside, from the Hindu perspective itself. It is only in this way that we can begin to have some feel for this multi-faceted and astonishingly rich tradition. Further, our approach will be mainly philosophical and theological in the broadest senses of these terms, though on occasion we may venture remarks which are sociological, anthropological, etc., when they seem appropriate. And we shall give a large place to textual, mainly but by no means exclusively Sanskritic, evidence in our study. I have already suggested reasons for this approach in terms of the relationship between Sanskrit and Brahminic culture.

But this study cannot presume to be anything like exhaustive. The Ancient Banyan is too vast in space and time, too complex to be dealt with comprehensively within the pages of a library, let along a single volume. Here the cobweb analogy comes to mind. One can at best hope to link various nodes of this great tradition by connecting strands of information and analysis in the manner of a cobweb, in which there are far more gaps than solid substance. But, as in a cobweb, we can at least try to make the connections coherently so that the whole picture hangs together. We now embark on this daunting task.

Part I

Guiding voices

2 The voice of scripture as Veda

I

'Scripture' in Hinduism, basically an oral authority. Two historical challenges to orthodox norms. The context of the Vedas; 'Aryans' and Harappans. Origins of the Veda; its content and divisions. Early Vedic religion as sacrificial ritual. The ritual: a 'resonant' and empowering performance. Homology and nyāsa. *Development of the Veda; some lists. The Upaniṣads, Vedānta and Pūrvamīmāṃsā. The place of ritual in Hinduism.*

Let us begin our understanding of religious Hinduism by considering the question of the guiding voices to which the Hindu ear has traditionally been attentive. We can conveniently divide this topic into three headings: the voice of scripture; the voice of tradition; and the voice of experience. In this and the next chapter we shall enquire into the voice of (canonical) scripture.

'Scripture' is perhaps a misleading word. It comes from *scribere* in Latin, which means 'to write'. The equivalent Sanskrit term which we have in mind for scripture in general is *śabda*, which comes from *śabd*: to make a sound, to call. For Hindus, 'scripture' in its most authoritative form is what has been heard and transmitted orally, not what has been written. No doubt in India, down the centuries, scripture has been written down for incidental purposes. But as such it loses vitality; the sacred word springs to life and exerts power when it is spoken and heard. This is why we can quite appropriately speak of the *voice* of scripture in the context of Hinduism. In the history of Christendom, the dominant medium of communicating truth and value has arguably been the written word; the elders of the community have exercised authority by referring to what has been decisively written, either in scripture or in numerous councils or official promulgations of some kind. In this sense, Hinduism is not a religion of the book. In Hinduism, the dominant medium of communicating authoritatively has been by word of mouth: the dominant source, that which has been heard. This is not to say that the medium of seeing has not been important. It has, but in different ways, as we shall appreciate in the course of this book. Traditionally, seeing has not been enough.

There are different weights and dimensions to scriptural authority in Hinduism. Traditionally, in Brahminic Hinduism the sacred word *par excellence* has been the Veda. The Veda is canonical scripture: that which is theoretically the norm for saving knowledge. Veda comes from the root *vid*, to know. Thus the Veda refers to that normative knowledge which saves the human being from the predicament of unfulfilled existence, in this world or hereafter. As such, Veda is a religious term. There are many different views in Hinduism as to what the saving content of Vedic knowledge is and how it works. In due course we shall enquire into some of these views. But there is broad agreement under the umbrella of Brahminic Hinduism (wide-ranging as it is) that *in theory* at least, the Vedas are the source of saving knowledge, even though (a) in practice most Hindus have had no direct access to the Vedas, either in written form or aurally; and (b) for all practical purposes many branches of Hinduism resort to alternative scriptures which seem to have no direct connection with the Vedas.

In the nineteenth century, Vedic authority encountered what may be described as an 'un-Hindu' challenge of massive proportions. Only once before perhaps in the history of subcontinental Hinduism has there been something comparable in scale and intensity.[1] We shall come to this, but in the nineteenth century the Ancient Banyan underwent a far-reaching upheaval, so much so that it was shaken to the core of much of its extensive root-system. But the banyan being what it is – a universe of interlocking worlds in which shock waves to the whole are distributed and absorbed through mutual support between the parts – Hinduism survived, and in some respects was strengthened and imbued with fresh vitality. In fact Hinduism was undergoing what it had successfully weathered countless times before: it was adapting to new influences and circumstances. The major difference was that this time the changes went deeper and further, and the new growth was the result of interaction with western stimuli. We shall say more about this in Chapter 3.

The earlier challenge occurred as Buddhism spread in India in the aftermath of Gautama the Buddha's teaching. Encountering both these challenges introduced a 'modernist' mentality into religious Hinduism. By this I mean that after a painful and not fully resolved power struggle for the high ground among factions of the spokesmen of established authority, Hinduism became more pluralistic. Authority structures fragmented and were increasingly questioned; a rational critique of traditional religious practices was more in evidence; and a greater number of religious options opened up, while a corresponding backlash of revivalist tendencies appeared on the scene. This was the general reaction after both the Buddhist and the nineteenth-century modernist challenges.

The Buddhists (like the Jains, who made a lesser impact) were called *nāstikas*, i.e. those who said 'there is no such thing' (*na* + *asti*) as the authority of the Vedas. Their teaching was regarded as destructive of the whole established way of life, and its chaotic nature is emphasised in the story about the Benares Buddhists in Chapter 1. The Buddha challenged the rationale of Vedic sacrifice and its caste context. This resulted on the one hand in a reaffirmation within Hinduism of the importance of the sacrifice and of caste, and on the other, in far-reaching concessions by way of a reinterpretation of the salvific efficacy of these institutions. The course of Hinduism was changed; an increasing number of populist religious dimensions were opened up.

Whereas the Buddha's challenge came from within the macrocosm of Hindu culture, the challenge of the nineteenth century came from without: from the West. When this happened, it seemed that the opposition between faith and reason had become more fierce, and the tension between the forces for and against traditional Vedic authority more intense. It will be all the more instructive, therefore, to consider the status of the Vedas in their nineteenth-century setting if, in the context of their traditional significance, we wish to have an idea of their relevance for modern Hinduism. But first we need to know something of the origin, structure and content of the Vedas. This will be the major concern of this chapter.

The Vedas encapsulate the religious tradition in the subcontinent of the tribes of the ancient Aryans whom we introduced in Chapter 1. Where these tribes originated from is not clear. There is reason to believe that their ancestors came from the northern regions between the Black and Caspian Seas and then bifurcated westwards into Anatolia (which overlaps with much of modern Turkey) and south-eastwards into the regions that we call Iran today. The pointer to the Anatolian migration is clay tablets found in Hittite archives at modern Bogazkoy (ancient Hattusa), south of the Black Sea. These tablets, which are in Hittite cuneiform and are dated to about 1350 BCE, contain references to deities and numerals which have obvious verbal counterparts in the Aryan language(s) of the people who entered the Indian subcontinent. A further pointer, if not to origins then to interaction along the way, is the close religio-cultural kinship between the Indic-Aryans (i.e. those tribes which entered India) and the followers of the religion of the Avesta in ancient Iran.[2] The early strands of this religion would have been shaped by Zarathustra (or, to give his name its more familiar Greek ring, Zoroaster) by about the beginning of the first millennium BCE. The Indic-Aryans would already have pushed eastwards towards the Hindu Kush, having made their presence felt in the north and north-west by about 1200–1000 BCE.[3]

They had been encountering a more ancient indigenous civilisation centring round the riverine system of the Indus and with origins early in the third millennium BCE. Who were the makers of this civilisation? They were hardly likely to have been aboriginal, like older inhabitants in the interior of the subcontinent. But they had been present for many centuries and in the course of time had built up a comparatively advanced civilisation of vast extent, covering much of the land-mass in the greater north-east of the subcontinent and ranging westwards to the land between the Yamuna and the Ganges and southwards to the latitude of lower Saurashtra (now the Kathiawar peninsula). These peoples are called the Harappans (from the name of one of their foremost cities, Harappa, situated on the banks of the Ravi river, a tributary of the Indus in the north-east) with a lingua franca apparently belonging to the Dravidian family of languages. About 400 miles southwards, on the Indus, was located another chief city of this civilisation, known as Mohenjo-Daro; a number of other large urban sites have also been discovered. We will not go into the various stages and causes of the development and decline of the Indus valley civilisation, nor its architectural, technological, political, economic, and social features. We shall comment briefly on what appear to be some of its leading socio-religious aspects. This is still an obscure subject, for the pictographic script which was in use has yet to be satisfactorily deciphered.[4]

From artefacts unearthed, among the most interesting of which are thousands of miniature embossed seals, mainly of steatite, we conjecture that the Harappans had agricultural and/or vegetative and pastoral, including female, focuses of the divine. There are seals depicting, apparently in a religious context, the following motifs, though there are others: composite animals and/or semi-human figures (e.g. a human face with horns, and the trunk and tusks of an elephant attached to a body with the forepart of a ram and the hindpart of a tiger); a nude woman, upside down, with a plant issuing from between her legs; and an ox-like creature or bull (this is quite common). There is a famous scene of what appears to be a (probably ithyphallic) human figure sitting cross-legged on a kind of stool, with a three-horned head-dress and surrounded by various domesticated and wild animals, (ox, rhino, elephant, tiger, etc.). With some plausibility, this figure has been interpreted as a prototype of Śiva in his form as Lord of the Beasts (*paśupati*) in a yogic posture. Several appliqué terracotta figurines of nearly nude women have also been found. Does this indicate a goddess cult of some sort (not necessarily a fertility cult, which would perhaps require more prominently displayed sexual features)? Again, small stone rings and tubular objects have also been unearthed. Could these have been female and male religious sexual emblems? We cannot give clear answers to these and similar questions about the religion(s) of the Harappans as we are still in the realms of conjecture here. But it may well be that we have in all these apparently cultic representations prototypes of features of later Hinduism formed by a process of synthesis or osmosis as the more martial Aryans gradually intermingled and coexisted with the indigenous peoples that they finally overran. For the time being we must leave it here; we cannot allow even plausible conjecture to run unchecked.

In any case, the Aryan tribes would not have developed a wholly new religious outlook as they entered the subcontinent. In fact, they followed a religious tradition which centred on a sacrificial ritual in which various 'deities' – *devas* (masculine) and *devīs* (feminine) as they called them – or personified focuses of the transcendent as I shall refer to them[5] were invoked in collections of hymns (*ṛks*). (Since there were a number of tribes fanning eastwards and southwards and settling on the land there must have been more than one collection of these hymns.) It is the *Śākala recension of the Ṛk* (sometimes written *Rik*) Saṃhitā or 'collection' – often referred to by itself as the Ṛg (Rig) Veda – that has come down to us. There are 1,028 verse compositions in the *Ṛk* Saṃhitā, the overwhelming majority of which are invocatory hymns.

It is clear from changes in style and content that the corpus developed over several generations of settlers.[6] But the geographical provenance of the different layers of hymns is still subject to dispute. Indeed, some commentators even think that all the hymns were composed within the confines of the subcontinent. Thus one scholar has maintained:

> There can be little doubt that the bulk of the hymns cannot have been produced . . . in the Punjab, where the phenomena of the rains are poor and uninteresting and could not have given rise to the remarkable stress laid on these natural features by the Vedic poets. . . . We must seek for the main home of the Vedic Indian in the country afterwards famous as Kurukṣetra . . . and in the region of Ambāla, and the oldest hymns only, those to Dawn, can reasonably be supposed to have been composed while the invaders were still in the land of the five rivers [the Punjab].[7]

However, it is highly unlikely that no hymns were composed outside the subcontinent. It seems clear from the epigraphic and textual evidence available that the religion of the Vedic Indians was a 'going concern', even in the earliest stages known to us.

Some commentators, however, speculate too much in defence of the view that a hymnic core originated outside India. One puts forward the theory that 'the Indo-Aryans had formulated their association between light and religion from what they saw on the snow-covered plains of their original home, probably in south Russia, and took it with them to India where it was an intrusion'. He continues:

> the physical phenomenon [of dawn] as described in a personified form in the *Rig-Veda* is not normally seen in northern India, where dawn is a reddish flush without radiance. . . . But the Vedas were put in their final shape almost certainly in the Punjab, or in the region between the Sutlej and the Jumna. . . . Thus it would seem that the image of the Vedic Ushas [Dawn] was brought into India by the Aryans from a region where such mornings are a visible climatic phenomenon.[8]

Clearly we are in the realms of fancy here.

The hymns of the *Ṛk* Saṃhitā would have been edited into their final form by about 800 BCE. They are composed in an Indo-European language called Vedic Sanskrit, a precursor of classical Sanskrit, and are divided into ten 'books' or *maṇḍala*s, each of which is traditionally ascribed to an ancient priestly seer or to the family or families of such seers. From the religious point of view, a *maṇḍala* is a cycle or unit of space or time set apart for a specific purpose. This term points to the fact that the overall purpose of the hymns was to serve what lay at the heart of Vedic religion: the priestly sacrificial ritual (*yajña*). Here we are not concerned with Vedic religion so much as with how and why the Vedas as the spoken word are a source of religious authority.

It seems that the *Ṛk* Saṃhitā was compiled to act only as a record of sacred hymns. The way these hymns were used in the sacrificial ritual gave rise to two further Saṃhitās or collections: the *Sāma* and the *Yajur*. The *Sāma* Saṃhitā (sometimes simply called the *Sāma* Veda) has two divisions. The first consists of hymns, the majority those of the *Ṛk* Saṃhitā; the second consists of notated chants (*sāmans*) to which these hymns were set, contained in groupings called *gaṇas*. The *Yajur* Saṃhitā or Veda (again 'Veda' as understood in a restricted sense) contains hymns found in the *Ṛg*, as also prose and verse formulas (*yajurs*) which were muttered (as opposed to chanted) by the priests during the performance of the ritual.

There is a fourth Saṃhitā called the *Atharva*, but its content sets it apart from the other three. Though in parts it is very old, perhaps as old as the *Ṛk* Saṃhitā, and though it makes ample reference to *devas* and *devīs* of the *Ṛk*, it is largely composed of earthy verse-spells for protection against life's problems (fevers and sicknesses, enemies, sorcery, snake-bites, bad dreams, and so on), and for bringing something about (e.g. the goodwill of others, victory in battle, success in love, healthy cattle, good crops and rain, virility, and power in society); it also contains hymns of homage to gods. It seems that the distinctiveness of this Saṃhitā was the reason why at first it was not accorded an authority equal to that of the other three Saṃhitās. In early strands of Hindu thought, the *Ṛg*, *Yajur* and *Sāma* Vedas are sometimes lumped together without mention of an *Atharva* collection.[9] But by about 400–300 BCE the concept of 'the four Vedas' (*catur-vedāḥ*) as an authoritative bloc took hold, and the *Atharva* Veda is made to follow the same pattern of textual development as that of the other three Vedas. We will explore this development later. The fullest picture, therefore, of the Vedic Indian's conception of the transcendent, in its earliest phases, can be derived from the *Ṛk* Saṃhitā (since the *Yajur* and *Sāma* Saṃhitās are mainly ritualistic in function, and the *Atharva* Saṃhitā does not say much that is original about the transcendent). This is why reference to the *Ṛg* Veda overwhelmingly dominates studies of the beginning of Vedic religion.

Thus in the course of time, four Saṃhitās – the *Ṛk*, the *Yajur*, the *Sāma* and the *Atharva* – were established as a canonical bloc. To each were attached prose descriptions and explanations of various sacrificial rites, called Brāhmaṇas, in the process of which the ritual itself was cast in a new perspective. The Brāhmaṇas were followed by compositions called Āraṇyakas (mainly in prose) and Upaniṣads (which contain a substantial amount of verse) –

compositions which purported to represent progressively deeper reflection on the inner meaning and reality of the ritual. Thus, upon completion, this canon of sacred language consisted of four Vedas ('Veda' in its broad sense, sometimes collectively called 'the Veda') – the *Ṛk*, the *Yajur*, the *Sāma* and the *Atharva* – each traditionally divided into four segments: Saṃhitā, Brāhmaṇa, Āraṇyaka, and Upaniṣad. Though these four genres of texts are always represented, the actual literary development of a Veda may not always follow this neat division. The last of the Upaniṣads of the canon were composed by about 500 CE, so that from start to finish – that is, from the beginning of the compilation of the Saṃhitās to the composition of the latest Upaniṣads – the Vedas as a whole took something over a millennium and a half to develop (from *c.* 1200 BCE to *c.* 500 CE). They contain a vast and varied body of sacred language, all of which, in one way or another (sometimes quite indirectly), is concerned with the sacrificial ritual.

In its early stages, Vedic religion was dominated by the *performance* of sacrificial ritual (*yajña*). Here we must distinguish between what has been called the solemn and the non-solemn ritual. The solemn ritual as a whole was a varied and complex public affair, consisting in general of three kinds of sacrifice: (i) the oblation of grain (rice or barley) in some way; (ii) the oblation of an animal or animals (mainly goats), and (iii) the *soma* rituals. *Soma* was originally the juice of a hill or mountain plant,[10] which was strained and fermented and sometimes heated. It had heady qualities and was inbibed during the ritual, helping to initiate its votaries into the mystic vision of the meaning and power of sacred speech (*śabda*) in association with the gods of which the early seers speak. Thus from earliest recorded times religion on the subcontinent was no stranger to imbibed stimulants. The solemn ritual could be a highly complex affair, requiring from between four to sixteen priestly ministrants, and was to proliferate enormously in the course of time. Its performance required the installation, among other things, of three fires: the *gārhapatya* (household fire), the *āhavanīya* (fire-of-the-offering), and the *dakṣiṇāgni* (southern fire).[11]

The solemn *yajña* was performed with various objectives in mind, some explicit, some implicit; some tangible (e.g. wealth, health, victory in battle), some not so tangible (e.g. immortality). In essence, the sacrificial ritual consisted of the performance of specific actions, set to specific utterances mainly in (Sanskritic) metre, in a determinate place and time which were 'sacred', that is, which brought the world of the individuals involved in the ritual into contact with the transcendent. The *yajña*, especially the solemn variety, was the bridge between the empirical world and the divine world. We shall deal with the non-solemn ritual later.

It was the appropriate utterance of the sacred word (*vāc*) which suffused the sacrificial ritual with its inalienable power. The success of the ritual and the realisation of its objectives depended on the due utterance of the sacred word. The ritual was a *resonant* performance. Its vibrations resonated to the depths of human and divine reality, and attuned the human to the divine. This harmonisation effected cosmic and natural order. It prevented the heavens and their luminaries from crashing to earth and preserved the rhythms of nature: the regularity of day and night, the seasonal cycles, the round of birth, growth and reproduction, and in the process it bestowed welfare and the promise of immortality to the beneficiaries of the ritual. The verses of all the Saṃhitās, including those of the *Atharva* Saṃhitā, are in their various ways concerned with these things. And though a great many of these verse compositions, especially from the *Atharva*, may not have formed part of the *sacrificial* ritual, the reason of their efficacy is clear: ritual utterance. That is why even the spells of the *Atharva* Saṃhitā were considered to be efficacious and sacred. When uttered in the right context, i.e. ritualistically (though not necessarily as part of the sacrificial ritual) by those entitled to do so and with the appropriate intention, they resonated with power, they could accomplish their particular objectives as spells by unlocking and marshalling the inner potencies of things. Hence their twofold functional division: *svādhyāya-artham* (for purposes of private recitation), and *prayoga-artham* (for the sake of implementation). Even today, spells from the *Atharva* Veda have a popular following.

'Working' the ritual was no doubt a form of activity, but it was also an exercise of *knowledge.* If one was eligible to perform the ritual and had the know-how (it was not a matter of 'knowing-that'), one was, as we have seen, in a position of power in Vedic society. From this time on, the simple formula that religious knowledge equals this-worldly power continues to reverberate in one form or another throughout Hinduism. The content of this knowledge will change as context changes, and religious thinkers will argue about whether spiritual knowledge should be sought for personal power of some kind or for salvific ends, or at least about the relative merits of pursuing spiritual knowledge for power or for salvation, but the acknowledgement of the equation itself will surive. Thus, belief in the equation lies at the heart of an important practice mentioned repeatedly in the Upaniṣads. It may be called 'homology', which is a form of realising or experiencing a (supposedly) *real* correspondence between an aspect of the individual (the microcosm) and a feature of external reality (the macrocosm). Here is an example. The very first verse of the *BĀUp* converts the sacrificial horse (the individual) of the elaborate *aśvamedha* sacrifice into a cosmic symbol. Its head is identified or homologised with the dawn, its sight with the sun, its breath with the wind, its body with the year, its back with the sky, and so on. The adept is required to realise these correspondences by a spiritual discipline, the idea being that once this is done the adept will derive spiritual energy or merit equivalent to that generated by the actual performance of the *aśvamedha* ritual. The ritual has been interiorised, its external form emasculated.

Take another example, one which focuses on an aspect of *aśvamedha* homology, i.e. the correspondence between breath and wind. On a number of occasions the Upaniṣads homologise breath and wind. This is done by identifying certain speech acts or aspects of speech acts of the ritual with the wind or air, or by advocating breath control (*prāṇāyāma*). One who knows how to control breath can control the winds, for one is in control of the specific power or energy underlying breath and wind via the homology between the two. Varying degrees of mastery of this correspondence, that is, varying degrees of 'realising' it, result, for example, in varying degrees of control over the length of one's life (which depends on breath). Thus the *Chāndogya* Upaniṣad declares that the one who *knows* (*veda*) the *Gāyatrī* chant which is woven into the vital breaths (*prāṇa*s) controls these breaths (i.e. becomes a *prāṇī*) and lives a long and successful life (II.11.1,2). The older Upaniṣads in particular make many homologies of this kind.

Belief in homology, and the practice of realising (mentally and actually) this identification (called *nyāsa* in a number of traditions), has had and continues to have extensive currency. In Tantra (see p. 50), *nyāsa* played a central role in the spiritual discipline, whether for salvific reasons or for personal ends. It was believed that by progressively identifying with the Goddess, after first having mentally 'installed' her or features of her at various places in and about his person, the adept could gain control over the path to liberation or, if he so chose, over other people or aspects of nature. This was possible because there were homologies between the microcosm (himself) and the macrocosm (the world) in so far as both are emanations of a single source, the deity. By realising a homology the adept acquired control over its underlying power. On one level this was a purely natural process, since it is a fact of nature that these homologies exist. At this level, irrespective of ethical or religious considerations, the adept could tap into certain homologies and acquire the natural powers or accomplishments (*siddhi*s) that they generated such as control over the force of gravity (demonstrated by walking on water, flying through the air, etc.), becoming invisible, becoming immense or minute in size, and so on. Such know-how is neutral where the achieving of ethical ends is concerned; morally, it can be used for good or ill. It is only on the level of striving for salvation where mutual love between adept and deity comes into play that morality enters into the realisation of homologies. On the 'natural level', a similar view prevails in the classical yoga tradition (which in important respects influenced Tantric practice).

Belief in the validity of homology and *nyāsa* has been widely current, even in modern times. Thus it is believed that the advanced yogī or spiritual adept can decide when to die (for he has power over his vital force or *prāṇa*). The death of Swami Vivekananda (1863–1902), a leading figure of the Ramakrishna movement (see Chapter 3), is officially explained in this way. I have also heard it said that Christ was able to walk on water for similar reasons. In the Hindu family of religions the conviction that spiritual knowledge in the form of know-how brings mundane power of some kind is still common, and this brings us back to early Vedic religion.

The central goal of this religion was, as we have noted, the efficacious performance of the solemn ritual (*yajña* in its primary sense). To this end, the metrical compositions, mainly of the *Ṛk* Saṃhitā, were rendered into formulaic utterances, to be either muttered or chanted. This is the rationale for the *Yajur* and *Sāma* Saṃhitās. The priests lived and breathed the *yajña*. They specialised hereditarily in different aspects of ritual performance. They were *par excellence* the utterers of the sacred word, those who tapped its power as manifest in the sacrificial ritual. Not surprisingly, the *yajña* became increasingly elaborate, generally requiring the ordered participation of a number of priests. Different *śākhā*s or 'branches' of *yajña* performance and its interpretation (including Vedic recitation) developed under the heading of each Veda. Each *śākhā* had its priestly exponents whose job it was to preserve and propagate the content of their tradition. Yet as 'branches' they were part of the same Vedic enterprise, professionally drawing sustenance from the life-sap of Vedic practice and seeking, in common and by combining in the performance of the ritual, to accomplish its ends.

Though the *Ṛk* Saṃhitā has been transmitted in only one recension, the *Śākala*, as noted earlier, the *Yajur* has two traditions, the

'Dark' (*kṛṣṇa*, sometimes translated 'black') and the 'Bright' (*śukla*, sometimes translated 'white'). It seems that the Dark was so-called because its *yajurs* or formulas are admixed with explanatory comment, whereas the formulas of the Bright are unmixed in this way: its explanatory comment has been recorded separately in the form of the lengthy and important *Śatapatha* Brāhmaṇa. The Saṃhitā of the Bright *Yajur* Veda is called the *Vājasaneyī*, while the Saṃhitā of the Dark *Yajur* Veda has three complete recensions: the *Taittirīya*, the *Kāṭhaka* and the *Maitrāyaṇī*. The Saṃhitā of the *Sāma* Veda has come to us in three traditions of chant: those of the *Kauthuma*, the *Rāṇāyanīya* and the *Jaiminīya*. Two recensions of the *Atharva* Saṃhitā are extant: the *Paippalāda* and the *Śaunaka*, the latter being the more usually cited. It is almost impossible to assign dates to the final versions of the four Vedic Saṃhitās, since their material was subject to interpolation and addition. But we will not be far wrong if we fix a lower limit of about 750 BCE for the compilation of the bulk of the material, keeping in mind that most of the *Ṛk* Saṃhitā and portions of the *Atharva* are the oldest (*c*. 1200–800 BCE).

As the *yajña* and its priestly ministration became more complex and more subject to interpretation, various explanations of what was going on were appended to what were in effect the verse sections of the Saṃhitās. These were the Brāhmaṇas – so-called because they were concerned with the significance of the *brahman*, the inner power of the sacrificial utterance, which had come under the control of the professional priests, the Brahmins (also *brāhmaṇa*s in Sanskrit). We have noted that the *Śatapatha* Brāhmaṇa belongs to the Bright *Yajur* Veda. This Brāhmaṇa, which has two recensions (the *Kāṇva* and the *Mādhyaṃdina*), is the lengthiest Brāhmaṇa available and is usually taken to be the most representative of this genre of sacred language.[12] The *Ṛk* Saṃhitā has the *Aitareya* and the *Kauṣītakī* Brāhmaṇas; the *Pancaviṃśa* and the *Jaiminīya* represent the Brāhmaṇas of the *Sāma* Veda, while the *Atharva* Veda had attached to it the *Gopatha* Brāhmaṇa, apparently to make it conform to the pattern of the other three. This is not a complete list – we have left out some names, while tradition records a number of lost Saṃhitā recensions and Brāhmaṇas – but it gives a good idea of the range of the available corpus. The bulk of Brāhmaṇa text would have been redacted by about 600 BCE. One must remember that the compilation of the Saṃhitās and the redaction of the Brāhmaṇas, and indeed the composition and edition of what follows as scripture,[13] was a staggered process without too many neat boundaries of time and space. Thus the earlier Brāhmaṇas were being composed while portions of the Saṃhitās were still being finally edited, and texts reflecting the ongoing interpretation of the ritual continued to appear while the later Brāhmaṇas were still being redacted.

What were these post-Brāhmaṇa texts? The thinking of the Brāhmaṇas phased into a more symbolical reflection on the sacrificial ritual, which was expressed in (mainly prose) collections called Āraṇyakas. The Āraṇyakas themselves developed into the final stage of this increasingly interiorised reflection on the *yajña* and its world, which was recorded, both in verse and prose, in the Upaniṣads. Each Veda has its own Āraṇyakas and Upaniṣads. Thus the *Aitareya* Āraṇyaka, the *Aitareya* Upaniṣad and the later *Kauṣītakī* Āraṇyaka and its Upaniṣad belong to the *Ṛg* Veda. Both Upaniṣads are essentially prose compositions. The other three Vedas have reproduced a larger number of authoritative Āraṇyakas and Upaniṣads. The *Bṛhad-āraṇyaka* Upaniṣad belongs to the branch of the Bright *Yajur* Veda, and is actually a prose composite of Āraṇyaka and Upaniṣad as its name implies. This forms part of the last portion of the *Śatapatha* Brāhmaṇa and, like its source, exists in the two abovementioned recensions. Like the *Aitareya* this Upaniṣad contains some of the oldest Upanishadic material available. The *Taittirīya* Upaniṣad (which is an old prose Upaniṣad but not as old as the Upaniṣads mentioned) forms sections 7–9 of the *Taittirīya* Āraṇyaka which belongs to the *Taittirīya* branch of the Dark *Yajur* Veda. The last section (10) of the *Taittirīya* Āraṇyaka comprises the *Mahānārāyaṇa* Upaniṣad, which is a relatively late metrical composition.

The short *Īśa* and the fairly long *Kaṭha* and *Śvetāśvatara* Upaniṣads, all three metrical, belong to the *Yajur* Veda, the first being located as the last section of its *Vājasaneyī* (i.e. Bright) Saṃhitā, the latter two belonging to the *Taittirīya* branch of its Dark tradition. The *Kaṭha* seems to be the earliest (*c*. 400 BCE) and the *Śvetāśvatara* the latest of the three (*c*. 100 CE). Two other, later, metrical Upaniṣads, sometimes quoted as authoritative by classical theologians, belong to the *Yajur* Veda: the *Maitrī* or *Maitrāyaṇīya* and the *Subāla*. The former belongs to the Dark and the latter to the Bright tradition. Their dates are not clear, though they are probably not later than the first half of the first millennium CE.

The oldest Upaniṣad of the *Sāma* Veda is the *Chāndogya*. This long and important Upaniṣad is, by and large, not as old as the *Bṛhad-āraṇyaka*, but it is older than the *Taittirīya*. It is a prose composition and comprises the last two sections of the *Chāndogya* Brāhmaṇa which runs to ten sections in all. Keith notes that 'the first two sections of the [*Chāndogya*] are of the Āraṇyaka type, but as with texts attached to the Sāmaveda, generally do not bear that name' (1925/1970: 499). The *Kena* Upaniṣad, in part metrical, is old and belongs to the *Jaiminīya* or *Talavakāra* Brāhmaṇa of this Veda.

Finally, the *Muṇḍaka* Upaniṣad (old, metrical), and the *Praśna*, *Māṇḍūkya* and *Jābāla* Upaniṣads (all three in late prose) belong to the *Atharva* Veda. Once again, it must be stressed that this is not a complete list of the Āraṇyakas and Upaniṣads of the Vedic canon, yet it contains the names of the most authoritative Upaniṣads and most of the canonical compositions quoted by the classical Vedic theologians.[14] In date, the *Jābāla* can be grouped with the *Maitrī* and the *Subāla*. You may think that these lists and names are rather boring, and with justification. Yet they have their use. You may need to consult them for further study in view of the importance of the Vedas for an understanding of Hinduism; they also help to form an impression of the extent, complexity and development of Vedic scriptural tradition.

Now to a more interesting point. There is a general tendency to refer to the Upaniṣads collectively as the 'Vedānta' (i.e. *veda* + *anta* = end of the Vedas), where 'end' is understood both in its chronological and teleological senses. In other words, the Upaniṣads are assumed to be the last sections of the Vedas and to consummate Vedic meaning. But this generalisation is both inaccurate and misleading. It is inaccurate because, as we have already indicated, the Upaniṣads do not invariably bring the Vedic corpus to an end textually, though they do represent the latest genre of scriptural language. Thus the short but well-known *Aitareya* Upaniṣad of the *Ṛg* Veda is ensconced between chapters of the *Aitareya* Āraṇyaka, while the shorter *Īśa* Upaniṣad is appended to the *Vājasaneyī* Saṃhitā of the *Yajur* Veda.

The generalisation is misleading, because not every important tradition of religious Hinduism acknowledges the Upaniṣads as the quintessence of Vedic knowledge. This stance is adopted, *par excellence*, by a theological tradition itself called the Vedānta (or Uttara Mīmāṃsā, i.e. Later School of Vedic Exegesis), whose origins are contemporaneous with the composition of the latest authoritative Upaniṣads. The Vedāntins became one of the most important philosophical-theological exponents of religious Hinduism from about 500–700 CE, and remain so until this day. They maintained that it is not the performance of the ritual that is the goal of the Vedas, but the contemplative interiorisation of the ritual in one's life and being. The Upaniṣads reveal the method and the goal (which was called *Brahman*) of this interiorising process. *Brahman* is the sole underlying reality of all diversity; the Upaniṣads reveal the nature of *Brahman*, of our true self (*ātman*), and of the inner relationship between the two despite the misleading appearances of life in this world. This is the inner meaning of the *yajña*, the sacrificial ritual, which is the bridge between this world and immortality. The *yajña* performed externally is only the symbol of the *yajña* to be performed internally. The Vedantic schools differ in their views about the nature of *Brahman* and of the relationship between *Brahman* and *ātman*, but they all agree that it is the Upaniṣads that are the source of the saving knowledge concerning these realities. As such, they refer to the Upaniṣads as the *śiras* or 'head' of the body of the Vedas.

The classical Vedāntins were reacting to the position of the already strongly established Pūrva Mīmāṃsakas (followers of the Earlier School of Vedic Exegesis) who for their part maintained that it was the Saṃhitās and the Brāhmaṇas, portions of the Veda directly concerned with the *performance* – not the interiorisation – of the sacrificial ritual, which were the most important part of the Vedic corpus. The Pūrva Mīmāṃsakas were in no doubt that the saving knowledge inculcated by the Vedas centred on the implementation of the sacrificial ritual in all its variety and complexity. The proper performance of the *yajña* would bring tangible results, both for the individual or individuals who sponsored the ritual (either for earthly ends – progeny, wealth, success in various this-worldly enterprises – or for a satisfactory post-mortem existence), as well as for society at large, in the form of cosmic stability and social well-being. For the Pūrva Mīmāṃsakas the goals advocated by the Upaniṣads, i.e. the knowledge and attainment of *Brahman*, were esoteric and secondary, if at all realisable.

The Pūrva Mīmāṃsakas (sometimes called Karma Mīmāṃsakas because they regarded sacrificial action (*karman*) as all-important) divided the sacred word (*śabda*) into three headings from the point of view of the performance of the *yajña*: (i) *mantra* (the verse or prose formulas of the ritual); (ii) *vidhi* (the directives to act or not to act in a certain way in connection with ritual); and (iii) *arthavāda* (the different kinds of statements purporting to explain the ritual or the hidden reality underlying it). They maintained that Vedic language was essentially action-oriented, i.e. essentially *vidhi*-cum-*mantra*, telling us how to act, and not fact-assertive, i.e. giving information about the nature of transcendent being. The Upaniṣads, being concerned mainly with *arthavāda*, or explanation (*vāda*) about the nature of things (*artha*), and not action-to-be-performed (*kārya*), were of secondary importance. We shall not pursue this debate between the Pūrva Mīmāṃsakas and the Vedāntins further. Here the point is that to call the Upaniṣads the 'Vedānta' implies a value-judgement which has not been accepted by all prominent Hindu schools of thought, even though it may be the case today that the majority of the (religious) Hindu intelligentsia subscribe to some kind of Vedantic interpretation of the Vedas.

But this does not mean that the Pūrva Mīmāṃsakas either did not for long exert a powerful influence in the history of Hindu religious thought (as advocates of a rival position, they remained a thorn in the side for Vedāntin theologians for nearly a thousand years) or that their emphasis on liturgical performance did not surface and manifest itself in other ways both during and after the period of their philosophical prominence. The Pūrva Mīmāṃsaka emphasis on public religious ritual and its efficacy struck and reinforced an answering chord deep in Hindu minds. For nearly two-and-a-half millennia, the more or less widespread performance of the complex sacrificial ritual resonated to this chord, but during that time – textual evidence for this begins to surface two or three centuries before the beginning of the Common Era – a new outlet for the Hindu's love of ritual practice became evident: the liturgy of devotional cults to the deity. This kind of liturgy overlapped with another kind (Tantra), texts of which become prominent from about 500–600 CE. Concurrent with this, the proliferating rites of passage (*saṃskāra*s) continued apace throughout Hindudom. These phenomena will be discussed later in the book. Thus, though the performance of the solemn Vedic ritual on a large scale may have died down by about the sixteenth century,[15] it was the original Pūrva Mīmāṃsaka concern for ritual that stoked the continuing Hindu liturgical preoccupation with bells and smells, incense and flowers, rites and ceremonies, both in the temple and in the home. Hindus are inveterately ritual-minded – sometimes in an enlightened way, sometimes even to the point of superstition – and the model for ritual, embedded deep in their psyche, is the Vedic *yajña*, which for our purposes in this chapter leads us nicely to where it all started: the performance of the sacrificial ritual in the religion of the *Ṛk*, *Sāma* and *Yajur* Saṃhitās.

II

Immortality the Vedic goal. The shaping of the Vedic 'canon': historical, mythological and theological considerations; the role of Brahmā. Various traditional views about the Veda considered: Mīmaṃsā, Bhartṛhari, Tantra. A contemporary anecdote. Mantra*: its meaning, purpose and scope. Veda as* śruti.

For Hindus, Vedic religion encapsulates the earliest phase of the quest of saving knowledge in their history. According to this understanding, it was the knowledgeable implementation of the ritual in its private and public contexts which constituted saving knowledge. Saving knowledge was what achieved well-being (*svasti*) in its earthly or heavenly forms. Thus, if one desired victory in battle or long life or the wealth of many cattle, particular solemn rituals were prescribed; these or other sacrifices could also bring about a happy immortality in the next life. Though different rites had different objectives, many of which were concerned with aspects of earthly well-being as indicated, it is true to say that the *ultimate* goal of the Indic Aryan – the ultimate fruit of saving knowledge – became the well-being of *immortality* in a heavenly realm after death.[16] In other words, saving knowledge culminated in immortality (*amṛtatva*). The concept of immortality as the final goal of human existence changed both in the Vedas themselves and in their subsequent interpretation. Thus immortality as understood in the Upaniṣads (and by their interpreters, the Vedāntins) differs from the immortality intimated by the Saṃhitās. This may also be said about the *attainment* of immortality. In the religion of the Saṃhitās, immortality is attained by ritual performance, and in that of the Upaniṣads by the contemplative and recitative interiorisation of the ritual. But it is immortality, according to either understanding, and the way to attain it, that is the central concern of the Vedic corpus. Quite simply then, the Vedas were the source and norm of the sacred word as authoritative – the voice of scripture *par excellence* – because they were (and are) accepted by the literate Hindu community at large as the earliest complete and decisive repository of saving knowledge: the knowledge that revealed the way to the goal of human existence, namely immortality. We can now begin to appreciate the enormity of the challenge to traditional orthodoxy of the Buddha and his followers when they repudiated the authority of the Vedas and proposed a new understanding of how human fulfilment is to be attained.

We may ask, how did the Vedic canon come to be fixed, and by whom? Historically, there is no definite answer. Hinduism has never had such things as magisterial Councils empowered, on behalf of 'the faithful', to determine canonical texts, fix their meaning in verbal formulations, and hurl anathemas at dissenters. Doubtless the determiners and guardians of orthodoxy, the Brahmin priests, by taking account of various circumstances (e.g. challenges to their hegemony by dissenters inside and outside the caste system), had the dominant voice in determining the corpus. For this, the established tradition of memorising and propagating strands of the Vedas in the different *śākhās* or schools of Vedic recitation and interpretation would have played a crucial part. The compositions and reflections of eminent sages within the ambit of the *śākhās* would have developed the corpus. Redactors would have both edited and then located these compositions in already established parts of the Vedas. In any case, in comparison to the quite determinate scriptural canon of traditional Christianity and Islam, for example, the boundaries of the Vedic scriptures as they have come down to us are not particularly neat. Thus Śaṃkara (600–700 CE), the earliest Vedāntin theologian whose works have survived intact, has written commentaries on ten or so Upaniṣads to which he clearly accorded canonical status (and only on particular recensions of these, where recensions exist), though he supports his views by quoting from a few other Upaniṣads which he must also have regarded as authoritative.

To the Upanishadic corpus cited by Śaṃkara, Rāmānuja, who lived in the eleventh century and who was a leading theologian of another Vedantic tradition, adds a couple more. And other classical Vedañtin luminaries extend slightly the number of Upaniṣads that they recognise as authoritative. But for all its fluidity the Vedic corpus did have edges. We are all used to the concept of variants within a fixed scriptural canon. This, by and large, was the case within the Vedic corpus. Though there is some unclarity as regards exactly which were the variants and texts of the four Vedas at various points and in various traditions during the development of Hinduism, from the time of Śaṃkara at any rate there is remarkable unanimity among orthodox Hindus about the broad extent of the Vedic corpus. And with the passage of time, this unanimity became increasingly corporate. Antiquity, for Hindus, is a great guarantor of authenticity and authority.

If historically we are not clear about the formation of the Vedas, mythologically and theologically Hindu tradition has more definite answers. Let us start with mythology. Before we go any further, it is as well to point out here that 'myth' in this book is used in its technical sense, that is, to refer to a form of narrative that is the vehicle of different kinds of truth. 'Myth' is not being used in its everyday, degenerate sense of 'tall story', 'nonsensical or false tale'. Myth conveys truth: psychologically and sociologically about the myth-makers; religiously and historically about its subjects and themes, and their origins and contexts.

Mythologically, in traditional Brahminic Hinduism the origin of the Vedas has been associated with the deity Brahmā. We have already met Brahmā in the story about Divodāsa in Chapter 1 (see p. 15).[17] Lord Brahmā, you will recall, was one of Śiva's emissaries, sent to detect a flaw in king Divodāsa's dharmic armour which Śiva could exploit to oust him from his beloved city of Benares. It is significant that Brahmā went in the guise of a Brahmin priest, requesting the king's patronage for the performance of ten *aśvamedha* (or horse) sacrifices. The *aśvamedha* was an elaborate Vedic ritual. Ten such sacrifices complicated things enormously, and would severely test Divodāsa's adherence to *dharma*. In the event, Divodāsa complied flawlessly with Brahmā's request. Not only did the king's position in Benares remain impregnable, but to add fuel to fire, Brahmā himself decided to stay on in Benares, captivated as he was by the city's beauty. What interests us here is the association of Brahmā with the Vedic ritual.

It is generally assumed by scholars that Brahmā, as a Hindu deity, post-dates the earliest strands of Vedic religion and is a personification of *brahman*, understood either as the latent power encapsulated in the Vedic ritual, or as the supreme Spirit which is the ultimate concern of the Upaniṣads. However, according to some scholars, the late origin ascribed to Brahmā as a deity may be misconceived. There are some references to what could be a male persona of the divine (i.e. a *deva*), called Brahmā, in the *Ṛk* Saṃhitā. Two such references occur in the first hymn of the second *maṇḍala*. This is a hymn to the *deva* Agni (who manifests as fire) in which Agni is eulogised by ascribing to him various priestly functions, and indeed by 'identifying' him with other personae of the transcendent. There are many such identifications, but the third verse says: 'You, Agni, are Indra, best among the righteous! You are Viṣṇu of the mighty stride, adorable! You are "Brahmā", full of sacrificial wealth, O lord of the *brahman*! You are the Supporter; you favour us with kindness'.[18]

In this context *brahmā* is generally translated as pertaining to the priesthood in some way, but such a translation seems strained. In this verse Agni has already been unambiguously 'identified' with two *deva*s, Indra and Viṣṇu; semantic symmetry would require the referent of *brahmā* to be a third *deva*. This would make good sense of *rayivid* as 'abounding in the wealth that derives from the sacrifice or that is needed to institute the sacrifice'. In other words, according to this meaning Brahmā would be the *deva* who liberally bestows wealth, possessions, etc. by means of the sacrifice and/or who abounds in such wealth in the first place, just as Indra is the best among the righteous (or, 'among all beings': *vṛṣabhaḥ satām*) and Viṣṇu is he of the mighty stride (*urugāya*). The last part of the verse

– 'You are the Supporter (*tvaṃ vidhartaḥ*)' – could then be construed as amplifying the reference to Brahmā as a *deva*. Note that in later Hinduism, when Brahmā is well-established as a deity, he is distinctively referred to as supporting or fashioning/arranging the world. This interpretation of *brahmā* may well apply in the previous verse in which Agni is again referred to by this term.[19] Brahmā could have been the *deva* associated with the fashioning or support of the world through the *yajña*, in the religion of a particular tribe or group of tribes. Not universally acknowledged among the Aryans at first (hence his sparse appearance in the Saṃhitās), he could in the course of time have come to occupy a position of increasing prominence. In any case, however *brahmā* may be interpreted in all these instances, it is certainly a concept that is generally associated with the performance of the sacrificial ritual of Vedic religion, through which the world is continuously established.

In the course of time Brahmā became a persona in his own right and was identified with Prajāpati, the divine figure in the Brāhmaṇas and occasionally in post-Brāhmaṇa literature, who was responsible for the production and governance of all being ('*prajāpati*' means 'Lord/Progenitor of creatures'). As such, Brahmā often appears in the epics and other folkloric accounts (e.g. the Purāṇas), where he is usually described by such epithets as 'self-existent' (*svayaṃ-bhū*), 'the Supporter/Disposer' (*dhātṛ*, *vidhātṛ*), 'the Maker/Lord of the world' (*loka-kartṛ*, *jagat-pati*), and so on. Mythologically, it is in his capacity as maker of all being that Brahmā is regarded as producing the Vedas and the Vedic ritual (a throwback perhaps to the 'Brahmā' of the *Ṛk* Saṃhitā?).

In the *Brahmāṇḍa* Purāṇa (*c.* 300–900 CE; 1.2.8. vrs.1ff),[20] we are given a mythic account of how Brahmā produces all things:

> From his first [i.e. eastern] mouth, Brahmā measured out the Gāyatrī metre, the *Ṛg* [Veda], the Triple Praise and Rathaṃtara Chant, and the Agniṣṭoma among the sacrifices. Then from his southern mouth he emitted the sacrificial formulas [*yajur*s], the Triṣṭubh metre, the Chandas metre, the Fifteenfold Praise and what is known as the Great Chant. Then from his western mouth he emitted the chants [*sāman*s, of the *Sāma* Veda), the Jagatī metre, the Seventeenfold Praise as also the Vairūpya and Atirātra rituals. And from his fourth [northern] mouth he emitted the Twenty-One Praise, the *Atharva* [Veda], the Āptoryāma ritual and the Anuṣṭubh and Vairāja metres . . . [Brahmā] measured out the verses, the formulas and the chants so that the sacrifice may

be accomplished. Beings, high and low, were born from the limbs of Brahmā, for [he is] the Lord of beings [Prajāpati], who emits creation's stream, having first produced the fourfold order of the gods, the sages, the ancestors, and human beings.

This extract contains a number of points of interest. Note that the four Vedas are referred to in their traditional order: *Ṛg*, *Yajur*, *Sāma* and *Atharva*, and that an important place is given to various Vedic rituals and practices. In spite of the obvious proliferation of popular devotional cults, etc., the Vedic tradition was still central – at least by its binding and normative symbolic value. Further, Brahmā is depicted as having four mouths, facing east, west, south and north respectively. In fact, Brahmā is also known as 'four-faced' and 'four-mouthed' (*catur-mukha; catur-vaktra*) in folkloric tradition and iconographically he is usually portrayed as having four heads, one towards each cardinal point of the compass, four hands (with the text of the Veda in one hand) and riding a flying swan or goose (*haṃsa*), the symbol of discerning wisdom. His consort is said to be Vāc (sacred utterance personified) or Sarasvatī (the 'goddess' of learning). Though Brahmā has four heads, from which the four Vedas are progressively promulgated as described above, the mythic relationship between the heads and the Vedas is not as straightforward as might be desired. There are myths to tell us that Brahmā originally had *five* heads, one of which was chopped off by Śiva in punishment for a transgression. These myths seek to assert the supremacy of Śiva, and according to one version it was because Brahmā had claimed falsely that he had grasped the extent of Śiva's greatness that he was thus punished. But before we are led, almost imperceptibly, by a process of lateral thinking to a completely different topic along the tangled skein of Hindu myth, let us turn to more philosophical and theological considerations about the origin and status of the Vedas.

In this context the Pūrva Mīmāṃsakas and the Vedāntins, implacable adversaries over a number of aspects of Vedic interpretation, agree in a fundamental respect, and provide the dominant model in the history of Hindu thought to explain the Vedas' authority. Both traditions agree that the Vedas are eternal (*nitya*) and have no personal author (i.e. they are *apauruṣeya* or impersonal as to their composition), though there is disagreement about further particulars. For instance, though there is general agreement that the Vedas, namely the particular sounds and their precise verbal order in the corpus (including the variants), have always existed, there was disagreement between the Vedāntins and one faction of the Pūrva

Mīmāṃsakas about what we may call the Vedas' mode of explicit existence. The Vedāntins, in common with most Hindus who followed the 'high' tradition, believed that the universe is emitted, endures for a fixed time, and is then dissolved, in endless cycles (see below and Chapter 10 for further details). In this conception, the Vedas as we have them, and as part of the experienceable universe, would be subject to this regular process of dissolution and reproduction. While dissolved, however, they would not exist explicitly but only implicitly, as potentially manifestable in their traditional form, namely the form that we know. On the other hand, some Pūrva Mīmāṃsakas believed that there is no periodic production and dissolution of the world, and that the Vedas have always existed in their present form.

Be that as it may, one popular version of the 'creation-story' has it that at the beginning of a world cycle Brahmā reveals the Vedas to seven primeval sages (*ṛṣis*[21]), a class of beings different from the gods and humans who, rather than seeing with the mind's eye, hear with the mind's ear the precise accented syllables and pre-established order of words in the Vedic corpus. The sages receive the stream of the sacred utterance intact, and equally unswervingly pass the word on to human beings, for personal recitation, for implementation in the ritual and for contemplation. This is why Vedic utterance in its original Sanskritic form was thought to have such efficacy: it was not an artefact in any sense at all. It 'came down' with its intrinsic power, and could be harnessed through ritual practice of various kinds (especially by the priests in the solemn sacrifice), not only for particular worldly ends but ultimately for the attainment of immortality. We are now in a position to understand why, from earliest times, Vāc or sacred (i.e. ritual) utterance was likened to a cow.

For the Vedic Aryan, the cow was the symbol and currency of wealth; its energy could be harnessed for the production of food (milk and its derivatives, and various crops through tilling the earth) and for trade and transport. Thus the cow was also a symbol of security and well-being. Like the cow, Vāc gave prosperity and salvation if its power was properly harnessed – if, as in the case of the harnessed cow, human beings could follow in Vāc's footsteps through the agency of the priests. *This* is the origin of the notion of the sacred cow in the Hindu psyche, and not derivative ideas such as that of the early economic value of the cow, and so on.

There are many places in the *Ṛk* Saṃhitā where these ideas are intimated. For instance we have the following verse: 'By sacrifice they (the priests) walked the track of Speech (*vāc*). They found her entered within the sages. Having fetched her, they distributed her manifoldly. Seven celebrants chant her together' (10.71.3). Here Vāc is compared to a cow whose footsteps the priests walk. They discover her locked up within the seven primeval sages and make ritual use of her in various ways. Thus the notion of the seven primeval sages hearing the sacred utterance is clearly very ancient. Note that ritual utterance is not composed; it is discovered. The idea is that Vāc existed originally in unmanifest form, as an inexhaustible, powerful river dammed up and unflowing which then streams forth (through the mouths of Brahmā and/or the Sages), its purity and power intact, in the form of the Vedic syllables for the benefit of humankind.[22]

For the Vedāntin thinkers, who sought to interpret this image theologically, it is *Brahman*, the Godhead or the supreme Spirit and universal cause, who is the ultimate source or form of Vāc. It is *Brahman* who reveals the Veda to Brahmā who then promulgates it (with or without the agency of the Sages). But for the Vedāntins, even *Brahman* does not *compose* the Vedas; they exist as a residual power in *Brahman's* essence, and are only manifested by 'him',[23] again and again in their pre-established verbal order, at each world-production in the way described above. In accord with this point, Śaṃkara likens the periodic emission and withdrawal of the Vedas by *Brahman* at each world-production and dissolution to breathing in and breathing out – a natural process, so to speak, not a deliberate act of creative composition. In support, Śaṃkara quotes BĀUp II.4.10: 'Truly, it is from this (supreme Spirit) that all these (the Vedas and their attendant texts) are breathed out'.[24] Only an omniscient being can give vent to such all-encompassing knowledge.[25] Rāmānuja is more forthcoming:

> When the time for dissolution comes to an end, the Adorable One, the supreme Person, remembering the world as previously structured, decides to proliferate. Having differentiated the whole mass of non-conscious and conscious being previously collapsed within him as but his residual power, he brings the various (originative principles) into being as in previous (world-emissions) including Hiraṇyagarbha (i.e. Brahmā). Then, after searching out the Vedas arranged precisely in their traditional order, he imparts them as before to Brahmā, instructing him about the production of the world in the form of the gods etc., while he himself dwells within everything as the inner Spirit.[26]

And how does Brahmā go about his job? Rāmānuja tells us further:

> Prajāpati (i.e. Brahmā) first considers the forms and powers etc. of the (primeval) Sages who make the sacred utterances, and then produces the Sages endowed with their requisite forms and powers. He then commissions each to remember his specific utterances. For their part, the Sages, endowed with the requisite powers by Prajāpati, practise the austerities appropriate to each, and without formal study directly intuit the sacred utterances endowed with their established potencies, infallible in accent and sound, as produced by the succession (of Sages of former world-emissions).[27]

These extracts make it clear that neither the Sages, nor Brahmā, nor even the Lord (*Brahman*) himself, compose the Vedas. The Vedas are pre-existent, their verbal order, accents, sounds, inalienably pre-established. Ultimately the Vedas reside in the bosom of the Absolute, but they are only promulgated, not authored by *Brahman*, Brahmā and the Sages in succession. Hence the supreme Being is said to have searched them out (*āviṣkrtya*), while the Sages only 'intuit' (*paśyanti*) them. As such the Vedas are 'non-personal' (*apauruṣeya*), eternal (*nitya*), and self-authenticating. Madhva, a younger contemporary of Rāmānuja, from yet a third Vedantic school, reasons, 'The validity (of the Vedas) is autonomous, else (the fallacy of) infinite regress (would result in trying to establish their validity)'.[28] As we shall see, this doesn't mean, of course, that they do not require sustained and justified interpretation, for it is acknowledged that in many aspects they are obscure texts. This, in brief, is Vedantic theology's conception of 'revelation'.

Let us now consider the 'creative' power of the Word in the theology of the Sanskrit tradition. We have noted how, in Vedānta, the Word is, if one can put it this way, an aspect of the 'essence' rather than of the 'will' of *Brahman*. When the supreme Being decides to produce the world again after a periodic dissolution, the innate, divine power of the Word (*Vāc*) comes into effect. To illustrate this we can turn to Rāmānuja again. In the last extract Rāmānuja speaks of Vedic words having 'established potencies' (*vīryasiddha-*). What does he mean? The Mīmāṃsakas in general subscribed to the view that Vedic 'naming-words', that is, substantives paradigmatically referring to natural material beings, like *gau* (ox), *aśva* (horse), *vṛkṣa* (tree), are innately and eternally connected denotatively, not directly with the individual objects they signify, namely this or that ox, horse or tree, but with the '*ākṛtis*' of these objects. Thus the *ākṛti* is a sort of concrete universal, a metaphysical class-contour (rather like the Platonic *eidos*). The Vedic naming-word denotes particular objects through the *ākṛti* they instantiate. Thus even though particular objects come and go, and even if, by some calamity, all the existing objects instantiating some *ākṛti* were to be obliterated, the eternal and innate relationship between a naming-word and its *ākṛti* remains unaffected.

This means, in effect, that the (Sanskrit) Vedic naming-word, rooted as it is in the divine essence, has an established potency to 'real-ise' itself by the production of the particular object(s) it (indirectly) denotes. The supreme Spirit having decided to bring forth a fresh world, this potency is actualised in the production of the appropriate being(s). This is what is meant by the 'creative power' of the sacred Word in Vedānta. But note that theologically, Brahmā etc. have no more than an instrumental role to play in this process, even though mythologically this may not seem to be the case. Rāmānuja is clear about this: 'All Vedic (naming-)words make known their proper objects and senses as terminating in the supreme Spirit. For the Vedic words, having been successively extracted as before by the supreme Spirit from the Veda (pre-existing in him), are applied as before as names to the objects created by the supreme Spirit and find their fulfilment in him'.[29] In other words (here Rāmānuja again speaks representatively for Vedānta), it is *Brahman* and *Brahman* alone who is the universal originative cause by virtue of his immanent and sustaining causal agency in all secondary causes. The Vedic word was believed to have other innate powers, e.g. the capacity to heal and to charm, which could be released in the appropriate circumstances.

The tendency to view the primeval Word (*Vāc*) as 'creative' is by no means confined to Vedānta in classical thought. It is strong among the philosopher-grammarians. A seminal thinker in this regard was Bhartṛhari (*c.* sixth century CE). According to Bhartṛhari, the highest form of being is the soundless Word which is imbued with the power (*śakti*) to burst forth (*sphuṭ*) into creative expression. The Word-burst-forth (*sphoṭa*) is the immanent ground of the hierarchical manifestation, not only of all existing things but also of all meaning, down to the grossest forms. The *Sphoṭa* is also called the *Śabda-Brahman* or Word-Brahman, an idea which may be derived from the Upaniṣads (see *BĀUP* IV.1.2, *MaitrīUp* VI.22). Bhartṛhari's major work, the *Vākyapadīya*, is a profound and extensive treatise and continues to be studied today, not only for its historical value, but also, it is claimed, for insights into the nature of language in general and religious language in particular.

Bhartṛhari was a major influence on the many-streamed Tantric tradition. In its non-technical sense *tantra* means 'a loom'; in theory the exponents of this tradition regarded themselves as unravelling, as if on the loom of experience, the essential meaning and practices of the Veda with the help of numerous non-Vedic scriptures of their own.[30] In fact in both word and deed, Tantra is often far from easy to square with traditional Vedic religion (this relationship will be discussed at greater length in Chapter 4). Though the number of Tantric initiates has always been tiny, Tantric ideas have had a pervasive effect on both precept and practice in religious Hinduism. We shall give examples of this from time to time. Tantrics, who can belong to any of the three major traditions – Vaisnavism, Saivism and Saktism[31] – speak of their observance of the norms of these traditions or of Vedic religion as 'external', which they then seek to distil in private (i.e. 'internally') by means of their particular Tantric orientation.

> [The] original Word, identical to the primal divine Energy [*śakti*], is envisaged in [the] Tantric perspective as phonic energy (*vākśakti*), eternal, indestructible, and all-pervading, which however unfolds and evolves, bringing forth all the various aspects and stages of the cosmos. This word, this sound, is endowed with a creative force . . . the Word precedes the object, it brings it forth, it is the energy that upholds it, its innermost nature, that into which it will dissolve at the time of the cosmic resorption. The process of emanation, related to speech, is variously described depending upon texts and schools; however, it appears generally as unfolding from an initial luminous vibration or sound (*nāda*), which is an extremely subtle state of pure phonic energy, which through a series of transformations and condensations will become less subtle, forming a concentrate or a drop (*bindu*) of sound-energy, from which, when it divides itself, worlds, humans, and language will come forth . . . . All this, of course, being valid both on the cosmic and on the human level, and animated with a double movement: the outward movement of emanation, converting itself into a movement of return to the source.[32]

The outstanding thinker of the Tantric tradition is arguably the polymathic Abhinavagupta (eleventh century), who espoused a form of non-dualist Kashmirian Saivism. Abhinavagupta develops a theory according to which the transcendent Word evolves through four stages, from the subtle to the gross. The highest level is *Parāvāc* which 'appears as the primordial, uncreated Word, the very essence of the highest reality, ever-present and all-pervading. She is identical with . . . luminous, pure consciousness' (Padoux 1990: 172). The next stage is *Paśyantī* which 'is the initial, undifferentiated moment of consciousness which precedes dualistic cognitive awareness, a moment – when what expresses and what is expressed are not yet divided' (1900: 190). This is followed by *Madhyamā*, the 'Intermediate' stage. Here, 'linguistic consciousness appears: "phonemes, words and sentences" are present, and consequently also the division in "expressing" and "expressed" resulting from convention (*saṃketa*) that is proper to speech' (1990: 205). The last level is *Vaikharī*, the Corporeal: 'that stage where differentiation is fully manifested, and which is linked with time since with it the process of language becomes fully manifest' (p. 216).

The different theories mentioned here about the creative power of Sanskritic sound have had long histories and are by no means defunct today among traditional Hindu thinkers.[33] We mention them not only because they still have currency, but because they illustrate how Sanskritic Hinduism has a rich and sophisticated history of articulate reflection about the sacred Word. Their effect was to perpetuate in the popular imagination the mystique that Sanskrit, especially when ritually uttered, is inherently and uniquely transformative and regenerative. This mystique continues to exercise great influence among many Hindus. Here is an anecdote, related to me by a Sanskritist friend, to illustrate this.

In the English city in which he lived, this Sanskritist had become friendly with a middle-class, elderly Hindu couple. In time the husband died and his widow asked my friend to officiate at the cremation, since no local Hindu priest was available. 'But I am neither a Hindu nor a priest', protested the Sanskritist. No matter, he was a friend, and so long as he read from the Scriptures, in Sanskrit, the old lady would be content. And so it happened. At the ceremony, my friend read from the *Bhagavadgītā* (Ch. 12), also translating into English, and the bereaved were entirely satisfied. But the story is not over.

About a week later my friend received a telephone call from a Hindu gentleman who was a complete stranger. The caller had heard what he had done at the cremation and made a similar request on behalf of a Hindu family who had recently been bereaved. Taken aback, the Sanskritist pointed to his lack of traditional credentials for the job. He was assured that this was no problem, so long as there was a scriptural reading in Sanskrit. The power of Sanskrit is all-consuming.[34]

It is a characteristic belief of religious Hindus that the power of the Sanskritic Word is encapsulated in the *mantra*. This term has a disputed etymology, with a complex history, meaning and application.[35] But in Hindu religion it is pervasive and of central importance. The term is often explained as deriving from some word meaning to save, e.g. *tṝ*, to pass over, float, and *trai*, to protect, rescue. *Man* has to do with the mind, so laconically the *man-tra* is a rescuing or protecting mental instrument of some kind. But in the multifarious Hindu family of religions, the types, efficacies and uses of *mantra*s in this capacity are manifold, even within a particular tradition. All we can do here is give some idea of this device's rationale and versatility.

We noted earlier that the hymns of the Saṃhitās are called *mantra*s. Many were used, in a highly ritualised way, as utterance in both the solemn sacrifice and the non-solemn ritual (e.g. rites of passage and other domestic rites; see chapters 4 and 10); others were used as spells and charms. In other words, they had an innate potency to produce specific results or 'fruits' (*phala*) which would materialise provided that they were applied with the requisite know-how (the mental part) and in the appropriate context, which could mean – depending on circumstances – taking care to conform to a code of ritual purity by fasting, abstaining from sexual intercourse, etc., pronouncing, thinking or intending in a certain way, making certain ritual gestures, using certain implements, and so on. It was not necessary to understand discursively, at the level of efficacy of the performance of the *yajña* or the casting of the spell, etc., what was being said or done. The *mantra* would release its power if it were appropriately unlocked, or if the right key were used.[36] So in early Vedic religion there was a *mechanical* dimension to the implementation of *mantra*; this aspect has persisted to the present day not only in so-called Vedic contexts, but also in most other contexts in which *mantra*s are used (e.g. Tantra, folk-religion).

But from early times a more reflective dimension was added to the significance of the *mantra*. This is clearly evident in the Upaniṣads. The Upaniṣads, you will recall, represent a tendency to interiorise the sacrifice and its utterance. So here, without losing its mechanistic efficacy, *mantra*, or rather the mental seed contained in the early understanding of *mantra*, develops a conscious dimension which bridges the gulf between the finite and the infinite, appearance and reality, the individual and the cosmic. Henceforth, in various ways and on different levels, both intra- and inter-religiously in the different Hindu traditions, the *mantra* will encapsulate, or consummate, or represent, or give access to supra-human levels of existence and experience, right up to the ultimate Reality. As such, the *mantra* is a sort of 'time-bomb', realising its power either gradually in accordance with the mantrin's, i.e. legitimate user's, increasing conformity to the rules for its use, or in other cases, explosively in a moment of time-transcending fruition (on both physical and spiritual levels: the spell has worked, the flash of insight or identity-experience has occurred). The *mantra* may be meaningful or nonsensical, particular or universal, unique to one (e.g. given by the guru) or general – there are many different kinds and interpretations of *mantras* – but by and large it is an *attuning* instrument, i.e. efficaciously attuning the mantrin's being/consciousness to a particular objective, however temporal or transcendent, narrow or expansive this may be.

A classic and pervasive example of a *mantra* is the syllable Om (pronounced 'Oh-m').[37] A whole, if short Upaniṣad – the *Māṇḍūkya* – is dedicated to its understanding. Its constituent phonemes, *a*, *u*, and *m* – which combine in Sanskrit to produce the sound 'Om' – are distinguished and valorised in relation to different levels of being and experience, as are the integral sound and the syllable's 'trans-aural' dimension. The *Māṇḍūkya* concludes by declaring, '*Doing* the OM (i.e. interiorising it by recitation and reflection) is (to be one with) the (underlying) Spirit itself. He who knows thus (i.e. the full meaning of Om) becomes one with the Spirit'. In short, if you experience Om in depth, you attain ultimate fulfilment; it has this innate capacity. We may mention here too the *Gāyatrī mantra*, one of the most symbolic and sacred of Brahminic Hinduism, symbolic, that is, of the traditional values of twice-born status and all that this implies in the context of the ambivalent relationship between orthodox Brahminism and various counter-cultures of Hinduism. The *Gāyatrī* (also called the *Sāvitrī*) is as follows:

> Om. Bhūr bhuvaḥ svaḥ. Tat savitur vareṇyaṃ bhargo
> devasya dhīmahi dhiyo yo naḥ pracodayāt.
> 'Om. Earth, atmosphere, heaven.[38] Let us think on that
> desirable splendour of the celestial Inspirer.[39] May he stimulate
> us to insightful thoughts.'

Today the *Gāyatrī* is chanted widely, and often at cultural functions, though not as exclusively as in the past.[40] Indeed, one can buy colourful posters of 'Gāyatrī Devī', the goddess Gāyatrī, depicted as a gorgeously dressed beautiful young woman with five heads and ten hands bearing various objects, and seated on a full-blown lotus, with her *mantra* inscribed below (see Chapter 11 for comments on Hindu iconography).

With so much emphasis on sacred sound, one can understand why another term for the Veda in traditional 'high' Hinduism[41] is *śruti*, 'hearing (the to-be-heard)'. The Veda is the hearing of the increate, eternal salvific Word in the human situation. Those who resonate to the Veda in their lives will attain ultimate well-being, i.e. they will be 'saved'. How is this done? How is the Veda to be understood? How has access to the Vedas been determined? What is their modern relevance? Have there been challenges or substitutes in respect of Vedic authority? We will try to answer these questions in succeeding chapters.

3 The voice of scripture as Veda and 'Veda'

Scope of saving instruction in ancient times – an Upanishadic example. Narrowing the scope and opening back doors. The Veda: a symbol of saving authority. Ways of claiming/substituting Vedic authority: Veda and 'Veda'. The Veda also a contrastive symbol of saving knowledge. Modern regenerators of Vedic authority, 'reformist' and 'revivalist': Ram Mohan Roy, Swami Vivekananda, Swami Dayananda Sarasvati, Radhakrishnan. Contemporary relevance of the Veda as authority symbol.

For by far the greater part of the first thousand years, until the time when Buddhism and Jainism became a significant combined challenge to traditional ideas, the religion of Vedic sacrifice prevailed in Aryan-dominated society. Though the most elaborate sacrifices, being expensive affairs, could be instituted only by men of substance, in theory most people, male and female, could participate directly in some way in Vedic sacrifice and/or ritual. And even those who were marginalised in this respect – those who were reckoned to be within the caste system but as unworthy to sacrifice, namely, the Śūdras or not 'twice-born' – acknowledged the authority of the Vedas. There was hardly a viable alternative within the pale of Vedic *dharma*. Moreover, there is evidence that until fairly late in the thousand-year period, Śūdras in the right circumstances could be instructed in Upanishadic teaching (without necessarily being able to participate in Vedic ritual). There is a story to this effect in *ChāndUp* IV.1.1ff. The story goes something like this.

There was once a man of princely estate, Jānaśruti, who was both generous and pious. One night some wild geese were flying by his residence when one said to another: 'Watch it, Bhallākṣa! Jānaśruti's light has spread like day. Don't go near or it'll burn you.' (This was probably an allusion to many flaming torches lighting up Jānaśruti's residence, perhaps on the occasion of some festival.) The second goose said to the first, 'Who's Jānaśruti? You talk as if he were Raikva-of-the-cart'.

'Who's he?' returned the first.

His friend replied that Raikva was a spiritual winner if ever there was one. Just as in a game of dice the player with the highest throw wins all, so to Raikva accrued the merits of the good deeds of all lesser mortals. In other words, Raikva's religious knowledge gave him unparalleled spiritual power. Now Jānaśruti overheard this conversation, and resolved to be taught by Raikva. So he sent a servant to find Raikva-of-the-cart. Eventually the servant found Raikva, a Brahmin, sitting under his customary shelter, a cart. (Just as the ancient Greek philosopher, Diogenes, is reputed to have lived in a tub of sorts, so, we are to assume, Raikva the holy man lived under a cart.) Raikva was scratching away at some itches. He may have been a spiritual winner, but he scratched like the rest of us. (The Upaniṣads are not without a sense of humour.) The servant went back and reported Raikva's whereabouts to his master. Jānaśruti turned up with 600 cows, a splendid gold ornament and a mule-drawn cart (Raikva liked carts). Jānásruti hoped that these gifts would induce Raikva to instruct him in the knowledge of the deity (*devatā*) he worshipped.

But Raikva would have none of it. A Brahmin himself, he dismissed Jānaśruti summarily: 'Hey, Śūdra, be off with your necklace and cart, not to mention the cows!' Note that Raikva called Jānaśruti a 'Śūdra', that is, a member of the lowest caste, which was deemed unfit to participate in Vedic ritual. Jānaśruti, who did not repudiate this description, humbly returned with a more generous gift, this time offering the sage the necklace and cart as before, but in addition a thousand cows, the revenue of a village in perpetuity, and a girl for a wife. This offer was acceptable. The Upaniṣad says that tilting up the girl's face, the pleased sage acceded to Jānaśruti's request, remarking, 'There was no need for these other things, Śūdra; by this face alone you will make my acquaintance!' 'Then' concludes the text, 'he discoursed with him'.

In the interests of maintaining an orthodox image, the classical Vedāntin theologians affected to be unhappy with the idea of a Brahmin revealing his Upanishadic secrets to a Śūdra. So, as theologians sometimes do, they resorted to exegetical legerdemain and tried to interpret *śūdra* not literally but metaphorically. But there is no call to do this. It seems clear that Raikva, who addresses Jānaśruti as 'Śūdra' twice, the second time to accede to his request, is speaking matter-of-factly. In India there have always been Śūdra men of importance like Jānaśruti; history even attests to Śūdra rulers and dynasties. So it seems reasonable to conclude from this that, in ancient India, there was flexibility as to the Śūdra's eligibility for instruction in religious knowledge. Indeed, tongue in cheek, the Upaniṣad suggests that it was up to the Brahmin to determine the limits of this flexibility. In modern Hinduism, such passages tend to become grist to the mill of those reformers who seek to abolish the post-Upanishadic taboos which rendered the *śruti* the monopoly of a few, and to open it up to one and all as the basis of egalitarian socio-religious change.

This flexibility diminished once the Buddhist challenge began to bite (*c.* fourth century BCE). Vedic religion, repudiated by the Buddhists, was put on the defensive. On the one hand the citadel of Vedic orthodoxy, ruled now by the Brahmins as its undisputed champions, hardened its defences. Rules and regulations discriminating between those who were and those who were not eligible within the caste system to participate in the ritual use of the Vedas were drawn up in legalistic compilations called *Dharma* Sūtras and *Dharma* Śāstras. This voice of authority will be discussed in Chapter 4. On the other hand however, back doors to salvific well-being began to appear in the citadel.

The reader will often have occasion to note how Hinduism is *par excellence* a religion of the back door. The great, multi-level edifice of religious Hinduism is dotted with back doors. Some of these accesses are tiny, opening – if not closing – esoterically in the course of history to allow a thin trickle of humanity to pass through. Others are grander, busier affairs; time has made some of these far more popular thoroughfares than the formal entrances of ancient orthodoxy. Indeed, regular usage has, for all practical purposes, sometimes converted a back door into a front entrance. And often presiding over each doorway, as guardian of the path, is the Brahmin. So it was with some of the back doors in the citadel of Hindu orthodoxy after the Buddha. These appeared in the guise of popular, Brahminised devotional (i.e. *bhakti*) cults which offered salvific passage irrespective of one's eligibility to use the Vedas ritually. As such, they gradually began to supplant the traditional *yajña*-oriented access to salvation on a popular basis.

This is not to say that the ritual use of the Vedas died out. *Yajña*-oriented religion, as practised by the Pūrva–Mīmāmsakas, was followed by an increasingly small but still religiously powerful Brahminised upper-caste minority. Then there were the Vedāntins, whose influence and numbers increased from the early centuries of the Common Era. For the Vedāntins the Vedic ritual was not to be abandoned. Rather, it was to be practised in the light of Vedānta, that is, as a stepping-stone to the more insight-oriented religion of the Upaniṣads. In any case, for both camps, the Vedas were still the active, normative source of saving knowledge. The whole point of the Vedantic enterprise was to claim the backing of *śruti* (as culminating in the Upaniṣads), and to this end Vedantic theologians generally embarked on detailed exegeses of Upanishadic texts.

But, for reasons we shall go into later, there were still large sections of the population who were denied direct access to the Vedas (women and Śūdras, for example) or who belonged to religious traditions in which spiritual sustenance was *de facto* derived from scriptures that were not the Vedas. It is important to note that in many cases, for these people too, the Vedas acted as *the* representative *symbol* of scriptural authority.

In fact it became the done thing to claim the sanction of 'the Vedas' as a sign of orthodox standing. Non-canonical sacred texts from earliest times abound in formal acknowledgements of the authority of the Vedas. The *Mahābhārata* (*c*. 400 BCE–*c*. 400 CE, abbr. Mbh), one of Hinduism's two great epic compositions in Sanskrit, typifies this tendency. Indeed, as part of its hyperbolic claim to orthodox standing, it goes so far as to make itself equal to the Vedas. 'This work' it says of itself, 'is on a par with the Vedas and is supremely purifying. This ancient lore, praised by the seers, is the best of tales worth listening to' (Mbh 1. 56.15). On occasion, the Mbh refers to itself as the 'Fifth Veda'. The other great story, the *Rāmāyaṇa* (composed largely between 400 BCE and 300 CE), also makes numerous deferential references to the Vedas. Its central figure, the hero Rāma (who in later strata of the work is regarded as the descent of God Viṣṇu) is characterised as the champion of Vedic *dharma* and of the authority of the Vedas. Subsequently through the centuries, in well-known reconstructions of the Rāma story, this image of Rāma is preserved, no less so than in Tulsīdās' late-sixteenth-century vernacular version, the *Rāmcaritmānas* – one of the most influential religious texts of popular northern Hinduism. Here, Tulsī gives an enlarged meaning to the term 'Veda'. It stands not only for the *śruti* but also for officially non-canonical sacred texts (e.g. the Purāṇas) which themselves claim to be in accord with and to elucidate the *śruti*. Thus Veda seems to take on two senses for Tulsī, a strict sense and a broad sense. The point is that from earliest times the Veda retained its status as the unchallengeable authority-symbol for scripture.

In fact going a step further, it became a theological move in some traditions to extend the concept of Veda so as to include in its strict or primary meaning reference to texts which would otherwise seem to be clearly extra-Vedic. By this device the scriptural authority of the Vedas is shared by these texts, making it possible for the latter to legitimise as Vedic a religious experience or way of life in itself not obviously arising out of the former. We can exemplify this tendency by turning to the ancient and still vigorous tradition of Tamil Śaiva Siddhānta.

In his well-known *Love of God according to Sáiva Siddhānta*,[1] Mariasusai Dhavamony writes: 'The *Śaiva Siddhānta* recognises four categories of writings as belonging to its sacred canon: the Vedas, comprising both the Samhitās and the Upanishads, the twenty-eight *Śaiva* Āgamas, the twelve *Tirumuṟai*, and the fourteen *Meykaṇṭa* Śāstras' (Dhavamony 1971: 4). We know something about the Vedas already. The twenty-eight Śaiva *Āgama*s exist in both Tamil and Sanskrit,[2] and for the most part give information about all that is required for the Śaiva Siddhānta way of life. Thus they instruct about the different modes of liberation in relation to Śiva and the means to attain these, about the nature of Śiva as the divine reality and as the origin and end of all things, about our relationship with Śiva in this life, about the rituals etc. in his worship, and about the construction of temples and images. The oldest of the *Āgama*s can be dated to around the sixth century CE.

The twelve *Tirumuṟai* are devotional compositions (in Tamil) by a number of Śaiva poet-mystics. They were compiled in the tenth century, although they contain material going back to a century or two BCE. They are sometimes referred to by their adherents as the 'Tamil Veda', a clear attempt to legitimise their contents as orthodox as a kind of extension of the traditional Veda. Finally, the fourteen *Meykaṇṭa* Śāstras are Tamil theological works (ranging from the twelfth to fourteenth centuries CE) by six teachers from within the Śaiva Siddhānta tradition. We shall refer to these and to the *Tirumuṟai* again in Chapter 6.

It is to the relationship between the Vedas and the *Āgama*s in Śaiva Siddhānta that we now turn. On the one hand, the *Āgama*s contain a number of remarks which appear to state that the religion of the Vedas is either to be rejected in favour of or supplanted by whole-hearted devotion to Śiva and its recommended practices. On the other hand, this repudiation is balanced by the claim that the prescribed devotion sums up the import of the Vedas and brings out their true meaning. A detailed analysis of how this is so is not given, yet Śaiva Siddhāntins have always found it important to make this claim. Thus Dhavamony quotes Tirumūlar, one of the contributors to the *Tirumuṟai*, as saying:

> The Vedas and the Āgamas are both true and both are the word of God. The first is a general treatise and the second a special one. When examined and where difference is perceived by some between the Vedānta and the Siddhānta, the wise will perceive no such difference.
>
> (Dhavamony 1971: 4)

The theologian Śrīkaṇṭha Śivācārya declared that there was no difference between the Vedas and the Śaiva *Āgamas.* He continues, 'Accordingly Śiva Āgama is twofold, one being intended for the three higher castes, the other being intended for all. The Vedas are intended for people of the three classes, and the other for all' (1971: 4).

Thus by the distinction between either 'general' and 'special revelation' or restricted and unrestrictied scriptural access (as in the case of Śaiva Siddhānta) or by means of some other device, the primary canonical status of the traditional Vedas is often extended to extra-Vedic texts. What is happening here is that the scriptural authority of the Vedas is being made to leap-frog, usually over an exegetical gap (rarely via an interpretive bridge), into a new textual locus to legitimise teaching that to all intents and purposes seems to be very different from what we find in the 'true' Vedas.

Let me give another example, this time taken from the thought of the philosophical theologian Vallabha (late fifteenth century), a south Indian Brahmin whose views continue to be influential for a number of religious communities especially in the northern half of India. By the time Vallabha came on the scene in the Vedantic tradition, devotion to Kṛṣṇa as the focus of a monotheistic faith had grown and developed in a range of micro-centres, at levels high and low, of the Ancient Banyan. Literary and popular works, including songs and poems, propagated this devotion; what may be called a multi-faceted Kṛṣṇa-cult had become a going concern. Vallabha's theology drew from and contributed to this tradition. This is relevant for our understanding of his view of scripture.

'Vallabha begins [his work, the Tattva-artha-dīpa-nibandha, abbr. TADN] by making clear he follows a four-fold canon embodying *Veda, Brahma Sūtra, Bhagavad Gītā and Bhāgavata Purāṇa*'.[3] Vallabha uses the term *pramāṇa* which means 'authoritative source of valid cognition' to refer to these four works as the source of our knowledge of the divine being. As we shall see more clearly in

Chapters 4 and 5, strictly speaking, in Vedānta the last three works named are *smṛti*, i.e. tradition which is supposed to corroborate the Veda; the Veda alone is *śruti*, or scripture in its most authoritative sense. In effect Vallabha is dissolving this distinction with respect to these four works and enlarging the concept of 'Veda', if not of *śruti* (which now just becomes a formal description of how one of these four scriptures, namely 'Veda in the strict sense', was transmitted), so as to cover all four texts. This is clear when he says that the fourfold canon produces valid cognition only when it is seen to make sense as a coherent whole (v. 28).

How is this done, since from the point of view of content, the four texts seem to be quite disparate? Vallabha now provides a kind of interpretive bridge for the authority of *śruti* to leap-frog into the other texts and legitimise his acceptance of Kṛṣṇa as the ultimate focus of all scripture:

> In the early part of the Veda Kṛṣṇa is intimated in the form of the sacrifice, in the later [Upanishadic] portion he appears as Brahman; [in the *Gītā* he appears more clearly] as the *avatārin* [namely, as God in human form], while in the *Bhāgavata* Purāṇa, Kṛṣṇa [appears clearly as himself].[4]

Thus Vallabha espouses the idea of progressive revelation through scripture. For him, the *Gītā* is the interpretive key to this divine self-disclosure; ostensibly containing the words of the Lord himself, it allows us to make sense of what scripturally and theologically (not chronologically) precedes and follows it, namely the Veda proper and the *Bhāgavata* Purāṇa respectively. Vallabha declares: 'The Lord's words in the Gītā are the criterion . . . it is in this way that the sense of the Vedas is determined'.[5] However, we cannot agree when it is said that Vallabha 'reverses the traditional scriptural hierarchy, dethroning the Veda and replacing it with the Bhagavad Gītā'.[6] On the contrary, the Veda is affirmed as the standard of scriptural authority; this is why, as the quotation makes clear, it is important for Vallabha to show that a key is needed to unlock the Veda's true meaning. It is no doubt in the *Gītā* that he locates this key, but the *Gītā* is given scriptural and interpretive significance only in so far as it basks in the authority of the Vedas and is alleged to reveal their purport.

Similar strategies were followed in the Brahminic Śrī-Vaiṣṇava tradition of the South. F. Hardy has shown how devotional Tamil songs of Caṭakōpaṉ, better known as Nammāḻvār (seventh to eighth centuries CE), one of the founding figures of the southern Vaiṣṇava *bhakti* of the time, were adopted by Śrī-Vaiṣṇavas as the (real) 'Tamil Veda'.[7] And Nammālvār is traditionally reputed to be a Śūdra! From beginnings in which these works were regarded as clarifying and then summarising for all, high and low caste alike, the teaching of the otherwise forbidding and obscure *śruti*, Hardy traces how the Tamil Veda was regarded as *consummating*, and for some even supplanting, the Vedas proper.[8]

This phenomenon of formal Vedic authority catapulting into all sorts of apparently alien contexts has been a common one in Hindu traditions which have sought some form of Brahminic sanction, and is current even today. It features, for example, in the Swaminarayan religion, a fairly influential faith established in the first half of the nineteenth century and predominantly Gujarati in its appeal. Here both Sanskrit and Gujarati works, including the Vedas which are formally given priority status, exist in a complex relationship of primary and secondary scriptures. It remains unclear, however, exactly which texts are included in what seems to be an extended concept of 'Veda'.[9]

We must also point out here that the Vedas can become a *contrastive* symbol of religious authority. This happens among Hindus who wish to oppose their religious norms and symbols to Brahminic values. Such people are often but not necessarily from low castes. The 'barttamān-panthīs' among the so-called Hindu Bāuls are a case in point. Though there are various groups of these Bāuls, religiously they are classified as Vaiṣṇava, mostly low-caste but also numbering Brahmin followers and sympathisers. They may be placed loosely in the Tantric tradition. The *sādhana* or spiritual discipline of the barttamān-panthīs, in spite of numerous variations, is generally claimed to be anti-Vedic, being based on texts and practices which the more 'orthodox' or Veda-inclined profess to abhor.[10] Indeed, the anti-Veda bias of the *sādhana* is supposed to account for its efficaciousness. Thus one way or another, the Vedas emerge with a high profile in the context of religious authority.

Historically, the authority of the Vedas was appealed to in defence not only of religious orthodoxy but also of political legitimacy. Instances of rulers performing Vedic sacrifices, especially the *aśvamedha* or horse-sacrifice (an elaborate ritual by which its patron affirmed territorial sovereignty), dot the historical and geographical landscape of the subcontinent. Thus Puṣyamitra (second century BCE), the Brahmin founder of the Śuṅga dynasty which at first controlled much of the Ganges valley and parts of northern India, is said to have performed two *aśvamedha* sacrifices. In the first century

BCE, Śatakarṇī, a notable king of the Śatavāhana dynasty (based in the north-western Deccan), after a number of expansionist military campaigns, 'performed a horse-sacrifice to establish his claim to an empire'.[11] Again, among the Pallavas who came to power in the sixth century CE in the South, at a time when we may speak more or less of the pan-Aryanisation of the subcontinent, kings

> took high-sounding titles . . . such as *dharma-maharajadhiraja* (great king of kings ruling in accordance with the *dharma*), and the more unusual *aggitoma-vajapey-assamedha-yaji* (he who has performed the *agnishtoma, vajapeya*, and *ashvamedha* sacrifices), which sounds rather like a self-conscious declaration of conformity with Vedic ideas.[12]

And so on. The royal performance of these sacrifices would have been a public event, designed to display to maximum effect the king's adherence to the *dharma* of the Vedas. This would have reinforced, in the public eye, the symbolic value of Vedic authority as final. Of course once the northern subcontinent and the central Deccan came under Muslim rule, such attestations of the Veda would no longer have been feasible.

Except for outposts of Vedic chanting in various parts of India, and for specialist study of the *śruti* in scattered contexts, and indeed, for the generally undiminished status of the Vedas as *the* scriptural authority symbol, the Vedas had ceased to be a source of religious inspiration for the majority of Hindus by the beginning of the nineteenth century. It was the untiring efforts of a remarkable man, Ram Mohan Roy, for social and religious reform in the Bengal of the early nineteenth century, that gave Vedic religion a new lease of life among his compatriots.

Under the influence of British rule, the subcontinent had just entered a period which was to bring far-reaching changes to Hinduism. In effect the British had displaced Muslim paramountcy; the way was clear for a new kind of cultural interaction between Hindus and those who controlled their political destiny. The bridgehead for this interaction was in and around Calcutta (in the Presidency of Bengal), the capital city of British India. Socially well-placed Bengalis increasingly realised that it would only be through English education that they and their children could hope to come to terms with British rule. The demand for English education among these Bengalis increased inexorably, thereby introducing new ideas concerning history, freedom, patriotism, society and religion. Whereas in the past an uncritical orthodoxy, controlled by the Brahmins, tended to prevail in socio-religious matters, now rational inquiry, deployed not least by reformist Hindus themselves, began to challenge the old ways. As a result Hinduism would never be the same again. Much of the credit must be given to Ram Mohan for initiating this transformation.

Ram Mohan was born in a Brahmin home in 1774 in the village of Radhanagar in a Bengal firmly under British rule. As a youth he had been deeply influenced by the monotheism of Islam and formal studies in Samkarite Advaita, a tradition of monistic interpretation of the Upaniṣads. In time, he learned English and drank deeply of the current social, philosophical and religious ideas streaming in from the West. By 1815 he had become a man of means, the result of sound business dealings in the ambit of the British East India Company. He took up residence in Calcutta, the hub of British influence, with a view to devoting himself to the social, moral and religious reform of his people.

On the basis of classicist assumptions, British scholars had reached the conclusion that the culture of ancient India was a far superior thing to the life-style of the Hindus around them. The following judgement by Sir William Jones (1746–93), an influential administrator–scholar, is typical: 'nor can we reasonably doubt, how degenerate and abased so ever the Hindus may now appear, that in some early age they were splendid in arts and arms, happy in government, wise in legislation, and eminent in various knowledge'.[13] Many with a vested interest in India, Hindus included, accepted this contrast. Ram Mohan was no exception.

Spurred on by the criticism of contemporary Hindu religion made by British missionaries, administrators and scholars (for which, indeed, he had some sympathy), Ram Mohan was keen to rehabilitate his ancestral faith. Hinduism had become degenerate, he maintained, because it had fallen into the grip of self-seeking priests who played on the fears and superstitions of a people largely ignorant of their religion's original high standards of belief and practice. The priests, he argued, based their teachings not on the Vedas, the original revelation of the Hindus, but on secondary religious texts such as the Purāṇas and Tantras. Ram Mohan's early studies in the monotheism of Islam and in Advaita, as well as a growing appreciation of Unitarian Christianity, led him to locate the revelational high point of the Vedas in the Upaniṣads. Ram Mohan alleged that the Hindus, misled by the Brahmins, had deviated from their ancient faith in the 'one, true God', author and provider of the universe, who desired all to walk the path of egalitarian virtue irrespective of sex and race. Ram Mohan claimed that this teaching was enshrined in the Upaniṣads no less than in the Scriptures of the world's great religions. Instead, Hindus now adhered to a religion of rampant polytheism, idolatry and ritualism, which was riddled with the canker of priestcraft and such abominable social practices as suttee, and caste and sex discrimination. The remedy was to revert to the insights of the Upaniṣads.

Ram Mohan was on strong ground. He knew that implicit in his position was an appeal to a distinction that the orthodox couldn't challenge, the distinction, that is, between the authority of the *śruti* and the authority of all other sacred texts. Nothing could match the former authority, which was supreme. If he could show that the *śruti*, in the form of the Upaniṣads, inculcated a vision of the transcendent that was anything but polytheistic and idolatrous, then the religion of contemporary Hinduism with its attendant evils would be overthrown.

Ram Mohan was a Vedāntin; but he was also a rationalist. He believed that all scriptures, including the Vedas, must be interpreted, not dogmatically but on the basis of rational criteria which gave due attention to historical context, semantic developments of style and content, and contemporary sociological and other influences. Thus where the Vedas were concerned it suited Ram Mohan's purposes to appeal to their paramount authority as scripture, but not to other features traditionally bolstering this authority, e.g. the mystical efficacy of Sanskritic sound, the method of the Vedas' promulgation and their characteristics as eternal and unauthored (see Chapter 2).

To achieve his reformist goals, Ram Mohan embarked on a campaign of translating and disseminating, mainly in Bengali and English, his rationalist interpretation of Upanishadic religion. It was by drawing on the authority of the *śruti* that he ceaselessly waged his battles to improve the social, moral and religious condition of his compatriots. An outstanding success in this regard was his contribution to the campaign to legally prohibit suttee, which was outlawed in 1829 when Lord William Bentinck was Governor-General. In fact it has been suggested that Ram Mohan's professed Vedantism (as also his espousal of a Unitarian interpretation of the Christian scriptures) was based on utilitarian motives rather than on personal commitment. There may well have been a utilitarian colouring to Ram Mohan's faith. But there is also no reason to doubt the sincerity of his religious beliefs. One can appreciate the utilitarian value of one's faith while at the same time being convinced of its genuineness.

In 1828, in order to further his aims, he had established the

Brahmo Sabha ('the Assembly of Brahman'). Here, 'Brahman' designated the supreme Being of the Upaniṣads. Among its various activities, the Sabha held religious services to which all who were interested were welcome, irrespective of caste and sex. These services generally began with formal Vedic chanting by Brahmins in the presence of Brahmins (it is said that the chanters, orthodox south Indians, refused to perform otherwise[14]), but continued with Bengalis expounding Upanishadic texts to the congregation at large. Note that these texts were no less a part than the Vedic chants of the Vedic canon. Thus did Ram Mohan both authenticate and propagate his message. Renamed the Brahmo *Samaj* some years later, this society played a crucial role in fashioning the shape of modern Hinduism by becoming one of the most potent instruments for westernising and lasting socio-religious reform in nineteenth-century India.

It is important to note that for all his avowed susceptibility to Muslim and Christian teaching, Ram Mohan regarded himself as a Hindu seeking to reform Hinduism from within. Hence the declared Vedantic basis of his reformist efforts.[15] It was Ram Mohan who started the process of restoring the Vedas to public consciousness in modern India, both as an object of study and as a source of religious inspiration. Ram Mohan regenerated the Vedantic tradition which, at least among educated Hindus today, is one of the most popular options for religious commitment. Veiled by Sanskrit, hedged round by taboos of access, jealously guarded by the priests, for centuries the *śruti* had lain smouldering in the religious life of the people. Ram Mohan started the process of dismantling the taboos, of opening up and exposing the *śruti* to the winds of change. In time, many both inside and outside the Samaj were to contribute to this process, so that once again the Vedas became the active basis of numerous ideologies for socio-religious change. In this way they played an important part in the creation of modern India, thus affecting either directly or indirectly the lives of the population at large.

There were two other well-known figures who contributed enduringly to the resurgence of Vedic religion in the nineteenth century. The first may be regarded as heir to the conceptual influences of the Brahmo Samaj, the second as a visionary outside this tradition. Swami Vivekananda,[16] whose original name was Narendranath Datta, was born in Calcutta in 1863. He was exposed to English education in his formative years and as a young man moved about in the circles of the Brahmo Samaj, especially in the movement's most westernising, reformist faction. He soon came under the spell of the mystic, Ramakrishna, whom he followed until the latter's death in 1886. After this, Vivekananda became a leading figure among Ramakrishna's devotees, preaching what he believed to be his Master's teaching and helping give it an organisational form. He was a sensation at the Parliament of Religions in Chicago in 1893. This launched him as a religious teacher of repute in the West, especially in the United States which he visited more than once. It also helped him to establish the Ramakrishna Mission in India, run by an Order of monks. The aim of the Mission was to perpetuate Ramakrishna's teaching. With its headquarters on the western bank of the Hooghly at Belur in the northern outskirts of Calcutta, the Mission currently has branches not only in the rest of India but throughout the world. By the time Vivekananda died in 1902, he and his teaching had become well known among the educated in India for whom his international standing acted as a counterbalance to the humiliation of colonial rule. Vivekananda and his message played an inspiring role in the early stages of the Indian nationalist movement.

In his numerous writings and speeches, Vivekananda based his teaching on an Advaitic interpretation of the Upaniṣads. At the innermost level of being – the level of Spirit – all humanity is one, outer differences of race, religion, sex and condition of life being of no lasting value. Vivekananda based his egalitarian ethic on this idea. He quoted and commented upon Upanishadic texts frequently in elaboration of his views. Here again the *śruti*, in the form of the Upaniṣads, had a leavening impact on the minds of many who played a not unimportant part in fashioning the new nation.

Among those who propagated Vedic religion in the nineteenth century, our second figure of note is Swami Dayananda Sarasvati (1824–83). Dayananda was born in the region of Kathiawar (part of the modern state of Gujarat), of Brahmin stock in a home in which the traditional icon-worship of Śiva was followed. He started the study of Sanskrit and Vedic texts from an early age. He once related how while still a boy, he was taken by his father to attend an all-night vigil in a temple of Śiva. Late into the night, struggling to stay awake while others, including his father, had nodded off one by one, he noticed some mice nibbling at the offerings made to Śiva's icon. This led him to question image-worship and all that it stood for. If Śiva cannot protect his offerings from some mice, he thought, how can he give solace and protection to his devotees? Deaths in the family and an attempt to marry him off induced him to leave home while still a young man to seek life's meaning. He travelled around as a traditional renouncer, studying and debating the sacred texts in Sanskrit and became increasingly attracted to an Advaitic interpretation of the Upaniṣads. He also practised classical Yoga with a will. Icon-worship he rejected.

From 1860, for about two-and-a-half years, he sat at the feet of a holy man, a well-known Sanskritist named Virjanand Sarasvati. Through this association his knowledge of classical Sanskrit grammar in particular deepened and he is believed to have derived the idea of dividing the sacred texts into two categories: (i) *arṣa*, namely, those that were revealed via the *ṛṣis* or ancient sages and hence were infallibly authoritative; and (ii) *anarṣa*, i.e. those which had no such derivation and were therefore not infallible. The historical point of division between the two categories was the supposed cataclysmic war around which the story of the Mahābhārata is spun. This war was supposed to have plunged a more or less religiously homogeneous people and polity into fragmented chaos. Post-Mahābhārata-war India lost its original high religious and social ideals and the process of Hindu degeneration began, giving rise to casteism, priestcraft, sex-discrimination, polytheism, idolatry, and so on. It was during this time that such religious texts as the Purāṇas, Tantras, etc. were produced; these shared the venality and falsehood of the religion which spawned them and which they helped to foster. The *śruti*, on the other hand, antedated this war and remained intact as a source of revealed truth. In time, Dayananda's attention was turned from the Upaniṣads to the Saṃhitā portion of the Vedas as the repository of the purest, most original Aryan truth. The principle that ancient India was the golden age of the Hindu tradition was very much in force.

For a few months in 1872–3, Dayananda paid a visit to Calcutta at the invitation of leading figures in the Adi Brahmo Samaj. The way the Brahmo movement successfully and influentially communicated its policies convinced him that he would have to change his own image. He relinquished the renouncer's garb, put on conventional clothes and started perfecting his Hindi with a view to propagating his teaching in this northern lingua franca.

Dayananda's teaching, as relevant for our purposes, contained the following points. The Vedas, not least the Saṃhitās – especially the hymns of the *Ṛg* Veda – are the source and model of all truth. The Vedas, which are innocent of icon-worship, declare the existence of but one formless supreme Being who is their source and who fashioned the world. God is omniscient, omnipotent, eternal, imperishable, benevolent, blissful, and so on; but the deity is also coexistent with *prakṛti* or primeval energy from which the world is fashioned, and with individual spiritual selves or *jīvas* who are subject to the law of karma and rebirth. Further, the state of *mokṣa* or liberation is not permanent but temporary, souls enjoying their heavenly reward and then falling back into the cycle of rebirth. This view is unique in Hindu thought.

The Vedas also provide the blueprint not only for all religious truth, but also for all scientific discoveries. The ancient Aryans knew all about such marvellous things as steamships and the telegraph. This scientific knowledge was lost after the Mahābhārata war, only to be rediscovered in modern times. Dayananda did not live in an age of historical–critical interpretation of sacred texts[17] as do his followers and sympathisers of today. Nevertheless, even some of the apparently educated among these maintain that the ancient Aryans were familiar with at least the basics of what the rest of us think are modern scientific inventions (including the aeroplane now[18]). The Swami's doctrinal *magnum opus*, written in lively style in chaste Sanskritic Hindi, is called the *Satyārth Prakāś* ('A Declaration of Truth's Meaning'),[19] first published in 1875 but finally revised by 1883, the year Dayananda died.

After one or two false starts, in 1875 Dayananda succeeded in establishing a society to institutionalise his views in Bombay. It was called the Arya Samaj. But it was in the Punjab in 1877, in a milieu of well-to-do merchant castes and professionals, that the Arya Samaj got off the ground. Those who became Aryas were seeking a genuine Hindu identity (they rejected the westernised life-style of the Brahmos who were influential in the area) compatible with the technological progressiveness of the times. They believed they found it in the Samaj, for Samaj ideology traded, on the one hand, on the traditional authority of the Vedas and, on the other, on the Vedas' supposed progressiveness. Though some Sanskritic rituals, derived from the Vedas it was claimed, were practised in Arya gatherings, these did not have the rationale of the ancient Vedic *yajña*. They were essentially symbolic performances, putting their adherents in mind of their claimed Vedic past. All this is a far cry from the Vedic religion of ancient India, but the high profile that the Samaj gave to the Vedas and their authority cannot be denied.

The Arya Samaj became an influential movement mainly in north-western India. From the outset, it reflected the militant missionary thrust of its founder's writings. Before long it was to express this zeal politically. Aryas played a significant role in the nationalist movement. The Arya Samaj is still an important religio–political force today, retaining on the whole its abrasive image. As a religious movement its activities have been confined mainly to the northern half of India, in both urban and rural settings. Politically, however, its influence has been somewhat more pervasive, elements of the Arya Samaj being associated with aspects of militant Hindu fundamentalism in the subcontinent.

It must not be thought that while Ram Mohan and others were adapting the Vedas to new purposes by their rationalist approach, the orthodox pandits remained silent spectators. They raised a cry of protest at this flouting of tradition. The innovators carried on regardless. But at another level of Hinduism orthodoxy fought back, showing that the traditional approach to the Vedas was also alive and well. This is quite typical of the Ancient Banyan. While new branches push out in one place, tough old roots survive doggedly elsewhere.

We catch a glimpse into orthodox thinking about the authority of the Vedas in the first half of the nineteenth century through a controversy at the time in Sanskrit over a polemical treatise called the *Mataparīkṣā* ('Test of Doctrines'). The *Mataparīkṣā* (which eventually saw three editions, the first in 1839) was written by a Scottish Episcopalian, John Muir (1810–82). At the time Muir was a civil servant in the East India Company. Muir purported to test for the true religion on the basis of certain criteria, rationally applied. Not surprisingly, it was the religion of the Christians which was found to pass the test, while that of the Hindus in particular was adjudged to fail. It is not our purpose here to enquire into the details of the controversy or into whether Muir's enterprise can be said to have succeeded.[20] What interests us is how some pandits responded, especially in their use of the Vedas.

Allowing for some individual variations, the pandits in general show remarkable unanimity in their attitude to the Vedas. Most if not all of the basic ingredients of a traditional approach are present: that the Vedas are from God/*Brahman*, but that they are essentially eternal and unauthored; that at each production of the world they are promulgated by Brahmā and/or the seers; that Sanskrit is their original, sacrosanct language; that the Vedas are above reason, but that they may be defended and elucidated with the help of reason; and that in this light the Bible, or any other scripture for that matter, is no match for the authority and truth of what they say. One pandit averred, 'If there is to be belief in a text, then let the Veda be relied on, for it has been current on earth from the time of creation'.[21] All other scriptures, it is implied, are newcomers and hence lacking in authority by comparison. Elsewhere he says, 'It is on the basis of the cognitive authority of the Vedas (*vedapramāṇatvāt*) that other [Hindu] scriptures have such authority'.[22] And another pandit declared: 'Having first accepted the things of scripture as true, one should then establish them by reasoning . . . . Reasoning conforms to scripture, not scripture to reasoning. Scripture is self-validating (*svataḥpramāṇaka*) whereas reasoning exists to understand scripture'.[23] So the old approach had its champions while the new was gaining ground. Even today the old approach is far from moribund; scriptural literalism or regarding scripture as the template of all truth are trends with many followers in all religious traditions. The Vedas have not escaped such adulation.

We cannot end this brief discussion about the influence of the Vedas in modern times without mention at least of one of Hinduism's best known contemporary thinkers. This is Sarvepalli Radhakrishnan (1888–1975), who was not only a philosopher in his own right but also President of India from 1962–7. Radhakrishnan was something of an eclectic, ranging widely among the philosophies and religions of the world in articulating his views. Like Ram Mohan he believed that rationalist criteria must be brought to bear in the interpretation of religious scriptures. So he could write, in perhaps his most enduring original work,

> Every revealed scripture seems to contain in it a large mass of elements which scientific criticism and historical knowledge require us to discard and there is no reason why we should accept it at all. Truth is greater than any revelation.[24]

On the other hand, his whole thought was structured on an Advaitic interpretation of the Upaniṣads. Again and again, in his numerous writings, he quotes from the Upaniṣads to substantiate a point. He goes so far as to say that the 'germinal conceptions' of Hinduism 'are contained in the Vedānta standard . . . . The Vedānta is not a religion, but religion itself in its most universal and deepest significance'.[25] However, it was the Vedānta as interpreted from his own Advaitic or monistic point of view that he had in mind here. On this basis he endorses an ascending scale of truth for the religions of the world. The closer a religious ideal is to monism the higher up the scale it is.

> The worshippers of the [monistic] Absolute are the highest in rank; second to them are the worshippers of the personal God; then come the worshippers of the incarnations like Rāma, Kṛṣṇa, Buddha; below them are those who worship ancestors, deities and sages, and lowest of all are the worshippers of the petty forces and spirits.[26]

Whatever we may think of Radhakrishnan's philosophy of religion,[27] there is no doubt that his writings helped reinforce the image of the traditional religious authority of the Vedas in a modern rationalist context, not only among the educated in India but also in the wider world.

The Vedas, therefore, are far from having to be written off on the modern Indian scene. On the contrary, Vedic religion, in one form or another, has helped bring that multi-faceted phenomenon we know as modern India, not to speak of modern Hinduism, to birth. Gone are the days of the widespread performance of the *yajña*, it is true, or of the mentality, certainly among the educated and the rapidly increasing middle classes of Hindu society, that the study and implementation of the Vedas are the special preserve of Brahmin pandits. Ram Mohan Roy and others saw to that. Nevertheless, as we have seen, Vedic religion, or at least religion based on the Vedas in some way, has staged a powerful comeback. And the mentality of the Saṃhitās that ritual is a source of power is still very much in force among Hindus at large. The Ancient Banyan continues to regenerate and to adapt itself.

Nor must it be thought that there is no place even for traditional uses of the Vedas. Aspects of Vedic ritual and utterance still figure importantly in various contexts, as we shall have occasion to note. Many Hindus still recite from the Veda as part of their daily religious observances. For instance, near sources of flowing water, such as rivers and even street hydrants, it is still possible to see pious men, clad only in a loin-cloth after their morning ablutions, stand facing the early sun and reciting the sacred *Gāyatrī mantra* as countless generations have done before them. We shall give other examples in due course.

Finally, as part of the process of Sanskritisation, recourse to the authority of the Vedas in some form continues to service attempts made by low castes to raise their estimation in the caste hierarchy. It has been shown, for instance, that contrary to age-old rulings Brahmins are not loath to recite mantras from the Veda for Śūdra clients. Other studies make it clear that castes traditionally described as 'untouchable' are seeking a higher standing in the hierarchy by abandoning ancestral so-called unorthodox socio-religious practices and adopting forms of religion and ritual in conformity with those of Sanskritic Hinduism. The norms of Vedic religion would figure large in this process.[28] And there is every reason to believe that what is happening in this respect today has always been a feature of historical Hinduism. The contemporary Hindu, high and low, in city and in village, is attentive to the voice of Vedic authority in many ways. And the strains of this voice echo in Hindu communities throughout the world. It is no accident then that (at the time of writing) it is still possible to find displayed in a glass-topped cabinet in a room in the Maheshwaranath temple compound in the distant island of Mauritius, a large, open volume in Sanskrit with excerpts from the four Vedas. It is clear that this impressive tome is intended to function as a potent, overarching symbol of Hinduism's ancient roots – a symbol which by wondrous twists and turns authorises, some 3,000 years after its creation, the dispensation of salvation through popular temple cults.

But the voice of Vedic authority, fundamental though it is in Hinduism, has always been appealed to so variously and for such diverse ends that it cannot stand alone. How to interpret it? What exactly is it saying in this or that circumstance of life? How should one respond to it? The voice of the Vedas has had to be clarified and popularised by attentiveness to other guiding voices. We will consider these issues in Chapter 4.

4 The voice of tradition: Varṇāśrama dharma

I

Smṛti: *meaning, purpose, scope. Six divisions in the 'great' tradition proposed. (i) The Vedāṅga: meaning and content; relevance. The 'sūtra'. (ii) Gṛhya Sūtras: scope, content and relevance. (iii) The* dharma *Codes.* Dharma, *an 'action concept'. The Codes as authoritative. Distinction between Dharma Sūtras and Śāstras. Elusive meaning of* dharma *as prescriptive and descriptive.* Varṇāśrama dharma *as male-oriented. Two tensions of* dharma *to be considered: (a) order/chaos, and (b) choice/necessity. The Vedic origins: 'caste' an expression of this tension. Caste as* varṇa. Varṇa *as ideal construct and 'natural' hierarchy. The plight of the Śūdras.*

The voice of *śruti*, or alternatively of what passes for primary scripture, cannot be interpreted without due attention to the voices of tradition and experience. 'Tradition' is a large word and seems to include 'experience' of all kinds. By 'tradition' here we mean something more specific. The Sanskrit term we have in mind is *smṛti.* Whereas *śruti* in traditional orthodoxy refers to the 'hearing' of the inviolable word as we have seen, *smṛti* refers literally to the 'remembering' (of the memorable), remembering the wisdom of the past. By 'experience and tradition' in 'the voices of experience and tradition' we mean individual experience and collective experience respectively. In other words, 'tradition' stands for the collective experience that has been recorded, codified and ratified for posterity by the elders of the community or society. It will occur to one that in contrast to *śruti, smṛti* seems to lack a fixed reference. Remembering of exactly what, you may ask; and by whom; and for how long? And why 'remembering' (*smṛti*)? Let us answer the last question first, as this will help us to deal with the others. Our normative frame of reference in this and subsequent chapters will be the Sanskritic tradition of which many basic trends also apply, with due modification, to other contexts. We will demonstrate this connection on a number of occasions.

Remembering is eminently a personal experience. One remembers what one has done. Through memory one can appropriate and relive one's past, and learn from experience. These marks – appropriation, reliving, learning and guidance – are all included in the sense of *smṛti*. *Smṛti* refers to that store of group experience by which the community appropriates and relives its past, learns from it and is guided by it. In so far as *smṛti* has to do with experience it is personal (*pauruṣeya*), unlike *śruti* which, being regarded as impersonal (*apauruṣeya*) or at least sacrosanct, is accorded a pre-established form. In so far as *smṛti* is humanly authored, it is generally fallible and liable to change. It is also liable to criticism. As such it is a selective term. Sometimes, what is *smṛti* for you may not be recognised as such by me; or rather, though it may be necessary for both of us to recognise the authority of a particular slice of *smṛti*, we may weight this authority differently according to the particular traditions out of which we come or the exigencies of the situation. *Smṛti* is the medium through which we hear the voice of *śruti*; it is interpretive, selective, collaborative, flexible. *Śruti* and *Smṛti* – or their equivalents, namely primary scripture and tradition – are the axes by which the religious authority of Hinduism has been transmitted.

For Hindus, *smṛti* recalls exemplary figures and events of 'the past', whether these be inside or outside our human world. These figures may be human or non-human, and they may exemplify virtue or vice, as we shall see. *Smṛti* has pronounced on the origination and transmission of almost every branch of human expertise. Its concerns include how to use words, how to read the heavens, how to tend elephants, how to make love, how to make war, how to make temples, how to worship, how to go on pilgrimage (and where and why), how to dance, how to sing; how to classify men, women, horses, gems, snakes, herbs, dreams, drama, diseases, metre, temple images, castes, kings, ascetics, sex organs, dance movements, rituals, time, offences, penances, heavens, hells. *Smṛti* deals with the founding of ancient dynasties and their ending; with the origination and destruction of the world; with rites of passage, the goals and stages of life, the rites of cremation. *Smṛti* prescribes and cautions in all matters of *dharma*: in the *dharma* of husbands, in the *dharma* of wives (and co-wives), in the *dharma* of ascetics and in the *dharma* of courtesans, in the *dharma* of things moving and unmoving, in the complex, multi-faceted, multi-layered *dharma* of caste, in the *dharma* of peace, in the *dharma* of war (and in the *dharma* of spies too); in the *dharma* of eating, drinking, having sex, seeing, handling, washing, worshipping, purifying; in a word, in the *dharma* of living and in the *dharma* of dying. *Smṛti* is a great story-teller, codifier, teacher, punisher, rewarder, foreteller, guide.

Smṛti may be understood in two senses: first, in a restrictive sense, second, somewhat loosely. Understood restrictively, the term denotes the traditional wisdom that supports and illuminates *śruti* (or primary scripture) in some way. *Smṛti* can support *śruti* directly or indirectly through stories about gods, saints and sacred events, cautionary tales, graphic descriptions of heavenly and hellish states, didactic discourses, the elaboration of codes of *dharma*, the sanctioning of reward or punishment for observing or violating *dharma*, recording the development of human expertise in prosody, phonetics, astronomy, love-making, war-waging, temple-building, icon-shaping, philosophy and theology (so that ritual and *dharma* may be practised appropriately), and so on. Of course, implementing *smṛti* is a highly subjective exercise. What may be suitable corroborative *smṛti* material for my interpretation of *śruti* may be quite unsuitable for yours; or you may use the same material in a different way. For *smṛti* to function in the restrictive sense of the term, what matters is the intention seen to be underlying the material being considered. An item of *smṛti* may not seem to focus on *śruti* at all (e.g. a treatise on erotics or grammar or astronomy), but it is regarded as *smṛti* because it is seen as intended, implicitly or explicitly, to further the aims of *śruti*. For instance, it may do this by enabling *dharma* to be followed, for it is only on a dharmic basis that *śruti* may be implemented.[1] Of course, there is a vast literary and oral tradition that may be viewed as *śruti*-oriented which is not *smṛti*. This is because the individual elements of this tradition are not regarded as having the appropriate authority. For something to be appealed to effectively as *smṛti*, it must be accepted as duly authoritative by all concerned.

Smṛti in its broader sense applies to authoritative tradition in a secular context. As can be imagined, this tradition too is wide-ranging and vast. Seminal works of poetry and drama – e.g. the compositions of the great poet and dramatist Kālidāsa (*c.* fourth century CE), of logic and other skills, and so on – fall under this heading. As has been indicated, the dividing line between *smṛti* in the broader and narrower senses is often hazy. For example, the grammarian Pāṇini's *Aṣṭādhyāyī* may be cited as an example of a borderline case (see p. 78).

Thus *smṛti* is a catch-all category and, whether it acts in the name of the Veda or not, it makes the cumulative wisdom of the past accessible to the Hindu community in general and to Hindu communities in particular, so that one and all can get on with the business of living in the proper way.

As such, *smṛti* in the restrictive sense is not entirely amorphous. In the course of many centuries a number of divisions of *smṛti* has come down to us – much of which has been committed to writing, much just transmitted by word of mouth or by practice. Here it may be useful to distinguish again between a 'great' tradition and a 'little' tradition, or a 'high' tradition and a 'low' tradition of *smṛti*. The former category is Sanskritic and Brahminic; the Brahmins, as the framers and preservers of the norm, have produced and/or ratified it. This does not make this tradition easy to define since, as we have intimated already, the Brahmins are not a homogeneous group. There can be much factionalism or disunity among them, exacerbated by exigencies of time and place. Nevertheless, there are texts and practices in the 'high' tradition which enjoy a relatively universal authority status as *smṛti*. Note that though we have said that the 'high' tradition has been ratified, if not always formed, by the Brahmins, this does not mean that claims are not made in the case of some texts or codes of behaviour that they originated with the deity itself (either God or Goddess). Such claims may of course be valid in the eyes of faith, though not necessarily to the scrutiny of reason. Hindus are sometimes able to argue in a sophisticated way that a particular knowledge or custom has been inspired by the deity and communicated through 'incarnations' or divinely appointed human agents. In this way they ascribe to it an authority enhanced by direct divine co-operation. The *Mānava* Dharma Śāstra and the *Bhagavadgītā* (see Chapter 5) may be cited as examples of such lore.

The 'little' or 'low' tradition of *smṛti* would refer to works and/or customs enjoying only localised authority, or authority dispersed not 'vertically' through different social strata but shared 'horizontally' in a layer or closely related layers of Hindu society. To complicate matters further, though such instances of *smṛti* (the term may not be used in these contexts) may not originate with Brahmins, they may well have their approval and even participation. There are many examples in the Ancient Banyan – replete as it is with greater or smaller micro-centres of community life and layer upon layer of social branching – of *smṛti*'s 'little' tradition. Let us now examine some of the main divisions of *smṛti* in the 'high' tradition, and in the process give examples of *smṛti* in the more localised context.

Smṛti in the Sanskritic tradition may for convenience be divided into six categories, though in some cases the subject matter of these categories overlaps. They are: the Vedāṅga; the Gṛhya Sūtras; the Dharma Sūtras and Śāstras; Itihāsa; the Purāṇas; and a catch-all category which we shall call the 'Prasthāna-vākyas'. It will be necessary to review each in turn, not only so that one may have an idea of the variety and range of *smṛti*, but also so that a clearer picture can be formed of the relation between the 'great' tradition and the 'little' tradition within *smṛti*.

The Vedāṅga

This is a category largely concerned with the preservation and propagation especially of the earlier sacrificial section of the Veda and its concerns. The Veda has been likened to a torso with head; six disciplines have been compared to its 'limbs' (*aṅga*). The Vedāṅga are the limbs of the Veda in that they support the Veda, protect it and help to implement it ritually. These six disciplines are: (i) *śikṣā*, which deals with the proper articulation of Vedic texts and with phonetics in general; (ii) *chandas*, which deals with the intricacies of Vedic metre. A well-known work in this category is the *Chandaḥśāstra* of Piṅgalanāga, *c.* fifth to sixth century BCE, though this work also deals with vernacular metres; (iii) *vyākaraṇa* or grammar, the representative text here being the outstanding grammarian, Pāṇini's, *Aṣṭādhyāyī*. Pāṇini, who was an inhabitant of the extreme north-west, seems to have lived four or five centuries before the beginning of the Common Era and his work was of momentous import for the history of Sanskrit grammar. So great was his authority that none of the works of the grammarian predecessors to whom he refers are extant; they seem not to have been worth preserving. The *Aṣṭādhyāyī*, comprising about 4,000 sūtras or aphorisms, presents itself as a general treatise on grammar rather than as being specifically tied to the Veda. But because it can (and often has) been seen to serve the understanding of Vedic grammar, and because it is without doubt the cream of a long tradition of grammatical works associated directly with the elucidation of the Veda, it may be included in this division as the 'representative' text.

We should also mention the Prātiśākhyas at this point. These are ancient works composed with the preservation of the form and text of the Vedic Saṃhitās in mind. The genre was pre-Paninian, comprising numerous texts, each Prātiśākhya intended to deal with questions of grammar, phonetics and metre in the context of a particular branch or tradition of Saṃhitā practice. Today, however, comparatively few of these texts exist, and they seem to have been revised or composed after Pāṇini's time. Each of the four Saṃhitās is still served, however, (though with varying degrees of comprehensiveness), the extant *Ṛgveda* Prātiśākhya – ascribed to the grammarian Śaunaka but apparently the work of more than one hand – being the most comprehensive.

The fourth discipline is (iv) *nirukta* or 'etymology', or more precisely 'the analysis of semantic content'.[2] This category is specifically concerned with explaining the meaning of contentious Vedic words. Its most eminent exponent as known to us is Yāska, who may have lived before Pāṇini and who produced an analysis of the meaning of mainly abstruse Vedic words as found in the earliest lexicographical text we have, the *Nighaṇṭu*. Yāska's work, which is also called the *Nirukta*, 'contains lengthy discussions of linguistic and philosophical import';[3] (v) *jyotiṣa*, which comprises astronomical-cum-astrological texts devised to fix the most auspicious days and times for the performance of the various Vedic sacrificial and other rituals, is next. An early extant work in this category is Lagadha's brief *Jyotiṣavedāṅga (c.* 400 BCE). A later, more astronomical treatise is the well-known *Āryabhatīya* (sixth century CE), which in one place attributes the passing of the day to the rotation of the earth; and (vi) *kalpa*, a large division, usually regarded as co-extensive with compositions known as Śrauta Sūtras. *Śrauta* is a derivative of *śruti*; hence, as the name implies, the Śrauta Sūtras revolve around the *yajña* or solemn sacrificial ritual, which is the chief concern of the early portion of *śruti.* According to some authorities, *kalpa* (i.e. the 'Kalpa Sūtras') refers not only to the Śrauta Sūtras but also to the Sūtras of the next two divisions, namely the Gṛhya Sūtras and the Dharma Sūtras. Yet others distinguish between the Śrauta Sūtras on the one hand, and the Smārta Sūtras on the other, a generic name for the Gṛhya and Dharma Sūtras.[4] These distinctions draw our attention to an important point: that is, that originally a branch or school of Vedic study had its own 'set' of Śrauta, Gṛhya and Dharma Sūtras; and in some cases sets, or parts of sets, seem to have been shared. Many of these sets, or parts of them (there were a great many Vedic schools in ancient times) have been lost, though a representative sample remains.

The Śrauta Sūtras contain detail about the sacrificial ritual: types, goals, times, duration, liturgy; the fees to be paid to the priests for the different sacrifices; the penances to be performed if rules pertaining to them were transgressed, etc. The Sūtras continually either quote or allude to Saṃhitā texts[5] which were to be used with the different rites. In this connection there were Mantra-Saṃhitās, i.e. collections of relevant Vedic texts in unabridged form, which the priests could consult as they performed one ritual or other. Well-known Śrauta Sūtras include the *Āśvalāyana* and *Śāṅkhāyana* Śrauta Sūtras (of the *Ṛg* Veda), the *Lāṭyāyana* and *Drāhyāyaṇa* Śrauta Sūtras (of the *Sāma* Veda), the *Kātyāyana* Śrauta Sūtra, which belongs to the *Vājasaneya* Saṃhitā of the 'White' *Yajur* Veda and the *Baudhāyana, Āpastamba* and *Vaikhānasa* Śrauta Sūtras of the 'Black' *Yajur* Veda. Many of these names, as in the case of the reputed authors of other ancient treatises, may well be patronymics.[6]

Taken collectively, the most seminal extant works of the Vedāṅgas range from about 600 BCE to about a century after the beginning of the Common Era.[7] It would, I think, be true to say that most of the material so far mentioned, especially of the first five categories of the Vedāṅga, has traditionally been the preserve of specialist Brahmins – for the most part the abstruse and rarefied activity of Hinduism's ivory towers. Most Brahmins themselves, let alone other Hindus, would have been totally uncomprehending in these towers of specialisation. That is not to say that this activity was unimportant, or that it did not significantly influence the community at large. It reinforced the centrality of the solemn ritual (and the Veda), and the crucial position of Brahminic authority for the ritual's performance and transmission. Schools of Vedic performance proliferated and established an active image of Brahminic presence in society. But the development of the Vedāṅga also enabled the horizons of 'the Vedic way of life' to be adjusted continually to meet changing circumstances (that is, it helped define and implement the ideal form of life for different groups of people in a range of situations, which would enable Vedic ritual and Vedic thinking to flourish). Not only did the solemn ritual ramify into domestic ritual through their common intermediaries, the Brahmins, but the ethos of the ritual as such began to be a normative influence for the life of the community. We can begin to understand now, and we shall do so more clearly later on, in what sense the Veda was seen to be 'the root of *dharma*'. Today, with the sharp decline of the performance of traditional Vedic ritual, many aspects of the Vedāṅga have ceased to have any extensive priestly relevance. But they still live another life of specialisation. They are now the preserve of Indological scholars – revealing glimpses of a psyche of the past which helps make sense of basic aspects of the Hindu mentality of the present, and surprising us by their linguistic sophistication, and challenging, shaping, and informing general theories of human language in ways which otherwise would not have been possible.

The term 'sūtra' has often cropped up. In linguistic as well as other contexts, it is important. A short explanation here of the 'sūtra' as a characteristic vehicle of Hindu wisdom will not be out of place. 'Sūtra' has been derived from the root *siv*, to sew, and means 'thread', or in our context, a more or less short thread of sounds (a sūtra can consist of a single word) conveying meaning in a condensed form.[8] There is a Sanskrit verse to the effect that the sūtra is to be short, grammatically simple, incorrigible, and as pithy as possible.[9] Thus sūtras are often aphoristic and require elucidation by means of commentary. The *Brahma* Sūtras, for example, comprise a text of about 550 individual sūtras (the number cannot be given exactly because there are different ways of dividing the sūtras up) on which many contending commentaries have been written. The very first sūtra runs as follows: *athāto brahmajijñāsā*. There are two compounds here, each consisting of two words, i.e. *atha* + *ataḥ* and *brahma* + *jijñāsā*. The whole sūtra means literally 'Now (*atha*), therefore (*ataḥ*), critical inquiry (*jijñāsā*) into Brahman (*brahma*)'.

The classical Vedantic theologians have commented on each word, often to different effect. Why does the text start with the word 'now'? they ask first. Because, says Śaṃkara, what ought to have preceded is the fulfilling of four prerequisites by the prospective inquirer into *Brahman*. Śaṃkara goes on to mention these prerequisites. Rāmānuja disagrees. He declares that 'now' intimates that a study of the Sage Jaimini's treatise on *dharma* has preceded; so for him the text begins with the implication, '*Now*, after *dharma* has been studied, we shall inquire into *Brahman*'. In *his* commentary Madhva gives another interpretation of 'now'; *atha*, he says, is an auspicious term, and that is why it inaugurates the *Brahma* Sūtras. And so it goes on. Because the sūtra is so condensed and usually aphoristic in meaning, it enables sometimes widely divergent commentaries to be written.

The reason for the popularity of the sūtra as a means of storing and passing on lore in Hinduism is not difficult to find. The sūtra attests to the fact that Hindu wisdom has traditionally been transmitted orally, and it facilitates such transmission. The sūtra is a memory device. It is far easier to remember a sūtra or collection of sūtras than a normally rendered, and far more verbose, text. Further, the sūtra points to the fact that Brahminic wisdom was more or less safeguarded knowledge and transmitted as such. Its pearls were not meant to be cast before swine, namely, those unfit or unprepared to receive it. The sūtra form enclosed Establishment wisdom, enabling it to be unlocked only in the appropriate circumstances. It was a vehicle and symbol of authority.

The Gṛhya Sūtras

Gṛhya means 'domestic'. The Gṛhya Sūtras are condensed codifications of domestic ritual ostensibly directed at the three top strata of Hindu society – the Brahmins, the Kṣatriyas and the Vaiśyas – giving instructions on how the domestic fire (called the *aupāsana*, in contrast to the three sacrificial fires of the solemn ritual) is to be established, and describing rites and practices to be followed under its symbolic influence. The Gṛhya Sūtras are a pot-pourri of counsel. Not only do they describe the performance of major and minor rites of passage (e.g. ceremonies at birth and death, the naming of a child, investiture of the sacred thread, marriage), but they are also concerned with such things as how a father, returning from a journey, is to greet his male and female children, how one should keep a fast, ward off various diseases, choose the soil on which to build a house, make love to one's wife to produce male offspring, etc. Here we have many examples of the Vedic non-solemn rites alluded to earlier.[10] Note that most of these rules and ceremonies are male-oriented, in keeping with the traditional emphasis of Hindu society. The Gṛhya Sūtras are closely associated with the *śruti*, and frequently quote from it. In effect these quotations ratify and solemnise the practices being recommended. The Sūtras are far from exhaustive; they purport to provide a ritual framework, a guideline, for the domestic life of the righteous (especially male) upper-caste Hindu who observes Vedic *dharma*. As such, they are complementary to the *śruti* which centres round the performance, not of domestic observances, but of the solemn sacrificial ritual.

In general, like the Śrauta Sūtras, the Gṛhya Sūtras are associated with particular schools or branches of Vedic study. On the whole they are very ancient texts. Linguistically they post-date the Vedic Saṃhitās but are earlier than the later Upaniṣads. But this refers to when the rites that they deal with were formally codified. Many of the rites themselves seem to have roots as ancient, if not more so, than the Vedic ritual. There is nothing surprising in this, for there is every reason to suppose that domestic ritual would have been in force in Aryan society simultaneously with the performance of the Vedic sacrifice.

As part of *smṛti*, the Gṛhya Sūtras are not sacrosanct in the way *śruti* is. They hold up an ideal, Brahminic code of domestic practice, and any two Gṛhya Sūtras often differ in various details in their descriptions of the same rite or custom. How far real life deviated from the ideal they recommended is not known. No doubt only a small fraction of those eligible would have sought to adhere to their recommendations to any comprehensive degree; most individuals would have followed the Gṛhya Sūtras highly selectively, according to how circumstances of one kind or another dictated. This is the way of human nature and this is precisely the situation today. Some of the rites of the Gṛhya Sūtras – mainly the major and some of the minor rites of passage – are still followed selectively and often in a highly condensed or symbolic form by Hindus (see Chapter 10), but hardly anyone maintains the ritual domestic fire any more. The Gṛhya Sūtras are ascribed to ancient authorities, and tend to be named after these. Some of the most important are the *Śāṅkhāyana* Gṛhyhasūtra, the *Āśvalāyana* Gṛhyasūtra, the *Pāraskara* Gṛhyasūtra, the *Āpastamba* Gṛhyasūtra and the *Gobhila* Gṛhyasūtra.

The Dharma Sūtras and Śāstras

We come now to *dharma*, one of the most important 'action concepts' in the history of religious Hinduism. By action concept I mean an idea that is a reference point for everyday implementation; that is, *dharma* functions as a normative concept[11] which has been promulgated, ratified and constantly re-worked by those in authority in society, mainly the Brahmins. It was first formally articulated in treatises consisting largely of rules and regulations so as to express the socio-religious ideal that these authoritative persons had in mind. This ideal could have a vested interest, of course. Thus all authoritative treatises on *dharma* grant socio-religious and, on occasion, even economic privileges to the upper strata of society, representatively males and especially Brahmins. Further, this ideal has operated at different levels of influence. Some treatises on *dharma* have enjoyed a very wide, almost pan-Hindu authority; others have been more localised in their influence. For example, the *Mānava* Dharma Śāstra (sometimes referred to as The *Manu Smṛti*, or Law, Code or Institutes of Manu (abbr. Manu) – composed mainly between *c.* 200 BCE–200 CE[12]) may well have derived from a text of the Mānava clan which celebrated their ancestry from Manu, the legendary progenitor of the human race. The present text seems to have emerged from an ancient non-sectarian law school, its author(s) no doubt adapting and extending Mānava law code for general use. As such, the *Manu Smṛti* came to have a very wide authority in Hindu society at large and has traditionally been the most quoted of the Dharma Śāstras, by Hindus and non-Hindus alike. It retained its authoritative status until well into the nineteenth century. In many cases it was even reckoned to have the force of law for their Hindu subjects by British administrators, until its rulings were supplanted by British norms of justice. Vijñāneśvara's *Mitākṣara*, on the other hand, another treatise on *dharma* (eleventh to twelfth century) was strongly influential on a large scale in Bengal and areas of northern India until recent times. Indeed, it is still referred to as normative when possible within the current framework of secular law among certain, mainly Brahmin, communities. Some of the ancient *dharma* books, especially Manu, are far from being a dead letter in India today. In so far as traditional-minded Brahmins are looked up to as teachers by other castes (e.g. when they act as family or temple priests), they continue to consult either the more authoritative ancient codifiers (such as Manu) or material from the endless chain of *paddhati*s or manuals which claim to be based on the ancient authorities as adaptations for local use. This is just one example of how the little tradition derives from the great.

The fact that there are a number of ancient authoritative treatises on *dharma* (not to mention a great many *paddhati*s) shows that no one treatise had *unquestioned* authority, even in localised circumstances. Hindus are practical people; they also relish debate (*saṃvāda*). One *dharma* text could be pitted against another, and often was, not only by those who dispensed *dharma*, as it were, but also by those at the receiving end. *Dharma* has always been manipulable, though too often to the advantage of males and the higher castes. This is because the *dharma* of the treatises has usually been seen as a norm, and has only selectively been translated into reality. It is now time to enquire, from the historical perspective, into what *dharma* has meant to Hindus. This will help us to understand the term's modern connotations.

The title *Dharma Sūtras and Śāstras* is usually translated as 'The Law Books', but this is unsatisfactory for two reasons. First, it does not distinguish between 'Śāstra' and 'Sūtra' in this context; and second, 'Law' is a very inadequate translation for *dharma*. We have seen what 'sūtra' means; 'śāstra' in general means authoritative composition, scriptural or otherwise. In the context of the treatises on *dharma*, some of the main differences between the Sūtras and the Śāstras are as follows. In general, although the Dharma Sūtras are older and more succinct than the Śāstras, they are not necessarily more authoritative. The former are in prose or in prose mixed with verse, whereas the latter are almost entirely verse texts. Further, Dharma Sūtras are each associated with a particular Veda, while the Dharma Śāstras are more or less independent in this respect. As to subject matter, like the Gṛhya Sūtras, both the Dharma Sūtras and Śāstras are meant to serve as guidelines only and are not exhaustive (though the Śāstras deal more comprehensively than the Sūtras with some topics, e.g. the duties of a king and criminal law – and may add some of their own, e.g. how the world is produced, how certain mixed castes arise, etc.).

However, both Sūtras and Śāstras have many topics in common, e.g. the codes of conduct governing some of the main rites of passage (for instance, 'initiation' or the investiture of the sacred thread, marriage) and the oblations-to-the-dead (*śrāddha*); which occupations the four caste orders may follow, in normal and in straitened circumstances; how one may fall from caste and be reinstated and ways of incurring and cleansing ritual impurity; types of purifying agent (e.g. fire, water, earth, various emissions of the cow) and how they work; the status of women; the penances (*prāyaścitta*) to be performed for infringing various rules of *dharma*, the laws of inheritance, debt, etc.; the duties of kings, and so on. While both kinds of texts have these topics in common, their treatment of these topics often differs, though it would be taking us too far afield to pursue this difference here.

It is believed that in ancient times there were a great many Dharma Sūtra texts (almost every Vedic branch and sub-branch had its own Dharma Codes, some differing only in detail, others apparently held in common). Comparatively few of these Codes are extant today. Some of these are as follows: the *Gautama* Dharma Sūtra (associated with the *Sāma* Veda), the *Baudhāyana, Āpastamba*, and *Vaikhānasa* Dharma Sūtras (associated with different schools of the *Yajur* Veda), and the *Vāsiṣṭha* Dharma Sūtra (associated with the *Ṛg* Veda). Except for the last named text which is relatively late (*c.* beginning of the Common Era), the other Dharma Sūtras may be dated from about sixth to third century BCE. The oldest portions of the *Viṣṇu* Dharma Sutra (associated with the *Yajur* Veda) may belong to a century or two before the beginning of the Common Era. Among the Dharma Śāstras which, unlike the Sūtras may well have derived from law schools, in addition to the Code of Manu which is the oldest extant, we may name the *Yājñavalkya Smṛti (c.* beginning of the Common Era) and the *Nārada Smṛti (c.* second to fourth century CE).[13]

Now to our second point. If 'law' is an inadequate translation of *dharma*, what exactly does *dharma* mean? Let us begin our study of *dharma* by enquiring into its traditional meaning and context; we can then go on to consider, in this and subsequent chapters, how *dharma* was articulated in the life of the people, and some contemporary nuances of the term. The word *dharma* comes from the Sanskrit root *dhṛ*, which means 'to support', 'to undergird', 'to establish'. *Dharma*, then, is that which 'bears up' in some way or other. In some contexts, e.g. the social or civic, the word could well be translated by 'law', but not in others. For traditionally Hindus have also spoken of the *dharma* of something in the sense of the essential characteristic, the basic property, of that thing. Hence the *dharma* of fire is to burn, the *dharma* of the human spirit or *ātman* has been (for most Hindu philosophers) 'consciousness'. 'Burning' and 'consciousness' are the outstanding natural marks of fire and the *ātman* respectively, the characteristics that establish them for what they are, that bear up to scrutiny. This sense of *dharma* is descriptive, not prescriptive. Thus we see that *dharma* can have physical, moral, social and religious connotations, depending on context. *Dharma* is that which properly undergirds or establishes something from a certain point of view, prescriptively and/or descriptively. In fact, one often finds that this semantic ambivalence gives an elusive meaning to the term.

Socio-religiously, *dharma* is that which acceptably upholds private and public life, which establishes social, moral and religious order, or at least which characterises the nature of something. This is why the word has been variously translated as 'law', 'virtue', 'merit', 'propriety', 'morality', 'religion', etc.[14] (with the negative *adharma* taking on contrary meanings). In fact, it was from the nineteenth century, once Hinduism came into systematic, often abrasive contact with Christianity under British rule, that *dharma* (and its vernacular forms) acquired the connotations of the western term 'religion'. Even today this is only one of the term's connotations, adding to its multi-faceted meaning, and making it even more necessary to be alert to the context in which it is being used.

Throughout the history of Hinduism, Hindus have been obsessed with trying to understand, analyse, interpret, determine, codify, articulate and debate *dharma*. This process of shaping and mapping out will continue for as long as Hinduism exists. This is because the implementation of *dharma* is integral to the structure of Hindu living. At the heart of this concept has lain the awareness of two tensions: between order and chaos, and between choice and necessity. We will consider the first tension in this chapter and in Chapter 5; in Chapter 8 we will enquire into the second.

Hindus have always been alive to the struggle between order and chaos, the focal point of which has been placed in a religious context. As the ancient Aryans began extending their way of life eastwards and southwards, and settling the land, this struggle must have been very real to them. The forces of chaos, natural and otherwise – mighty rivers and thunderstorms, blazing sun and searing drought, the impenetrable darkness of night, unpredictable seasonal variations and harvests, disease, human enmity, battles, death – figure starkly in their religious hymns and could be coped with only through some controlling power. The Vedic Indians found this power in the sacrificial ritual: the sacrosanct and integrated combination of word and deed. The ritual generated *ṛta* or order out of surrounding *anṛta* or disorder. This opposition was also expressed by the terms *satya* and *asatya* and increasingly (by the time we come to the period of the Dharma Sūtras) by *dharma* and *adharma*. However, these pairs often had overlapping nuances of meaning and their understanding did not develop in linear progression (thus both the Vedic Saṃhitās and the authoritative Upaniṣads, for example, make use of all six terms, though with varying degrees of frequency and emphasis). *Ṛta* and *anṛta* stood for order and disorder (among other meanings) in natural or cosmic as well as moral dimensions of life. This semantic polyvalence reappeared and was strengthened in the pairs *satya-asatya* and *dharma-adharma*. Although the ancient Aryans invoked a number of *devas* (gods) to foster aspects of order in their lives, the *deva* who chiefly presided over *ṛta* they called Varuṇa. In the Saṃhitās, Varuṇa is 'lord of the sea' (RV.1.25.7); he has tamed the amorphous, lawless waters (RV.7.64.2; AV.5.24.4–5); he rules all worlds (RV.8.42.1); he has measured them out (RV.5.85.5); he is 'true to his Law' (RV.1.25.8); all-seeing (RV.1.25.16; AV.4.16.1ff); the one whose precepts are true (AV.1.10.1). We can see from these references how Varuṇa was considered sufficiently competent to preside over moral and natural order. Poignant are the passages where Varuṇa the Righteous is beseeched to grant friendship, mercy, protection (RV.2.28.3; 2.28.10; 7.86.2), and forgiveness (RV.7.86.4ff; 7.89.1ff).

The concept of *dharma*, of moulding order out of chaos, developed from these early, complex Vedic roots. In a socio-religious context, the rationale underlying it first surfaces in a late hymn of the *Ṛg* Veda (10.90, the hymn of the generative sacrifice of the cosmic Person). This hymn depicts how out of the cosmic Person (*puruṣa*), sacrificed 'in the beginning' by the *devas*, different features of our universe (the creative word, animal life, human life and social order, heavenly bodies, etc.) were produced. This original sacrifice contained the norms (*dharmāṇi*, v. 16) of all subsequent sacrifice. For our purposes, v. 12 is significant. For it tells how the cosmic Person was apportioned to give rise to the prototypical caste hierarchy. 'His mouth became the Brahmin, his arms became those who protect and rule (*rājanya*), his thighs became those who trade (*vaiśya*), from his feet those who serve (*śūdra*) were born'. Note how the caste hierarchy – and its hierarchical nature is very clear – is set in a religious context, in the context of the normative, primeval sacrifice of the cosmic Person; caste is given a sacrosanct status. Further, it is implied that this hierarchy is somehow organic and natural. These features of the caste order were not lost on the *dharma*-codifiers, not least on the influential Manu (who clearly alludes to this *Ṛg* Vedic verse in I.87[15]); they reverberate in Hindu thinking about caste down the ages to the present day. Again and again in Hindu texts, which seek to express normative socio-religious values or to preserve or reinstate Hindu *dharma*, this ancient Vedic verse is invoked. In fact, a great deal of formal *dharma* literature may be regarded as the attempt of the orthodox to elaborate this verse in terms of what they regard as the ideal life-style. It lies at the heart of the bitter debates between modern social reformers and conservative revivalists. It is time now to look more closely at the traditional link between *dharma* and caste.

First we must clarify the concept of caste. Hitherto we have spoken somewhat vaguely but acceptably I believe, for the general purposes we have had in mind, of 'caste' in the sense of a religiously sanctioned, stratified social order. We must now be more specific. With respect to caste in this sense, two Sanskritic terms in particular are relevant: *varṇa* and *jāti*.[16] We will deal with *varṇa* in this chapter and *jāti* in Chapter 5.

Varṇa generally refers to the appearance of something (its form and colour), and we find the term used with significance in the *Ṛg* Veda to differentiate the Vedic Indians, who called themselves 'noble ones' (*āryas*), from the other peoples they encountered (chiefly the Harappans to begin with). Two examples are RV 2.12.4 and 3.34.9. Both texts come from hymns to the martial *deva*, Indra, special protector of Aryans in battle. In the first text Indra is praised for scattering the 'inferior Dāsa "*varṇa*" ' ('colour, race'; *dāsaṃ varṇam adharam*); in the second, he is celebrated for having taken possession of the 'golden' or better portion (*hiraṇyayam* . . .

bhogam; perhaps a reference to the lighter-skinned Aryans) and for smiting the Dasyus while he watches over the 'Aryan *varṇa*'. Elsewhere, we are told exactly why these Dāsas or Dasyus are to be despised. Not only do they look different (e.g. RV 5.29.10 probably refers to 'noseless' (*anāsaḥ*), i.e. snub-nosed Dasyus) but they speak and worship differently (e.g. RV 7.6.3, 7.21.5), and therefore unacceptably. Thus it apears that in the beginning *varṇa* was a term which had racial, indeed racist, connotations. It heralded a Hindu preoccupation with social and religious hierarchisation based on natural attributes.

The Śrauta, Gṛhya and Dharma Sūtras (but especially the Dharma Sūtras and Śāstras) ratify socio-religious stratification in terms of a four-tiered ideal called the *catur-varṇa*, i.e. the four *varṇas* or 'caste-orders', made up, in descending order, of Brahmins, Kṣatriyas, Vaiśyas and Śūdras. This follows the hierarchy mentioned in RV 10.90.12 (where *rājanya* has the sense of 'Kṣatriya'). It seems that from very early times the prevailing view was that membership of each *varṇa* was generally to be determined by birth. Once functioning as a Brahmin or priest became hereditary, the other strata were likewise linked with hereditary occupations. One was born into the caste hierarchy. The following observations, in accordance with the intentions of the authoritative texts, must be taken to apply representatively to men. We will comment on the status of women in due course.

In theory, the Brahmins had the most exalted status and were set up as the unattainable model of society in many respects. This is because, by hereditary occupation, they presided over the most important form of available power: that of the sacrificial ritual which was the source of temporal and spiritual well-being. The Veda itself attests to the pre-eminence of Brahmins. For example, the *Śatapatha* Brāhmaṇa not infrequently refers to Brahmins as 'gods among humans' or 'human gods' (*mānuṣyadevāḥ*).[17] They were the earthly counterparts of the *devas* in heaven, and as a caste ritually the most pure. The *dharma*-codifiers reinforced this status. Manu says (10.3): 'The Brahmin is the lord of the *varṇas* because of his superiority, the pre-eminence of his origin (from the cosmic Person), his protection of the precepts (enjoined by religion) and the distinctiveness of rite (marking the development of different phases of his life)'. The Brahmin's special duty is to serve the Veda by reciting, practising and teaching it – he originated from the *mouth* of the cosmic Person – with all that this entails, namely performance of the sacrificial and domestic ritual, living an exemplary life, receiving donations so that the donor can acquire merit, etc.

The Kṣatriya is next in the hierarchy. Ideally it is from the Kṣatriya order that the king and rulers of society are to be drawn, as are also those who physically protect the community. The duty of the ruler is to ensure that justice reigns and that a suitable milieu prevails for all members of society to observe their appropriate *dharma*. If necessary this is to be achieved by force of arms. In the history of Hinduism the ideal of the warrior who is prepared to make any sacrifice to protect society out of a sense of *dharma* has been a potent one. In important and sometimes sinister ways this ideal is being reinterpreted in modern Hindu society, in particular in the waves of fundamentalism being whipped up in the country. This gives fresh impetus to reconsider the current image of Hinduism which westerners tend to have, especially as a result of publicity given to the views of Gandhi, i.e. that it is a religion devoted to non-violence (*ahiṃsā*). Hindus themselves are generally aware that their religion teaches a much more complex relationship between violence and non-violence than this image suggests. In fact Hindu literature and tradition often glorify or condone violence (in the form of ritual animal sacrifice, righteous war, etc.). On the other hand, many texts recommend non-violence (*ahiṃsā*). We will comment on this tension in another context.

Next in order is the Vaiśya *varṇa*. The particular duty of the Vaiśya is to engage in trade and commerce, to build up a flourishing community so that *dharma* can be established on a sound economic basis. After all, the Vaiśya is supposed to have originated from the thighs of the cosmic person; thus the Vaiśya is meant to prop up society, to give it economic mobility.

The first three *varṇas* are regarded as 'twice-born' (*dvija*). The first birth is physical; the second birth is spiritual, the result of initiation into Vedic study generally during childhood, which renders the initiate eligible to practise Vedic and Veda-based ritual and to be sanctified by religiously sanctioned rites of passage. The *Āpastamba* Dharma Sūtra says: '(The teacher) gives birth to the (student) through knowledge. That is the best birth' (1.1.1.15–16).[18] Thus, although members of each of the twice-born *varṇas* are enjoined to practise a particular form of livelihood (and the specific virtues stemming from this), as twice-born they have many duties and practices in common. Further, the *dharma* texts allow for flexibility in the practice of one's livelihood in straitened circumstances.[19] In Chapter 8 we will consider some of the main features of Hindu ethics, chiefly in terms of the teachings of the śāstras.

Much has been made in Hinduism of the privileges (and sometimes of the responsibilities) of twice-born status, though it has not always been clear, as we shall see presently, exactly to whom this status applies. The mark of the twice-born is the sacred thread (*yajñopavīta*), a triple-braided loop[20] usually worn over the left shoulder and under the right armpit as the result of initiation.[21] This and other aspects of twice-born life will be considered in Chapter 10.

Finally, the Śūdra belongs to the lowest *varṇa*, which is emphatically not twice-born. In other words, by birth, members of this *varṇa* were not eligible to be initiated into the rights and responsibilities of a life based directly on the Veda. Fearful punishments were prescribed for Śūdras who had the temerity to utter words of the Veda; the twice-born were not even permitted to recite the Veda in their presence.[22] As to livelihood, 'Śūdras must serve the three higher (*varṇa*s), for (as the Veda declares), they came forth from the feet (of the primordial Person)'.[23] Although, as we shall see later, Śūdras could acquire virtue and win ethical approval, they were generally reviled and were often the referent of unfavourable comparisons, the norm of a despised socio-religious status. In fact their humanity was discriminated against in highly objectionable ways. This was because they were regarded by the twice-born as ritually polluting agents; this was supposed to be a *natural* characteristic which could be controlled and even overcome by a web of socio-religious taboos maintained by both sides of the twice-born divide, but which required constant monitoring lest it actualise its potential. Here we have the roots of untouchability in its modern form.

Further, the later *dharma* books in particular insinuate that the Śūdras have a natural proclivity to certain kinds of vice, which they must seek to overcome by the cultivation of the corresponding virtues. There was not much that the Śūdras were allowed to do about such stereotyping except acquiesce, strive to heed their betters and so hope to win approval in this life and a higher (twice-born) *varṇa* in the next.[24] By the time of Manu the idea had taken hold that the underlying reason for being born in a particular caste was karma, or the way in which moral actions of previous lives matured in the present one. Belief in rebirth was a necessary component of this way of thinking. We shall examine the teaching of karma and rebirth in Chapter 8.

Who were the Śūdras? We don't rightly know, although a number of suggestions have been made, namely that they were generally drawn from the ranks of the colonised Harappans and other indigenous peoples (the '*Dāsa*s' and '*Dasyu*s' of the Vedic hymns);[25] that they included those who had been disgraced or socially ostracised for some reason; and that they were the products of frowned-upon marriages or unions, or a combination of these criteria. In any case, they formed a useful category, socially, religiously and psychologically, as scapegoats for a hierarchical-minded, purity-conscious élite. In many ways this rationale obtains even in contemporary Hindu society.

II

Dharma *as ashramic ideal. The* aikāśramya *view and the fourfold progressive view. The progressive view outlined. Comments on the place of women in traditional Sanskritic Hinduism up to modern times. Loss of caste: meaning and scope. An important distinction.*

So far we have considered *varṇa-dharma*, the *dharma* of caste in its theoretical aspect. There was another side to this idealised code of practice known as *āśrama-dharma*. *Āśrama* means 'stopping-' or 'resting-place' and refers to four stages of life open to twice-born males. These are (i) *brahmacarya*, the stage of the religious student; (ii) *gārhasthya*, the stage of the householder; (iii) *vānaprastha*, the stage of the forest-dweller; and (iv) *saṃnyāsa*, the stage of the renouncer.

Books on Hinduism sometimes give the impression that the codes are unanimous in instructing all twice-born males to enter each of these stages in the given order. But this is not the case. The earliest Dharma Sūtras seem to regard a life in *one āśrama* as desirable (the so-called *aikāśramya* view), following a period of instruction by the teacher after initiation (*upanayana*). The *āśrama* favoured in these Sūtras is that of the householder – after all, it was this way of life that was generally indispensable for the viability of society in accordance with Vedic tradition.[26] The other *āśramas* were permitted and endorsed, but there was no pressure to enter them. The quaternary-*āśrama* view in its progressive form came to predominate in time – this is reflected in the later Codes – and we will now give an idea of the practices of each *āśrama* of this developed view.

Brahmacarya

The religious student of the first *āśrama* was called a *brahmacārin*, that is, one who walks the path (*cārin*) of *brahma*, the Veda's central concern, in the sense both of the supreme reality and of the inherent power of the sacred word. We can understand now why this stage became the first in a man's life – it preserved the centrality of the Veda in one's existence, it made the Aryan religion a going concern and, if one wants to be a little cynical, it maintained the authority of the Brahmins who were the guardians of this religion. In order to enter this *āśrama*, a youth born into one of the three top *varṇas* had to be initiated into his second birth, usually by a Brahmin teacher in good standing.[27] In a hymn extolling the *brahmacārin*, the *Atharva* Veda says, 'The teacher initiating the student makes him an embryo within; he bears him in his belly for three nights'.[28] This process of 'being born again' meant that he was now empowered to utter, study and ponder the Veda, first as a disciple of his teacher and then on his own for the rest of his life (provided he did not lose caste). Even if he entered the other *āśramas*, he was to exercise this prerogative in one way or another.

According to the Codes, one is to be initiated while still young (from about 8, 11 and 12 years for a Brahmin, Kṣatriya and Vaiśya respectively), though if initiation is delayed after about 16, 22 and 24 years, one is excommunicated unless and until a penance has been performed. After this, initiation may take place. After initiation one is ordinarily to reside with the teacher, hence this stage is sometimes called *ācāryakula* (residing in the family of the teacher). The period of residence may be from one year to an indefinite stay. Thus it was possible to be a *brahmacārin* for life, absorbed in the study and practice of the Veda. Doubtless this option was followed only in a very few cases, either separately or in the company of the teacher, the latter also having a say presumably in how long he was prepared to tolerate his pupil(s).

On entering *brahmacarya*, the student had entered the school of life in a serious way. He had formally come of age religiously, but spiritually, psychologically and socially he had much to learn. As can be imagined, the teacher and his family[29] had a very important part to play in this formation. Not only was the student initiated into the recitation and understanding of the Veda and Vedic rites in greater or lesser degree (depending on the length of time he stayed with the teacher), he was also trained in a detailed code of behaviour governing his relationships with men and women in various walks of life. The student had to follow a strict regimen, with rules governing how he was to conduct himself in the presence of the teacher or the teacher's wife, how to dress, how and what to eat, etc.; he was to cultivate especially the virtues of celibacy (of mind and body),[30] truthfulness, obedience and humility. He was to be self-controlled internally and externally, shunning dancing, singing, exuberance of any kind, preening himself in any way (by the use of ornaments, unguents, etc.), and so on. He was to beg regularly for food and offer it to his teacher. This utter reverence for the teacher was symbolised in the literature by the expression 'approaching the teacher with fuel in hand'; that is, the student was to gather wood regularly to light the sacred fire of the teacher's home in which Vedic rites would be observed. By this act he expressed his subservience to the teacher in the spiritual relationship thus far described. Historically, this relationship lies at the root of the modern phenomenon of the Hindu guru which we will consider in Chapter 7. But subservience did not mean servility, as it often seems to in the modern context. We will return to this matter later.

Gārhasthya

When the student finished his tutelage, he was to give his teacher a fee (*dakṣiṇā*) such as his family could afford – perhaps a cow or cows, some gold, or a parasol to keep off sun and rain – and then take a ritual bath. This made him a *snātaka*, i.e. someone who had thus ritually bathed after completing the *brahmacarya* stage. He then returned home; this returning, celebrated ritually, was called *samāvartana*. Under certain conditions the *snātaka* phase could be protracted (for the fulfilling of vows, pilgrimages, etc.). *Snātaka* Brahmins in particular were to be shown great respect; they were supposed to be granted free passage throughout the land notwithstanding hostile political boundaries. One comes across instances in literature of fugitives and others, not least from the Kṣatriya caste, disguising themselves as *snātaka*s in order to escape capture.

The *snātaka* phase lay at the threshold of the next *āśrama*, that of marriage and of being a householder (*gārhasthya*; in some contexts *snātaka* just referred to a twice-born male, married or not, who had duly completed *brahmacarya*). The Codes speak very warmly of *gārhasthya*. As it was crucial to the stability and propagation of the social order, this *āśrama* was regarded as the foundation of the other three stages. 'From what is laid down in Veda and *smṛti*' declares Manu, 'it is the householder among the members of these (four stages) who is said to be the best, for he supports those of the other three (groups). Just as all kinds of river find rest in the ocean, so members of the different stages find rest in the householder' (6.89–90).[31] Indeed, some codes suggest that one could not proceed to the other two *āśrama*s without fulfilling the obligations of this stage, for the householder was the foundation of Aryan *dharma*. Together with his wife (ideally of the same caste order) he both financed and practised Vedic rites. And the maintenance of Vedic rites implied the perpetuation of society and the establishing of world order, which included a state of affairs even today of great importance for a Hindu – a state of harmony between those who live in this life and those who live on as ancestral spirits before either being reborn in different forms or achieving final liberation.

The special duties of the householder were summed up in his obligation to perform regularly the five *mahāyajña*s or 'great sacrifices'. This obligation is described variously in the Codes, but the principle is the same. The householder is to celebrate ritually the *deva*s, the ancestors, life in this world, human existence, and *Brahman* (as embodied in the Veda). By this the whole order of being, thrown into relief against the backdrop of potential non-being, is affirmed. As an expression of this affirmation the householder, together with his wife (or co-wives), is enjoined to keep and activate the sacred fires, both solemn and domestic (the *deva*s, the manes and Brahman-qua-Veda are thereby satisfied), as well as to procreate, and wherever possible, to protect life and offer hospitality to guests, especially Brahmins (by so doing, human life and the world are affirmed).

Exceptions were made, of course, some showing inconsistency. Thus animal sacrifice and other forms of killing, e.g. by a Kṣatriya in battle, or punishment by execution, were permissible, so long as these were seen to protect the Vedic way of life or to be in accord with Vedic dictates. Inconsistency arose when meat-eating by slaughter was permitted, as it was earlier on. But by the time of Manu, meat-eating and the slaughter of animals was frowned upon if not condemned by the traditionally orthodox, probably in response to mounting Buddhist and Jain criticism.[32] The householder had a particular duty to offer hospitality and to protect vulnerable life, but even this was not to be indiscriminate. For instance, quite elaborate rules were devised as to what being a guest meant and how different kinds of guests in the different *varṇa*s were to be treated; and though abortion was in general roundly condemned, medical texts permitted it in the name of *dharma* to save the life of the mother.[33]

In the course of time and as the religion of *bhakti* or single-minded devotion to God developed, the obligation to perform the *mahāyajña*s was reinterpreted somewhat. Although in many cases the order of creation continued to be seen as multi-dimensional (the gods being viewed either as expressions of the underlying One or as supra-human beings of some kind), for the *bhakta* or (sectarian) theist the one supreme Being became the source, mainstay and end of all finite being. We will examine this issue when we discuss Hindu theology and worship. In later (post-Manu) texts, there was a tendency to regard the performance of the *mahāyajña*s as in general discharging one's debts to the ancestors, to the sages who propagated and inspired Vedic religion, to society and the world, and to God.[34] This continues to be a popular belief among educated Hindus and in books on Hinduism written by Hindus.

Vānaprasthya

If a twice-born male wished, he could go on to become a 'forest-dweller' (*vanaprastha*) and/or ascetic (*saṃnyāsin*). Generally, the stage of forest-dweller (or *vaikhānasa* as it is sometimes called[35]) is mentioned as coming first. The idea is that from now on the individual who so wishes progressively detaches himself from the concerns of the world with a view to achieving serenity in this existence and post-mortem fulfilment outside the cycle of life. He starts by putting his household affairs in order; then he departs to a secluded place, usually outside inhabited areas (hence *vana*, 'forest', *prastha*, 'dweller'). He may take his wife or go alone. If he goes alone, he must first provide for his wife and children.[36] It seems that if he goes alone, the wife (or wives) should acquiesce.

The texts describe an increasingly austere life in this state, merging into the complete mental and physical renunciation which characterises the final *āśrama*. Thus the forest-dweller is to remain celibate, sparsely clothed, practising austerity, dependence on nature, and begging (for food). He is not to hoard food unduly and should provide for visitors in his forest retreat so far as he is able. He is to recite the Veda (even if it is only the sacred syllable 'Om') and keep the sacred fire. He may cook his food and, according to some early traditions, eat meat that he has not killed himself. He is to gradually adopt a more strict regimen, becoming more and more of an ascetic, refraining from all self-indulgence and cooked food, and eating only vegetarian food. He is on the threshold of the fourth and last stage, that of the renouncer.

Saṃnyāsa

In this *āśrama* – sometimes called *bhaikṣya* (mendicancy) – the forest-dweller ceases to tend the sacred fire. In fact, by a special rite he incorporates the sacred fire(s) into himself; henceforth, fuelled by his austerities, he is to be a living fire, his spirit shining through as a smokeless flame.[37] Utterly detached from material and mental possessions and from family, he becomes a wanderer and begs for his sustenance. He is to be without guile. The text says that, rather than making for a homestead where the kitchen smoke is visible (in expectation of freshly prepared and tasty food), he is to beg, without importuning, at a dwelling where no kitchen smoke is to be seen. He is to recite the Veda, even if it is only a few sacred words, utterly impervious to the *dvandvas*, those opposites of worldly existence – heat and cold, bitter and sweet, male and female, affection and hatred, desire and aversion, joy and sorrow, life and death – in which ordinary mortals live and move and have their being. So disciplined, and desiring harm to no being, when he dies he will pass out of the cycle of life into immortality, his accumulated demerit consumed by the fire of his austerities. Some passages allow him to encompass his own death in his wanderings by the gradual reduction of food as he makes his final, 'great journey' (*mahā-prasthāna*) through life.

But it was recognised that the way of the forest-dweller and the renouncer was the way of but a few; it was commended without being enforced, and a man could just as well live out his days 'under the roof of his sons'.

This in short was the righteous life-style for twice-born males envisaged by the codifiers. It was called *āśrama-dharma*, and the whole two-sided construct was known as *varṇāśrama-dharma (varṇa + āśrama dharma)*. How roundly implemented was this socio-religious construct by twice-born males in Hindu society it is impossible to say. There is no doubt that it was widely deferred to as a comprehensive *ideal* until recent times, until, in fact, the rationalist and modernising critiques of the nineteenth century. There can also be no doubt that in practice it must have been subject to swingeing adaptation according to how time, place, circumstance and temperament varied. The influence of this orthodox, Vedic ground plan in contemporary times will be considered later.

Let us now consider the place of women in the traditional Hindu view of life, with reference to the modern context. At first, the Aryan woman had some individual standing in early Vedic times. It was intended that she take part in the solemn ritual and presumably share in its immortalising power.[38] The *Śatapatha* Brāhmaṇa clearly implies that a man is incomplete if his wife does not sacrifice with him, and that it is as 'a whole' that a husband should strive for the highest sacrificial goal (5.2.1.10). The *Taittirīya* Brāhmaṇa declares that without a wife a sacrificer is ineligible to sacrifice.[39] In Vedic religion, woman was man's *saha-dharmiṇī* (partner in *dharma*), and it was as a unit (*dampatī*) that they were supposed to perform the sacrificial ritual. However, it is also clear that if a woman was not quite an adjunct to her husband in the unity of the sacrificial act, she was his junior partner. Rarely, if ever, could she perform the solemn ritual independently of him. Further, it was only as a wife that she was empowered to function as a complement in this context. Later works, e.g. the *Rāmāyaṇa*, indicate that wives could act by themselves in certain rites of domestic or non-solemn worship. However, even here, instances cited are generally for or on behalf of the husband. This idea of wives being the subordinate partner of the husband in matters of worship has persisted into contemporary times. I know from personal experience that in Bengal, for instance, even western-educated women who are anti-traditionalist in many respects are reluctant to or will not take part in, say, the ritual worship before the image of the Goddess during the Durgā Pūjā, Bengal's great autumnal festival, if their husband is barred from this by some ritual impediment such as a death in the family.

Nevertheless, to return to ancient times, there was scope for a woman in her own right to be formally initiated into Vedic study and to discourse on the Veda. This could not apply to Śūdra women, of course. But it seems that in early Vedic times women of the three upper *varṇa*s were permitted or expected to undergo some formal *brahmacarya* discipline, i.e. studying the Veda, before marriage. By thus ratifying the caste status of women the *varṇa*-system would be preserved. But as study of the Veda grew more elaborate, marriage – at least for girls – presented an obstacle. Boys could wait longer to be wed while studying the Veda, but the sooner girls got married off the better. The reason is depressingly familiar; it has its cultural counterparts around the world. There was a growing, exclusivist tendency to regard women as sources of ritual impurity and as naturally weak not only physically but also morally. To offset these frailties, women had to be protected and controlled – by men. Marriage, male-dominated marriage, was the institution in which this was to be done.

But before this kind of thinking reached fever pitch, women were still allowed to show their prowess in an activity that brought prestige, power and even wealth, and that as such was fast becoming a male preserve – knowledge of the Veda. Most women, still mere girls, were married off usually in their early teens, more or less concomitant with a formal initiation rite; they then devoted themselves, as one text says, to such expertise as women acquire (*strī- prajñā*).[40] Clearly this was not expertise in the Veda. But others were permitted, even after marriage, to pursue the prestigious occupation of studying and expounding the Veda. The former type of woman was known as a *sadyovadhū* (namely a 'bride', *vadhū*, married (off) 'without delay', *sadyas*), the latter as a *brahmavādinī*, or discourser on Brahman.

The *Bṛhadāraṇyaka* Upaniṣad gives us a glimpse of what being a *brahmavādinī* could mean. It tells of a great sacrifice held under the patronage of Janaka, king of Videha, at which many Brahmins were present (BAUp III.1.1ff). Janaka, who presumably prided himself on being a patron of learning, combined the occasion with a contest to discover who was the most scripturally learned Brahmin in the group. (Holy quizzes of this kind were not uncommon on such occasions.) He offered a fabulous prize to the winner: a thousand cows, with ten gold coins tied to each horn.

Let us cut this long story short. The chief contender was a sage called Yājñavalkya. He had a number of challengers, and he kept silencing them one by one. In due course, Gārgī Vācaknavī threw down the gauntlet.[41]

> 'Now, respected Brahmins,' she said, 'I shall ask him two questions. If he can answer them, none of you can defeat him in quizzes about *Brahman*.'
>
> 'Ask, Gārgī,' said Yājñavalkya.
>
> What impresses is how she asked.
>
> 'Yājñavalkya,' she said, 'Like a warrior son of Kāśi or Videha (this doubtless with a sidelong glance at Janaka), might stand against you having strung his untaut bow and taken up two arrows deadly to the foe, even so do I confront you with two questions. Give me the answers.'

We shall not go into what Gārgī asked, or the details of what happened (she lost). But she was clearly a woman of spirit and self-esteem, and the nature of Yājñavalkya's answer shows that he respected her, both for her spirit and her learning.[42] With the passage of time, as the tendency to denigrate women intensified, the likes of Gārgī became few and far between.

By the time of Manu, marriage was the only *āśrama*, if it could be called that, which was in practice open to women. Various rites could be performed for them, but without Vedic utterances (see e.g. Manu 2.66) and in general they were regarded as wells of ritual pollution (exacerbated by such distinctive phenomena as menstruation and childbirth) and as symbols and instigators *par excellence* of lust and other vices.[43] All women, irrespective of *varṇa*, were cast more or less in the same mould as virtual nonentities in their own right both socially and religiously. They were granted little or no independence; they were barred from studying the Vedas; and they were marginalised from *śrauta* ritual. As time went by, their religion consisted of *smārta* ritual in the sense of such practices as worship before images in the home and in the temple, the observance of vows and fasts, attending and participating in rites of passage, the recitation and enactment of texts that were not officially part of the Vedas, and so on. They were respected not as women but as child-bearers (i.e. wives) and child-rearers (i.e. mothers). Once again Manu can be quoted to good effect. 'Night and day women must be kept dependent by their menfolk, and if they become attached to worldly things they must be kept under one's control. Protected in childhood by her father, in youth by her husband, and in old age by her sons, a woman is not fit for independence' (9.2–3).[44]

Their code of *dharma* was also male-oriented. 'For women the marriage injunction is reckoned (equal to) a Vedic rite, as is service of the husband to living with the guru (which follows the initiation into Vedic study for boys), and housework to tending the sacred fire' (2.67). Marriage (*vivāha*), service of the husband (*patiseva*) and housework (*gṛhārtha*) made up the broad parameters of *strī-dharma*, woman's ethical path. These were her surrogates for involvement with the Veda which was the traditional means to ultimate fulfilment and immortality and now the domain of men. Remember, Manu does not stand alone. Manu summed up a longstanding tradition which it then reinforced and helped to perpetuate. It was not long before women and Śūdras were normatively lumped together as subject to a host of social and religious disabilities. This association continued down the centuries and persists in many conservative minds, not excluding those of women, to the present day.

By Manu's time, the grandest thing a woman could do was to be chastely married and to spend the rest of her days serving her husband. Though Manu pronounces that ideally the husband should act as if marriages are made in heaven, and that mutual fidelity should sum up the married life,[45] the balance of the relationship as a whole is made very clear. The husband is the wife's lord and master, more or less literally her 'god' (or superman).[46]

If, as earnest proof of her devotion as a true wife (*satī*) she agreed to be concremated with her husband when he predeceased her,[47] well and good; otherwise she was to pass the rest of her days in self-effacing widowhood. Manu does not prescribe suttee, but he rules that a widow should mortify herself until death, honouring the memory of her husband (5.157–8). In the later śāstras suttee is prescribed, though it was not legally enforceable (*dharma* texts made recommendations, not state law). Suttee, in fact, was positively forbidden in certain circumstances.[48] Further, it must be pointed out that suttee was never widespread and that not uncommonly, from early times, women practised suttee willingly.[49] They were much admired for this, of course, and such immolations were commemorated down the centuries by the erection of stone tablets and other shrines. Many are visible in various parts of India today.

There is a moving account in the *Mahābhārata* of how Mādrī, the junior wife of the prince Pāṇḍu, argued (successfully) with her senior co-wife, Kuntī, to be allowed to join her dead husband's body on the funeral pyre so that she could be happy in heaven with him.[50] There are also records by foreigners and Indians of wives, especially of rulers and from warrior clans, willingly committing suttee on the death of their husbands. But by the nineteenth century, especially in Bengal, the practice had on the whole become corrupt. It was often enforced in horrible ways, not least by moral and psychological pressure. The reasons for this varied. Greed for the inheritance of the widow was no doubt a potent factor, as was the felt need of the victim's family or caste to display credentials of orthodoxy in the face of real or supposed challenges to these at a time of great social turmoil. The suttee was the scapegoat. There is the story of Ram Mohan Roy as a youth, looking on in horror at the enforced suttee of a relative, the pathetic shrieks of the victim ringing in his ears as she was beaten down by poles on the burning funeral pyre.[51] As we have noted in Chapter 3, it was Ram Mohan who played a prominent part in securing the legal abolition of suttee.[52] Note that in bringing about this reform, as in so many others, Brahmins and other upper-caste Hindus took the lead.

Subsequently, the emancipation of women became one of the most important and emotive issues for nineteenth-century Hindu reformers. Campaigns to 'liberate' women were not monolithic, of course; all sorts of reasons were at work in the minds of the protagonists (overwhelmingly men), and no doubt a great deal of goodwill was involved. But withal, in the process women still tended to be regarded as 'the field' over which battles for male authority were fought. Here the Victorian attitudes of the British to the relationship between the sexes played an important part.

Today, it seems, suttee is moribund, but not dead. On 4 September

1987, Roop Kanwar, a young matriculate Rajput wife, created a furore in India by willingly committing suttee on the funeral pyre of her husband. This deed activated age-old dormant attitudes throughout the land. Traditionalists and revivalists, for their own reasons, hailed the event. Some politicians condoned it, others condemned it; feminists and others, man and woman, from all walks of life, were outraged. Roop Kanwar's place of sacrifice has become a thriving shrine, and the controversy smoulders on.[53] But so far she has been the exception that has proved the rule: today, suttee is a thing of the past – if not some of the thinking behind it.

By the beginning of the Christian era one or two 'back doors' had begun to appear for a kind of religious rehabilitation of women. The Buddhists, who were growing in religious influence, allowed women to become nuns – somewhat grudgingly and hedged with a lot of qualifications, it is true – but to be a nun was an honourable Buddhist vocation. Sociologically as a response perhaps, the 'Hindus', i.e. those who followed Vedic *dharma*, while not favouring the nunnery for their womenfolk, made it possible for women to play an increasingly important part in the devotional theistic traditions that began to develop. These *bhakti* religions did not start off as orthodox in the traditional sense. But many soon became Brahminised and thus were accommodated to a changing view of orthodoxy. One of the earliest texts of this new devotional orthodoxy was the *Bhagavadgītā (c.* the time of Manu). Chapter 9, v. 32 is significant for our purposes. The Lord Kṛṣṇa, God in human form, is talking to his devotee, Arjuna. 'For even those, Arjuna, whose birth results from demerit (*pāpayonayaḥ*) – women, Vaiśyas and Śūdras too – reach the highest goal once they've sought refuge in me,' he says.[54] We note the concessionary form of the statement; nevertheless, love of God conquered all disabilities and women could reach the highest religious goal, namely communion with the Lord, if they sought refuge in him. *Bhakti* religion was subsequently to enable women to acquire a measure of religious independence, and there is a sporadic record of women achieving renown in one tradition or another for their devotional fervour.

Thus the Śaiva Nayanar and the Vaiṣṇava Āḻvār *bhakti* movements of the South (*c.* fifth to ninth century CE) gave prominence to one or two women as founder figures (e.g. Karaikkal Ammaiyar and Aṇṭāḷ respectively). In the mediaeval South, from about the twelfth century, the Liṅgāyats or Vīraśaivas maintained that male and female members of their community were equal; some of the most poignant and inspirational devotional hymns of this tradition have been composed by women. Moreover, in contemporary times Liṅgāyats have acknowledged a woman as their religious head. In the Tantric and Śākta traditions, in which the Goddess figures prominently, a special place is given to female sexuality in religious contexts as the expression of *śakti*, divine power. Thus the Kāpālikas or Skull-bearers (who rose to prominence by about the first millennium of the CE) accorded salvific importance to female sexuality and to female companions of male ascetics. In similar vein, in the East, mediaeval Bengali Chaitanyaism[55] encouraged devotees (including men) in some Vaiṣṇava circles to adopt the roles of female associates of Kṛṣṇa during his sojourn on earth, in their religious worship of him as supreme Being. In the mediaeval *bhakti* efflorescence of the North, there were powerful examples of women who were regarded as recipients of saving grace, e.g. the Rajput princess, Mīrābāī (sixteenth century), who composed intensely personal love poems to Kṛṣṇa, and Śabarī, the outcaste woman devotee of Rāma in Tulsīdās' momentous *Rāmcaritmānas*. These are some examples of the ways in which women in Hinduism have salvaged some religious esteem.

Nor has this esteem existed exclusively in a religious context. It was possible for women to express their individuality in social contexts as well. In the course of history, a number of cases are recorded of women wielding political power, either as rulers in their own right, as regents, or as the power behind the throne. Human nature being what it is, there was scope too for a strong-minded woman to exert influence over her menfolk domestically – as wife, lover, mother, daughter. Female lovers (including wives) in particular, had considerable opportunity, even dharmic latitude, to be forceful in their sexual relationships.[56] And who can doubt that in real life a resourceful woman was quite capable of establishing in many ways satisfactory relationships, if not the upper hand, with the men in her life? But it is equally true that the flexibility she had for independence/individuality had to be nurtured, at best, within the strict parameters of a general Manu-like attitude to women, more or less irrespective of the theology which prevailed in her milieu, and that this attitude has been dominant in Hindu society from early to modern times. Even today it exerts a powerful, one is tempted to say all-powerful, residual influence in the minds of most Hindus. Besides, the religious esteem of which we have spoken must be qualified in important ways. It is an ambivalent esteem and is not as straightforward as it may sound. We will return to this point later in the book.

Today, however, progress in the emancipation of Hindu women

certainly has been made in crucial ways: legislatively, socially and religiously. This progress is most noticeable in westernised, middle- and upper-class circles. This can be illustrated in the case of widows. In Hindu society today there is still a widespread bias against (Hindu) widows remarrying. Nevertheless, widows of a westernised background seem to find it easier than their more traditionally placed counterparts to overcome this bias and to gain self-respect not only by establishing successful careers for themselves but also by sometimes remarrying. Their less fortunate counterparts in rural and other contexts still labour under the weight of tradition, both as regards the way that they perceive their own status and the way this is perceived by their peers. They feel that after the death of their husbands they have become a burden to their families, that they live on sufferance and are inauspicious.[57] Their social milieu encourages them to feel guilty in some way for encompassing their husbands' early demise, and to live ascetic, joyless existences. Their *raison d'être* (namely the husband) having passed away, some succumb to internal or external pressures to leave home and await death in an environment thought to be conducive to a holy end. One can still see in a number of ancient places of pilgrimage, not least Benares, the pathetic sight of generally elderly widows clad in drab, white saris (the traditional garb of the widow) living together in austere hostels, grimly eking out their remaining days as derelicts of society. One could give other examples of the lingering effects of traditional discrimination against Hindu women.

As citizens however, Indian Hindu women have the same fundamental rights as their menfolk under the law, even when this affects former religious male prerogatives. For instance, except for the very traditional, the ban on women studying the Vedas is a dead letter. In Indian universities and other institutions of learning today, women (as also male non-twice-born) teachers and scholars make valuable contributions. And there are many other instances of women striving successfully to hold their own.

We must add here that, according to the Codes, twice-born men and women, and even Śūdras for some authorities, could 'lose caste' if they failed in specific ways to live according to *dharma*. There is no unanimity about the list of transgressions which caused this condition, not only because views changed but also because opinions differed. There seems to have been general agreement, however, that certain kinds of dharmic violation incurred 'loss of caste', e.g. some kinds of killing (in particular of a Brahmin, or abortion), of sexual intercourse (particularly with one's guru's wife, or incest) or of eating or drinking (e.g. the drinking of alcohol by a Brahmin); consorting with outcastes; and recidivism of one sort or another. Loss of caste was a terrible thing to happen, but there was no unanimity as to what this meant. Gautama speaks of being fallen (*patita*; or of 'falling', *patana*), a state brought about by a number of violations, including those mentioned above.[58] Being fallen means having lost (i) the right to live according to the Veda-based rites and actions of the twice-born; and consequently (ii) the fulfilment that results, in the hereafter, from such a life.[59] But loss of caste was also a terrible thing because of the social penalties it incurred, which included isolation from one's community.

In reality, the fear of loss of caste was pervasive and acute until well into the twentieth century. Its sting lay mainly in its public effects, of course, for the unfortunate individual or family was socially ostracised until such time as due penance was made. It mainly occurred over the two Ms, i.e. marriage and meals, in other words, through prohibited marital and commensal relations (e.g. marrying out of caste or eating with/taking water or food from the 'wrong' people). Because the prospect of loss of caste was usually traumatic, it could prompt extreme behaviour for its avoidance. Thus parents would go to absurd or cruel lengths to prevent offspring from incurring loss of caste by undesirable marriages. Loss of caste also prompted extreme behaviour in its enforcement. One comes across harrowing examples of this. Here is a proclamation of caste excommunication by the Kapole Banyas (a merchant caste) against a member of their community. It was issued not so very long ago, on 14 May 1871 in Bombay.

> That as the custom of widow remarriage is not in our caste, and as such remarriage is contrary to the immemorial practice of our caste, and is opposed to what we conscientiously believe to be the law enjoined by our religious Shastras, the said Madhowdas Rugnathdas having married the said widow, Dhunkorebai, they have rendered themselves ineligible for such social intercourse as that of eating and drinking with the caste, and of giving and receiving in marriage. Therefore no member of the caste shall hold such intercourse with them.
>
> That if any member of the Kapole caste will eat or drink with the said Madhowdas Rugnathdas or Bai Dhunkore, or hold such intercourse with them as that of giving and receiving in marriage, such member shall render himself equally ineligible for holding such intercourse with the caste, and no such intercourse shall be held with him.

> That if it be proved hereafter that any member or members of our caste had aided, or taken part in, the remarriage of Madhowdas Rugnathdas with Dunkorebai, the caste shall not hold with such member or members any such intercourse as is stated above.[60]

By one fell stroke, one was debarred from one's own community, including family and friends, and from the solace and support that this implied. Couple this with the fact that for similar social and religious reasons, members of commensurate castes were generally equally reluctant to associate with the excommunicates. Today the fear of losing caste is neither as pervasive nor as acute as in the past. But it continues to exist in varying intensities and in different ways among different strata of Hindus. It is most in evidence in rural communities, among the uneducated and among the traditionalists. One still reads of cases where outrage or dishonour adjudged to have occurred by actions incurring loss of caste (especially out-of-caste marriages) results in the murder of an offending party (by a member of either faction).

Although various penances were prescribed to recover caste in the Codes, there seems to be no unanimity (in fact, there is confusion) as to how effective or far-reaching these penances were (did they apply to all the relevant transgressions and to men as well as to women? Did some of the penances necessarily imply death?). Different, that is more extreme, standards of penance and punishment tended to apply to Śūdra transgressors in so far as they lacked twice-born status. As in the past, so it is today, that what is decided by the elders or the pandits of the community, consulting tradition, circumstances and their law manuals, determines recovery or continued loss of caste. Here, as one would expect, many circumstantial, sometimes opposing, considerations come into effect to produce a decision.

One must also keep in mind that traditionally in so far as *dharma* was given a naturalistic dimension, it could be transgressed not only intentionally but also unintentionally. This view is still current. Thus menstruation made a woman ritually impure, and contact with her in this condition made one also impure whether or not one knew it at the time and intended the contact or not. Penances were prescribed for both kinds of transgressions. This is an additional reason for saying that Hindu *dharma* is not co-extensive with Hindu morality, if morality is to be confined to the sphere of intentional activity. We shall comment on the relationship between *dharma* and morality in Chapter 8. We note here, however, that the Codes prescribe a general morality for all as the framework within which one's particular morality as a man or woman, or as a member of one or other of the castes/*varṇa*s, was to be followed. This too will be dealt with later. We will continue our particular discussion on caste in the context of our general discussion on tradition in Chapter 5.

5 The voice of tradition: 'Caste' and narrative

I

Varṇāśrama dharma *challenged by the reality of* varṇa-saṃkara *('caste' intermingling); implications. Two views: caste as determined by heredity, and caste as determined by behaviour. The concept of* jāti; jāti *and* varṇa. *Untouchability, unconstitutional yet widespread, especially rurally. How untouchability manifests itself. The Dalits;* śūddhi. *Modern interpreters of* dharma *and caste: Ram Mohan Roy, Swami Dayananda Sarasvati, M. K. Gandhi. Gandhi and Sant Mat. A fresh look at* smṛti.

The *varṇāśrama* system – and the *dharma* that it inculcated – was an idealised hierarchical construct, an expression of the Hindu passion for order. But in real life things didn't quite follow the ideal. Real life was a little more chaotic, the 'fit' between the ideal and the actual often being far from exact, much depending on time, place and circumstance. We have a number of clues in the *dharma* texts themselves (and in other sources) that in real life the ideal was being challenged.

One source of this challenge was unapproved sexual union. The ideal union recommended for wedlock was between partners of the same caste status.[1] Such marriages and their offspring were regular. When partners of different castes produced children, what was technically known as *varṇa-saṃkara* or 'caste-mixing' occurred. This could happen in various ways, licitly (e.g. through wedlock) and illicitly (e.g. through adultery). In general such unions and their offspring were frowned upon in the Codes, the extent of disapproval shown usually being proportionate to the degree of caste disparity perceived between the partners. When a man cohabited with a woman of lower caste, the union was described as *anuloma*, lit. 'with the sweep of the hair' (note the naturalistic image). When the woman belonged to a higher caste the union was *pratiloma*, that is, 'against the sweep of the hair', and more reprehensible. In *anuloma* unions, which could be licit, the offspring of a Brahmin man and a Kṣatriya woman, say, had higher caste status than the child of a Brahmin man and a Śūdra woman. In *pratiloma* unions, some of which seem grudgingly to have been recognised as licit, the reverse occurred: the higher the caste status of the woman, the more base-born the offspring. Thus the Caṇḍāla (the son of a Śūdra father and a Brahmin mother) was a byword for degradation.

A number of the Codes, especially the *dharma*-Śāstras, take great pains to describe and name various combinations of inter-caste progeny (including combinations between the progeny of mixed castes). Many of these mixed castes were ritually so impure that their presence or touch, or food taken from their hands or vessels, drastically polluted a member of a twice-born *varṇa*, and as such were anathema.[2] In the context of the Codes' description of *varṇa-saṃkara* it is important to note two points: first, many of the offspring of such unions, especially the more despised, were accorded undesirable congenital physical or moral characteristics simply by virtue of their 'base' birth;[3] particular occupations were also enjoined on or associated with them.[4] The naturalistic character of caste comes to the fore in all of this. It is essential to understand this in order to appreciate not only how deep-rooted the caste phenomenon and its implications are in the Hindu psyche, but also how difficult and commendable it may be to try to eradicate this phenomenon, in however limited a manner. The second point is this: casteing a child was basically a patrilineal affair; it was the father's caste that most mattered.[5] In fact, in traditional Hinduism the woman was often referred to as the field (*kṣetra*) in which the man sowed the seed. It was generally thought that though the quality of the field deserved consideration, the quality of the crop really depended on the quality of the seed.[6] Patriarchy triumphed then – as it does now.

But the elaborate effort that the Codes made first to classify and then to disapprove of *varṇa-saṃkara* indicates not only that the ideal they were propagating was under fire, but that caste intermingling was going on all the time. The Codes' treatment of *varṇa-saṃkara* can be regarded as a form of damage containment. It offered a pattern for perceiving and evaluating *varṇa-saṃkara*; the extent of the 'match' between this pattern and what was happening in real life can only be a matter for speculation.

Why was *varṇa-saṃkara* such an issue? In early Vedic times it seems that it was a priority to preserve the racial purity of the Aryan peoples. The Dharma Code of *Vasiṣṭha* hints at this when it says bluntly, 'The attractive girl (*rāmā*) of dark complexion (*kṛṣṇavarṇā*) (becomes a wife) for pleasure (*ramaṇāya*), not for *dharma*' (18.18). Such marriages (liaisons?) seem to have been tolerated socially, but they were hardly dharmic. But, in time, intermingling of peoples became established so that *varṇa* lost its original racial emphasis and acquired predominantly socio-religious connotations as a hierarchical term. It was no longer possible to tell caste on the basis of appearance.[7] *Varṇa-saṃkara* was now discouraged mainly for social and religious reasons.

In the *Bhagavadgītā*, in which *dharma* is understood in a new light, the warrior, Arjuna, gives *varṇa-saṃkara* as one of the reasons why war is undesirable. 'When the family is destroyed (by war through the death of its menfolk),' he says, 'longstanding family-laws (*dharmāḥ*) are destroyed. With the destruction of this Code (*dharma*), lawlessness (*adharma*) rules the whole family. When such lawlessness rules, the women of the family are corrupted. When they are vitiated, *varṇa-saṃkara* takes place. Such mixing leads to hell for the family and its destroyers. For the ancestral spirits of both parties fall, deprived of their libations and food-offerings' (1.40–2). So *varṇa-saṃkara* was bad because it wrecked lineal succession which in turn left one's ancestors, bereft of their post-mortem rites, duly uncared for. This was most undesirable, for as unassuaged ghosts (or *pretas*) they were likely to take revenge on their living descendants (see Chapter 10). Further, the balance of nature was now disrupted and all sorts of personal and natural calamities could occur. Last but not least, keep in mind that today's earthling is tomorrow's ancestor; one does not wish to be left hanging in the air, so to speak, when one's turn comes. (The Codes and their successors, the *paddhatis*, find a way of getting round the lineal disruption that life's vagaries throw up: male relatives and even daughters are deemed 'dharmic sons' eligible to perform the required rites). Even today, in a great many Hindu minds not overly influenced by modernising forces, it remains important to perform and to be seen to perform rites for one's dead. The reasons for this are religious, social and, not least, psychological. And since dharmic offspring are required for the performance of funeral and ancestral rites, even today there remains generally a strong bias against marriage outside certain caste boundaries. The demarcating of these boundaries in individual cases is, of course, subject to circumstance. The more traditional, and generally the more rural, are the more strict.[8]

Still, caste miscegenation was unstoppable, and this became an obstacle to the implementation of any ideal construct of a socio-religious hierarchy based on naturalistic or hereditary principles. Another obstacle was the view that it was the *quality of one's behaviour* that determined one's standing in the community, not one's status at birth. This view was expressed within the framework of the *varṇa* hierarchy, or rather the Brahmin/non-Brahmin divide, but it is of sound pedigree, being internal to the authoritative texts themselves. It may well have gained strength in orthodox circles as the Hindu response to the Buddhist challenge to caste, for the early Buddhists tended to interpret *varṇa* on behavioural rather than on naturalistic or hereditary grounds.

There is early and classic evidence of this view in a story of the *Chāndogya* Upaniṣad (IV.4.1–5). The youth, Satyakāma (i.e. 'Truth-lover'), wished to study the Veda as a *brahmacārin*. He asked his mother, Jabālā, for details of his lineage so that a teacher could duly accept him. Jabālā makes a confession: 'I don't know your clan (*gotra*), my dear; when I was young I moved about a great deal as a maidservant, and so had you. So I don't know your clan. But my name's Jabālā, and your name is Satyakāma, so say that you are Satyakāma Jābāla'.

So Satyakāma goes to the teacher Gautama and asks to be received as his pupil. Gautama questions him about his lineage. Satyakāma says that he does not know, repeating his mother's words in full. Then Gautama replies, 'One who is a non-Brahmin could not speak thus. Bring the fuel, my son, I'll take you on; you have not departed from the truth.' For Gautama, that was credential enough to study the Veda. Credit all round: to the mother no less than to the son for their love of the truth (no doubt Gautama had the mother in mind when he associated truth-telling with what being a Brahmin was all about); and credit to the teacher for appreciating the fact and acting in defiance of custom. Thus has religious Hinduism always been able to rise above a sterile orthodoxy.

This view that one's social standing (in terms of *varṇa*) is, or ought to be, a consequence of character rather than of birth runs as an undercurrent in the family of religions comprising Hinduism. Even Manu, otherwise so uncompromisingly in favour of the hereditary-naturalistic principle, allows a glimpse or two of it. Thus Manu 2.157 declares that a Brahmin unschooled in the Veda (*anadhīyāna*) is a Brahmin in name only, just as an elephant made of wood or a deer made of leather are not the real thing. In similar vein the Law Code of Baudhāyana says: 'The offence of insulting a Brahmin cannot be made against the fool ignorant of the Veda. For one does not pass by a blazing fire in order to offer an oblation in ashes!'.[9] Again, the non-hereditary view of social standing finds expression in other authoritative *smṛti* works, like the Mbh.[10] And the tendency in the increasingly popular and pervasive *bhakti* traditions beginning with the concession of *Gītā* 9.32 (see Chapter 4) to regard (low) caste as no barrier to attaining final salvation from this life, gave valuable support to this view.

However, it was in the beginning of the nineteenth century, with the work of Ram Mohan Roy, that the first systematic steps were taken to draw the sting out of the hereditary view of caste. In time these steps became the tramp of many feet culminating in the struggle led by Gandhi to uplift India's millions of untouchables. During this process it was not always the case that caste was reinterpreted by reformers according to the behavioural criterion; on occasion some endorsed or tolerated the concept of an ideal caste hierarchy while attacking the privileges and discriminations of the existing social system. We shall return to this point later, when we take up the question of the untouchables, on p. 114.

Ideal constructs apart, in real life the caste system was developing into a highly complex, multi-level social system, with elaborate rules of marriage within or outside the clan and eating-relationships, based on perceived disparities of ritual purity or impurity, and centring round a notional relationship between one's *jāti* and *varṇa*. *Jāti* and *varṇa* must be understood as representative terms for the actual and the ideal, for in the texts at any rate, a strict distinction is not preserved between them; sometimes they are used apparently interchangeably. In India today, the notion of *jāti* is used among Hindus (and even among Sikhs, Christians, Muslims and others, so ingrained is this concept) in identifying one's social status. For Hindus, *jāti* is not only a social term, it also has religious, economic, occupational, psychological and other connotations as and when the context demands.[11]

Jāti in Sanskrit comes from the root *jan, janatilte* which means 'to beget', 'to produce', and refers not only to origin but also to the group or class to which something belongs. For our purposes, *jāti* is the social stratum in which one is born. It is fixed by birth and associated with strict parameters of occupation available to one and of groupings within which one may marry or share food and water. Whereas there are only four *varṇas*, there are many hundreds of *jātis*. For instance, there are numerous *jātis* of Brahmin alone, which are mutually governed by elaborate rules of commensality and marriage.[12] These relationships are often defined by local tradition and the occupations associated with the 'castes' or *jāti*s[13] concerned. Thus, in various parts of the country, there are Brahmin *jāti*s occupationally associated with certain aspects of the funeral ceremony which are forbidden to intermarry or interdine with other Brahmin *jāti*s on the grounds that the former are ritually inferior and even polluting to the latter. The privileges of superiority here are often fiercely protected. If this can be the case among Brahmins, imagine how distinctions of superiority may be (and often are) preserved between Brahmin and other twice-born castes, and even more so between the twice-born and those who cannot claim this status. Thus the concept of twice-born still evokes powerful reactions in India.

The relationship between *jāti* and *varṇa* is a complex one. In theory the four *varṇa*s are affirmed; in practice it is not always easy to relate a particular *jāti* to the *varṇa* hierarchy. Brahmin castes belong to the Brahmin *varṇa* of course, notwithstanding distinctions of ritual purity and social superiority among them. But, in many cases where non-Brahmin castes are concerned, it is just not relevant to ask to which *varṇa* they belong. What are relevant are the established rules of intermarriage and commensality that have built up between and within the lineages of these castes, notwithstanding theoretical claims they may make to belong to a particular *varṇa*. In Bengal, for instance, there are three main upper castes: the Brahmins, the Baidyas and the Kāyasthas. There may be no dispute about the *varṇa* of the Brahmins, but it is hardly relevant to ask to which *varṇa* the other two castes belong. Some claim that the Kṣatriya and Vaiśya *varṇa*s are virtually defunct in Bengal; others that the Baidyas are ex-Brahmins and the Kāyasthas are Śūdras. Yet Kāyasthas sometimes claim the sacred thread, and have even gone to court to enforce their claim. These are contentious issues, yet these three castes regard each other as the three top castes of Bengal (with the Brahmins indisputably at the head), and apply traditional codes of behaviour in their mutual relationships, which often extend to intermarriage, without reference to formal *varṇa* placements. From this we see that, as of old, the Brahmin/non-Brahmin divide is a peculiarly significant one; and this is the case not only in Bengal but in India as a whole. Brahmin family priests often determine to their own and to their clients' satisfaction the *varṇa*s to which the latter belong so that various rites and rituals may be carried out on request.[14] Needless to say, such pronouncements do not always meet with general approval.

Even within castes which are not supposed to be twice-born there are taboos of interrelationship. Among these castes, some are regarded as untouchable, but not all. Even among so-called untouchable castes, some will refuse to 'take water from the hands' of others (the mark of decisively superior ritual status).

The name of a caste may derive from an occupation traditionally associated with that caste (even though most of the members of that caste may actually be engaged in other occupations), or from a particular ancestor, village, historical event, etc. Sometimes the position of a particular caste relative to other castes is contested. This happens either when the caste itself seeks upward mobility (a caste may rarely seek to downgrade itself in order to take advantage of certain government concessions), or when other castes challenge its claimed status. Upward mobility is sought by such devices as the caste refusing to perform certain traditional occupations, refusing to take water from another caste, claiming higher ancestry, Sanskritising some of its ritual and other practices, or a combination of these. A caste's position in the ladder is the result both of its self-perception and of its standing in the eyes of other concerned castes. Usually this position is not under question – traditions of caste placement die hard – though there may be some jostling for status between contiguous castes. In India, the most invidious consequences of the caste system in its present form are evident with regard to the way the so-called untouchables are treated. It is important to consider this question, albeit briefly.

The untouchables of today are the product of many centuries of the evolution of the caste system in ways that are often historically still obscure. Nevertheless, this evolution has been based on various features inherent in the *varṇa* system such as the distinction between those who are twice-born and those who are not, hereditary occupations, and notions of ritual purity connected with these occupations. We have already seen how the Śūdra, who was 'born to serve the twice born', tended to be regarded as a source of ritual impurity by the Codes. The polluting influence of some of the mixed castes, particularly the Caṇḍāla, was particularly stressed, not only because of what they were but also because of the jobs that they were supposed to do. Caṇḍālas and those of similar rank were to be shunned by almost everybody else; they were to live outside village boundaries and to carry distinguishing marks for easy identification.[15]

It was this kind of separatist thinking on the part of the more privileged that engendered Hindu India's untouchables, among whom there are many castes today. Altogether, about 15 per cent of the

Indian population, or over 115 million people, are designated 'untouchable' (i.e. as being members of the 'Scheduled Castes' in the language of the Indian Constitution). Most thus designated live in rural areas (see Note 8). And it is in the villages that the discriminations of untouchability are most evident, notwithstanding the declaration of the Indian Constitution that 'the State shall not discriminate against any citizen on grounds . . . of religion, race, caste, sex, place of birth' (Article 15) and the enactment of laws to back this up (especially the Protection of Civil Rights Act, 1976). It is particularly in the villages that many untouchables are still found living at the margins of society or even beyond, literally and metaphorically, and plying trades that the upper castes deem polluting and which are economically disadvantageous.

Ancient customs live long in the village milieu. This is because the village community more than any other is bound up as a whole with the land, and the ways of such communities take longest to change. It is specially so in the Indian village; most castes of the Indian village live in connection with the land in one way or another, even Brahmins who are often landowners (though some may practise their priestly calling).[16] This dependence on the land is such that, by and large, village transactions, namely the exchange of goods and services between people, are still bound up, not so much with cash currency, as with an established barter system at the heart of which lie staple crops of the area. The barter system and caste interdependence reinforce each other in so far as caste is more or less inflexibly tied to occupation in the rural context. Reinforcing caste interdependence in this context means reinforcing the traditional caste hierarchy at the bottom of which, of course, are the low castes and the untouchables. These groups are thus trapped in their positions by a self-perpetuating vicious circle, made all the more unrelenting by centuries of psychological and religious pressure. It is by no means uncommon to read reports today of untouchables being ill-treated, attacked, raped or killed in rural areas by so-called 'caste' Hindus (i.e. higher-caste, even upper-caste Hindus) because they have been regarded as stepping out of line by their assailants.[17] Such deviation is perceived as threatening to the general 'social security' of the whole village, in which upper-caste privilege is entrenched.[18] Again, because untouchables in particular have been regarded as defiling by most members of Hindu society, they have traditionally been denied access to temples and other holy places. This has forced them to build their own temples and shrines, especially in the villages, and to run these with priests drawn from their own ranks. (Moral: by no means all who officiate as priests in Hinduism are Brahmins.)

This is not to say that things have been rosy for the untouchables in the towns and cities. In fairly large-scale ancient habitations, now citified, the living plan often follows the same pattern as in the villages. For example, in the holy city of Hardwar and its environs, on the banks of India's most sacred River Ganges, the highest castes, namely the Brahmin priests, etc., live closest to the ritually pure confines of the river, while the lower castes live further and further away in proportion to their increasing ritual impurity.[19] Modern urban areas are not designed in this way, and in the cosmopolitan bustle of a modern city, untouchables have a greater freedom to live and work without the old constraints. Even in such an environment however, they usually drift into the most menial jobs and the few who find themselves in a position to seek betterment not infrequently encounter more or less subtle forms of discrimination. Further, marriage between twice-born and non-twice-born (let alone an untouchable) in any environment, is discouraged by Hindu society and is therefore very rare.

What exactly does it mean to be 'untouchable'? This varies from village to village, from caste to caste, from region to region, even from city to city. But the general picture in the village context a generation ago is given in the following statement which describes the position of the Camārs of Madhopur, a village in Uttar Pradesh some 25 miles from Benares. The Camārs, says the author,

> have long stood near the bottom of the regional society of Uttar Pradesh in wealth, power, and caste position. . . . In Madhopur . . . a Camār's touch does not ordinarily carry defilement to the body of another. When most high-caste persons refer to a Camār as 'untouchable', they mean only that they cannot take food or water from him, and that his touch will pollute food, water, and the utensils used for food and water. Camārs are regarded as defiled especially because of their repugnant traditional occupations of skinning, tanning, and midwifery, and because of their reputation for eating carrion beef.[20]

By and large this conception of untouchability is not uncommon in village India today.

But it is important to note that things are changing for the better – not always as quickly or as peacefully as one would wish, but inexorably all the same. Legislation against discrimination helps (it would help more if it were enforced more); so does India's interaction with the West. Technological progress, city planning on western lines, foreign travel and exposure to western forms of life by means of film and television, and social and political processes such as democracy, feminism, etc. are forcing Hindu India to take stock of traditional usages and to make changes. Further, change is aided by the fact that many low-caste and untouchable groups have banded together in unions, societies, and so on, within the context of India's democratic Constitution, to struggle to improve their lot. Untouchables are becoming increasingly aware of the legal, political and religious options open to them to ameliorate their condition, as well as increasingly impatient. There are untouchable groups who refer to themselves as 'Dalit', i.e. 'the oppressed', some of which are becoming politically more and more militant.[21] Even such a thing as 'Dalit theology' is beginning to take shape.[22] In short, untouchables have become more articulate, not only politically but also in other ways. Some have expressed in biting verse their painful experiences or defiant hopes for change.

One lodges this protest against the higher castes:
'We've lived our whole lives at your doors,
But we never met each other.
You were inside, we were outside.
You were in the temple, we were on the steps
Because you thought us Untouchable.

But those days are over.

We've begun a new life.
We've found our own temples,
Regained our lost faith.
Our gods are where we are.
All are equal here . . .

This faith is going to
Penetrate every corner of the world.
Now *you* can scream.

It's fallen! It's fallen!
Brahmin *dharma* has been overthrown.
You lit your own pyre.
What can you do now?'[23]

Another, under the title *Jat* (i.e. 'Caste'), recalls:

'When I knew nothing, I knew
My caste was despised . . . .

The Patil had kicked my father,
Cursed my mother.
They did not even raise their heads,
But I felt this "caste" in my heart.
When I climbed the step to school,
Then too I knew my caste was low.
I used to sit outside, the others inside.
My skin would suddenly shiver with little thorns,
My eyes could not hold back the tears.
Our lips must smile when they cursed . . . .
How is caste? Where is it?
It isn't seen, so does it live inside the body?
All the questions float like smoke,
And the wick of thought is sputtering.
But when I knew nothing, then I knew
My caste was low.'[24]

Many untouchables have also converted to Islam, Buddhism and Christianity in the hope of a less disadvantaged way of life. This has alarmed the more jingoistic Hindu groups, some of which have sought to communicate with the untouchables in terms of 'Suddhi' movements. *Śuddhi* means 'purifying'; the aim here is to receive apostates back into the fold of Hinduism by purifying them ritually. At the same time, to make the reconversion palatable, these groups profess to be in favour of remedying at least the more outstanding of the traditional disabilities of untouchability. Requiring purification on the one hand and offering concessions on the other is a back-handed way of going about things, to say the least.[25]

The basis for a new, more humane way of thinking about caste was laid, as already noted, in the early nineteenth century by Ram Mohan Roy. Ram Mohan was opposed not so much to the institution of caste as to its chronic divisiveness. Hindus could not take their place amongst the peoples of the world, counter the incoming disruptive cultural challenges of the West, acquire self-esteem and capitalise on their great religious and cultural past if they allowed the disintegrating influence of caste- and sex-discrimination to continue. Ram Mohan sensed that with the advent of British rule it was inevitable that India, especially the Hindu India of the great majority, must now face a future of coming to terms with the West. The isolated existence of the past was gone for ever. This future could be one either of dialogue with Western values and ideas or of studied rejection and separatist development. The latter alternative would only hasten India's ruin, degraded as Hindu culture already was by the evils of casteism, priestcraft, ritualism, polytheism, religious infanticide, discrimination against women, and so on. For Ram Mohan, dialogue was the only way forward for India to emerge renewed, purified, strengthened.

It is of great importance to appreciate that Ram Mohan sought to renew Hinduism *from within.* This is what motivated all his attempts at social and religious reform. To achieve his goal Ram Mohan began the process of reinterpreting the pervasive action concept of *dharma.* For Roy, *dharma* ceased to be an individualistic affair, bound up with introspective, dogmatic socio-religious taboos. It became the expression of a rationalist ideal, based on egalitarian religious principles and the ethic of the Golden Rule. All may have equal access to the One True God, and the religious destiny of all is ultimately the same, though not all can be socially equal. Ram Mohan hardly envisaged a classless society; the Victorian values of his political masters and the heritage of traditional Hinduism's social norms were too strong for that. What he envisaged was the elimination of all inhumane discrimination based on birth and sex. The new order to which age-old Hindu norms and practices would now have to accommodate would be based on rational rather than on dogmatic principles. Ram Mohan's views lived on in the Brahmo Samaj. In this fissiparous movement they underwent the vagaries of reinterpretation and adaptation, but their leavening influence crept over the land.

Thanks to Ram Mohan, a new question hung over Hinduism in the nineteenth century. His successors, whether reformers or revivalists, were forced to take stock of their ancestral faith and to query its horizons. We will single out two of these successors for consideration here: Swami Dayananda Sarasvati and M. K. Gandhi.

Dayananda has already received attention in Chapter 3 in another context. His views on caste, which continue to have influence, deserve comment. Dayananda made a powerful if somewhat ambivalent plea for reinterpreting caste according to qualities, not birth. The plea was powerful because it went straight to the point. Caste, Dayananda taught, should be determined only in terms of the traditional *varṇa* categories; the innumerable *jāti*s which had mushroomed in the land should be dispensed with. This teaching was ambivalent, because *varṇa*-placement was to be determined by the wise (*vidvān*) backed by authority after due examination of the individual's 'qualities, actions and nature' (*guṇa, karma* and *svabhāva*). The age for this examination should be 16 years old for a woman and 25 years old for a man.[26] Imponderables here about the workability of the scheme abound. In particular, what is the relationship between 'qualities, action and nature', as criteria for the determination of one's *varṇa*? Is 'nature' something changeable? If not, have we reverted to some hereditary criterion of caste? Is 'nature' to be overruled by 'qualities and actions'? May one be re-examined later in life and so have one's caste position changed? Dayananda's ideas on caste were hardly practicable, and so it has proved. But for those prepared to consider his views there is a strong incentive to question the rationale of the traditional caste system and to act accordingly. Dayananda's stance on caste broadly reflects his understanding of *dharma*. For him as for Ram Mohan, *dharma* is a concept with universalist dimensions, no longer to be swallowed up by the ritualistic and other minutiae of traditional Hindu practice. Rather, it signifies a religio-moral way of life, and in some contexts carries the connotations of the term 'religion'.[27] *Dharma* is best lived out, of course, within Hindu parameters based on his own thought so far as Dayananda is concerned.

We come now to Mohandas Karamchand Gandhi (1869–1948), familiarly known as the 'Mahātmā' (Great Soul). Gandhi, perhaps more than any other Hindu in modern times, is noteworthy for his untiring efforts to improve the lot of those disadvantaged by the socio-religious excesses of Hinduism, namely, not only the untouchables, but also women. Gandhi's work (and its efficacy) needs to be appreciated in terms of its historical context. I remarked earlier that Ram Mohan Roy laid the basis, in the nineteenth century, for a more humane attitude to caste. True enough, but there is more to it than that. For the most part Ram Mohan and his peer-successors worked *from above*, directly addressing the higher social strata of the Ancient Banyan in the hope that their influence would percolate down. But, for centuries before Ram Mohan's time, a 'movement' had developed in the northern half of the land which leavened Brahminic *dharma* and thinking *from below*, on a populist level. Gandhi was heir as much to the latter approach as to the former; perhaps this explains why he had such a comprehensive impact.

This movement, which has been called 'Sant Mat', i.e. the View of the Sants or poet-saints who assumed prominence across an east-west swathe from about the late thirteenth century, was not homogeneous. Rather it was a pastiche of socio-religious attitudes based on the kind of devotional religion (*bhakti*) first expressed about a millennium earlier in the *Bhagavadgītā*. Yet Sant Mat was characterised by most if not all of the following features, namely a tendency to sit loosely to sectarian boundaries and iconic worship, and to Brahminic ideas of caste and precedence; to call upon God by non-exclusive names (even across religious divides, though there seems to be a preference for Vaiṣṇava epithets[28]); to express core teaching verbally in pithy, vernacular verse (mostly in forms of Hindi); to regard the devotional uttering of the divine Name as having intrinsic saving power; to regard the externals of birth and ritual as having no religious value; and to reckon true religion as a matter of loving and surrendering to God who dwells in the heart.[29] Many of the Sants, some of them women, came from low castes; some were even untouchables. Not surprisingly, they did not take kindly to the idea that ritual purity and caste status determined access to salvation. Sant religion was a religion of the heart, accessible to all. Here is a typical verse from Kabīr, Sant *par excellence*, on caste.

> Kabīr asks derisively:
> 'Pandit, look in your heart for knowledge.
> Tell me where untouchability
> came from, since you believe in it. . . .
> Eighty-four hundred thousand vessels
> decay into dust, while the potter
> keeps slapping clay
> on the wheel, and with a touch
> cuts each one off.
> We eat by touching, we wash
> by touching, from a touch
> the world was born.
> So who's untouched?' asks Kabīr.[30]

Perhaps only a small fraction of religious Hindus have formally followed Sant Mat. This does not mean that the tradition has not considerably influenced northern Hindus across the caste and sect spectrum over the centuries. Today many can quote sayings from one Sant or other. Cassettes of *bhajan*s or devotional songs attributed to well-known past Sants, including women (e.g. Mirābāī, late fifteenth century), have a large market not only in India but in Hindu communities around the world. The leading singers of these *bhajan*s perform to a busy globe-trotting schedule, and have star-rating in the media. The lives of many ordinary Hindus have no doubt been leavened by the liberating social and religious teachings of the Sants, yet when it comes to the crunch, age-old counter-influences continue to dominate – the influences of institutionalised caste practice, and Sanskritising tendencies among lower castes to win social respectability.[31] Nevertheless, Sant Mat has always retained considerable socio-religious transformative potential, and together with parallel counter-discriminatory forces in the South (e.g. the ideas of the Tamil Siddhas and original Vīraśaiva teaching) could be actualised to change society from below. This is where Gandhi comes in.

Gandhi was not low-caste; he came from a merchant background. And I am not going to deny that his thinking was shaped by a combination of Indian (including Brahminic), Christian and other sources. This is not the place to analyse these sources.[32] But there can be no doubt that guiding elements in his views derived from the *Bhagavadgītā* and the Sant tradition, especially from Kabīr and Narasiṃha Mehta, a fifteenth-century poet-saint of Gujarat (Gandhi's homeland). Gandhi makes significant references to Mehta. For example, in articles in Gujarati in *Navajīvan* (5 and 12 December 1920), he quotes one of Mehta's lyrics, and concludes from this that it is *dharma* to reject untouchability and 'the very limit of *adharma* to refuse to touch *Antyajas* (= untouchables) however clean.'[33] The 1920s were a seminal period in Gandhi's life.[34]

In suiting the action to the word Gandhi sometimes suffered life-threatening persecution. Regarded by some as a latter-day Sant, he gave a new name to the untouchables, 'Harijans', which means 'the begotten of God'.[35] This name has come into general usage in India. It is also used by a number of untouchable societies and groups when referring to themselves. But there are some untouchables, notably among the Dalits, who object to it; quite understandably, they find it patronising. Further, untouchables and others have begun to criticise Gandhi, sometimes vehemently, for expressing support for the varnashramic ideal which they regard as the root of caste oppression and untouchability. According to these critics Gandhi reprehensibly and ineffectually only treated the symptoms of the disease; he didn't attack its cause. This is to do an injustice to Gandhi on at least two counts. First, by action and word Gandhi consistently made no bones about the fact, even at the risk of personal danger, that he abhorred caste discrimination, especially untouchability. But he had other items on his social agenda, e.g. rehabilitating Hindu religion from within so that Hindu self-esteem could be raised and divisiveness countered in the nationalist cause. For this he believed it necessary to uphold the varnashramic ideal. To criticise Gandhi for not rationally resolving the apparent conflict between repudiating caste discrimination and upholding the concept of *varṇāśrama dharma* is to criticise him for what he was not – an analytic philosopher. In fact he claimed to have neither the interest nor the talent for philosophy proper. Gandhi was *par excellence* a thinking activist.

Second, by his tactics, irrespective of their philosophical underpinning or lack of it, Gandhi was the first to have a mass impact throughout the land in raising social awareness about the evils of institutionalised discrimination, especially against untouchables and women. This must not be underestimated. Much of whatever progress has come about in challenging discrimination has stemmed from this. But on the whole, in the face of Hindu India's ultra-tenacious caste mentality, this progress has been limited. As noted already, caste discrimination, often crude and brutal, is entrenched in village and town life.[36] The Gandhian struggle for human equality, which so many inside and outside government endorse by word but not by deed, still has a long way to go.

Selectively no doubt, but pervasively, the words and actions of outstanding figures like Ram Mohan, Dayananda and Gandhi, purporting as they do to interpret scripture and religious *dharma* in the modern age, carry the authority of latter-day *smṛti*. For some, their socio-religious message mediates an otherwise closed, irrelevant or remote scripture: indeed it becomes the human face of scripture (it becomes 'Veda' or its equivalent); for others it tempers the understanding of whatever scriptural corpus they have access to. This shows that *smṛti* is becoming increasingly open-ended; not only the content but the parameters of the concept are fluid. In modern times *smṛti* is being opened up in two ways: (i) by the critical use of reason and (ii) by technology.

Reason

It is true that for Hindus in general authority grows with age – the older some teaching is the more its authority tends to be respected. But in modern times, Ram Mohan and others have introduced a new element into the reckoning of religious authority – a rational critique. By this I do not wish to imply that, traditionally, reason had no role to play in the religious quest. We have already intimated that it had a vital role, and we shall enquire more fully into this in later chapters. But the deployment of reason in understanding the claims of religion had become stunted well before the beginning of the eighteenth century. An unthinking malaise had permeated the religious enterprise. In any case, the use of interpretive reason had always been mainly the preserve of pandits. Thanks to the approach of the likes of Ram Mohan, Dayananda, Vivekananda, Gandhi, etc. it has become not only rejuvenated but common property. And this has influenced the popular understanding of scripture and the assimilation of its teaching. On one level, Hinduism has become more pluralistic and selective than ever. Perhaps this has helped to prompt the reaction of closing ranks under the banner of *hindutva* on the one hand, and of greater sectarianism in other contexts on the other. The melting-pot of religious Hinduism continues to boil over; what will emerge remains to be seen.

Technology

To the more traditional means of communicating *smṛti* by writing (and printing) and word of mouth, technology has added a new dimension – the aural and audio-visual medium. By this I mean radio, film and television. Today, these media reach not only into city homes but also into urban slums[37] and into every village. We have already noted the popularity of devotional cassettes; but who can say that the addresses of a Gandhi or some other supposed saintly person heard on radio, or films like Richard Attenborough's celebrated portrayal of the Mahātmā, do not play a similar role in diffusing religious lore (*smṛti*) to the populace at large? *Smṛti* is a resource-in-the-making.

These comments on *smṛti's* changing content and its modes of communication lead us on to its next category – that of '*itihāsa*', or sacred narrative. After dealing with *itihāsa's* (Brahminic) representative works and some of their variants, we will consider the changing circumstances of its transmission. We shall also note how in certain contexts what is technically *smṛti* or collaborative lore for Brahminic orthodoxy may be invested with an intrinsic saving power, with or without the connivance or ratification of this orthodoxy. In other words, how, in the context of what is officially *smṛti* according to the 'high' tradition, there may be parallels to the phenomenon of Veda-extension (and Veda-substitution) in non-Brahminised or not significantly Brahminised 'low' tradition.

II

(*iv*) Smṛti *as sacred narrative* (itihāsa): *meaning. The* Rāmāyaṇa *and* Mahābhārata: *their concern with* dharma; *Kṣatriya bias, Brahmin editing, wide-ranging appeal. The* Rāmāyaṇa: *form and content. The character and role of Rāma. The* Mahābhārata: *form and content. The* Bhagavadgītā *and* Harivaṃśa. *Religious and cultural adaptability of the epics exemplified by the* Rāmāyaṇa *up to present times. Recitation and enactment. Narrative and the little tradition: the story of Pābūjī, the* Manasā Maṅgal.

Itihāsa

The Sanskrit can mean literally 'Thus (*iti*), indeed (*ha*), it was (*āsa*)'; an irony, because as we shall see, it could hardly have been thus. The term for 'history' in the modern sense in some vernaculars has been derived from this word – a greater irony because *itihāsa* in its traditional sense is clearly intended to mean the 'Once upon a time' of story-telling.[38] Itihāsa is narrative which has been transformed by editing into sacred narrative. Western scholars tend to translate it by 'epic'. In the Sanskritic tradition two compositions represent itihāsa: Vālmīki's *Rāmāyaṇa* and Vyāsa's *Mahābhārata.*

Vālmīki and Vyāsa are only the reputed authors of these two compositions in Hindu tradition. They are legendary figures of a distant past, though Vālmīki may have a little more historicity on his side. After all, as tradition has it, having started life as a bandit before turning to religion, he acquired his name from the ant-hill (*valmīka*) which grew about him while he was engrossed in meditation. 'Vyāsa' on the other hand simply means 'the arranger', 'compiler'. Much is credited to him: not only the *Mahābhārata* and works of philosophical import but also the division of the Vedas in their present form. In fact, neither the *Rāmāyaṇa* nor the *Mahābhārata* in their familiar historical forms are the work of a single hand. Both have long existed in at least two major recensions (northern and southern), with appreciable chunks of unrepeated material in each recension, and took shape by way of numerous interpolations and additions. Recent scholarship, which has produced 'critical editions'[39] of both epics, has agreed on more or less similar dates for each: *c.* 400 BCE–400 CE for the *Mahābhārata* and *c.* 400 BCE–300 CE for the *Rāmāyaṇa.*

We have seen how the *Dharma* Sūtras and Śāstras are formally concerned with describing *dharma.* It is important to note that the epics also focus on *dharma*, but informally; that is, not by stringing together lists of 'shoulds' and 'shouldn'ts' but chiefly through narrative and sometimes by didactic passages. The word *dharma* is ubiquitous in them, and their chief characters openly question its meaning in their eventful lives.

The epics started from a distinctive perspective. Whereas the Codes were doubtless originally composed by Brahmins, the epics stem from eulogies of *Kṣatriya* derring-do first propagated by non-Brahmin professional bards. Their principal characters, male and female, are generally of the Kṣatriya *varṇa*. Thus there is a Kṣatriya bias in the epics' treatment of *dharma.* This does not mean that they do not appeal to society at large. For though their *dharma* is not the somewhat artificial *dharma* of the Codes which is largely that of acquiring ritual purity, and to a lesser extent, of attaining *mokṣa* or ultimate liberation from the world, it is chiefly the *dharma* of living life to the full, of coping with love and hate, war and peace, wealth, ambition and power, in short, of what Hindus call 'gain' (*artha*) and 'desire' (*kāma*), and this is of course in one way or another of interest and relevance to all sections of society.[40] But the epics are not silent about the ethics of liberation. Hindus have always understood pretty well (in theory, at any rate) that there can be no ethical pursuit of particular objectives except against the horizon of *mokṣa*. Hence the epics have important things to say about the means to salvation. The *Bhagavadgītā*, traditionally a part of the *Mahābhārata*, is a case in point; the *Rāmāyaṇa*, as we shall see, waxes strong on saving devotion to Rāma. Rather, it is a question of *dharma*'s immediate focus.

Further, the epics have been Brahminised. At the hands of their Brahmin editors, which is how they have been ratified and popularised, their stories are allowed to unfold in a framework of generally Brahminic ideals. The Brahmin *varṇa* is acknowledged as the highest; the Kṣatriya heroes observe Brahminic rules of precedence and protect Brahminic interests. The stamp of Brahminic approval emerges interestingly in epic religion. On the one hand, traditional Vedic religion is still deferred to; on the other hand, an alternative religion (or religions?) of *bhakti* or devotion to God, of cult places, sacred fords, and even images on occasion, of portents and austerities, makes its appearance, generally in quite late strata of the composition. In both cases, irrespective of the non-Brahminic roots that may be discerned in some of these features, Brahminic authority sits astride the religious teaching.

Both epics are composed in verse, mainly the *śloka*, also called the *anuṣṭubh* metre, consisting of two lines of sixteen syllables each (or four quarter-verses of eight syllables each).[41] The *Mahābhārata* is by far the longer of the two. Traditionally, it is said to be 100,000 couplets long, although, oral narrative being what it is, this number has not been adhered to. Still, it is an enormous work.[42] The *Rāmāyaṇa* is only about a quarter of its length.[43] Let us consider the *Rāmāyaṇa* first.

In its traditional form, the *Rāmāyaṇa* consists of seven books (*kāṇḍas*), though scholars generally agree that most of the first and last books, as well as other parts in between, are later additions to the narrative. This does not mean, however, as we shall explain, that the gist of the opening and concluding books is extraneous to what intervenes in a religious sense. As its title implies (*Rāma +āyana*: 'The Coming of Rāma'), the *Rāmāyaṇa* tells the story of the coming of the Kṣatriya hero, Rāma, on to the world stage. To give an idea of its story-line and chief characters, we summarise as follows:

King Daśaratha, descendant of Ikṣvāku (the founder of the solar dynasty[44]), rules from Ayodhyā[45] in the Kingdom of Kosala; he is childless and advancing in age. To beget heirs he performs the *aśvamedha*[46] *and putreṣṭi* ('son-seeking') sacrifices. Meanwhile, the gods are meeting to discuss the depradations of the ogre king of Laṅkā, Rāvaṇa, who is oppressing both them and the earth. Rāvaṇa has obtained a boon that he cannot be killed by any but human hands, and there is no one on earth to despatch him. The gods petition Viṣṇu, who agrees to take birth as the offspring of Daśaratha by the king's three wives. (Thus the Vedic *yajña* is endorsed as the occasion of divine descent to earth.) Half of Viṣṇu descends as Rāma by queen Kausalyā; a quarter of Viṣṇu is born as Bharata from queen Kaikeyī, while the remaining quarter descends as the twins Lakṣmaṇa and Śatrughna from queen Sumitrā. The four brothers grow up amicably in Ayodhyā, Rāma outshining his siblings.

When Rāma is 15 years old the sage Viśvāmitra comes from his forest hermitage to Ayodhyā; he wants Rāma to get rid of some ogres who are obstructing his sacrifices. Daśaratha agrees and Rāma, accompanied by Lakṣmaṇa, sets off for the hermitage. Attested by a sage, he has begun his 'public' career as the upholder of Vedic *dharma.* But we shall see that there is more to it than that. Rāma does what is required of him and on the way back home accompanies Viśvāmitra to the court of king Janaka of Mithilā (capital of Videha).[47] Janaka has two treasures in particular (or three if you include Yājñavalkya): the god Śiva's great bow which no one can string, and his daughter, Sītā (who in fact was not born in the usual way but was found by Janaka as a baby in a furrow). Rāma breaks the bow and is given Sītā in marriage. The ceremony (which also includes the weddings of Rāma's three younger brothers to Sītā's sister and cousins in the presence of Daśaratha) is a grand affair. Eventually, all return to Ayodhyā.

Daśaratha wants to make Rāma his successor, but queen Kaikeyī, Bharata's mother, egged on by her maid Mantharā, has other plans. She invokes two boons granted her earlier by the king; with one she wants Bharata and not Rāma to be made king, with the other Rāma is to be exiled to the Daṇḍaka forest for fourteen years. Daśaratha is distraught, but as a king he must abide by his word. In the name of *dharma*, Rāma calmly agrees to honour his father's promise; equally in the name of *dharma*, Lakṣmaṇa argues spiritedly that it should not be obeyed. But Rāma is unmoved and resolves to enter banishment alone. There are famous passages in which Sītā in particular argues that she cannot but follow her lord, and she and Lakṣmaṇa prevail upon Rāma to allow them to accompany him to the forest. After they leave, much to the regret of the citizens of Ayodhyā, Daśaratha dies of a broken heart.

Bharata, who has been away, is aghast when he hears what has happened. He has no intention of usurping the throne and hastens to Rāma's bivouac to implore him to become king. The *dharma* of the situation is discussed once more. Rāma's determination to carry out his exile remains unbroken. For his part, Bharata resolves to rule the kingdom as Rāma's representative, and carries back his brother's sandals as the symbol and proxy of his authority. Rāma's obedience and unswerving fidelity to his word, Sītā's plea to accompany him in exile, Lakṣmaṇa's loving devotion to Rāma, the incident of the sandals, are among the most favourite instances of noble behaviour in Hindu tradition. But we will move on with the story. Rāvaṇa is waiting in the wings.

For ten years, Rāma and his companions had lived relatively peacefully in the forest, Rāma acting as protector of its sages from the various ogres roaming about. But trouble really starts when the ogress Śūrpaṇakhā, Rāvaṇa's sister, espies Rāma and tries unsuccessfully to seduce him. She fails similarly with Lakṣmaṇa. So she threatens Sītā, and Rāma instructs his brother to cut off Śūrpaṇakhā's nose and ears in punishment. The humiliated and enraged ogress seeks revenge, in due course getting Rāvaṇa to agree to abduct Sītā and leave the hapless Rāma to face this grievous loss. In order to accomplish this end, Rāvaṇa persuades an ogre, Mārīca, to lure Rāma away from Sītā in the guise of a beautiful deer. At Sītā's behest, Rāma hunts the deer and pierces Mārīca with an arrow who with his last gasp imitates Rāma's voice. Lakṣmaṇa sets out to investigate, leaving Sītā alone to be carried off by Rāvaṇa.

Rāvaṇa imprisons Sītā in his island stronghold of Laṅkā.[48] There she is given a year to decide whether to submit to Rāvaṇa or die. Rāma discovers what has happened and makes an alliance with Sugrīva, the banished brother of the monkey king Vālin. Rāma controversially assists Sugrīva to kill Vālin and in return Sugrīva, now king in Vālin's place, sends search parties to find Sītā.

Hanumān, a monkey noted more perhaps for his physical prowess than his intellect (in the epic at any rate, and who had earlier acted as

Sugrīva's contact with Rāma and Lakṣmaṇa), leads the group which learns where Sītā is being held. Hanumān agrees to cross over to Laṅkā and investigate. He reaches Laṅkā in marvellous fashion (by becoming immense and leaping over the sea!), finds Sītā and reassures her, and after various adventures (which includes torching Laṅkā with his flaming tail which Rāvaṇa had set on fire as a punishment – another much-loved episode) returns to the mainland. Sītā, who has remained faithful to Rāma, has informed Hanumān that there are only two months left before Rāvaṇa is due to carry out his threat.

Apprised of Sītā's whereabouts, Rāma, Lakṣmaṇa and their allies come to land's end before Laṅkā. Here, Vibhīṣaṇa, Rāvaṇa's brother, joins them as the side upholding *dharma*. They cross over to Laṅkā (the monkeys throw boulders into the sea to make this possible), and in due course a terrific battle is fought with Rāvaṇa and his forces. Here great deeds are done, in the course of which Rāma and Lakṣmaṇa are felled. Hanumān is despatched to a mountain to procure a rare healing herb, which he cannot find. So he returns with the whole mountain, thus enabling our two combatants to be revived.[49] Eventually, Rāma kills Rāvaṇa, installs Vibhīṣaṇa as king of Laṅkā, and rescues Sītā. The conditions are now set for Rāmarājya, or the dharmic rule of Rāma, to begin. Sītā proves by a fire ordeal that she has remained faithful to Rāma, and they return to Ayodhyā where Rāma, gladly restored to his kingdom by Bharata, is made king amid great rejoicing. But rumours spread casting doubt on Sītā's fidelity in Laṅkā. Rāma, the symbol of *dharma*, who cannot allow the reputation of his reign to be tarnished, is forced to send his pregnant wife into exile. She is given protection by Vālmīki (the author of the *Rāmāyaṇa*) and gives birth to two sons in his hermitage. Eventually, Rāma seeks to reinstate Sītā who again protests her innocence by calling upon the earth to swallow her. The earth takes back its own (remember Sītā was born from a furrow) and Sītā is finally lost to Rāma. The glorious rule of Rāma (*rāmarājya*) continues not without a further personal tragedy for Rāma through his devotion to *dharma*: Rāma is forced to banish his beloved brother, Lakṣmaṇa. Eventually Rāma leaves his sons in charge of the kingdom and returns to heaven to resume his identity as Viṣṇu.[50]

Here, in summary, are the colourful and exuberant episodes of a great story beloved of Hindus across sectarian boundaries for generations and generations. A tale of heroes and villains – including animals and ogres – of war and passion, devotion and duty, wondrous feats and fell deeds. And at the centre of it all is undoubtedly the figure of Rāma, the very model of *dharma* in its different aspects: dutiful king (even at the cost of personal tragedy), protector of the vulnerable, avenger of the wronged, obedient son, faithful husband, loving brother, magnanimous enemy. His compassion and friendship extend to the disadvantaged, to animals and even to conciliatory ogres. Thus, at the beginning of his exile, he accepts the assistance of and embraces Guha, the low-caste chief of the Niṣādas; in the forest he is gracious to Śabarī, the low-caste woman ascetic; he befriends the monkeys in his journey southwards towards Laṅkā; and he welcomes the ogre Vibhīṣaṇa who acknowledges his righteous cause.

So Rāma is the model of *dharma* – a *dharma* that cannot but be regarded as orthodox, i.e. as justified by the Vedas. For both in the story and, with the passage of time outside it, has not his brand of *dharma* been approved by the Brahmins, the official agents of the Vedas? Does he not endorse Veda-based sacrifice by protecting the sages who practise it? Has he not married according to caste requirements and ratified the traditional status of the husband? Is he not respectful of Brahmins and does he not enact his Kṣatriya *dharma* by championing a righteous cause, etc.?

The answser is yes, to all these questions. But Rāma also expands, almost subverts on occasion, the traditional orthodox understanding of *dharma*. For he fraternises with those on the margins of Aryan society: the low castes, 'talking animals' and 'friendly ogres' (tribes outside the Aryan pale?). But the crowning 'subversion' of all is that in his person he so takes over the religious concern of the epic as to become the focus for the numerous *bhakti* religions or religions of saving devotion which subsequently spring up in his name. In other words, in the *Rāmāyaṇa* the seeds are sown for a devotional faith which in effect acts as an alternative to traditional, *yajña*-based Vedic religion.

This is where the last strata of the *Rāmāyaṇa*, which include the first and the last chapters, become relevant. Scholars affirm that Books 2–5 emphasise a human Rāma and that it is only in later strata of the epic's composition that Rāma's divine origin and status are clearly attested. However, in a religious sense this is not to the point, for Hindus have traditionally regarded the epic as a unitary text and seen the references to Rāma as an embodiment of the supreme Being (in those portions of the text designated by scholars as additions) as theological *clarifications* of Rāma's divine status in the epic as a whole. When the god Brahmā addresses Rāma (in 6.105.13–28) as 'the imperishable *Brahman*, the Truth . . . beyond the (created) worlds . . . the supreme Person (*puruṣottamaḥ*) . . . Protector and refuge . . . the essence of the Vedas (*vedātmā*) . . . the one whose origin and end no one knows', as the one who appears in all beings, in Brahmins and in cows, as the one whose body the whole world is (*jagatsarvaṃ śarīraṃ te*), as the God whose devotees will never see defeat, then he but voices the sentiments of later generations of Hindus who follow the story with religious fervour. This is the Vālmīki-*Rāmāyaṇa* of Hindu devotion, the original setting of the Rāma that we must come to terms with. I have further comments to make on the Rāma story, but these can wait until after we have considered the other great Hindu epic, the *Mahābhārata.*

The *Mahābhārata* and the *Rāmāyaṇa* have two separate story-lines, there being no intrinsic connection between them.[51] About three times the length of its counterpart, the *Mahābhārata* is an even more exuberant example of the story-teller's art – it is divided into no less than eighteen books or *parvans* – and we shall have to exercise a corresponding ruthlessness in our summary of its main events and characters.[52]

The *Mahābhārata* is the great (*mahā*) tale of the *Bhāratas*, a clan, this time of the lunar dynasty, which derived its name from Bharata (no relation to the Bharata of the other epic), a descendant of Pūru whose line is traced to Yayāti, descendant of Purūravas, descendant of Soma, the moon god. The story is as follows.

Śaṃtanu, a scion of Bharata, is king of the ancestral realm of Kurukṣetra, which is situated between the Ganges and Yamuna rivers in north India not far from the foothills of the Himalayas, and where he rules from his capital, Hāstinapura. One of his sons, Bhīṣma, his first-born, cannot succeed him. He gave up his right to the throne (and took a vow of celibacy – hence 'Bhīṣma': 'Awesome') in favour of the male heirs of a late marriage of his father to Satyavatī, daughter of the chief of a fisher tribe. It was only on this condition that Saytavatī's father agreed to the marriage. Śaṃtanu has two sons by Satyavatī: Citrāṅgada, who dies unmarried and childless, and Vicitravīrya, who marries two sisters, Ambikā and Ambālikā. Vicitravīrya also dies childless and leaves Queen Satyavatī, who lost her husband before Vicitravīrya came of age, with something of a problem regarding succession to the throne. But before marrying Śaṃtanu she has had a liaison with the Sage Parāśara, which resulted in the birth of Dvaipāyana or Vyāsa (the original reciter of the epic who lives the life of a hermit). Since Bhīṣma is bound by his vow of celibacy, Satyavatī calls upon her son Dvaipāyana to father heirs to the throne by Ambikā and Ambālikā in the name of Vicitravīrya, their dead husband, according to the current law of levirate. Dvaipāyana agrees, since it is of vital importance for the kingdom to have heirs. By Ambikā he begets Dhṛtarāṣṭra who is born blind, since Ambikā shut her eyes during intercourse because of Dvaipāyana's grim appearance. By Ambālikā he begets Pāṇḍu who is born pale (*pāṇḍu*), because *his* mother blanched at the sight of Dvaipāyana. For good measure the hermit fathers a third male child, Vidura, by a maidservant of the palace, and then goes his way.

Dhṛtarāṣṭra, though the first-born, cannot become king because he is blind. He marries Gāndhārī and, in wondrous fashion, they have a hundred sons and one daughter. The eldest son is called Duryodhana who grows up to become power-hungry and arrogant in the extreme. As can be imagined, he plays a big part in the story.

Pāṇḍu, who becomes king, has two wives, Kuntī and Mādrī. But he dare not father any children by them because a sage has cursed him to die in the act of intercourse. So, renouncing his throne to Dhṛtarāṣṭra, he goes off with his wives to live in the forest. Kuntī, however, had earlier received a boon of invoking any celestial or god to do her bidding. Pāṇḍu is informed of this and, faced with the prospect of dying childless and his royal line becoming extinct, he instructs her to implement her boon and beget sons for him according to the law of levirate. So Kuntī invokes the celestials Dharma, Vāyu and Indra and they father three sons in Pāṇḍu's name: Yudhiṣṭhira, Bhīma and Arjuna respectively. Mādrī, Kuntī's co-wife, is loath to deny Pāṇḍu progeny through her; so she gets Kuntī to implement her boon once more on her behalf. Mādrī chooses the Aśvins, a celestial pair, and they beget the twins Nakula and Sahadeva by her. Thus Pāṇḍu has five heirs known as the Pāṇḍavas, and they become the potential rivals, for the throne of Kurukṣetra, of the sons of Dhṛtarāṣṭra who are known as the Kauravas.[53] But Pāṇḍu succumbs to the curse (the hapless Mādrī, who is the occasion for this, willingly commits suttee on his funeral pyre), and Kuntī and the five boys return to Hāstinapura where they are brought up with Dhṛtarāṣṭra's sons.

The story pivots now on the struggle for succession between the Kauravas and the Pāṇḍavas. We are told how Dhṛtarāṣṭra, the blind ruler, while acknowledging that the Pāṇḍavas have a claim to the throne, is blind to the *dharma* of the situation by his infatuation for his son, Duryodhana. Duryodhana plots to win the throne (to do this he tries to have the Pāṇḍavas killed, most notably by scheming to have them burnt to death in a house built of lacquer in a distant town, but they escape with Vidura's help). The Pāṇḍavas then form an alliance with two bordering peoples, the Vṛṣṇis (of whom Kṛṣṇa Vāsudeva, the embodied deity of the *Gītā*, is a chief) and the Pāñcālas. Arjuna wins Draupadī, daughter of the Pāñcāla king, for his wife and by a remarkable occurrence she becomes the joint wife of the Pāṇḍavas. The kingdom of Kurukṣetra is divided between the Kauravas and the Pāṇḍavas, the latter being given the wild tract of the Khāṇḍava forest, where they rule from their capital, Indraprastha. When he visits Indraprastha, Duryodhana is humiliated in the Pāṇḍavas' palace and challenges Yudhiṣṭhira to a game of dice in his own capital. The fateful game of dice is played (for Yudhiṣṭhira, model of *dharma* though he may be, has a fatal flaw in his character: he is addicted to gambling). With the help of his uncle, Śakuni, who cheats, Duryodhana wins from Yudhiṣṭhira all his wealth, his four brothers, Yudhiṣṭhira himself and finally Draupadī, their joint wife; subsequently, the Pāṇḍavas and Draupadī are humiliated in the Kaurava assembly hall.[54] The dicing match is nullified by Dhṛtarāṣṭra, the king, but with one final throw Duryodhana succeeds in having the Pāṇḍavas banished for thirteen years. The Pāṇḍavas live out those years, eventually having their claim to the realm rebuffed. Deciding that there is no other solution, they prepare for war (at this point Kṛṣṇa offers the two parties a choice: one side can have his troops, the other side can employ him in the role of non-combatant adviser. Duryodhana chooses the warriors, Arjuna chooses Kṛṣṇa).

We are then told how both sides, eighteen armies in all, meet on the battlefield of Kurukṣetra and how Kṛṣṇa, as Arjuna's charioteer, uses this opportunity to explain the *dharma* of spiritual combat to his friend in the form of the *Bhagavadgītā*, revealing in the process that he is God in human form. The great battle is fought for eighteen days, a terrible, remorseless, devious, incident-laden conflict in which most of the heroes of both sides are slain. Bhīma, whose larger-than-life character bears a distinct resemblance to that of Hanumān, rips open Duḥśāsana's breast and drinks his warm blood to avenge Draupadī's humiliation in the Kaurava assembly hall. During the course of the battle, the 'wise Bhīṣma, dying on a bed of arrows, interminably expounds on the varieties of *dharma* in what must be the longest deathbed sermon on record'.[55] On the last day Duryodhana himself is felled by Bhīma in violation of the Kṣatriya code and dies the following day, leaving only Kṛṣṇa and the Pāṇḍavas to survive the battle. The Pāṇḍavas are then reconciled with Dhṛtarāṣṭra, and Yudhiṣṭhira asserts his supremacy by performing the horse-sacrifice. Some years later Dhṛtarāṣṭra, Gāndhārī his wife, and Kuntī (mother of the three eldest Pāṇḍavas) repair to the forest to live a hermit's life, and die subsequently in a fire. Years later, Kṛṣṇa destroys the men of his tribe after they indulge in a drunken brawl in which his own son is killed. Subsequently, Kṛṣṇa, while meditating, is slain mistakenly by a hunter and, on hearing of Kṛṣṇa's death, the Pāṇḍavas and Draupadī resolve to leave the world, and eventually attain heaven.[56]

This is but the skeletal outline of a tale that can itself be likened to a great and luxuriant *aśvattha (ficus religiosa)*, the holy fig tree of the Hindus. It is a story containing many myths about well-known figures and events barely, if at all, connected to the main story-line or characters. Yet there does seem to have been a historical seed to this tree. It is believed that a great internecine war did take place in north India in about 800–700 BCE; a number of individuals who then became some of the main characters of the epic may well have taken part. These would have included Kṛṣṇa, who becomes *the avatāra* of the *Mahābhārata*. Two of the choicest fruits of this great epic tree are the *Bhagavadgītā* and the *Harivaṃśa*.

The *Bhagavadgītā* (lit. 'Song of the Lord'), or abbreviated to Gītā, is in the form of a dialogue (the standard text has 700 stanzas) between Kṛṣṇa and his close friend, Arjuna.[57] Kṛṣṇa, who had earlier promised to be a non-combatant in the fighting, acts as Arjuna's charioteer. As the battle is about to start, Arjuna, a great warrior, recoils from the prospect of fighting not only his kith and kin, but a number of revered elders. Kṛṣṇa uses this pretext to explain to him the true *dharma* of life's spiritual combat. In the process he reveals himself to be the supreme Godhead, and explains how he is the origin, mainstay and goal of all created being and how his devotees attain to ultimate salvation in loving communion with him. For the first time in Hindu religious teaching, the *Gītā* mentions a doctrine of the *avatāra*, namely of periodic descent by the deity in embodied form for the welfare of the world. Kṛṣṇa declares:

> Being unborn, my Spirit is imperishable. As God of all being and established in my creation, I take birth by my spiritual power. For whenever *dharma* wanes, Arjuna, and *adharma* grows strong, then do I generate an embodied self. For the protection of the good and the destruction of evil-doers, and for the establishing of right I take birth age after age. (4.6–8)

The *Bhagavadgītā* is a seminal text for much of Vaiṣṇava devotional theology, at least where the Sanskrit tradition is concerned. Composed probably between 150 BCE and 250 CE, it has been regarded as a self-contained text by a long line of Hindu thinkers and spirtual gurus, many of whom have produced virtually word-for-word commentaries or shorter reflections on its meaning. In itself, the *Gītā* is a revealing comment on the relationship between *smṛti* and *śruti*. It is not part of the canonical Veda; as such it cannot be regarded strictly as *śruti*. Yet in its own context, in Sanskrit or in translation, it has functioned as 'the word of God' for a great many Hindus down the centuries and across sectarian divides with the same meaning that this phrase has evoked scripturally for Christians in their traditions. Its open-endedness, an authentic mark of religious depth, has generated commentaries ranging from the monistic to the starkly dualistic. It retains its religious importance today, and continues to be interpreted by both scholars and teachers according to their own purposes. Susceptible to various interpretations it may be, yet there are limits to interpretive open-endedness. There seems to be no doubt that the *Gītā* is a genuinely devotional text, telling of the soul's immortality and of a caring God's saving and reassuring love for each individual, so that monistic interpretations appear strained.[58] The *Gītā* continues to give comfort in crisis situations. I have attended Hindu funerals in Britain at which a reading of passages from the *Gītā*, usually accompanied by a translation into English or the relevant Indian vernacular, plays a central part in the proceedings.

Is the *Gītā* an interpolation in the *Mahābhārata*, as some scholars maintain? For Hindu devotionalism, this is not a relevant question. The *Gītā* has come down to us as part of the great epic; that is its traditional matrix. And if scholars point to a difference between the Kṛṣṇa of the *Gītā* and the Kṛṣṇa of other parts of the epic, the one being clearly a sober manifestation of the Godhead, the other a transparently human, somewhat erratic figure, the mind of devotion remains unfazed. Hindus are quite used to the idea of the *deus absconditus*, the hidden God, whose divinity lies obscured by the distorting veils of mundane existence only to burst forth on occasion in all its splendour and power. So it is with the Rāma of the *Rāmāyaṇa* and with the Kṛṣṇa of the *Mahābhārata*.

The *Harivaṃśa* (i.e. '[About] the Family of Hari=Kṛṣṇa') has passed into tradition as a supplement of the *Mahābhārata*. A comparatively late work (produced towards the end of the time-span allotted the epic), it is specially well-known for giving details about Kṛṣṇa's birth and youthful exploits near the northern city of Mathurā, and his later sojourn to the city of Dvārakā in the west. We are told how he was born, and, with his brother Balarāma, escaped the clutches of his wicked cousin, King Kaṃsa, who wanted to kill him. (Kaṃsa had been told by a sage that he would die at the hands of Kṛṣṇa's parents' eighth child, which Kṛṣṇa was.) Lots of adventures follow of the young Kṛṣṇa (and Balarāma), while they were being brought up by their foster parents, Nanda and Yaśodā, in a community of cowherds on the banks of the Yamunā river. These include favourite tales of the killing and subjugating of anti-gods, ogres, etc.[59] Kaṃsa is duly killed as foretold, and eventually Kṛṣṇa establishes the city of Dvārakā on the mid-western coast, where he enjoys the company of his numerous wives. We are told how he comes by them and some of the activities of his sons. Clearly the main purpose of the *Harivaṃśa* is to offer fuller information than was generally available about the life of Kṛṣṇa, whose cult seems to have been flourishing by the time of its composition.

Unlike the great epics of the West, e.g. the Illiad and the Odyssey, the *Rāmāyaṇa* and the *Mahābhārata* are not a relic of the past, of interest only to classicists and literati. The chief episodes and characters of the *Rāmāyaṇa* and the *Mahābhārata* are part of the very sap of the Ancient Banyan, coursing through the system, nourishing its growth and manifesting variously at different levels and centres. Thus Vālmīki's story of Rāma has been adapted to suit different philosophical and devotional tastes. Though there is little if any hard evidence to show that Rāma cults based on Vālmīki's Rāma existed earlier than about a millennium after the redaction of the epic, this does not mean that such cults had not been around in some form or other. Further, devotion to Rāma as a divine figure certainly existed during this early period. The devotional content of the 'later strata' of the *Rāmāyaṇa* itself bears this out, and other forms of evidence exist.[60] The first sign of a Rāma *cult* that we have seems to be a community of devotees who are thought to have produced the Sanskrit *Adhyātma Rāmāyaṇa* – an adaptation of the Rāma story – in North India in about the fifteenth century. This group has been regarded as the precursor of the important present-day Rāmānandin sect for which the *Adhyātma Rāmāyaṇa* is a central scripture. The Rāma of the *Adhyātma* is more a manifestation of the Godhead itself than only one of a number of divine *avatāras*. He combines in himself the roles of the supreme *Brahman* of the Vedānta (the *Adhyātma* acknowledges the authority of the Veda and claims to speak in harmony with it) and the personal focus of saving grace. This is not spelled out systematically, but then the *Adhyātma* makes no claims to being a systematic treatise. In Vālmīki's *Rāmāyaṇa*,

> Rāma's dharma had applied in principle to all; here [in the *Adhyātma*] Rāma's grace applies in principle to all. There, those living directly under Rāmarājya [or Rāma's rule] (the citizens of Ayodhyā) had held an immediate advantage; here, the devotees of Rāma have an immediate advantage.[61]

A trend is at work here: that of making Rāma the supreme source and focus of saving grace.

In fact, devotion in Rāma's name followed two courses in the India of the second millennium CE. These two courses do not exist in isolation from each other; in their historical meanderings they have often intersected in style of approach and content, and at most represent two basic kinds of attitudes. In one, the Name became a central or acknowledged symbol for the very essence of deity, for a personal, loving, accessible God who lives in the hearts of all. Here there is little or no theology of Rāma as an *avatāra*, or recourse to iconic worship of Rāma. The Rāma of this devotional path is not rooted in Vālmīki's story. By and large this was the way of the Sants. So it was that Mahātma Gandhi could gasp, '*Hay Rām!*' ('Oh God!') as the assassin's bullets pierced his body.

In the other course, the Rāma story was adapted in some way, and Rāma and/or some other member of his Vaiṣṇava circle (e.g. Hanumān, Lakṣmaṇa) was viewed as the focus of salvation. An iconic cult could be associated with this devotion. As noted, the devotion of the *Adhyātma Rāmāyaṇa* falls into this category. But the *Adhyātma* is in Sanskrit, and as such could have only limited direct religious influence. For a far wider impact a suitable text in the vernacular was required; north India received this in the form of Tulsīdās' immensely popular *Rāmcaritmānas (Rām-carit-mānas)*.[62]

Tulsīdās' origins, as in the case of many other traditional Hindu figures, are shrouded in legend. He was born of Brahmin stock probably in the first half of the sixteenth century in a part of north India in which eastern Hindi was spoken. He seems to have lost his parents while still very young, and grew up in poverty. He had a guru who inculcated devotion in him to a Rāma based on Vālmīki's story. The *Rāmcaritmānas* was begun in Ayodhyā (Rāma's birthplace) perhaps in 1574 and completed in Benares some years later. Tulsī became famous for this composition; he wrote at least ten other works, and died in Benares, probably in the early 1620s.

Though the basic story-line is on the whole the same, there are significant differences of content between Tulsī's *Rāmcaritmānas* and Vālmīki's *Rāmāyaṇa*. It is not necessary to go into these here.

Suffice it to say that Tulsī's great work is clearly intended to weave together different influences and sources. These include the *Adhyātma Rāmāyaṇa* (from which Tulsī seems to have taken the idea that the Sītā abducted by Rāvaṇa was not the real Sītā but an illusory substitute), devotion to Śiva, an approach similar to the devotion to Kṛṣṇa's childhood exploits (paralleled by Tulsī's treatment of Rāma's childhood), Sant-like devotion to Rāma's Name as salvific in its own right, and so on. But in his insistence that everything, including devotion to Śiva and other religious figures, e.g. Sītā and Lakṣmaṇa, must converge in single-minded devotion to Rāma, Tulsī makes no compromise.

The *Rāmcaritmānas* consists of about 10,000 lines composed in an eastern Hindi dialect called Avadhī.[63] That it is not in Sanskrit but in straightforward vernacular verse is significant. It could thus have a mass appeal; it could easily be memorised and quoted. It could, in short, fire and shape a devotion that could exist independently, that is, that no longer required a knowledge of Sanskrit sources or the ministrations of their official intermediaries to be viable. This is exactly what happened. The *Rāmcaritmānas* is not a text overtly subversive of traditional orthodoxy. In fact it formally acknowledges the props of this orthodoxy: the sacrosanct status of the Vedas, the authority of the Brahmins and their *varṇa*-superiority, in short, the framework of *varṇāśrama dharma*. Yet, by its message in the vernacular that devotion to Rāma conquers all, it has nurtured the 'subversive' seed of Vālmīki's text against the traditional order. In working within the framework of orthodoxy, it succeeded in bursting through this framework and before long was itself embraced as orthodox by the sentinels of Hindu orthodoxy, the Brahmins. It helped to extend the boundaries and understanding of orthodoxy in religious Hinduism.

Today it is quite acceptable, at least within the pluralistic *bhakti* tradition, to base one's religious orientation on the *Rāmcaritmānas*, so much so that for many Hindus today this work has become the chief mould and platform of their religious way of life. This is not done by an explicit repudiation of the Vedas and their traditional trappings. It is done rather in the manner discussed in Chapter 3: by implicitly or explicitly claiming that the *Rāmcaritmānas* distils traditional Vedic teaching and makes it relevant.

This is yet another example of the way *śruti* and a vernacular source (officially *smṛti*) can relate to each other: not by outright rejection or condemnation – though this *has* happened, of course, especially where surrogate scriptures of low castes are concerned –

but by semantic and/or teleological accommodation, encroachment, substitution, or revision. This may be called the 'appeasement' syndrome as regards *śruti*.

Hindu tradition in fact contains many *Rāmāyaṇa*s and *Mahābhārata*s. If each epic may be spoken of as having a *svarūpa* or intrinsic form (and this is not necessarily some 'critical edition'), then it is the nature of this *svarūpa* to manifest through a range of *bahurūpa*s or multiple forms embodied in particular vernaculars, linguistic styles and other adaptations.

We can exemplify this cultural pluriformity by the Bengali version of the *Rāmāyaṇa*, attributed to Krittivās (early fifteenth century), and of the *Mahābhārata*, ascribed to Kāśirām (early seventeeth century). As in the case of the *Rāmcaritmānas*, these are not attempts at faithful translations of Sanskrit sources – this is not the point of such renderings – but creative reconstructions of traditional themes and stories in a relevant context. Their aim is to make the ancient epics, accessible in their Sanskrit forms to only a few, live anew in a popular, vernacular garb. 'Their interest is ethical, not literary, and the world they reproduce is not the ancient India of Vālmīki and Vyāsa but the Bengal of their own day'.[64] These two adaptations were extremely popular in Bengali-speaking areas for generations, and being composed in the *payār* metre, the stock rhyming couplet of Bengali poetry, were easily committed to memory in whole or in part from an early age. Dineshchandra Sen, in his *The Bengali Rāmāyaṇas*, reveals that 'at 7 years of age I had committed almost the whole of Krittivās' *Rāmāyaṇa* to memory without any conscious effort'.[65]

This custom of memorising these sacred texts has persisted in Bengal to modern times, with parallels throughout Hindu India. The well-known scholar Tarapada Mukherjee (1928–1990), who grew up in rural Bengal before the partition of Independence, writes:

> What I say . . . is based on my personal experience. I was born and brought up (until I was 16) in a village which is now in Bangladesh. What I say is . . . true in respect of that part of the country during that period.
>
> Bengali children learn the stories of the epics from their mothers or grandmothers or aunts before they can read or write. When they are in their teens they begin to recite or chant the metrical adaptations of the Ramayana by Krittivasa and the Mahabharata by Kasiramdas. Before becoming an adult the child recites the two texts several times either for his own pleasure or for the benefit of

> his elders for whom it is a pious act to listen to these scriptures. For months I have recited the Mahabharata to a group of old women, some of whom could not read the texts themselves . . . .
>
> Girls of 11 or 12 must know the stories of the two sacred books. They must demonstrate their knowledge of the Ramayana and the Mahabharata before they are accepted as brides in a respectable family.[66]

Smṛti means 'Remembrance', the heritage of the past being creatively relived, renewed, memorised and passed on. Mukherjee speaks of this custom being prevalent among 'respectable' families, that is, the upper castes; it was not current among labourers and artisans. Today, no doubt, it is in rapid decline. But for the lower, as well as for the upper castes, other ways had been established for imbibing the popular myths and stories and for becoming familiar with the various didactic characters of religious Hinduism. Some of these ways have currency even today, and new ones are continually being devised. We now turn to these other ways, old and new.

An immemorial, popular, and still current custom for transmitting religious folklore among the community at large has been the public reciting and/or enacting of sacred texts. The recitation, which is called *pāṭha*, may or may not be in Sanskrit; if it is it is usually accompanied by a gloss in the appropriate vernacular. *Pāṭha* can go on for short periods or for days; in the latter event, there may be a chain of *pāṭhaka*s (readers/reciters). The venue may be a temple courtyard in a city or village, or in any open space, including the courtyard or house of a patron, a public hall, theatre, etc., and *pāṭha* may even be broadcast on radio or television.[67]

Enacting the sacred texts is also widespread. There are variations here also, e.g. impromptu performances on street corners; advertised performances in theatres; village performances, sometimes under the aegis of a patron, often by wandering minstrels and acting troupes; television serials (and their video spin-offs). The material selected for recitation and enactment is selective of course, for the range is immense, but not entirely arbitrary. It is usually drawn from popular folklore, often from epics, including the *Rāmāyaṇa* and the *Mahābhārata*, and the Purāṇas (see Chapter 6), or from local well-known tales.

The performers tend to be 'professionals' in one of two senses. They usually either belong to a particular caste which has traditionally dedicated itself or some of its members to this form of livelihood, or they are members of a professional troupe in the modern, western sense. In the first instance, the style of presentation is traditional, innovation being permitted only minimally and within an established framework. Such professionals tend to be active only in rural areas, although occasionally they may be hired for work in towns and cities. We will consider an example of such traditional presentation shortly. As to the other group, the more modern professionals, street and workshop theatre seems to be on the increase, particularly in metropolitan areas. In this kind of enactment, the style is not predetermined; characters and themes of traditional religion may be presented in a 'creative' way or used to project a topical message. No matter. One way or another, by traditional or modern methods, religious Hindus are able to grow in a knowledge of their ancestral faith by these processes of acculturation.

Let us examine some examples of such enactment in order to appreciate more clearly how *smṛti* functions. First, we will consider the Rāmlīlā of northern India. This is a celebration of the Rāma story during the great autumnal festival of Daśahrā. Episodes of the story are enacted for up to a week or so accompanied by a recitation based on Tulsīdās' *Rāmcaritmānas*. The Rāmlīlā is supposed to have been started by a disciple of Tulsī in about 1625, though there is evidence to indicate that the practice of acting out incidents from the lives of various divine descents was already current in some parts. The performers tend not to be professionals; those who act the roles of Rāma, his brothers and Sītā are usually Brahmin youths, chosen for the purity symbolised by their caste. The Rāmlīlā, which is performed on a more or less grand scale by hundreds of communities mainly across north India, is extremely popular and is attended by all. Being part of the occasion, even as a member of the audience, is regarded as a pious act; in the process the Rāma story and devotion to Rāma gain currency.

Yet these celebrations are not lacking in enjoyment. They have strong entertainment value, and often contain impromptu humour and slapstick. There is nothing here of the great solemnity, say, of Christian parallels. I have witnessed well-known Bengali reconstructions of the Rāma story which are nothing short of hilarious send-ups, not of deity, but of the prevailing social élite. Yet the familiar sacred characters – not excluding Rāma – become the vehicle of this intention. In fact, such reconstructions work only because of the contrasts or exaggerations they depict with regard to the original setting. All this helps to explain why the term *līlā*, which has connotations of 'sportiveness' and 'joyful celebration', is often associated with such enactment (hence Rām*līlā*). Hindus are rarely cowed or overawed – at least for long – by the lives of their saints, *devas* or deities. Because such lives are usually full of marvels and wondrous characters and tend not to end in tragedy, their enactment is a delight, an occasion for easy familiarity and for vicarious participation. The enactment is also a communal act; one way, if you like, of seeing the Hindu community at prayer.

This means that, *līlā* notwithstanding, such enactments are not without serious purpose. Their Bengali description, namely *jātrā*, brings this out. At the time of great festivals (e.g. the Durgā Pūjā, Bengal's equivalent of Daśahrā) *jātrās* have been, and to some extent still are, popular in Bengal. *Jātrā* can also mean a purposeful journey of some kind, or a pilgrimage, and this is what these plays are. Their characters may be larger than life, they may consciously seek to entertain, but a serious purpose underlies them. They sacralise space and time, drawing the audience into the religious event they celebrate; they instruct and inform, renew and perpetuate a cultural identity, and bestow the spiritual fruit of participation (not least in the form of merit or good karma).

The more modern methods of enacting the sacred themes are portrayed in the recent television serials in India of the *Rāmāyaṇa* and the *Mahābhārata*. These have had protracted runs: 93 weekly instalments for the *Mahābhārata* and 78 for the *Rāmāyaṇa*. Both productions leave much to be desired: acting, dialogue and technique are poor; liberties have been taken with the ancient sources (which much of their audience is not to know, of course); subtleties have been blunted, especially with regard to the relationship between *dharma* and fate; and bowdlerised and textually ill-founded idealisations, many arguably socially retrograde, abound. Yet, though in Hindi, the main language of northern India, they have taken India by storm. It seems that the whole country, from the communal village television set to the urban skylines bristling with antennae, has been faithfully tuned to these productions, week after week, month after month. Whole sets of each have been given as nuptial presents: one hears that cabinet meetings, weddings and even railway schedules have been rearranged so as not to interfere with viewing hours. These broadcasts have set an important precedent – the mass dissemination of traditionally popular *smṛti* sources. Both serials have been acquired for public viewing by television companies around the world (thus in the early 1990s, the *Mahābhārata* was being shown weekly, with a repeat, on British television). For many, unless fresh interpretations and presentations of the epics are produced for television so that the self-correcting and creative techniques of oral transmission are perpetuated, these productions will become the definitive *Mahābhārata* and *Rāmāyaṇa*, supplanting the traditional sources if not substituting for the Scriptures altogether. They will become a religious norm, 'like scriptures on celluloid',[68] as the producer of the *Rāmāyaṇa* has commented. The consequences are yet to be assessed.

Let us consider now how what is, from the traditional Brahminic point of view, no more than *smṛti*, and a fairly localised instance at that, can yet function as a 'Veda' or scripture substitute, even though no reference may be made to the Vedas proper at all. This is the performance of the epic of Pābūjī.[69]

Pābūjī seems to have been a historical figure – the Rajpūt chief, in the early fourteenth century, of a village and its environs in what is now the state of Rajasthan. The epic that has grown around Pābūjī is a complex but stirring one. It tells of various battles he fought to safeguard his tiny realm or the honour of various members of his family (even to the extent of raiding Rāvaṇa, the ogre-king of Laṅkā, for she-camels!), of the complicated events of Pābūjī's prospective marriage, and of his eventual ascension into heaven in a palanquin. The story embraces feats performed by Pābūjī's companions (one at least of whom resembles Bhīma and Hanumān in nature) and a (posthumous) nephew; Deval, a form of the Goddess, also plays a prominent part. It is all very entertaining and rather long (its narration, with breaks, can run to twelve hours and starts invariably at nightfall). The epic is sung, at times chanted, in a Rajasthani dialect, by a professional male performer (*bhopo*) of the Nāyak caste, who usually accompanies himself on a simple fiddle. This instrument can be played with great skill. A companion, often the *bhopo's* wife, may also be in attendance. At times the singer performs dancing movements. The epic is enacted throughout Rajasthan by a number of these wandering reciters and is still popular.[70] Castes below that of the Brahmin follow the epic, including the upper-caste Rajpūts and Jāṭs, and most commonly the lower-caste, pastoral Rebārīs. The Nāyak caste of the *bhopo* is among the lowest in the hierarchy of Rajasthan, and is listed officially as a scheduled-caste.

Though not devoid of virtuosity and entertainment – good-natured banter between performer and audience is commonplace – in theory the performance is basically a religious event for those concerned. This revolves around the *paṛ*, a large painted cloth scroll of about 15 ft by 5 ft. The *paṛ* depicts scenes from the life of Pābūjī, who is generally regarded as divine by the audience, and acts as a backdrop to which the epic is sung. Indeed it acts as a mobile temple icon; its installation before each performance is accompanied by various rituals associated with temple worship such as cleaning the place of worship, burning incense and circling a flame (*ārati*) in front of Pābūjī's image by the *bhopo*, and the making of cash offerings. In other words, Pābūjī is believed to be present at least when the *paṛ* icon is activated during the performance, and the role of the *bhopo* is not simply that of epic singer but also of priest. This demonstrates yet again that Hinduism has different forms of priesthood depending on context, ranging from the traditional practices of Brahmins to the ministry of low castes and untouchables.

In fact, it seems that the cult of Pābūjī is beginning to be Sanskritised, e.g. by associating the epic of Pābūjī with the Rāma story, and Pābūjī himself, in images of the *paṛ*, with established deities of the 'great tradition', and by regarding Pābūjī and other characters as *avatāra*s of Sanskritic deities and personages, though Brahmin involvement is still minimal. Pābūjī seems to be worshipped for very worldly ends, e.g. sound health or its recovery, prosperity, a good marriage, a successful childbirth, and so on. Traditional Brahminic spirituality of *mokṣa* and mention of the Vedas is still virtually absent. Pābūjī may become 'Brahminically respectable' in time. At present his epic takes the place of *śruti* for his worshippers; it may well be their main if not only source of religious sustenance and orientation. There are of course other examples of such epics and their transmission.[71]

Finally, a further example of *smṛti* of the 'little' tradition is the *maṅgal* narratives of Bengal. This is a type of religious epic narrative in Bengali verse based on reworked folklore. *Maṅgal* narrative celebrates popular, local deities and/or their devotees, though not exclusively, and 'were generally composed . . . for semi-musical and semi-dramatic performance by professional singers called *gāyak* or *maṅgal gāyak*.'[72] There are *maṅgal*s in honour of the goddesses Manasā (who guards against snake-bite), Caṇḍī (who is identified with Durgā), Śītalā (who protects from smallpox), the god Dakṣiṇ Rāy (who protects from tigers), and so on. We shall comment on the theology underlying these deities in Chapter 12. For now we note that

> While the [*Maṅgal* myths] were – and still are – enjoyed by the common people, they were produced by (and to a certain extent for) those of the upper classes who could only accept these new deities once they and their myths had been reworked and brought into harmony with orthodoxy.
>
> (Smith 1976: 1)

Thus the *Maṅgal*s have been more or less consistently Sanskritised. It is generally impossible to identify source myths or stories, since in the way of the transmission of oral narrative, each *Maṅgal* has come down to us in more than one variant, though common elements of a story can be discerned. As an indication, we shall give an outline of some of the main elements of the *Manasā Maṅgal*, the 'oldest of the *maṅgal* poems . . . [which] assumed the form we now have it in by the end of the fifteenth century' (Smith 1976: 17).

Śiva's seed trickles to the underworld and gives birth to Manasā, who is made queen of the *nāga*s, serpentine beings and hence representatives of snakes, though Manasā herself is always depicted in human form. She introduces her cult to cowherds and fishermen. But to make her cult universal, Śiva tells her, she must win the worship of Cāndo, a spice merchant. Sonakā, Cāndo's wife, is won over, but not Cāndo. In fact most of the story tells of the running conflict between Cāndo and Manasā, she trying every device to make him worship her, he steadfastly refusing. Manasā, having destroyed Cāndo's fortunes, eventually kills Cāndo's six sons and threatens that she will kill Lakhāi, the seventh, on his wedding night. Lakhāi is to be married to the resourceful Behulā. Cāndo builds an iron chamber to protect the couple on their wedding night, but Manasā carries out her threat. One of her snakes more or less inadvertently kills Lakhāi. Next follows an account of how the faithful Behulā accompanies the corpse of her husband on a long journey to the dwelling of the gods to ask for the restoration of his life. After many adventures, she reaches her destination and pleases Śiva by her dancing. He grants her a boon which results in the summoning of Manasā and the restoration not only of Cāndo's fortunes but of all his sons to life. Cāndo acknowledges Manasā, and finally Manasā, Behulā and Lakhāi depart to the world of the gods. It is noteworthy that 'Brahmans play no role in the myth except as propagandist window dressing' (Smith 1976: 64); nevertheless, the *Manasā Maṅgal* is at a more advanced stage of Sanskritisation than the epic of Pābūjī, and consequently as *smṛti* it is more integrated with the great tradition. For many worshippers of Manasā she is a manifestation of Devī, the source Goddess.

We will conclude our discussion of *smṛti* and its bearing on primary scripture for Hindus in Chapter 6.

6 The voice of tradition: folklore and the intellectual heritage

(v) Smṛti *as Purāṇa. Meaning: classification, origins and contents. Interpreting the Purāṇas; some examples. Purāṇas as saving texts: a story. Puranic composition: variety and scope. (vi)* Smṛti *as 'prasthāna-vākya'; meaning. Prasthāna-vākya as exemplified in the six perspectives of Mīmāṃsā (Pūrva and Uttara), Nyāya, Vaiśeṣika, Sāṃkhya and Yoga. Actual plurality of Perspectives (*darśanas*) in Hindu tradition with corresponding plurality of prasthāna-vākyas. The context of the* puruṣārthas: artha, kāma, dharma *and* mokṣa*; the extended context.*

Purāṇa

The next category in our division of *smṛti* is Purāṇa, meaning something old or ancient; here the word refers to a textual, i.e. oral or written, repository of folklore. In fact, *purāṇa* refers primarily to members of a group of Sanskrit texts, traditionally eighteen in number, although as is often the case in Hinduism, the candidates contending for inclusion in the collection are more numerous than the figure sanctioned by tradition. There are also supposed to be eighteen Upa-Purāṇas or sub-Purāṇas – no doubt a way of accommodating the overflow – though the lists of the two collections can vary and it is not always clear on what grounds particular lists differ. There is a fluidity in such matters in Hindu tradition which is typical; preference of candidates for such lists are expressed according to circumstances and the dictates of the religious tradition in which one finds oneself.

Nevertheless, the drawing up of a Purāṇa list is not wholly arbitrary. Most of the names are fixed in most traditions. The following is a list of well-attested Purāṇas, well above eighteen in number (with putative dates CE for the bulk of the material in each Purāṇa given in parentheses): *Agni* (850), *Bhāgavata* (950), *Bhaviṣya* (500–1200), *Brahma* (900–1350), *Brahmāṇḍa* (350–950), *Brahmavaivarta* (750–1550), *Bṛhaddharma* (1250), *Bṛhannāradīya* (750–900), *Devī* (550–650), *Devībhāgavata* (850–1350), *Garuḍa* (900), *Harivaṃśa* (450), *Kālikā* (1350), *Kalki* (1500–1700), *Kūrma* (550–850), *Liṅga* (600–1000), *Mahābhāgavata* (1100), *Mārkaṇḍeya* (250), *Matsya* (250–500), *Narasiṃha* (400–500), *Padma* (750), *Sāmba* (500–800), *Saura* (950–1150), *Śiva* (750–1350), *Skanda* (700–1150), *Vāmana* (450–900), *Varāha* (750), *Vāyu* (350), and *Viṣṇu* (450).[1] Thus the traditional Purāṇas range from those compiled in about the third to fourth centuries CE (among which the *Mārkaṇḍeya, Matsya* and *Vāyu* seem to have the oldest material) to those redacted a few centuries ago (namely, the *Brahmavaivarta* and *Kalki*).

In fact, the Purāṇas are compilations of different kinds of material which has usually been several centuries in the making. The versions which have come down to us are not necessarily the original forms of this material, most of which had oral beginnings. The Purāṇas are almost entirely in verse, the standard metre being the same as that of the epics, the *śloka*. The term itself is ancient. The Saṃhitā of the Atharva Veda mentions *purāṇa* as part of a list of oral texts (11.7.24). There are references also in the classical Upaniṣads. For example (in *ChāndUp* VII.1.2), when recounting his learning, Nārada says that he is conversant with 'epic and Purāṇa' among other things. In *BĀUp* II.4.10, epic and Purāṇa are included with the four Vedas and the Upaniṣads in a list of different kinds of knowledge (see also IV.5.11). I think we can have a good idea of what *purāṇa* means in these references. First, it seems to signify a distinctive kind of composition (though we cannot be sure of its content); second, from the term's regular linkage with *itihāsa* (epic), we may conjecture that *itihāsa* and *purāṇa* refer to two genres of composition which were similar at least in form, i.e. both were records in verse. This linkage may well be grounds for assuming that like the epics, the Purāṇas originally reflected Kṣatriya interests, though probably, again like the epics, they were edited by Brahmins. Certainly the present Purāṇas contain material which may be regarded as Kṣatriya in concern, though there can be no doubt that Brahmins have had the last word in the compilation.[2]

As a genre of composition the Purāṇas were supposed to deal characteristically with five topics (called the *pañca-lakṣaṇa*s or five defining marks of Puranic subject matter). These are: the production of being (*sarga*), its dissolution and re-formation (*pratisarga*), genealogies of gods, sages, and other ancients (*vaṃśa*), the ages of the different human ancestors (*manvantaras*), and the history of the lunar and solar dynasties (*vaṃśānucarita*).[3] The problem is not so much that most of present Puranic material does not conform to the *pañcalakṣaṇa* criterion as that it contains so much else besides, although one reason for dating the *Brahmāṇḍa, Matsya, Vāyu* and *Viṣṇu* Purāṇas among the earliest is that their material can be seen to conform most to the *pañcalakṣaṇa* test.

The *Agni* Purāṇa stands out as being particularly comprehensive in its scope. There is hardly anything that it does not deal with: it treats of *avatāras* of Viṣṇu; summarises the *Rāmāyaṇa* and the *Mahābhārata*; recounts incidents from Kṛṣṇa's childhood; describes innumerable vows, rites, rituals and forms of worship directed at various deities including the Goddess; discusses various aspects of *dharma* and how merit is to be gained in various ways; lists different kinds of images and their chief characteristics (not excluding details about their pedestals) and describes their modes of installation and consecration; advises on how a city is to be established; comments on the sanctity of certain cities and rivers (e.g. Benares and the Ganges), on the topography of India, indeed on the topography of the world; instructs on how to cast spells (e.g. to encompass an enemy's death), how to atone for wrongs done, the various forms of marriage; describes the characteristics of different types of women, gems, diseases, snakes; of the art of warfare on horseback, healing (including the cure for dysentery in infants, and of diseases to which horses and elephants are prone), dancing, rhetoric, diplomacy, divining dreams, and so on; it *also* treats of *pañcalakṣaṇa* topics and a great many things not mentioned hitherto. The Purāṇas often have this encompassing quality, though not perhaps with the eclat of the *Agni* Purāṇa. Collectively, they are a veritable repository of the accumulated wisdom of the past, not least of a great many myths, which we will briefly discuss in Chapter 7. The Purāṇas are 'knowledge stored up' (*smṛta*), so that the past may be pondered upon. Although much of this knowledge, especially its technological features (e.g. the making and use of weapons and medicines) may be regarded today as either obsolete or just misguided, there are still important ways, as we will note, in which the Purāṇas provide guidelines for future courses of action.

We can now appreciate more fully why so many Purāṇas were crammed with such wide-ranging data. They became convenient holdalls for information which their compilers, the Brahmins, deemed useful for the welfare of society.[4] They are Brahminic in so far as they propagate Brahminic norms and values: they uphold the *varṇa* hierarchy, Brahminic codes of *dharma*, and so on. But as we have indicated, they also contain much material that does not seem to have originated with the Brahmins but points to beliefs and practices which developed a momentum outside the traditional Brahminic pale. Such material needed Brahminic ratification if the Brahmins were to remain in control; it received Brahminic approval 'by the back door' and subsequently became a part of the authoritative tradition.[5]

It is not always easy to identify this material. This is because in the past there was a difference between what Brahmins were expected or recommended to do by the normative texts and what they actually did do. Here is an example from ancient literature. We would expect the archery teacher of the five Pāṇḍava boys and their Kaurava cousins to be a Kṣatriya; surely such expertise was the preserve of the warrior caste. The *Mahābhārata* assures us, however, without apology, that it was Droṇa the Brahmin who was the youths' guru in this skill. This may have been an exception to the rule, but it indicates that exceptions could be made and often didn't raise too many eyebrows. And most Brahmins of today don't take too seriously a great many more traditional expectations.

Nevertheless, we can assume that what the Purāṇas say about the healing of diseases, the making of images, the use of arms on horseback, and so on refers originally to activities which in general were the domain of groups or castes outside the Brahmin community. The Purāṇas also say a great deal about a form of religion (or perhaps, form*s* of religion) which was not part of the traditional Brahminic sacrificial cult and which was becoming increasingly popular soon after the beginning of the Common Era. It consisted of pilgrimages and visits to holy sites and rivers, of temples and shrines, and of the worship of images. The worship of the Goddess was an important feature of this kind of religion, and the Purāṇas duly record it. In time, such religious practice was legitimised as 'Vedic' (by the technique of Vedic authority leap-frogging into another context; see Chapter 3) and presided over to a large extent by Brahmins, a situation which continues to the present day. Indeed, in Hinduism throughout the world it is this kind of religion which is by far the most dominant today.

Because the Purāṇas are holdall texts, often with a mix of material, they invite an interpretively selective approach religiously. But if one is, first, to escape the charge of handling one's sources arbitrarily, and second, to give one's Puranic interpretations a semblance of authority, an attempt must be made to justify the approach taken. It is therefore necessary to work out a coherent method of interpreting the texts. For example, this is how the theologian Rāmānuja sets about his task. He says:

> The *Matsya* Purāṇa states that some Brahmā-[ruled] ages are of mixed quality, some have an excess of the quality of goodness (*sattva*), others of passion (*rajas*), and still others of ignorance (*tamas*). Once the ages have thus been distinguished, the grandeur of the beings with an excess alternately of *sattva, rajas* and *tamas* is described, and we are told also that the way Brahmā, himself consisting [during one age] of an excess of one quality and during another of another, brings this about is explained in the Purāṇas correspondingly constituted . . . . To be specific, we are told that 'The grandeur of Agni and Śiva is proclaimed in the tamasic ages [or Purāṇas]; one declares the greater grandeur of Brahmā in the rajasic, and the still greater grandeur of Hari[=Viṣṇu] in the sattvic ages. In these ages those perfected in Yoga will reach the highest goal. In the mixed ages, [it is the grandeur of the goddess] Sarasvatī [that is proclaimed]'. This means that because Brahmā himself is the first creature (*kṣetrajña-*), in some Brahmā-periods *sattva* predominates, in others *rajas*, and in still others *tamas* . . . . Thus, with regard to the Purāṇas Brahmā has proclaimed, when a contradiction arises between a Purāṇa proclaimed when *sattva* predominated and any other, it is the Purāṇa of the sattvic period that is true while the opposing one is false. This rule for interpreting the Purāṇas has, in fact, been laid down by Brahmā himself during his sattvic phase.[6]

Rāmānuja was a Vaiṣṇava, i.e., for him Viṣṇu was God, the ultimate reality, the supreme Being. All other *deva*s or gods were, like the demiurge Brahmā, no more than creatures. Thus it is no surprise that Rāmānuja gives so much interpretive weight to the *Matsya* statements showing preference for Purāṇas exalting Viṣṇu. It was only on this basis that he could try to make the Purāṇas cohere in the service of his theology. The more arbitrarily selective with the Purāṇas one is, the less authoritatively do they support one's views (for one can always find in them some opposing view). If some Purāṇa is to be given a doctrinally authoritative status, it must be interpreted according to criteria based on a pre-established attitude of faith.

It is interesting to note that in modern times there are a number of religious groups which approach the Purāṇas precisely in this way. Consider, for example, ISKCON (the International Society for Krishna Consciousness, known popularly as the Hare Krishna movement)[7] or the Swaminarayan faith, both of which are relatively modern expressions of Hindu religion. For both faiths it is the *Bhāgavata* Purāṇa (especially its tenth section or canto) which occupies pride of place among the Purāṇas. This is because their founders came from religious traditions which already accorded doctrinal priority to this text. In its present form, the *Bhāgavata* Purāṇa can be given a fairly late date (*c*. tenth to eleventh century), though this does not mean that it does not draw upon much older material. This Purāṇa treats its wide range of topics consistently from one angle, namely that of exalting Kṛṣṇa Vāsudeva (the Kṛṣṇa of the *Mahābhārata*) as 'the Supreme Personality of Godhead' (the standard description used by the Bengali founder of the Hare Krishna movement, A. C. Bhaktivedanta Swami Prabhupada).[8] As the Purāṇa itself declares: 'The Vedas bear on Vāsudeva alone, and so do all feasts and sacrifices. All spiritual discipline converges on Vāsudeva, as does every rite and ceremony. Knowledge is fulfilled in Vāsudeva and so is asceticism. *Dharma* is oriented to Vāsudeva, and salvation comes only from him' (I.2.28–9).

For ISKCON, devotion to the person of Kṛṣṇa especially through the incidents of his childhood and youth as depicted in the tenth canto of the *Bhāgavata* Purāṇa consummates traditional Vedic religion – another example of the 'Vedicisation', without the building of strong hermeneutic bridges, of what appear to be, if not anti-Vedic, then extra-Vedic texts or elements. This is sometimes done in a disarming manner. I once attended a public demonstration of a solemn Vedic sacrifice performed by a Hare Krishna minister. Everything was set up with as much attention to traditional detail as was practicable. The altar was built in the right shape, facing the right direction and with the requisite number of bricks, and the sacrificial implements and other paraphernalia (down to the deerskin on which the minister would sit) were duly assembled. Then the ritual began to the accompaniment of the Vedic chants. Soon a fire was blazing, at intervals whooshed into leaping flames with liberal splashings of clarified butter (*ghee*). However, at the end of the invocations to the traditional Vedic *deva*s or 'gods', the names of Rādhā and Kṛṣṇa (the dual deity of Isconites) were regularly added as a *pièce de résistance*. This was done with a panache that would have taken the breath away of the ancient Vedic priests, for the simple reason that the Vedas proper make no mention of a divine couple called Rādhā and Kṛṣṇa. For the Swaminarayan faith too, the tenth canto of the *Bhāgavata* Purāṇa has a special devotional significance.

As in the case of the epics, the reading or recitation of the whole or parts of a Purāṇa is recommended, usually by the Purāṇa itself, as conducive to salvation and as the means for release from sin. Psychologically this can be a greatly comforting experience. Often the Purāṇas go to extremes in endorsing this recommendation. Here is an example from the *Śiva* Purāṇa.[9]

Once there was a Brahmin called Devarāja. He was an out and out reprobate – a very bad thing in any case, but especially for a Brahmin who is supposed to be 'a god among humans'. In fact, Devarāja means 'King of the gods', so the Purāṇa really intends to drive its point home. Devarāja did everything a Brahmin shouldn't do. He didn't know the Scriptures; he didn't say his prayers; he sold liquor; he robbed people of their money by deceiving and sometimes killing them. His life-style made him rich, yet he used none of his ill-gotten wealth in the cause of *dharma*. He became infatuated with a prostitute and married her, more or less putting aside his first wife. When he wasn't making money he was making love to his new wife. Wealth (*artha*) and lust (*kāma*), beyond the bounds of *dharma*, quite overpowered him. What prospect of release (*mokṣa*) did he have?

One day he went so far as to kill his mother, father and first wife while they slept, and to steal their money. After this, in the company of his willing partner, he threw all restraint to the winds. He drank liquor; he ate forbidden foods (the Purāṇa doesn't mention the word 'beef', but who knows what he ate?). He didn't care; *dharma* meant nothing to him.

One day he visited a town with a Śiva temple where he decided to stay for a while. In this temple, the *Śiva* Purāṇa was being constantly recited by Brahmins to devout hearers. Devarāja couldn't help but overhear. As fate would have it he was struck down by a fever, and after a month, he died. Not surprisingly, the messengers of Yama, the Lord of death, came for him and led him to the city of Yama, a place of gruesome torments. But help was at hand. The servants of Śiva flew to the rescue, entered the city, beat up Yama's messengers and made preparations to take Devarāja away in a 'marvellous celestial chariot', to Śiva's glorious mountain home.

By this time, Yama had come out to see what all the fuss was about and saw Devarāja about to depart with his victorious companions. He knew the score: far from objecting, he honoured his 'guests' and allowed them to spirit Devarāja away from under his nose. The moral of this story is clear, but the *Śiva* Purāṇa makes it even clearer. 'Precious is the reciting of the *Shiva Purana*, the highest purification, by the mere hearing of which even a very evil person attains Release', it declares, continuing:

> It [i.e. the *Shiva Purana*] is the great place of the eternal Shiva, the highest dwelling, the high spot; those who know the Vedas, say that it stands above all worlds. That evil man who, in his greed for money, injured many Brahmins, Kshatriyas, Vaishyas, Shudras, and even other creatures that breathe, the man who killed his mother and father and wife, who slept with a whore and drank wine, the Brahmin Devaraja went there and in a moment became released.[10]

And in their own distinctive ways, all the other Purāṇas make a similar claim. Here we see *smṛti* virtually usurping the saving power of traditional Vedic religion, but in the name of the Vedas, an instance of the 'appeasement' syndrome mentioned earlier.

Today, the practice of formally reading or reciting sacred texts (Purāṇas included) continues apace, sometimes on a grand scale publicly. For example, in August 1990, in Leicester (England), large extracts of the *Bhāgavata* Purāṇa were recited in a school playing-field (renamed 'Rameshwar' for the occasion).[11] The event was sponsored by an anonymous donor and lasted for eleven days; the reciter, a Gujarati Brahmin living in Bombay, was flown over for the occasion. An average of 10,000 people attended daily, with about three times that number at the weekends. The Sanskrit text was explained in Gujarati with some Hindi and English interspersed. There were similar recitations in the country in 1990 and in preceding years.[12] We have already commented on the nature of such recitations in another context.

Although the classical Purāṇas are in Sanskrit, as in the case of epic composition, there are also vernacular Purāṇas. In fact, the parallel is exact. 'There are actually two types of vernacular Purāṇas: those that have been translated, however freely, from Sanskrit originals and those that originated independently.'[13] Brockington goes on to point out that a number of these vernacular Purāṇas have played an important part in the development not only of the vernacular but also, as can be imagined, of various aspects of culture in different parts of India. In fact, the Purāṇic tradition also includes many so-called *māhātmyas*:

> The term *māhātmya* applies to those texts [not necessarily committed to writing] which are composed with the specific purpose of proclaiming the 'greatness' of a variety of things: a place, an auspicious time, a deity, a ritual activity such as . . . pilgrimage or . . . donation, etc.[14]

One may add countless *sthalapurāṇas*, i.e. folkloric accounts about a particular temple, shrine, holy place, etc. (usually in the possession of the place concerned), and many caste Purāṇas, namely similar accounts purporting to relate the glories, 'history', special figures and events of particular caste groupings.

We come finally to the last category of *smṛti* mentioned – that of the prasthāna-vākyas.

THE PRASTHĀNA-VĀKYAS

In Sanskrit, *prasthāna* can mean source, basis, journey. This is all to the good, for the prasthāna-vākyas are seminal or source texts – not falling under any of the *smṛti* categories already listed – which are regarded as supportive of what passes for primary scripture in the tradition concerned. In some way their followers depend upon them in their spiritual journey through life. It is in this sense that they are source and journey texts or *statements* ('prasthāna-*vākyas*'). In the Hindu tradition, there are a great many collections of prasthāna-vākyas. They may be of greater or lesser extent, composed in Sanskrit or in the vernacular, and function on different levels of the religious journey. They may relate to the rest of *smṛti* and to primary scripture in a number of complex ways: by corroborating, expatiating, balancing, illuminating, filling in gaps. What may be regarded as prasthāna-vākyas by one person may not be regarded as such by another. Different traditions, sects, and cults tend to resort to different prasthāna-vākyas, though sometimes two or more groups may share the same prasthāna-vākyas but may prioritise them differently. Let us give some examples.

One often comes across a reference in religious Hinduism to 'six orthodox perspectives on life'. These are called the *ṣaḍ-darśanas* (*ṣad* means 'six' and *darśana* stands for 'perspective', a total orientation in life). Scripturally, the *ṣaḍ-darśanas* have in common a formal acknowledgement of the Vedas as *śruti*. In practice, however, the founding or leading figures of some of the *darśanas* at least, have been more interested in working out virtually independent perspectives on life, independent, that is, of sustained Vedic exegesis. For these the Vedas are formally invoked as ratifying their methods and conclusions. It is important to note that however systematically they may seek to deploy rational argument, the luminaries of all the *darśanas* treat them as soteriologies, i.e. as systems of 'salvation', so it is not accurate to call these *darśanas* simply 'philosophies of life'.

The six *darśanas* provide a good context to exemplify what

we mean by prasthāna-vākyas. The prasthāna-vākyas of all these *darśanas* are in Sanskrit, since they belong to what may be called the 'high tradition' of Hinduism.[15]

We begin with two sub-divisions of the tradition known as Mīmāṃsā or Scriptural Exegesis, namely (i) the Pūrva Mīmāṃsā or the Prior School of Exegesis, and (ii) the Uttara Mīmāṃsā or the Later School of Exegesis, another name for which is Vedānta. As the alternative name for Uttara Mīmāṃsā indicates, for members of this school scriptural teaching culminates in the Vedānta or Upaniṣads, the 'later' portion of the Vedas. By contrast, for the Pūrva Mīmāṃsā it is the earlier or prior section of the Vedas, namely the hymns and Brāhmaṇas, which have greatest import (see Chapter 2). 'Pūrva' and 'Uttara' are thus not only chronological terms but also theological expressions, for 'Pūrva' can mean not only prior (in time), but also religiously prior or basic, while 'Uttara' can mean superior as well as subsequent in time.

Both these schools of Mīmāṃsā have wielded a pervasive and powerful influence in Hindu tradition, and can be divided further into sub-schools of thought (the greater number falling under Vedānta). Under Pūrva Mīmāṃsā, two renowned sub-schools are those of Prabhākara (*c.* fifth to sixth century CE) and Kumārila Bhaṭṭa (*c.* eighth century).[16] Under Vedānta there have been a number of well-known sub-schools, some of which have splintered further. These include the traditions of Śaṃkara, Rāmānuja, Madhva, Nimbarka, Vallabha and Caitanya – luminaries from the eighth to sixteenth centuries who continue to attract significant followings. New forms of Vedānta continue to appear. Thus the thought of Radhakrishnan (see Chapter 3) is professedly Vedānta-based if also wide-ranging and eclectic; no school seems to have been initiated by this thinker. On the other hand, Aurobindo Ghose (1872–1950) – or Sri Aurobindo, as he is called – does seem to have a distinctive following in India and elsewhere, with headquarters at the Aurobindo Ashram in Pondicherry on the Coromandel coast south of Madras. Another Vedānta-inspired organisation, with branches around the world, is the Ramakrishna Math (monastic foundation) and Mission which Swami Vivekananda (see Chapter 3) helped to establish in the name of his guru Ramakrishna Paramahamsa (1834–86). As noted before, this is based at Belur close to metropolitan Calcutta. Doctrinally, the monks of this Order profess to be Advaitins and defer to Śaṃkara.

The main prasthāna-vākya of the Pūrva Mīmāṃsā tradition is the *Mīmāṃsā* Sūtras, attributed to the Sage Jaimini. This text, which numbers over 2,600 sūtras, may be dated to about the beginning of the Common Era, and in a number of respects sums up a long tradition of thought on the nature of Vedic exegesis. It is concerned chiefly with the meaning and implementation of *dharma*, understood as right action, especially the Vedic solemn ritual, or *karman* in the strictest sense; hence the Pūrva Mīmāṃsā is sometimes called the Karma-Mīmāṃsā. The *Mīmāṃsā* Sūtras have acted as a decisive reference point for subsequent analysis and commentary by a long line of Pūrva Mīmāṃsakas. In the process a fairly comprehensive view (i.e. *darśana*) of life's meaning and goal was worked out.

The corresponding prasthāna-vākya of the Uttara Mīmāṃsā or Vedānta tradition is known as the *Brahma* Sūtras. Numbering about 550 aphorisms (the precise number depending on the way in which some of the sūtras are interpreted), the text sets out the nature and means of attaining *Brahman*, the ultimate reality of the Upaniṣads. The *Brahma* Sūtras seem to have been composed around the first to second centuries CE and are attributed to the thinker Bādarāyaṇa.[17] Whereas the *Mīmāṃsā* Sūtras recommend ritual action as the means of ultimate fulfilment, the *Brahma* Sūtras stress the need for knowledge (*jñāna, vidyā*) of *Brahman* as the means to final liberation (*mokṣa, mukti*) from entanglement in the flow of individual existence (*saṃsāra*). The *Brahma* Sūtras have generated a vast commentarial literature which continues to be studied by Indologists as a vital portion of the Hindu intellectual heritage, not least as a basis for inter-religious dialogue (with specific reference to Christianity in India and the West).

It is important to appreciate, however, that for the classical Vedantic theologian the *Mīmāṃsā* Sūtras were not to be discounted as irrelevant. Though these theologians regarded knowledge (variously interpreted) as crucial for attaining liberation (also variously interpreted) and as superseding the performance of the sacrificial ritual, the latter had its place. In one way or another it was regarded as a stepping-stone to the attainment of liberating knowledge. In other words, the Vedantic aspirant was expected to recognise the scope and goal of Jaimini's Sūtras (in the light of Vedantic teaching, of course).[18] This meant that these Sūtras had authority as a kind of prasthāna-vākya, but an authority subordinate to that of the *Brahma* Sūtras. In fact, in the context of *smṛti*, the Vedāntins appealed variously to the authority of not only the two Sūtra collections mentioned, but also the (Sanskrit) epics (especially the *Bhagavadgītā*), selected Purāṇas and other sources.[19] Latter-day Vedāntins have been far more eclectic, ranging widely even into western thought to construct their world views.

The next two classical *darśanas* may also be taken together. They are (iii) Nyāya, which means 'reasoning', and (iv) Vaiśeṣika, which means 'pertaining to individuality or particularity'. Again, both traditions claim to be Vedic, and also have seminal prasthāna-vākyas with a long tradition of commentary and sub-commentary, especially in the case of Nyāya. The Naiyāyikas, i.e. those who follow the Nyāya tradition, regard the *Nyāya* Sūtras of Gautama (*c*. beginning of the CE) as the philosophical source text for their system. The corresponding prasthāna-vākyas of the Vaiśeṣikas are the *Vaiśeṣika* Sūtras attributed to Kaṇāda (produced probably a century or two earlier than the *Nyāya* Sūtras) and a later composition, the so-called *Bhāṣya* or commentary on the *Vaiśeṣika* Sūtras by Praśastapāda, but in fact a more or less independent work dealing in large measure with topics from the Sūtras. Both systems are highly analytical and in basic ways not incompatible philosophically, the Nyāya stressing epistemological issues and procedures, the Vaiśeṣika ontological questions and distinctions about the nature of reality.[20] By about the seventh century CE, their proponents (and adversaries) tended to conflate both systems, marrying the epistemological interests of the one with the ontological concerns of the other, and giving additional grounds for talking of Nyāya-Vaiśeṣika in one breath. In fact, many of the logical techniques and conceptual insights yielded by Nyāya-Vaiśeṣika in the course of time were adopted as standard philosophical assets by traditional Hindu thinkers. Nyāya, the dominant system of the two, is divided into two phases. The Old School represents the first phase, and continues till the beginning of the thirteenth century when the Bengali logician Gaṅgeśa's momentous *Tattva-cintāmaṇi* inaugurated the New School, in which, to oversimplify, it was not so much *what* was said as *how* it was said as precisely as possible, that mattered. The whole Nyāya-Vaiśeṣika enterprise consists of a long tracery of commentary and sub-commentary of amazing complexity, with particular works acting variously as primary and secondary commentarial departure points (in the role of subordinate prasthāna-vākyas) for different commentators. It is an interesting fact that Nyāya techniques and insights are beginning to attract the attention of western logicians and philosophers as a result of more or less adequate attempts made in fairly recent times to translate Nyāya into a western idiom.[21].

We come finally to the last two of the so-called orthodox systems: (v) Sāṃkhya, and (vi) Yoga. These may also be paired because of a similarity of perspective. The prasthāna-vākyas of classical Sāṃkhya and Yoga are the Sūtras of Īśvarakṛṣṇa and Patañjali respectively. Both are brief compositions, unlike the more extensive *Nyāya* and *Vaiśeṣika* Sūtras, and are the result of already longstanding traditions of thought and practice. Īśvarakṛṣṇa's work is known as the *Sāṃkhya Kārikā* and may be dated to the second to fourth century CE, whereas Patañjali's *Yoga* Sūtras seem to have been composed about two centuries earlier. The *Sāṃkhya Kārikā* describes twenty-five categories of existence in terms of two fundamentally different principles of being (also accepted by Yoga): *prakṛti*, which may be translated loosely as 'the principle of energy and matter' and which contains twenty-four kinds of being, and *puruṣa* or spirit (the twenty-fifth category). *Puruṣa* is characterised as unfractured consciousness and bliss; *prakṛti* is the source not only of physical forces but also of what is known as mental experience, namely, our fragmented experiences of different kinds of awareness, structured in terms of subject, object and knowing act, of emotions (e.g. joy and sorrow, love and hatred), of feelings (e.g. hot/cold, sweet/sour, pain/pleasure), etc. The aim of Sāṃkhya is to guide the aspirant, by an arduous and single-minded process of self-realisation, to distinguish the congenitally conflated realms of *puruṣa and prakṛti* constituting his being, so that his individual *puruṣa* or spirit (his 'real', trans-empirical self) may be released from the cycle of rebirth (*saṃsāra*). Later, we will discuss in more detail the relationship between *puruṣa* and *prakṛti*, and the releasing process. The liberated state of classical Sāṃkhya is one of absolute spiritual self-containment. There is no talk of God.[22]

The goal of the classical Yoga system is absolute self-mastery, that is, *puruṣa*'s mastery over the entangling and spiritually blinding forces of *prakṛti*, by a practical discipline of meditative techniques. In the course of time Sāṃkhya theory was seen to interlock with Yoga practice, though both systems retained distinctive features (thus there is no place for a supreme *Puruṣa* or God in classical Sāṃkhya, whereas classical Yoga theory and practice accommodate a kind of Īśvara or God).[23] Once more there is a tradition of commentarial literature in both systems. We shall say something on *yoga* as a process in contrast to Yoga as a classical system of thought and practice in Chapter 12.

Unlike the two Mīmāṃsā traditions, the other *darśana*s are not overly concerned to show that they derive from the Veda. Indeed, unlike Mīmāṃsā, they are conspicuously short of sustained Vedic exegesis so that it is difficult to appreciate their Vedic credentials.

They might be regarded as orthodox, in a loose sense of the word, to the extent that in their several ways they prepare the ground for a sustained Vedic interpretation, by developing methods for thinking correctly and precisely, for distinguishing and classifying kinds of being, and for analysing mental states and controlling and integrating mind and body. But like the two Mīmāṃsās, each claims both to be based on the Veda and to provide *the* life-orientation that results in ultimate well-being (for their conception of liberation see Chapter 11). This they do, not only by vigorously arguing against one another, but also by sub-schools in a particular tradition no less vigorously arguing amongst themselves. After all, the Vedas are dense and recondite texts and cry out for interpretation – and often get bewilderingly discordant ones. Is there not an old Hindu saying that the gods love obscure things? So do philosophers and theologians.

Further, the six systems developed not only through *intra*-religious polemic so to speak, but also by *inter*-religious debate with other traditions both Hindu, e.g. the *Pañcarātra* school of Vaiṣṇavism, various Śaiva denominations, and non-Hindu or avowedly anti-Vedic, like Materialism, Jainism and Buddhism. In fact, talk of only six orthodox systems is misconceived. There are many more *darśana*s or religious perspectives on life even within high Hinduism, i.e. the traditions which formally acknowledged the religious authority of the Vedas. And 'orthodox' in this context is a highly debatable word. These other *darśana*s also had their prasthāna-vākyas. Consider, for example, the *Śaiva Siddhānta* tradition first mentioned in Chapter 3. Here, as explained, the Vedas and the Āgamas act jointly as primary scripture. But it was stated (in Dhavamony's quotation) that the *Tirumuṟai* and the *Meykaṇṭa* Śāstras are also part of 'the scriptural canon'. This can only be as secondary scripture, as, in fact, prasthāna-vākyas, the first inspiring devotion, the second acting as the basis for a systematic articulation of the tradition. Indeed, if we take the alternative name for the *Tirumuṟai* seriously, namely, the Tamil Veda, then only the Śāstras can be deemed prasthāna-vākyas. In our usage, 'prasthāna vākya' refers only to those sources, written or oral, which do not count for primary scripture, and which, as not falling under any other category of *smṛti* mentioned, serve to support primary scripture in some way.

It has already been pointed out that prasthāna-vākyas may function at different levels of the spiritual journey. We need to say more on this. First, however, we have to provide a context. In Sanskritic Hinduism the goals of human existence are sometimes said to be fourfold. These goals, or *puruṣārtha*s, are: *artha* or prosperity, *kāma* or gratification, *dharma*, here to be understood as religious merit, and *mokṣa* or liberation from *saṃsāra*. Though one often comes across this division in traditional literature there is nothing sacrosanct about it in that many Hindus simply do not make much of it, unlike modern Hindu (and non-Hindu) commentators on Hinduism. The order in which the first three goals are traditionally listed varies, as does their precise meanings.[24] It is perhaps useful to note that when the list, especially of the first three goals, was first formulated some centuries before the beginning of the Common Era (*mokṣa* being added at a later date), *artha* is likely to have meant the means required to fund the Vedic sacrifice,[25] *kāma* the satisfaction gained from the fruits of the sacrifice, and *dharma* the merit acquired by regular and proper performance of the solemn ritual. In other words, these three goals centred round the Vedic sacrificial cult, still the religious norm of the time. As alternative cults gained currency, the meaning of the *puruṣārtha*s changed according to context. With the rise of *saṃnyāsa* (the renunciation of worldly ties) as a religious objective – the early classical Upaniṣads mark this trend – *mokṣa*, interpreted variously as the transcending of the traditional ritualistic mentality, was added to the list as the fourth goal, and the relationship between *mokṣa* and the other three *puruṣārtha*s takes on revealing philosophical implications. More will be said about this relationship later. Here we point out that, in typical Hindu fashion, the original list was not discarded but reinterpreted.

However, the pursuit of *artha* and *kāma* was set in an ethical context very early on. *Artha* and *kāma* (and perforce *dharma*) were never recommended as goals to be sought for their own sake *irrespective* of an ethical code of practice. This is implied, for instance, in the *Bhagavadgītā* 7.11. The Lord Kṛṣṇa says: 'I am the *kāma* (you experience) for things, but not as opposed to *dharma*.'[26] The dharmic context of the four goals was affirmed throughout the tradition. Today it is common for *artha* to be interpreted as worldly success, *kāma* as aesthetic (and sensual) satisfaction, and *dharma* as virtue, whether in the cause of enlightened self-interest or when pursued for disinterested ends. The interpretation of the *puruṣārtha*s has been enlarged, although their ethical context has been retained. We shall return to this later.

It is now time to relate the *puruṣārtha*s to the notion of the prasthāna-vākya. In Brahminic tradition various writings are associated with the articulation and attainment of each *puruṣārtha* in such a way as to be, in effect, the prasthāna-vākya for each pursuit. For example, consider the *Artha Śāstra*, a well-known Sanskrit work of some 5,000 sūtras attributed to Kauṭilya, an expert on politics.

It is the general view that the *Artha Śāstra* was written in the third to fourth century BCE by an adviser of the king Candragupta Maurya. A fairly recent study has claimed with plausibility, however, that the text has come down to us as a compilation of the first or second century CE.[27] Whichever position is nearer the truth, there can be no doubt that the classical text itself was preceded by a developed tradition of thought on polity. The very first sūtra declares: 'This particular treatise on *artha* has been produced after collecting as many authoritative texts as possible by former teachers on the acquisition and preservation of territory.' Moreover, the text refers to a number of other teachers by name. As the sūtra quoted intimates, *artha* here has to do with well-being in the context of 'the acquisition and preservation of territory', that is, in a well-ordered and stable state. Over fifteen chapters Kauṭilya's work expounds *artha* by concentrating directly on what the king and his chief officials should do to run a successful state. Only indirectly, then, has the material well-being of a member (indeed, an 'aryan' member) of such a state been described.

The meaning of *artha* in the text is already considerably broad. The work tells us, among other things, how princes, including the heir, should be raised, educated and treated; councillors tested and appointed by the king; wars begun, conducted or averted; enemies won over, undermined or overthrown; taxes levied, criminals punished, calamities dealt with; and how the king's chief officials function (namely the king's chaplain and the ministers of revenue, records, audits, taxes, mines, courtesans, gold control, agriculture, the armoury, shipping, cattle, elephants, etc.).

As a treatise on material well-being (in the context of a stable and well-run state) rather than on ethics, the *Artha Śāstra* is not concerned to justify its recommendations by moral discussion. But it does postulate a moral framework for the pursuit of *artha*. The alternative name for the genre of literature for which it was a model, namely *Daṇḍa Nīti* ('The Code of the Rod') indicates as much. Further, we are told (1.4.11–14),

> For the Rod, used wisely, endows one's subjects with *dharma, artha* and *kāma*. Used badly, out of passion or anger or disregard, it enrages even forest-anchorites and wandering ascetics, leave alone householders! If not used at all, it gives rise to the Law of the Fish (*matsya-nyāya*): for, in the absence of the wielder of the Rod, the stronger swallows the weak.[28]

Thus those in power were expected to ensure the right moral ambience for general well-being, spiritual as well as physical, or else the Law of the Fish would take over. True, but one wonders at the moral context implied here, for at times the end seems to justify the means. Thus not only spies, double agents and courtesans, but even monks and nuns are encouraged to dissemble for the sake of a stable regime. Perhaps it was believed that this end was so important that all else justified it.

There is one other feature of the *Artha Śāstra* which deserves a mention. The text seems clearly to imply that political and religious authority were to be kept apart. There was to be no established religion, though this does not mean that in the course of history Hindu rulers did not try to favour or enforce a particular faith, even by means of persecution. On the whole, however, rulers have followed this directive, thus adding to the image of Hindu religious tolerance. Perhaps this tradition helps to explain why independence from colonial rule could be negotiated in terms of a 'secular' state, which in the Indian context simply means that while one has the right to practise a religion, no particular religion is constitutionally privileged. This puts into perspective those Hindu religiously political forces today which seem to wish to act against the weight of history.

Not only politicians but others among the educated, such as theologians, were expected to be cognisant of the gist of what *artha*-literature taught. After all, material well-being was the basis of a stable society in which religion could be freely pursued and patronised. People needed *artha*, if not to service the increasingly disused (though still deferred to) Vedic sacrificial ritual, then to finance the inevitable and numerous rites of passage, domestic and temple worship, the building of images and temples, the maintenance of pilgrimage centres and shrines, and so on. The paraphernalia of religious worship was ubiquitous and constant and could be costly, not to mention the priest's fees which continued to figure on every religious agenda. In its way, the *Artha Śāstra* and its various copies, with their more or less localised influence, were a sort of prasthāna-vākya in a religious context. Their moral implications were a matter of circumstantial interpretation.

Just as there were prasthāna-vākyas for *artha, dharma* and *mokṣa* (in the sense of fulfilment in a transcendent context, e.g. the seminal texts of the various *darśana*s), so there were prasthāna-vākyas for *kāma* or gratification. The Hindus leave nothing to chance. The model for this is the *Kāma Sūtra*, well-known in the West by name if not by content.

This treatise, which is based to some extent on the *Artha Śāstra* and which has been dated to the third or fourth centuries CE, has been ascribed to the Sage Vātsyāyana (also called Mallanāga). It too may be a compilation of sorts; in any case, it mentions various earlier authorities by name and makes clear that it is preceded by a long tradition of thought on the subject.

The *Kāma Sūtra* is a fairly extensive work (thirty-six short chapters under seven headings) and deals with *kāma* in the general sense of the pleasurable awareness that arises from 'hearing, touch, sight, taste and smell in appropriate contact with their distinctive objects, controlled by the mind in conjunction with the spiritual self'.[29] Sexual pleasure then, is only a part of *kāma*, though for the *Sūtra* it is a leading part. The *Sūtra* is directly addressed to the *nāgarika* or refined man. This is not to say that the less leisured, and even women and Śūdras (the cultured Śūdra was by no means a rare phenomenon in some contexts), were not expected to learn from it. Yet, allowing for time and circumstance, the *Sūtra* is less chauvinist than might be expected. Although the work is the product of men for the gratification of men, its aim is not to titillate (in this it succeeds), nor are women treated merely as sexual objects. Lovers from both sexes are expected to show sensitivity and understanding towards their partners.

As in the case of the *Artha Śāstra*, an ethical context for the pursuit of *kāma* is implied.

> One should (plan to) live for a hundred years and so should divide one's time so as to serve the three goals (listed as *dharma*, *artha* and *kāma*) in such a way that they inter-relate and do not harm one another (1.2.1). . . . When the three co-exist, the preceding goal is superior to the one which follows (i.e. *dharma* is superior to *artha* which is superior to *kāma*; 1.2.14).

Kāma is put in its place. Nevertheless, as in the case of the *Artha Śāstra*, some of the moral implications may seem disquieting. Not only are various sexual types and activities described, but also the arts of courting and seduction, the behaviour of courtesans, the preparation of aphrodisiacs, and so on. Clearly one of Vātsyāyana's aims was to classify dispassionately all the significant options and facts known to him under a particular topic. The treatise is a fund of cultural information for the period.

In the high tradition, the *Kāma Sūtra* became immensely authoritative and, either directly or through subsequent texts for which it was a prototype, it greatly influenced art, literature and drama,[30] as well as facets of religious imagery. Many a stylised description of the love between the Lord and his devotee, depicted in verse or sculpture, shows signs of the influence of the *Kāma Sūtra*. Today, it would have only a residual impact on urbanised society, intimating by its very presence that Hindu civilisation, far from being philistine, has a developed and refined tradition of enjoying life's pleasures in ethical context, and also insinuating its aesthetic ideals into religious and secular art.

And so it goes on. In the religious context there are prasthāna-vākyas, ancient and less so, similarly across a whole range of human activity. There are cautionary tales and animal fables, iconometric and iconographic treatises, texts for temple building and worship, dance and music, astrology and herbal lore, etc. It is remarkable that they still exert a pervasive if elusive influence among Hindus in all walks of life. Temples and images are still being built, aesthetic ideals enforced and assimilated, worship and Yoga practised, horoscopes and almanacs devised, children raised, traditional medical practitioners resorted to (not to mention the innumerable quacks and 'virility clinics' that infest the land), and so on.

Finally, we come to the third authoritative summons to which Hindus have traditionally been attentive when shaping their religious response in life: that of personal experience. This will be discussed in Chapter 7.

7 The voice of experience

I

Experience as based on the senses and reason. A story. Pravṛtti*: its ancient roots. Materialism in the high tradition. Worldly imagery as indicative of spiritual realities; various examples. Classical dance as a participative experience. An anecdote.* Nivṛtti. *The role of reason: reason, scripture and faith. Rationality recognised as a conditioned process.*

So far we have discussed various features of the 'public' voices of scripture and tradition (or collective experience) to which Hindus have been attentive in shaping their religious orientation. We must now do the same for the 'private' voice of personal experience. Hindu tradition has always insisted on this voice as a crucial component of one's religious response to life.

Here the evidence of the senses and of reason has always been given a vital role. Sense experience has generally been regarded as a necessary feature and stepping-stone of the religious vision. We have seen how positively the householder stage (gārhasthya) has been evaluated in the classical view. This implied the ethical cultivation of *artha* and *kāma*: in fact of sensuous and sensual experience. It is distinctive of Hindu savants to teach that in general one can best appreciate the innate spiritual limitations of worldly goals by first passing through the critical fires of the dharmic pursuit of *artha* and *kāma*. With respect to *kāma*, let me illustrate this with a story about Śaṃkara, the great champion of Advaita.

Tradition has it that Śaṃkara, from an early age, embraced the renouncer's life; this implied the vow of celibacy. While still a youth he would tour the land engaging in theological debate with rival teachers. On one occasion his opponent was the famous Ritualist or Pūrva Mīmāṃsaka, Maṇḍana Miśra. After a great contest, Śaṃkara got the better of him. But before he could claim victory, Bhāratī,

Maṇḍana's wife and also a reputed thinker, claimed that he would first have to defeat her in debate since she was the other part of Maṇḍana's team. Śaṃkara agreed. Things were going well for him until the canny Bhāratī led the debate into an area which required a personal knowledge of sex. The nonplussed celibate asked for a month's intermission, which was granted. Luckily, he heard about a king who, it seemed, had dropped dead on a hunting expedition, at which event his attendant queens had promptly fainted. By his superior yogic powers the great Advaitin projected his soul into the king's corpse (for so it was) while his own body remained in a state of suspended animation in his disciples' secret care. Imagine the joy of the waking ladies when they discovered that their lord (or Śaṃkara) hadn't died after all but instead seemed full of life. For the next month or so the 'king' was certainly not occupied with affairs of state. Then Śaṃkara's soul returned to his own body, the ex-king's queens were back where they started, and Śaṃkara, still celibate in his own body but suitably educated in the lore of sex, hurried back to resume his debate with Bhāratī. Needless to say, and no doubt to Bhāratī's surprise, Śaṃkara now knew what he was talking about, and of course won the debate. The story has a happy ending – at least for all the main participants: Maṇḍana, for one, became one of Śaṃkara's most famous disciples and exponents of Advaita, whose cause he strongly supported.

Let us not worry too much about the exploitative and manipulative elements of the story so far as Śaṃkara's behaviour is concerned. After all it is only a story, revealing more about the hagiographer than about Śaṃkara. We are interested in the relevant lesson that lurks beneath the surface, which is that it is indispensable, even for a celibate, to appreciate the place of *kāma* (and not only in its sexual connotations) in a well-ordered life. Such *kāma* is not to be just tolerated; on the contrary it is to be embraced, for repression, in the absence of sublimation, will lead to unhealthy consequences, spiritual and otherwise. Of course, the pursuit of *kāma* is not the highest religious goal and it is fraught with spiritual danger. But for the ordinary person its outright rejection is even more dangerous spiritually, while its ordered pursuit is conducive to spiritual progress. This understanding is very much in evidence today. It is common for religious teachers, including those respected for their celibate way of life, to be asked for and to give advice freely on domestic matters, including sexual, marital and financial problems. Usually, though not always, they evaluate the (restrained) seeking of *artha* and *kāma* positively. After all, as the weight of Hindu tradition teaches, without *artha* and *kāma* and their basis in the life of the householder, society falters and the religious enterprise as a whole grinds to a halt.

Thus *pravṛtti*, or engagement with the world, has an important role in the traditional Hindu religious vision. The roots of the Hindu accent on *pravṛtti* can be traced to the early Vedic religion of the Aryan peoples and possibly also to a Harappan contribution. As we have seen, the religion of the Aryans was strongly grounded in the affirmation of this-worldly images and realities. Aryan religion was concerned as much with well-being in this life as with immortality in a post-mortem existence. Typical of this attitude is the following prayer:

> O Agni! May our sacrifice yield abundant sheep, cows and horses. May it be fit for valiant men and be forever indestructible! Great hero, may it renew us and bring us many offspring. Firmly established, may it grant great wealth and be of wide assembly.
>
> (RV. 4.2.5)

Agni is the *deva* of fire, especially the sacrificial fire. So too invocations were made to the transcendent as manifesting in the sun, dawn, rivers, rain, the storm, in powers offering protection in war, sickness, death, etc. In Chapter 12 I will attempt to show that we are not talking of polytheism here – at least, not in a straightforward sense. On the contrary, early Vedic religion represents an attempt to relate to one transcendent reality perceived to manifest through many worldly phenomena. And, not without change and development it is true, the same approach is evident in the imagery of the Upaniṣads and subsequently in Hindu tradition.

The contribution of the developed Harappan civilisation encountered by the Aryans, on the other hand, is obscure. We have already noted in Chapter 2 that its script is yet to be deciphered, but from the pictorial use made of vegetation and (often composite) animals on numerous seals and from the clay figurines of what may be a goddess cult, we may perhaps conjecture that earthly experience played an important part in Harappan religion. It also appears that the later Hindu idea of *yoga* or harmonious union of different levels and facets of existence may have derived from this religion (one recalls the theme of the seated 'yogin'). Classical Yoga recommends the integration – and then transcendence – of sense-experience in the spiritual life.

In fact, at one extreme one can detect a prominent thread of materialist attitudes running throughout the Hindu cultural fabric. From earliest times there has been a tradition of materialist thinkers, who were called Cārvākas or Lokāyatas. They pointedly dismiss the spiritual realities and values of the dominant religious outlook, with its bolstering philosophies: Vedic and Brahminic authority, belief in and arguments for the existence of spirit or *ātman*, God, heaven, ultimate spiritual fulfilment, and so on. They have even rejected the validity of inference, the putative logical support of so many non-materialist conclusions, and they unabashedly advocated a hedonist way of life. Here are two quotations attributed to materialist thinkers. The first is on the nature and destiny of the human being by one Ajita Keśakambalin, a contemporary of the Buddha:

> Man is formed of the four elements. When he dies, earth returns to the aggregate of earth, water to water, fire to fire, and air to air, while his senses vanish into space. Four men with the bier take up the corpse: they gossip . . . as far as the burning-ground, where his bones turn the colour of a dove's wing and his sacrifices end in ashes. They are fools who preach almsgiving, and those who maintain the existence (of immaterial categories) speak vain and lying nonsense. When the body dies both fool and wise alike are cut off and perish. They do not survive after death.[1]

This is typical of Hindu materialist attitudes to the present day. And on religious belief and practice, here is another biting attack as quoted in the *Sarva-darśana-saṃgraha* (*c.* eighth century CE), a text noted for its summary of various world views, including that of the materialist.[2]

> There is neither heaven nor liberation nor spirit in the after-life,
> Nor do deeds appropriate to the castes and stages of life produce other-worldly fruit.
> The Agnihotra sacrifice, the three Vedas, and ascetic practices – smearing oneself with ashes, bearing three staves –
> Are Nature's way of providing a livelihood for those without virility or brains.
> If a beast slaughtered during the Jyotiṣṭoma sacrifice will go to heaven,
> Then why isn't his own father killed by the sacrificer during the rite?
> If [food-offerings during] the *śrāddha* rite gratified dead beings,
> Then oil would increase the flame of an extinguished lamp! . . .
> Enjoy life while you can, run up debts and feed on *ghee*,[3]
> Can you return [to face a reckoning] once the body is turned to ashes? . . .
> Whence rites for the dead are simply a means to a living laid down by Brahmins,
> There is no proof anywhere to the contrary.
> Those who implement the three Vedas are buffoons, rascals and revellers.[4]

These are extreme views of course, to be rejected at least from the standpoint of Brahminic Hinduism. But their presence in the cultural fabric acted as a constant challenge to Hindu religious teachers and their followers to reassess and deepen their commitment. Further, materialist critiques may well have encouraged Hindus to acknowledge that the goals of *artha* and *kāma* in the context of the *puruṣārtha*s were an integral part of the spiritual life. There is even a tendency in the 'high' Hindu tradition to think it requisite for renouncers to have enjoyed sensual experience at an earlier stage, the better to appreciate the meaning of their new way of life. For such experience, in proper context, produced a rounded personality by expending natural inclinations, and thus contributed to the contentment and welfare of society. In the fullness of time it would lead to the spiritualising if not transcending of worldly concerns.

Thus at least primary Hindu scriptures of all kinds are replete with imagery of worldly life. For example in the Upaniṣads, images of the sun, moon, fire, lightning, air, water, birds, flowers, insects, animals, eggs, various artefacts such as musical instruments and their sounding, giving birth, and even sex, are used positively to explain spiritual realities and relationships. 'As the spider emits its web, as small sparks shower from fire', says the *Bṛhadāraṇyaka* Upaniṣad (BAUp II.1.20), 'even so from this Spirit come forth all breaths, all worlds, all gods, all beings.' In the same Upaniṣad, when describing a mystical state, Yājñavalkya says: 'As a man deep in the embrace of a beloved wife knows nothing without or within, even so the one deep in the embrace of the intuitive self knows nothing without or within' (BAUp IV.3.21). In a famous passage (VI.1.3f), the *Chāndogya* Upaniṣad teaches that 'just as everything made of clay is known from but one lump of clay – the change (of shape of the clay) being only a designation based on speech while the truth is that it is really clay', so should we understand the relationship between the unknown, underlying source of all being and the objects of experience. Again:

> Know the spirit as the master of the chariot and the body as the chariot.
> Know the faculty of judgement as the charioteer, and the faculty of sensation as the reins.
> The senses themselves are called the horses, while objects are the paths for them.
> The wise say that the agent of experience is the conjunction of spirit, senses and the faculty of sensation.
> For the one who lacks understanding, with faculty of sensation always untrained,
> The senses are uncontrollable, like unruly horses for the charioteer.

But for the one who has understanding, with faculty of sensation ever trained,
The senses are controllable, like docile horses for the charioteer.
The one who lacks understanding, who is rampant, always unclean,
Does not attain the goal but moves along life's flow.
But the one who has understanding, who is restrained, ever pure,
Attains that goal from which one is not born again.

(*KaṭhUp* 3.3–8)

Based on the analogy of the war-chariot, which had two occupants, the combatant (i.e. the master of the chariot) and his charioteer who drove and manoeuvred the chariot, here is teaching about how the individual should function as a union of body and soul to reach the spiritual goal. And thus does the *Svetāśvatara* Upaniṣad (IV.4.) describe the Lord in his creative omnipresence:

You, the indigo bumble-bee,
The green parrot coppery-eyed,
The cloud with lightning in its belly,
The seasons and the seas.
Boundless, you abide in omnipresence,
You, from whom all worlds are born.

Not only the capacity, but the felt need to borrow, fashion, evoke and transform worldly images in order to share religious experience is characteristic of the Hindu image-maker, irrespective of sex, religious affiliation, position in society, or the language used. We have seen how the image of the spider emitting its web is used to express the relationship between the world and its maker. In marvellous imagery which plays on a similar theme to different effect, the Vīraśaiva (or Liṅgāyat) poet-saint Mahadevi (twelfth century CE) expresses in Kannada free verse her anguished devotion to Śiva, her Lord:

Like a silkworm weaving
her house with love
from her marrow,
and dying
in her body's threads
winding tight, round
and round,
I burn
desiring what the heart desires.
Cut through, O Lord,

my heart's greed,
and show me
your way out,
O Lord white as jasmine.[5]

Here is a poem entitled *Dust-temple* from the work of the religious visionary and Bengali poet, Rabindranath Tagore (1861–1941):

Chanting, incense, striving worship – cast all this aside,
Behind closed doors, in temple-corner – do you think to hide?

In darkness, hiding in your mind –
Whom will your secret worship find,

Look well about you, friend, and see – there's no God inside!

He's gone where peasant cleaving earth ploughs the ground anew,
Where rocks are split to forge a path, where they toil the whole year through,

In sun, in rain, with all He'll stand,
Look, there's mud on both His hands –

Come on, cast off those spotless clothes and like Him muck in too.

Deliverance?
Where's that, my friend, where's deliverance to be found?
The Lord himself is chained to all, the Lord is creation-bound.
Leave off your meditating, friend, flower-offerings are now amiss,
Torn clothes, dust that sticks – now it's time for this.

Be one with Him in the way of work, let sweat pour to the ground.[6]

These are but a few examples from an almost inexhaustible stock of verbal images of the way in which Hindus from different times, backgrounds and religious persuasions have called upon experience of the world to express and share their faith. There is a keen observance and appreciation of the world at work here, based on the assumption that life has a more or less transparent potential to reveal the sacred mysteries. We will touch on the rationale of this attitude later, but a line from Tagore's poem contains the philosophical clue: 'The Lord himself is chained to all, the Lord is creation-bound'. This refers to the pervasive belief that the power of the deity pervades all things and may be experienced accordingly.

It is not only verbal images that are used in this respect; lavish use is also made of visual and auditory images. The arts of painting, dance, instrumental music, recitation, sculpture and architecture, for instance, have traditionally been developed and patronised in large measure in the service of religion. This is still the case, with respect not only to the pan-Indian, so-called cultured modes of artistic expression but also the more localised, popular forms of these arts. The way in which the epic of Pābūjī is presented with its musical accompaniment (see Chapter 5) is a good example of the latter.

In fact, by using the world of sense experience as a means to grasp religious realities, a symbiotic relationship often exists in Hindu tradition between the different kinds of imagery used, as also between the images and forms of their artistic expression. The verbal imagery of love poems, for instance (drawn originally from erotic treatises like the *Kāma Sūtra*), may be used to express the relationship between the soul and God. As a somewhat extraordinary example we may consider the *Gītagovinda*, a famous Sanskrit poem composed by Jayadeva (twelfth century CE) who came from the area of Bengal. Ostensibly in language that is frankly erotic, the poet describes a passionate love affair between Kṛṣṇa and a favourite milk-maid lover, Rādhā.[7]

But this is not the whole picture. Various events, at different levels, are going on in the poem. The poem is both a literary and emotional experience, but it is also clearly intended to evoke religious experience. On the one hand, in refined language and imagery, a master poet depicts a passionate love affair between a man and a woman. On the other hand, the man is Kṛṣṇa, already established over many centuries in a Vaiṣṇava context as a devotional focus *par excellence* of a personal God who has assumed human form (the *Bhagavadgītā* had been composed at least a thousand years earlier). The woman is Rādhā, a figure who was coming into her own as Kṛṣṇa's female counterpart in a 'binitarian' conception of the deity.[8] It seems clear that at the time a number of *bhakti*-cults were using a developing mythology of an erotic relationship between Rādhā and Kṛṣṇa to sustain this conception. Jayadeva's poem both resulted from and fuelled this mentality.

Jayadeva explicitly places the poem in a theological context. The poem's Introduction lauds Kṛṣṇa as the subject of a number of well-known divine descents in embodied form into the world. In keeping with tradition, each descent or *avatāra* is depicted as having taken place for a specific reason, but in such a way as to disclose collectively a God who cares for the world, who wishes to protect it, to cleanse it of undesirable elements, a God keen to enter into a personal, saving relationship with the world. In short, a God of *pravṛtti*. Is it then stretching the imagination unduly to see Jayadeva's portrayal of the intimate, sensual relationship between the two lovers as intended to symbolise the desired relationship between the soul and its God, represented by Rādhā and Kṛṣṇa respectively – a relationship that rises to ecstatic and all-consuming heights? The poem's innuendoes that the lovers are involved in an illicit affair serve all the more poignantly to indicate that in our own lives nothing must stand in the way of whole-hearted commitment to our divine Lover, least of all conventional complacencies and expectations. Generations of Hindus, savants and laypeople alike, down to the present day, have drawn spiritual nourishment by interpreting the *Gītagovinda* in this light, and that is perhaps the most important consideration of all.

But the poem displays further wheels within wheels. After the Prologue, each section begins by recommending the musical mode and mood (*rāga*) that best evokes its content. So the poem can be set to music and enacted by dance.[9] Verbal, visual and aural imagery can blend in an integrated religious experience. In fact – and here a wider symbiosis is at work – the landscape of Hindu painting is dotted with portrayals, susceptible to a religious interpretation, from the *Gītagovinda* theme and others like it. Some of the finest of these are displayed in galleries around the world. Prints and contemporary paintings of these themes done in traditional style – some of them very beautiful – are easily available in India, and adorn numerous homes in the subcontinent and abroad.

We will comment here about classical Hindu dance. This evolved in a religious context and was given a high profile as part of temple worship. There are a number of basic regional and other styles as well as seminal texts,[10] but the point that we wish to stress is the participative nature of such dance. In form and content, the heart of dance as worship has always been expression (*abhinaya*). In highly stylised fashion, its aim is to enact stories and characteristics from religious sources and figures so as to evoke an emotional atmosphere in which the watchers participate. The watcher must be drawn into the changing mood and sentiment of the performance. Classically there are eight (sometimes a ninth is added) basic emotions (*bhāva*s) from which corresponding sentiments or *rasa*s arise. These *rasa*s are the erotic, the comic, the sympathetic/compassionate, the wrathful, the heroic, the fearsome, the repulsive, the wondrous, and the pacific. With consummate skill, the expert female or male dancer aims to evoke these *rasas* in the watcher as the content of the dance dictates, so as to enable the beholder to participate vicariously in the religious experience that the performance is. Thus the dance becomes a shared experience. It is not the aim of the dancer to express his or her own personality in the process; rather such individuality must be submerged in the atmosphere of the occasion.[11]

Not only Vaiṣṇava figures, but also those of Śiva and the Goddess are subject to the process of understanding the sacred mysteries by reference to worldly features. Śiva in particular, perhaps – though certainly not exclusively, as we have already intimated – is at home in a luxuriant mythology of the sensual. In this context his sexual appetite and prowess are more blatant than Kṛṣṇa's, and more shocking to conventional sensibilities. In imagery, Śiva is the 'erotic ascetic',[12] a figure of contrasts, the God of the unexpected. His best-known symbol is the *liṅga* or phallus, usually a smooth, aniconic shaft of black stone standing in the centre of a shallow, tear-drop shaped bowl of the same material, representing the female sexual organ or *yoni*: God at one with Goddess, God united with the loving soul, male with female, the reconciliation of opposites in a higher synthesis, the creative seed in the womb of becoming. These and other insights shower forth from the *liṅga-yoni* conjunction, its aniconic display itself a study of contrast – the warmth of sexual union sited in the cool shadow of a million canopied shrines around the land, in mighty temples and in little wayside grottoes or on the sidewalks of busy urban streets.[13]

I remember once trudging through paddy fields in the company of some pilgrims during the rainy season in Bengal. A great storm was brewing. Before long the rain lashed down under lowering black clouds; the wind whipped and howled about us. It was awesome. Since no shelter was at hand we continued our journey as best we could. Suddenly there was a thunderous flash as a bolt of lightning struck the field a short distance ahead. Some of the pilgrims cried out in terror; we instinctively huddled together for safety. But then an old woman smiled and said in Bengali, 'Don't be afraid. Can't you see that this is Mother's *māyā*?' In other words, can you not see that God our Mother is displaying her wondrous power?[14] This was meant to be a consoling thought, and it worked. It is not uncommon for Hindus to interpret elemental phenomena as manifestations of divine presence or agency.

In Goddess-dominated Tantric contexts too, sexual imagery looms large. Notwithstanding centuries of dampening outside influences,

Hindu minds still retain a robust naïvete about regarding the sensual as a more or less translucent veneer of the divine. This is manifested in all sorts of ways, some of which we have noted. But we must include in this epiphany the fulsome figures of the gods and goddesses populating temple facades or their terraced roofs, or housed in temple or domestic shrines. Wander about the tangled lanes of Kumartuli, the icon-making locality of Calcutta, for example. There, most of the year round, you can follow in the dank gloom of workshop after workshop the skilful emergence from its rough frame of straw and dark clay to its final painted, gorgeously apparelled, sensual form, the image of the god or goddess to be worshipped at some forthcoming festival. It has been claimed that the voluptuous aspect of the Hindu icon signifies the expansive influence of the spirit or *ātman* within. Perhaps. But it signifies no less the traditional Hindu idea of well-being, physical health and joy of life, an idea which continues to find its material expression in the mortal frames of those surrogate gods and goddesses of another popular pantheon, that of the Indian film-star.

I do not deny that there have always been world-denying trends in Hinduism, especially in the more cerebral religions of the 'high' tradition. Thus the philosophical theology of the monistic Advaita Vedānta tends to exalt an ascetic ideal according to which *pravṛtti* or a positive spiritual assessment of the world is denigrated in favour of *nivṛtti* or the path of withdrawal from the world (this has been allowed to unduly represent 'Hindu spirituality' for many westerners). In this perspective the reality of the world is deceptively evanescent, and devotion to God is a stepping-stone to a higher vision in which all (including divine) individuality dissolves, and only the pure, homogeneous Being of *Brahman*, the One, remains. In the way of the Christian Desert Fathers of old, the world and its symbol the body are viewed largely as the source of spiritual delusion and disaster. Here is a statement from the *Vivekacūḍāmaṇi*, a medieval and important Advaita Vedantic text, which encapsulates its normative perspective:

> Having realised the Form that is Being and untainted Awareness and Bliss, keep far away this (other) siren-form (i.e. the body), which is vile and senseless. Remember it no more; what's vomited out and then brought to mind can only repel.
>
> (v.414)

This is not to say that it is not characteristic of most traditions of Hinduism to teach that *pravṛtti* must be balanced by *nivṛtti*. It is a question of emphasis, and later Advaita Vedānta overwhelmingly emphasises *nivṛtti* at the expense of *pravṛtti*. Further, it must also be admitted that there are many traditional (Sanskritic) myths which denigrate sex and sensibility as a positive symbol of spiritual realities. These have had a pervasive effect on Hindus. But on the whole, largely through the impetus of the various *bhakti* movements in history, an ethical *pravṛtti* has a central place in Hindu spirituality. In the Hindu family of religions its role is sometimes dominant, sometimes recessive – depending on cult, phase of life, individual temperament – but it has always made its presence felt so that if the popular judgement that Hinduism is a world-denying religion is true, it is true in no obvious sense. In general, the Hindu attitude to the body and matter is an ambivalent one, with positive and negative sides. But there *is* a positive side to this tension, and it is a vibrant one.[15]

For the reflective person however, images are not enough. Their significance calls for interpretation through the process of critical analysis, and it is the job of the philosopher and the theologian to give the lead in this respect. Hence the thinking traditions of Hinduism have always given careful attention to the role of reason in religion. In his commentary on the *Bhagavadgītā* 18.66, Śaṃkara speaks representatively for Hindu philosophical theologians when he sketches out the relationship between faith and reason thus:

> The cognitive authority (*prāmāṇya*) of scripture (*śruti*) applies not to the objects of perception and other (sources of empirical knowledge) but to objects not known from such sources, such as the practice and fruit of the *Agnihotra* sacrifice and so on. For the cognitive authority of scripture concerns the vision of things unseen. . . . Even if a hundred scriptural utterances were to say that fire is cold or that it is not bright they would have no cognitive authority. If scripture were to say such things we would have to assume that it intended some other sense, else we would be understanding its cognitive authority amiss. For such utterances cannot be understood either as opposed to the other authoritative sources of knowledge or to their own true purport.

In short, it is not the business of scripture to challenge the evidence of the senses, inference, etc.; nor is it the business of such knowledge to challenge the scope of scripture, whose cognitive authority 'concerns the vision of things unseen'. With regard to our knowledge of the world, Śaṃkara is a realist; it is on this basis that he attacked the epistemology of the Mahāyāna Buddhists. The common supposition that Śaṃkara taught that the world is an illusion is a much too superficial reading of this thought. For Śaṃkara, the world is as real as we are; only the fabric of worldly reality of which we are an integral part has no ultimate reality status. We shall have more to say about Śaṃkara later. Here we make the point that, like Hindu thinkers in general, he was careful to distinguish the cognitive scope of scripture from the cognitive scope of empirical experience.

Scripture teaches us about verities outside the scope of empirical experience – about the existence and nature of the ultimate reality, about our relationship to it, about our relationship to one another in the light of the transcendent, about what happens after death, about beings beyond this world, about the other-worldly effects of religious observance, and so on. This is not to say that reason plays no important part in this understanding. It does. In his great teaching to his wife Maitreyī about the path to immortality, the Sage Yājñavalkya insists that the Spirit (*Ātman*) which underlies and validates all that we hold dear in life – spouse, offspring, social status, wealth, indeed everything – 'must be intuited, heard-about-and-listened-to, reflected upon and contemplated'. Only then will everything fall into place (*BĀUp* II.4.5). The journey of faith leading towards ultimate realisation necessarily includes reflection (*manana*), that is, the critical use of reason. Such advice echoes throughout Hinduism and was generally upheld by thinkers. Anyone who has read in the long history of Hindu philosophical theology and philosophy of religion will be clear about this. Reason has been called upon to substantiate faith, purify it of superstition, mark out its limits, render it plausible, refute opposing points of view (both religious and non-religious), and to provide justification for a critical commitment. How successful rationality has been in fulfilling this role during its chequered career in the various Hindu traditions is open to question. Thus we have seen that Ram Mohan Roy used rational argument to try and purge his ancestral faith of what he regarded as superstition. In debate, his Hindu opponents claimed equally to have used reason to demonstrate reason's rational limitations in defence of many of the same so-called superstitions.[16]

One rationality or more in Sanskritic Hinduism? One, at least in this respect that Hindu religious thinkers have largely maintained, at least implicitly, that reason and faith exist in a complementary relationship, that both are culture-conditioned functions, that there is no such thing as 'pure' reason; that is, a rationality that has not been nurtured within a particular perspective on the meaning of life which has itself conditioned the application of that rationality. Practical rationality is a conditioned thing.[17]

Thus on the foundational religious issue of whether an ultimate transcendent reality or god exists ('*Brahman*'), the Vedantic thinkers were quite representative when they argued that the existence of *Brahman* cannot be 'proved' by some process of pure reasoning. To argue that an omnipotent Being exists on the grounds, say, that it is the cause of the world, is to assume that the world as a whole is an 'effect' in the first place, and on what other than circular grounds can one assume that? And even if it were agreed that the world is an effect, could one argue from this to an *omnipotent* first cause, rather than to an indefinite hierarchy of causes, each member of the hierarchy being causally superior to its predecessor but never leading to an omnipotent first cause? No, they concluded. By this they implied that the plausibility of rational 'proofs' for the existence of *Brahman* is itself tradition-conditioned. One is properly apprised of the existence of *Brahman* as the origin, sustaining power and end of all things only on the basis of what scripture reveals. And the role of reason in this perception is to make that perception critically coherent from within and to justify it against other perceptions from its self-evaluating point of view.

This may prompt the objection that the later Naiyāyikas sought to prove the existence of an all-powerful God – not indeed a God who creates *ex nihilo* but a God who fashions the world from pre-existent matter – and that they claimed to have succeeded not on the basis of scriptural teaching but from arguments of universal or pure reason. Is not this the burden of the fifth chapter of the tenth-century logician, Udayana's, famous *Nyāya-kusumāñjali*? Not quite. All of Udayana's arguments rely, more or less explicitly, on tradition-specific assumptions to make their points. These assumptions include premisses affirming the pre-existence of material atoms from which *Īśvara*, or the deity, fashioned the world, the existence and infallibility of the Veda, the existence of the law of karma, and so on. And closer scrutiny of the Nyāya tradition in general makes it clear that the logicians made no claims for a universal reason and that, on the contrary, they were aware that the rational arguments they used had force only within a particular religio-cultural framework.

The Naiyāyikas knew perfectly well that some of their rational assumptions were acceptable only to those who shared the relevant views of their own particular tradition (e.g. the premiss that there were pre-existent material atoms was acceptable to the Vaiśeṣikas but not to either the Vedāntins or the Buddhists), while the rest were acceptable only to those within the Sanskritic–Brahminic framework of belief in the first instance (e.g. the authority of the Vedas was accepted by the Vedāntins but not by the Buddhists). Any other interpretation of their logic would render them philosophically naïve in the extreme, and they were certainly not that.[18] To revert to our example, the rationality of the arguments propounded by Udayana was an in-house rationality to some extent and a 'Sanskritic' rationality in general. It was not meant to be an exercise in 'pure' reason. And this characterises Hindu perception of the role of reason *vis-à-vis* faith at its best.

At its 'not-so-good', religious Hinduism has always had its share of unsophisticated literalists who are unresponsive to the moderating voice of reason. These literalists have sought uncritically, or cynically, to transplant ideas from the past into the present. A good example of this is the evocation in recent times of the *rāma-rājya* (Rule of Rama) idea derived from Vālmīki's *Rāmāyaṇa* (see Chapter 4) in connection with the so-called Ram-janma-bhumi/Babri-masjid affair. This concerns a conflict between Hindus and Muslims over the supposed birthplace of Rāma situated in close proximity to where a mosque stood in the city of Ayodhya.[19] It is ironic that a concept originally meant to express harmonious coexistence between humans and nature under the benign rule of Rāma, and which was in modern times carefully reinterpreted by Gandhi to encourage Hindus and Muslims to live together in amity, has become a leading element in a conception of *hindutva* ('Hinduness') which is intolerant *especially* of Muslim identity and presence.

We will not pursue this issue here. Let us return instead to our contention that it is distinctive of the Hindu intellectual tradition at its best to appreciate the conditioned nature of rationality. In this appreciation faith and reason condition one another mutually. One supports the other, not indeed in circular fashion (because there is no general tendency to 'prove' that faith depends on reason for its plausibility, or vice versa, in a question-begging way), but as an inescapable feature of the human condition. By this it was implied that the empiricist or the rationalist also could adopt their stance only on the basis of a similar faith interpretation of the world in which they lived. In other words, to say that only empirical or rational evidence is valid while religious belief lacks self-sustaining validity, is itself a view based on a faith stance about the kind of evidence that is acceptable in the first place. In fact, the rationality of one's religious faith is sustained by faith in one's rationality. One cannot perch on some rationally 'neutral' vantage-point so as to arbitrate on the truth of belief systems. This brings us to the way in which Hindus tend to understand the nature of truth, and by extension, to their appreciation of religious tolerance.

II

Truth. Truth and tolerance. The meaning of satya/sat. *Truth as conditioned. Truth and myth: an illustration. The pursuit of truth in the tradition. Gandhi's understanding of truth (*satyāgraha *and* ahiṃsā*). Orthopraxy and orthodoxy. The transmission of authority and truth: guru and disciple. Meaning of* guru. *The guru–disciple relationship: ideal and reality. Ramana Maharshi. Finding the guru. Images, qualifications and forms of the guru.*

For most religious Hindus, religious truth is truth in a sense not deviant from the use of the word in empirical judgements. This means that when the Vaiṣṇava asserts, for example, that it is true that Viṣṇu is Lord of the world, that it is true that the Scriptures teach us the way to salvation, that it is true that the law of karma and rebirth governs our lives, that the *Bhagavadgītā*'s analysis of the human condition is true, he or she is using the word 'true' in a sense that overlaps with the meaning given to the term when ordinary people claim that their empirical judgements are true. This is what the religious use of 'true' in Hinduism has in common with the secular use of 'true'. It is not the case that the religious meaning of 'true' in Hindu tradition is quite out of touch with the term's everyday meaning. One often comes across statements to the effect that 'truth' in (religious) Hinduism is a purely relative concept and that Hindus understand better than most that what one believes to be true religiously is an entirely subjective matter; that consequently Hindus advocate a 'believe-what-you-want' mentality where religious belief is concerned. 'It does not matter what you believe', they are supposed to say, 'what matters is how you believe. Believe sincerely and believe what you want. It's not worth arguing over. One view is as true as the next and leads to salvation just as effectively.' This is then vaunted as the Hindu ideal of religious tolerance, an ideal that members of all religious traditions would do well to follow.

As a description of what Hindus tend to mean by religious truth, this view is quite perversely at variance with the evidence of history and does scant justice to the often sustained, sometimes bitter doctrinal controversies which have been waged down the centuries not only among Hindus themselves but also between 'Hindus' and 'non-Hindus' (such as the Jains and Buddhists). Here is how Rāmānuja characterises the Advaitic position to which he was vigorously opposed:

> This view has been fabricated by means of various illogical and vicious arguments which cannot stand the test of sound reasoning, by those who lack the distinction of those virtues which bring down the blessings of the supreme Person of the Upaniṣads. Their whole minds have been infected by a residue of beginningless sin so that the nature of words and sentences and their proper meaning, as also the ways of correct reasoning which prescribe what one must do on the basis of the sources of knowledge like perception etc., are quite unknown to them. As such this view is to be scorned by those who know the truth (*yāthātmyavid*) on the basis of the texts and the various sources of knowledge supported by reasoning.[20]

Little tolerance is shown here, and there are many similar indictments from other authorities as a feature of their quest for religious truth. In fact for most Hindus, the pursuit of truth is regarded as an existential matter, in which the whole person is involved. No doubt truth has a propositional dimension. This is what is meant by saying that Hindus use the word 'true' in a religious context in a sense not deviant from its use in empirical judgements. The propositional side may be emphasised in some contexts more than in others, e.g. in the stating of facts. But Hindus have always understood that the existential dimension of truth cannot be divorced from propositional truth. Whenever something is perceived to be true, even when its 'propositional truth' is emphasised, the existential asserts itself in so far as what is perceived to be true demands to be acknowledged as such by the perceiver in sincerity and goodwill. Where the truth is given its due in this way the perceiver acts in good faith, and becomes worthy of praise as a person of integrity. Where truth is culpably not given its due, by evasion or prevarication or dissembling, the person concerned is in 'bad faith' and becomes worthy of censure as lacking in integrity. This is how the existential dimension of truth takes on a moral character. It is for this reason that Rāmānuja's statement has an implied *moral* condemnation. It is characteristic of the pre-modern mentality to assume that the dissenter against one's own view is in bad faith, that he or she *culpably* refuses to believe what, with suitable effort, can be perceived to be 'the truth' – the truth of one's own point of view, of course. And when truth is pursued in a *religious* framework, its existential–moral dimension is emphasised, for the goal here is soteriological: that is, the ultimate well-being of the individual is at stake. This is why the pursuit of truth in religion can become a passionate affair, and quite personal at times, as the quotation from Rāmānuja illustrates.

What I have tried to do here is to analyse the underlying rationale of the way that Hindus have tended traditionally to understand truth in religion, a rationale which accounts for the fact that, all along in its Sanskritic context – down to the present day – the same word, *satya* (or *sat*), has meant both truth and being or reality.[21] Not only in the Sanskritic but also, I suspect, in the Hindu psyche at large, this term evokes simultaneously propositional, personal and moral connotations, analytically separable but semantically unitary in the way discussed.

This synthetic understanding of truth has ancient roots. Here is an example of its religious use from the *Śatapatha* Brāhmaṇa (1.1.1.4): 'This (world) is twofold: there is no third; there is truth and untruth (*satyaṃ caivānṛtam ca*). Now the *deva*s are truth, humans untruth. So when one says, "I go from untruth to truth" one goes from humans to the *deva*s.' The context is the sacrificial ritual, the bridge from this conditioned and fragile life to the blissful immortality represented and enjoyed by the *deva*s. The idea was that during the ritual, the sacrificer received a foretaste of immortality in the life to come by sharing in the nature and company of the *deva*s. So the text goes on to tell sacrificers that they should speak the truth because then they will become like the gods.[22]

This text gives a clue to understanding a famous prayer found in the *Bṛhadāraṇyaka* Upaniṣad (I.3.28) which belongs to the samc Yajurvedic school as the *Śatapatha* Brāhmaṇa. The prayer runs:

> From untruth/the unreal (*asat*) lead me to the truth/real (*sat*), from the darkness lead me to the light, from death lead me to immortality.[23]

It has been shown that this prayer has been inserted into the Upaniṣad from Sāmavedic sources where it was originally used in the context of the Agniṣṭoma sacrifice.[24] The Upaniṣad gives it a more general invocatory role than it originally seems to have had. Be that as it may, it is a popular invocation in public functions in India today, and not only among Hindus.[25] On these occasions the words *asat* and *sat* may be translated in terms of either truth or being, implying that truth tends to have an existential dimension in the Indian mind. Old roots in the Ancient Banyan continue to produce green leaves. India has much to live up to in its official Sanskrit motto: *satyam eva jayate*, i.e. 'Truth [namely, speaking and living the truth] alone prevails'.

But in so far as the pursuit of truth is, or must be, a rational process, and in so far as rationality is perceived to be conditioned by various factors, one's grasp of truth is itself understood to be conditioned. Absolute or unconditioned truth, which is how the transcendent or God has sometimes been characterised in Hindu tradition, is not something that can be understood by the human mind, which is itself conditioned. Thus Hindu thinkers tend to regard the propositional grasp of truth – i.e. saying *what* is true – as necessarily partial and relative to one's perspective and circumstances. This makes the propositional grasp of truth in a particular situation provisional and continuously susceptible to modification and enlargement.

The way that myths reveal to the Hindu how truth can be grasped only partially and relatively will help to explain this. We have pointed out more than once the pervasiveness of myths and myth-making throughout religious Hinduism. Indeed, Hindu mythology is like an ancient banyan tree itself, inhabiting the whole phenomenon that we call religious Hinduism, the distinction between root-myths and branch-myths often blurred. Thus the life-sap and imagery of one myth system flows through or mingles with those of another, the whole tangled structure held together, not by the *same* mythic elements from end to end, but by a staggered process of overlapping, blending and resemblance between elements of one myth system and those of another, a process which characterises all the parts as parts of the same whole. Indeed, each salient myth system can be likened to the Ancient Banyan in so far as it is a sprawling conglomerate of different micro-centres (each generating a religious atmosphere of its own) organically unified, in the staggered way described above, by particular mythic elements (symbols, ideas, story-lines and variants of story-lines), and interacting with other micro-centres of the whole network.

It must be emphasised that by 'myth' we do not mean the word's degenerate but common meaning of 'fabrication' or 'fable'. 'Myth' in this context means 'a vehicle of enactment for individual or community through living symbols of story or narrative'. In other words, through myths or myth systems the individual and community are enabled, sometimes in paradoxical or cathartic ways, to participate (enact and re-enact), often by means of liturgy and ritual, in constructed sequences of events (story or narrative) inhabited by forms and figures – human or non-human, animate or inanimate (living symbols) – which represent good and evil, right and wrong, purity and pollution, life and death, etc. Through (re-)enactment of myth, individual and community can come to terms with a developing social and religious identity often in changing circumstances which threaten the security deriving from traditional perceptions, customs and behaviour patterns. Myths imply assumptions, evaluations, attitudes and assertions about reality and life in the world which define the self-image, ideals and goals of individual and community. In so far as they contain assertions about the nature of being (including human beings, the transcendent/God, salvation, etc.) they make truth claims and have a truth content.

It is important to note that in myths this truth content remains to be teased out by rational analysis. It often exists in contradictory, paradoxical or dialectical form in the tangled narrative skein of the myth system. Consider, for example, myths about Śiva. Śiva myths are characterised by the fact that some depict him as ascetic, others as erotic, and yet others as both. Not only the ordinary Śiva follower but the ordinary Hindu knows this. They know that Śiva is depicted in his mythology as an 'erotic ascetic' (though they may not quite put it this way).[26] This depiction takes place verbally and visually (e.g. iconographically). For example, in what has been called the myth of the pine forest, Śiva attempts to seduce the wives of ascetics practising their austerities there. He appears on the scene in the form of a provocative naked holy-man (the erotic aspect), hair matted, and body smeared with ashes from the cremation ground (the ascetic aspect). One interpretation claims that Śiva was actually trying to test the purity and singlemindedness of both sages and their wives. According to a variant of the myth, it is the wives who try to seduce Śiva. A number of layers of meaning historically, psychologically, sociologically, theologically – about the relationship between the divine and the human, between conflicting forces within us, between ascetic and non-ascetic, between priest (i.e. the Brahmin redactors of the myth) and ascetic (the sages, who represent a non-sacrificial, other-worldly ideal) etc. – can be and have been read into this myth system, for it has variants and a history.[27] Depending on the extent of knowledge of this myth, as well as individual circumstances and insight, the Hindu must try to analyse and understand the story with reference to his or her life, by ranging over the different levels and implications.

At the same time the Hindu is likely to be aware of a number of other ascetic/erotic mythic representations of Śiva. Consider one of the best known iconographic representations: Śiva as 'Lord of the Dance' (*Śiva Naṭarāja*). Perhaps the most famous depiction of Śiva in this role is of him poised dynamically on his right foot on a little human figure (known as *Muyalaka*) symbolising darkness and delusion, his left foot upraised and his four arms in various poses. The ascetic and the erotic features in this portrayal are largely implicit. Among the erotic we may include the dance itself (symbolising the dance of creation) and the serpent coiled about Śiva's person (symbolising fertility), while the ascetic features include the skull in Śiva's (usually matted) hair and the ring of flames framing his form (the fires of destruction), and perhaps the flame in his upper left hand (the flame that consumes or purifies?). The meaning derived from the *Śiva Naṭarāja* role will have to be integrated, on various levels, not least the rational, with Śiva's role in the myth of the pine forest. And so it continues in the context of a plethora of Śiva myths and representations available.

By his erotic behaviour Śiva symbolises, among other things, the fertile and super-abundant creativity of the deity in multi-faceted immanent relationship with the world; by his asceticism Śiva symbolises (through the concept of *tapas* or ascetic heat) the transcendent brooding power of the godhead not only to destroy all things by the periodic dissolutions of the world but to renew all things by a discharge of *tapas*. As the erotic ascetic, Śiva simultaneously symbolises not only the deity's power to create and to destroy, to sustain and to renew, to draw and to repel, but also the truth that these divine functions coexist in our lives and in the world under different guises. Further, this multi-faceted divine action is usually portrayed in a particular myth system by variant myths of one theme. The 'whole truth' which Śiva symbolises, then, must be pieced together from partial insights yielded by different myths and their variants in a composite, paradoxical picture continually being developed and modified through interrelation with the believer's variegated experience of life in the world. Sometimes the signals given by a myth appear contradictory, i.e. not amenable to rational synthesis. In recognising logic's limits, reason allows deeper recesses of the believer to envelop and be enveloped by the myth in an apprehension of reality in which there is at least an implicit realisation that truth can be systematically elusive in important ways.

In fact, in the pervasive context of myth, Hindus realise, by the process of acculturation which is so distinctive of the way they grow into their religion, that religious truth about the world or God or our relationship with God must be pieced together in a provisional manner. In other words, Hindus realise that our grasp of religious truth must be relative and partial. For most Hindus, this is an 'instinctive', more or less implicit, realisation. Acculturation can do no more. It is left to reflection and the philosophical–theological tradition to tease this realisation out, to seek to articulate it in particular contexts and in the form of particular theories as coherently as possible; this may happen with varying degrees of success. If, perhaps one should say, *as*, Hindus lose touch with their mythic heritage, their instinctive understanding of truth as partial and provisional will be greatly impoverished and this will have serious repercussions for their capacity to tolerate a wide variety of religious beliefs.

In order to preserve the mythic mentality it is not necessary to single out myths or to invent some and then attempt to infuse life into these stories by some artificial process – a devised ritual or celebration perhaps.[28] Religious myths do not survive this way. Their vitality is an aspect of the vitality of the religious tradition in which they are rooted; indeed, they are a source of religious vitality. A living myth can, for one reason or another, wither and die, or it can be revitalised in a new form, or continue from strength to strength in its old structure. The life-course of a particular myth is unpredictable, but it is bound up with the vitality of the mythic mentality of which it is an expression. I am not making a plea for the preservation of any particular myths or myth systems. It is the Hindu mythic mentality as such, in so far as it bears on the understanding of religious truth, that I am analysing – and celebrating. Whether this mythic mentality will last or wither, and where and how, remains to be seen.[29]

From our analysis of the way Hindu myths tend to function, we may regard the pursuit of religious truth in Hindu tradition paradigmatically as assimilative and open-ended. It is assimilative because, on the basis of the acknowledgement that one's grasp of propositional truth is provisional, it proceeds by *incorporating* 'alien' insights in terms of the complex thought structure of the receptor system. During this digestive process (which may be more or less integrated and more or less consistent), the 'alien' insights are likely to undergo transformation so as to be rendered compatible with the assimilative processes – the relevant assumptions, ideas, feelings, attitudes, myths, etc. – at work on them. Thus 'provisional' does not necessarily mean 'totally relativistic'. Provisional truth may still be adhered to as truth, as something illuminating a life or situation and, as such, worth adhering to while the assimilative process continues. At the same time, however, the receptor system itself is liable to change in relevant ways (some of which may be far-reaching) in the process of accommodation. The result of this mutual transformation cannot be predicted, because at each stage of the interaction a new synthesis of understanding emerges which must be tested for its truth value in and through the living, ongoing situation in which the individual, and the community of which the individual is a part, finds itself. This is how the Hindu view of truth ideally tends to be inherently open-ended.

Error, then, tends to become the untoward blocking or closing up of truth's natural momentum towards wider perceptions. This happens by mistaking the part for the whole in some way, either by concentrating unduly on the part (so that there is no larger perspective) or by taking the part out of the context of the whole.[30] Wrongdoing is culpable error, more or less deliberate in a more or less serious cause. As such it is the (more or less) conscious thwarting of truth's claims on one to be existentially open to it; that is, to be open in mind and heart to where one's honest search for truth may lead.

Gandhi, for one, understood this very well, and sought relentlessly to implement this understanding in his life. It is no accident that he entitled his autobiography *The Story of my* ***Experiments*** *with Truth* (emphasis added). The title must not be interpreted as a trivialisation of the quest for truth, as if truth is something to be trifled with by experimentation. On the contrary, as a study of his life will show, Gandhi was a most serious searcher after truth, at times exposing himself to misunderstanding, disgrace, and even death in the process. For Gandhi truth was something not only to be sought by the intellect but also to be lived, its provisional grasp at any one time the basis of a continuous exploration – hence the title of his autobiography – of its receding boundaries. The chief vehicle of this exploration was his action concept of '*satyāgraha*'. *Satyāgraha* means literally 'the laying hold of truth/reality', but for Gandhi it meant both 'laying hold of the truth to the best of one's ability' and 'truth's laying hold of one through the quality of one's life'. The more truth is allowed to grow in one in this integral way, the more one's grasp of the truth is enlarged to embrace other insights and perspectives in a vision which *under-stands* and seeks the welfare of the whole world. It is for this reason that Gandhi saw his other action concept of *ahiṃsā* (active benevolence towards all) as an integral part of truth-seeking, as the other side of *satyāgraha*. There is no room in this view for easy recourse to violence to settle differences, for such violence humiliates the victim and degrades the oppressor; there is no victor in the end.

One of Gandhi's chief contributions to the modern religious Hindu's self-understanding and search for truth is the assumption, to be built into one's religious quest, that the dissenter maintains his or her own point of view not out of bad faith – the traditional, pre-modern stance – but in good faith; that is, that unless there are clear reasons to the contrary, the dissenter acts and believes out of motives as sincere as one's own. Further, this assumption implies that the dissenter's view has a validity that one must try to understand and respond to sensitively. Thus the search for truth becomes a shared quest, based on mutual understanding and respect, notwithstanding differences that may remain. Gandhi's understanding of truth is a classic modern example of the way the underlying trends of what we have analysed as the ideal Hindu perception of truth converge. For Gandhi, the pursuit of truth was at the same time a path to salvation, the healing experience of which began along the way. So he preferred to say 'Truth is God' rather than 'God is Truth'. All believe in truth, he said, but not all believe in God.[31]

Because most Hindus have been instinctively trained by their tradition(s) to inject a dose of healthy relativism into their perception of the truth, they have acquired a reputation of showing tolerance in the sphere of dogma and creed. To be sure, this 'tolerance' is often an expression of indifference or reluctance to sift for truth, or of believing one thing and saying another in a misguided effort to please (Gandhi was hardly like that).[32] Or again, among the westernised, or partially westernised, this tolerance is sometimes an undiscerning acceptance of some view attributed to a modern teacher or movement. Thus to Ramakrishna, the nineteenth-century Sage, is attributed the saying that there are as many paths to salvation as there are points of view ('*jata mat tata path*', runs the Bengali jingle), and many profess to sympathise with this dictum, although on closer inspection some of his present followers can be seen to be advocating a quite definite path to liberation.[33] Ramakrishna himself was no philosopher, so that pronouncements he allegedly made should not be taken out of context.[34] All this notwithstanding, a genuine doctrinal tolerance, namely, a tolerance based on the view that one can learn from others and that one's religious stance is worth struggling for and adhering to but not killing for, is noticeable throughout traditional religious Hinduism.

The same Rāmānuja who inveighed against Advaita quotes with approval the following *smṛti*-text: 'Sāṃkhya, Yoga, the Vedas, Pañcarātra, Pāśupata – these are sources for knowing the Spirit; they are not to be dismissed by [hostile] argumentation.' In other words, one must acknowledge that these different traditions have something to teach about spiritual reality. But, Rāmānuja implies, that something can make sense only within the framework of his own position. Thus Sāṃkhya doctrine about the existence and nature of *prakṛti* and individual souls is acceptable only in so far as it can be accommodated into Rāmānuja's overview that Viṣṇu-Nārāyaṇa, the ultimate reality of his system, ensouls and rules all being. (Note the assimilative nature of this acceptance.) It is on his terms, then, that Rāmānuja is prepared to tolerate rival religious traditions.[35] Thus there *were* sticking points to his doctrinal tolerance.

In formulating their religious vision, some modern Hindus have given the impression of a more wide-ranging tolerance. Radhakrishnan, for example, has sought to accommodate most of the major religious traditions in his world view. But the assimilative (and not so open-ended) nature of his account soon becomes evident, for Radhakrishnan grades religious experience in a hierarchy headed by Advaitic experience (scripturally most authoritatively expressed, he declares, in the classical Upaniṣads), on the assumption that genuine religious experience finds its culmination in Advaita.[36]

Although Hindus were traditionally noted for their doctrinal tolerance they have not been perceived as tolerant in the practice of their religion. Hindus have always been far more rigid with respect to orthopraxy ('doing the right thing/behaving in the accredited way') than orthodoxy ('believing the right doctrine(s)'). We have indicated as much in the context of caste-*dharma*. This has applied not only to the upper castes, who have a vested interest in maintaining caste hierarchy, but also to the lower castes and even untouchables who have either sought to reinforce the hierarchical structure by attempts at Sanskritisation, or who have accepted it under the weight of centuries of despairing acquiescence. With the rise of the Dalit movement (see Chapter 5) and its ideology of 'counter-culture' – counter to Brahminic and Sanskritic Hinduism, that is – on the one hand, and the attempts of latter-day fundamentalists to define some homogenising essence of Hinduism on the other, this situation is changing. We await the outcome.

Orthopraxic intolerance is also manifest in Hinduism's reluctance to allow access to temples, especially their inner precincts, not only to untouchables[37] but also to those designated as non-Hindus (e.g. westerners). This is done on the grounds that the offerings to the deities will be rendered impure. One still comes across signs in and about temples warning that only Hindus may enter. The fact that foreigners are thus barred from access (sometimes in spite of protestations that they are 'converts' or sympathisers), is a clear sign that subliminally at least there is still a tendency to regard racial and cultural origin as criterial for what it is to be a Hindu. It must be said, however, that many Hindus – as opposed to ideologues and many temple authorities – welcome foreigners to participate in their festivals and other forms of worship. No doubt it is also the case that this official stand-offishness is the legacy of over-zealous colonials lampooning those 'much-maligned monsters',[38] 'the grotesque idols of the heathen'. But Hindu self-confidence, and western sensibilities for that matter, have come a long way since the Raj. Perhaps religious Hinduism can afford to slip the bonds of history in this regard.

In trying to fathom the voice of personal experience in the Hindu's religious life, we have had occasion to discuss a number of central ideas, including those of sense and sensibility, faith and reason, myth, truth and error, tolerance and intolerance. There is one final component of this voice that we must now consider: the significance of the guru.

The word 'guru' must be understood in its core sense. In order to get to this sense consider the following extract from the *Mahābhārata*. The narrator is eulogising his God, whom he describes as

> the primeval Person, sovereign . . . the True . . . *Brahman*, the manifest and unmanifest, the Eternal, being and becoming, All-pervasive, yet beyond being and becoming, the Maker of high and low, the Ancient . . . pure . . . Hṛṣīkeśa, Hari, *the Guru of that which moves and moves not*.[39]

At first sight, this seems a curious use of the term 'guru'. But in fact it takes us to the heart of the matter. Literally, 'guru' means 'weighty', 'heavy'. Perhaps it is clearer now why, seemingly as a high point of this paean of praise, the Lord is described as the Guru of all being. He is the mainstay, the unshakeable centre, the spiritual weight around which everything gravitates. So, to take up its popular meaning, the guru is an authoritative 'heavy' (in the most positive sense!) in one's life. In traditional Sanskrit literature, the elders of the community, including one's parents as the elders of the community that is the family, are often called gurus. In this context, when the text wishes to record approval of some individual, he or she is commended for their *guru-śuśrūṣā,* i.e. attentiveness to the elders – those to whom a debt of gratitude, service and reverence is owed for their guidance, nurture, stabilising influence, protection, and personal warmth.

In Chapter 4 we discussed the role of the guru as teacher and guide in the traditional context of *brahmacarya* or celibate studentship. We noted that the guru is to be deferred to as the 'spiritual father' of the person under his care. The student was supposed to respond with attentive service (*śuśrūṣā*), not servility. In the Sanskritic tradition, one is never servile towards a parent. On the contrary, the parent–child relationship (especially the mother–infant relationship) is one of tenderness, even of affectionate familiarity, notwithstanding the obligation to show respect and obedience to one's parents throughout life. A dominant image of this relationship is expressed by the term *vātsalya*, which means literally the tender and protective love that the cow shows to her calf (*vatsa*). In fact, the guru often addresses the disciple by the endearment, *vatsa*, 'child'.[40]

Thus the disciple may show deference to the guru, but servility is out of place. Indeed, one of the chief functions of the guru in the traditional guru–disciple relationship has been to encourage the disciple in a discipline of critical questioning on spiritual matters. A famous work entitled *Upadeśa Sāhasrī* (Teachings a-thousandfold), ascribed, in part mistakenly it appears, to Ṣaṃkara[41] records a conversation between the guru and his disciple in which the latter questions his teacher searchingly about ultimate truth and value.[42] The implication is that spiritual growth takes place through searching enquiry at the feet of the guru. One must sit at the guru's lotus-feet, as the saying goes, but not grovel before them.

Gradually, as the tradition developed, in the eyes of many service turned into servility, a servility expected and a servility willingly offered, so that today in Hinduism generally, it seems that it is unquestioning obedience to the guru that dominates the guru–disciple relationship. A sense of mutual responsibility seems to be lacking: responsibility on the guru's part to train the disciple in spiritual independence, and responsibility on the disciple's part to grow in this training. I believe that abrogation of responsibility in this way runs counter to the best traditions of the guru–disciple relationship.

But it need not be so. A well-known example of a modern guru living up to his responsibility of encouraging critical spiritual inquiry is Ramana Maharshi (1879–1950). Venkataram Aiyar, as he was originally called, was a Tamilian who at the age of 17 underwent a transforming experience in which his body seemed to die and fall away from his 'true self' or 'I' which he identified with the ultimate, deathless Spirit. The impact of this experience never left him. Soon he went to live the life of a renouncer on the sacred hill of Arunachala, near the town of Tiruvannamalai. In time disciples gathered and an ashram was founded. Ramana Maharshi never claimed to be a philosopher, but his religious vision, expressed unsystematically through conversations with disciples and an endless stream of visitors, is strongly Advaitic in tone. At the heart of these exchanges lay a central question which the enquirer was required to consider: 'Who am I?', that is, 'Who or what is the real I?' On the search for the answer depends the fulfilment of one's life.[43]

How does one come by a guru? This can happen in various ways. Sometimes the guru is 'inherited', that is, the person who acts as spiritual adviser to one's parents or family members automatically becomes one's own guide. Or if the sect to which one belongs has fixed procedures for appointing its spiritual guide, one may not have a choice in the matter.[44] In this case it may not be easy to develop a deep personal relationship with one's guru. In many sects or denominations there is a *guru-paraṃparā*, i.e. an official line of succession of spiritual preceptors. Some of these lines of succession stretch back (or are reputed to stretch back) many hundreds of years. It is often claimed that a particular *guru-paraṃparā* originates in some way with God or a representative (usually, but not always, in the distant past). This invests the teachings and institutional framework of the sect with inalienable authority, of course, although on occasion it is alleged, by breakaway groups, that this authority has been abused or the teachings distorted irremediably.

Sometimes the guru just arrives. Cometh the hour, cometh the guru; the guru seeks one out. This is how it was apparently with the Sage Ramakrishna during his spiritual development. Ramakrishna, the records say, had more than one guru, including a woman ascetic. The gurus who had the greatest influence on him sought him out at the appropriate time, instructed him, and eventually went their way. Thus one's spiritual preceptor can be a woman (women gurus are more in evidence in modern times), and one can have – not necessarily successively – more than one spiritual preceptor.

Although claims to the antiquity and/or divine origin of the guru's teaching tradition greatly enhance the guru's authority, the ultimate basis of this authority is spiritual experience. That is, the guru is to be deferred to because the guru is 'heavy' with spiritual wisdom. As such, if we may transpose metaphors, the guru, overwhelmed by compassionate love (*karuṇā, dayā*), gives birth, like a midwife, to spiritual experience in the disciple. The guru is often likened to a lamp which dispels the darkness of spiritual ignorance. Or the guru is described as the one who rouses the disciple from sleep (the sleep of spiritual unknowing). Or again, he or she is like the bee, gathering the honey of knowledge from the flowers of the Scriptures or sacred lore and feeding it to the disciple. The guru enables the disciple to progress towards the 'further shore' across the deceptive waters of life's stream (*saṃsāra*). And it is distinctive of the guru to be able to communicate inner peace and spiritual teaching to the disciple in a way appropriate to the latter's particular circumstances. This is called the skilful use of means. Ideally then, the guru has a uniquely personal relationship with each disciple based on mutual trust.

Because of this personal relationship, one person's guru may be another's imposter. Trust in the guru is often so great that the voice of the guru is regarded by the disciple as the voice of God; indeed, the guru may be openly revered as the divine presence in bodily form. When this happens, (i) universal claims may be made on behalf of the guru, namely that he or she is a/the *Jagad-guru* ('World Guru') or *Sad-guru* (the 'True Guru'[45]); and (ii) all sorts of dangers arise, not least the prospect of the disciple's abandoning personal responsibility to the guru.

Often, in this state, to show their unquestioning devotion, disciples shower the guru with gifts, many of them quite futile. To be sure, the guru needs to live and may quite legitimately accept gifts in cash or kind to live moderately, especially if the guru has a family. But according to the best traditions the guru lives an austere life and discourages gifts that appear unsuitable to such a life-style.

Is the guru necessary for achieving spiritual enlightenment? There are different views on this; further, it depends on the form that the guru is perceived to take. In traditional Brahminic Hinduism the guru was deemed necessary for salvation. He – it was usually a male – was required to belong to a twice-born caste (preferably the Brahmin) to initiate the disciple into the study of scripture (including the Vedas) and into the Vedic way of life (*dharma*).[46] But as Hinduism diversified, it was not necessarily so, and there are instances in Hindu literature and practice of persons from non-twice-born castes acting as gurus for people of the upper castes, or of 'caste gurus' taking on members of low or out-castes as disciples (this is not uncommon in the Tantric tradition). A tendency developed to regard someone with proven spiritual wisdom as transcending the barriers of caste and sex. In modern times, this tendency is more apparent. In many cases the caste of either guru or disciple is not a decisive consideration; often the guru openly repudiates caste. Low castes and untouchables, however, tend to follow gurus of their own socio-religious strata, but there are many exceptions.

A Hindu might often think the guru necessary for enlightenment but then ascribe the role of guru, either additionally or substitutively, to non-human things. Thus scripture may be reckoned as the guru, teaching and guiding the disciple through a discipline of reflective study or meditation. Rāmānuja has declared more than once that the Scriptures love those who resort to them with a love greater than that of a hundred mothers and fathers. Others regard some inner voice, perhaps the voice of conscience, as their guru (Gandhi sometimes spoke of an inner voice guiding him).[47] This may have derived from the well-known Hindu idea that God dwells within one as the 'inner controller' (*antar-yāmin*).[48]

Whatever the emphasis or form it may take, the voice of experience is generally regarded by Hindus as indispensable for shaping one's religious orientation. Combined with the voices of scripture and tradition, it issues to each attentive Hindu an invitation to spiritual growth and fulfilment. In each case the constituent strains of this call will be different, depending on personal background, individual response and other particulars. We cannot speak generally here of 'the Hindu call' to religion. No doubt sectarian and other group allegiances will impose their stamp. But in the end, each must respond to a voice uniquely beckoning to him or her. What we have sought to do is to tease out some of the main features that go to make up this triune, polytonic summons.

Part II

Reason and morality

8 A story with a tail

I

> Dharma: *the second tension considered through a story: the dicing incident in the* Mahābhārata. *The story unfolds. Draupadī's question. Roles and responses. The story, a good illustration of Hindu narrative and its function as* pāṭha.

We will now return to *dharma*. We have already considered this action concept as embodying the tension between order and chaos. We have seen that ideally and practically, prescriptively and descriptively, this tension takes in the relationship between being and non-being, the sexes, *varṇa* and *jāti* (from Brahmin to untouchable) and purity and impurity. But as already noted, there is another tension in the Hindu understanding of *dharma* – that between chance and necessity on the natural level, and freedom and determinism on the human. We shall concentrate on the latter, and it will be instructive to do so by means of a story.

This is the tale of one of the best-known and important episodes of the *Mahābhārata* narrative (see Chapter 5). The episode appears in the second book of the epic, the *Sabhā Parvan* or Book of the Assembly Hall (*sabhā* = assembly hall, assembly), and is about a dicing match played between Duryodhana, the arrogant, ambitious eldest son of king Dhṛtarāṣṭra, who reigns from Hāstinapura, and law-minded Yudhiṣṭhira, Dhṛtarāṣṭra's nephew, eldest of the five Pāṇḍava brothers and regent of the adjoining Khāṇḍava territory with its seat at Indraprastha. Now for the story.[1]

There is sporadic and increasing rivalry and enmity between the Kaurava brothers and their cousins, the five Pāṇḍavas. This has led to the separation of the two sides and an unequal partitioning of the kingdom. The Pāṇḍavas take up residence in the smaller portion, the still wild Khāṇḍava tract, and the Kauravas continue to live in the main part of the territory with their blind father, Dhṛtarāṣṭra, as king. Both sides defer to Dhṛtarāṣṭra as the ruling patriarch of the lineage, and in fact although Dhṛtarāṣṭra is inordinately fond of his eldest son, he is conscious of his role as father figure and guardian to the Pāṇḍavas (the royal heirs of Pāṇḍu, who has already died).

A fabulous assembly hall has been built in Indraprastha for the Pāṇḍavas by Maya, an anti-god who is a renowned architect. It was common for ruling or noble houses to have an assembly hall. At the centre of this open-plan complex was an arena for the men of the family and their male associates; here they would find entertainment or discuss life. The women were allowed to be present in the hall (female entertainers and lackeys had access as a matter of course), but they were generally confined to an outer section, and were expected to be on their best behaviour. Yudhiṣṭhira was going to inaugurate the assembly hall, and himself for that matter, by holding a great and solemn Vedic ritual, the *rājasūya* sacrifice, where he intended to declare himself a sort of titular emperor of greater India. The reason for this is not made clear; perhaps we have an irony of the story-teller – we know how rulers of underdeveloped kingdoms sometimes seek to aggrandise themselves. Yudhiṣṭhira needs as many rulers of other kingdoms as possible to acknowledge, at least theoretically, his imperial claim. Helped by his brothers and, with some wile, by his cousin and well-wisher Kṛṣṇa Vāsudeva (whom later tradition but not yet the *Sabhā Parvan*[2] reveals to be the God of the *Gītā*), dozens of kings acquiesce in the sacrifice by offering tributes. The Kauravas and one or two other ruling houses are exempt because they are family. Duryodhana, as the eldest son of Dhṛtarāṣṭra, is invited to the occasion and, not very wisely, is placed in charge of collecting the tributes.

Duryodhana has a difficult time. Already at odds with his cousins, his stay at Indraprastha raises his animosity to fever pitch. To begin with, he is humiliated by some of the marvellous contrivances of the Pāṇḍavas' assembly hall. He falls into water thinking it is a crystal floor, and he bumps into crystal thinking it is empty air. The Pāṇḍavas and their court (including their joint wife, Draupadī) add insult to injury by witnessing his embarrassment and finding it very funny. To cap it all, Duryodhana fumes at the number of kings offering tributes and the fabulous wealth they bring.

With his maternal uncle Śakuni who had accompanied him, Duryodhana returns to Hāstinapur, consumed with resentment and envy. 'Fate (*daiva*), I think, is supreme' he says bitterly, 'and human effort pointless when I see such glorious wealth offered to Kuntī's son [Yudhiṣṭhira]' (2.43.32). But he does not really believe this, and neither does his scheming uncle Śakuni. Together they hatch a plan to topple Yudhiṣṭhira from his high place and replace him with Duryodhana. Not by battle, says Śakuni, for the Pāṇḍavas are too good at that (besides, all the tributary rulers would have to take their side), and not by upsetting their own allies, adds Duryodhana (most if not all of them were busy sending tribute to Yudhiṣṭhira). Śakuni suggests a dicing match.

> The Kaunteya [Yudhiṣṭhira] loves gambling but he doesn't know how to play . . . . But I'm expert at gambling, there's none like me on earth. Challenge the Kaunteya to a game of dice . . . and for sure I'll wrest his glorious kingdom and wealth for you, bull among men.
> (2.44.18–20)

So, under the guise of fate, namely the dicing match, they will attempt to manipulate fate to their advantage. But first they must win the approval of Dhṛtarāṣṭra. They approach the blind king.

Duryodhana complains eloquently to his father about how miserable he is at his cousin's rise to fame and his own eclipse. Śakuni and he suggest a dicing match to turn the tables. Dhṛtarāṣṭra is doubtful. First he wants to ask Vidura's opinion on the matter. Vidura is his illegitimate half-brother and also his counsellor. He has great wisdom, says Dhṛtarāṣṭra, 'for, putting *dharma* first, he's far-sighted enough to see what's best. He will surely say what's right for both parties' (2.45.41–2). Duryodhana does not like this at all; he knows that Vidura will disapprove and he wants to put himself first, not *dharma*. So he accuses the one who looks to *dharma* first (Vidura) of disloyalty to the family, and threatens to kill himself if his father won't agree to his plan. And the blind king, 'knowing the evils of gambling', acquiesces 'because of his love for his son', and gives instructions that a grand hall be built for the dicing match. But he sends for Vidura to consult him all the same.

Meanwhile, Vidura learns of the intended dicing match and arrives hotfoot to advise against it. But it is too late. Dhṛtarāṣṭra has made up his mind to indulge his son and justifies his decision by making fate and the gods responsible.

> 'Don't worry, the gods in heaven will give us their blessing', he says. 'For good or bad, for better or for worse, let the friendly game take place; it's been ordained for sure. While Bhīshma and I are present nothing amiss ordained by fate will befall . . . . Fate is supreme, I think, so that this will happen.
> (2.45.53–7)

First the gods will help – either by overruling fate or contriving it; then, for better or for worse, the match must be played, for it has been ordained. Then he and Bhīṣma, his staunch and righteous adviser (here Dhṛtarāṣṭra is spreading the responsibility), will see to it that bad fortune is kept at bay; ultimately it is in the hands of fate again! Under the pretext of fate, of supra-human decree, and a bundle of weak arguments to cover up his son's weakness, he commands Vidura to summon the Pāṇḍavas to the contest. But Vidura is not fooled by Dhṛtarāṣṭra's appeal to fate. 'It is not so' (*naitad asti*), he thinks to himself as he dejectedly leaves the king's presence.

Dhṛtarāṣṭra has second thoughts; he knows that the contest will lead to trouble and he does not wish to have to preside over such trouble among his wards. So he again tries to persuade Duryodhana to give up his idea of the dicing match. But to no avail. Duryodhana launches into an impassioned description of his experiences at Indraprastha – his humiliations and the extent and variety of the tributary wealth. 'Son, coveting what belongs to another is the quick way to disaster' says the king, 'The one who abides by his own *dharma (svadharmastha)*, content with what he has, prospers' (2.50.6). 'Great king, the way of the Kṣatriya is fixed on victory' counters Duryodhana, 'whether there's *dharma* or *adharma* on his way' (2.50.15). He has quoted the Sage, Bṛhaspati who, according to tradition, taught the corrupting doctrine of materialism and self-gratification to bring about the ruin of the anti-gods and the demonically inclined. In his rage and envy, Duryodhana too thinks like a demon as his true motives surface again and again: 'The power, even of an insignificant enemy, gradually increases to excess, just as an anthill at the root of a tree devours the tree in the end' (2.50.24).

Finally, Dhṛtarāṣṭra, his 'mind obsessed with fate' (*daivasaṃmūḍhacetāḥ*), gives in, 'thinking fate supreme and unavoidable' (2.51.16). The hall is built, Vidura is overruled, and he is despatched to summon Yudhiṣṭhira to that 'friendly game of dice'. 'For this whole world runs under the sway of the Disposer's decree, not by itself', says the king (2.51.24).

When Yudhiṣṭhira receives the summons, he sees trouble ahead and asks Vidura's advice. Vidura's answer is direct: 'The game will lead to disaster,' he says, 'but do what you think best.' Yudhiṣṭhira accepts the invitation, but clearly this is not what he thinks best. He is told that Śakuni, master-gambler, and other tricksters await him. Yet he makes excuses for agreeing to play: the king, his 'father' has summoned him, he must obey; he knows Śakuni is waiting to challenge him, and he has taken a vow never to refuse a challenge.

This repeated appeal to determinism echoes the words of Dhṛtarāṣṭra: 'This world runs under the sway of the Disposer's decree' (2.52.14f.). It is significant that the most put-upon characters of this drama, the two most passive actors, who should have known better, appeal most to fate to justify their actions.

In the Introduction to his translation of the *Sabhā Parvan*, van Buitenen has argued plausibly that structurally the book requires Yudhiṣṭhira to play the dicing match because a token dicing game was a formal part of the *rājasūya* sacrifice. van Buitenen may well be right. But from the *story's* point of view, more specifically from the point of view of the tension between freedom and determinism in the context of *dharma*, we know perfectly well what led Yudhiṣṭhira to obey the summons. The text has been careful to tell us: Yudhiṣṭhira loves to gamble. This *adharmic* addiction is a big chink in his dharmic armour. This is why, again from the point of view of the book's structure, he is made to perform the *rājasūya* ritual – to justify the events that proceed from this flaw in his character – rather than the *aśvamedha* sacrifice, which would have been much more appropriate for his imperial aspirations. Dhṛtarāṣṭra has a passion for his son, and Yudhiṣṭhira has a passion for dice, and both can be quite decisive in covering up their actions when they want to indulge their passions. Thus they cover up by appealing to fate – even in the same words on one occasion. In fact, Yudhiṣṭhira admits as much. 'Fate blinds reason as light dazzles the eye. Man obeys the Disposer's sway as if bound with nooses', he says as he starts his journey to Hāstinapura (2.52.18). The complex human drama continues to unfold.

The Pāṇḍavas, together with Draupadī and their retinue, arrive at Hāstinapura where they are well received. Once they have rested, they proceed to the venue of the dicing match, the newly-built assembly hall, which is abuzz with anticipation. The protagonists take their places. Śakuni will play on behalf of Duryodhana; Yudhiṣṭhira will throw the dice himself. Before they begin, Yudhiṣṭhira solemnly warns Śakuni to play fair. 'Gambling is guile (*nikṛti*), an evil' he says piously, 'there's no prowess here for the nobility . . . Śakuni, don't defeat us dishonourably or basely.' Śakuni answers brilliantly, ruthlessly exposing Yudhiṣṭhira's addiction to the game. 'Indeed, the learned person confronts the unlearned, the knowledgeable the ignorant, by guile, Yudhiṣṭhira, yet people don't call it that. If you believe you're up against guile here then don't play – if you're afraid' (2.53.11–12). This is a masterly challenge, one which Yudhiṣṭhira cannot refuse. On the one hand, Śakuni practically admits that he will cheat. To each his own, he implies, and gambling is *my* skill;

beat me if you can. On the other hand, is Yudhiṣṭhira unwilling or unable to indulge his passion? And he a Kṣatriya, afraid in front of all these people? The dicing game has taken on the aspect of a surrogate duel between the two sides.

One wonders if Yudhiṣṭhira is so desperate to play that he cannot see through this trap, so desperate that, hoping against hope that Śakuni will not cheat, he actually hopes that luck (or fate) will decide the contest, not expert manipulation. Or is it that in spite of his doubts, he cannot back down now in front of a Kaurava crowd? We do not know. But he is determined (in more than one sense) to play. He has taken a vow never to refuse a challenge, he answers weakly, so he'll play. 'I stand bound by decree' (2.53.13), he says. But it is not clear by what decree. His own vow? (Is it *dharma* to stand by one's word even in the face of a dishonest challenge? This understanding of *dharma* will be contested). Fate's decree? (But this *has* been contested by the wise Vidura). The decree of the king-paterfamilias who summoned him – to a dishonest game? (The king described it as a 'friendly game', but already it is clearly more than that). In a highly charged atmosphere the dicing begins.

We will not recount the details. In all, twenty rounds must be played, and Yudhiṣṭhira loses consistently and mightily. Again and again we hear the refrain: 'Having heard (the stake), Śakuni addressed (the dice), resorted to guile, and cried "Won!" at Yudhiṣṭhira.' By round ten, Yudhiṣṭhira has lost much wealth – pearls, gold, his finely caparisoned chariot, a thousand elephants, male and female slaves, choice horses, a small army of chariots and their drivers, and so on. Vidura intervenes. He sees disaster ahead and does not mince his words. It is useless to appeal to Duryodhana to desist for, 'drunk with the dice game, he's besotted, oblivious to the situation' (2.54.5). He's a jackal (an inauspicious animal) who will cause conflict in the family and ruin to his house; he must be stopped at all costs. It is equally useless to appeal to Yudhiṣṭhira, though Vidura does not say this. After all, Yudhiṣṭhira is besotted too, but he is losing, and to pull out now would be to lose face. So Vidura appeals to the only person who can do something, the king Dhṛtarāṣṭra, whose authority all acknowledge. He says to him,

> For the sake of the family, one may abandon an individual. For the sake of the village one may abandon a family. For the country's sake, one may abandon a village. For the sake of the soul one may abandon the world!
>
> (2.55.10)

In other words, abandon Duryodhana! It is perfectly natural in Indian households even today for appeals to be made to the head of a family to override or influence decisions of more junior members, especially sons and daughters. Furthermore, Dhṛtarāṣṭra was the king, and ensconced in his own capital.[3]

But Duryodhana savagely intervenes, openly accusing Vidura of disloyalty. Besides, he exults in his nature; 'there is only one Guide' (*ekaḥ śāstā*), he concludes, 'the Guide who teaches the person as he lies in the womb. Commanded by that one I flow on, like water directed by a slope' (2.57.8). In fact, bold in the knowledge of his father's indulgence, he is actually repudiating his authority here to act as his guide. He will follow the bent of his own nature – his interpretation of his Kṣatriya nature, that is – formed in the womb. He has come so close to total victory over his enemies that nothing will thwart him now. Dhṛtarāṣṭra, glad that his son is winning, remains silent, and the game enters a new and more terrible phase.

Śakuni goads Yudhiṣṭhira to continue gambling. In four further throws Yudhiṣṭhira loses all his wealth, even his kingdom. There's no stopping Yudhiṣṭhira's (or Śakuni's) headlong progress now. Then Yudhiṣṭhira stakes Nakula, one of his twin brothers – and loses. Next he wagers Sahadeva, the other twin, who 'teaches the laws' (*dharmān*; 2.58.14) – and loses; then Arjuna, then Bhīma. Is he entitled to do this? Apparently he is, if his brothers acquiesce out of devotion and loyalty; he is their elder brother, the head of their family unit, their king. 'Won!' gloats Śakuni each time. 'You have lost much wealth, your brothers, and horses and elephants too', says Śakuni to Yudhiṣṭhira. 'Consider now, Kaunteya, if there's anything else that's left unwon'. '*I* am left', says Yudhiṣṭhira, and stakes himself, his freedom against servitude, to Duryodhana. They throw. 'Won!' rings out the familiar cry. If the match's symmetry is to be preserved, there is one throw left. And indeed the match is prolonged for one last, fateful round. With dastardly guile, Śakuni suggests the stake. 'There remains your beloved lady, and one throw is still unwon. Stake [Draupadī] and through her win back yourself [and everything else].' For a moment Yudhiṣṭhira muses on Draupadī's charms. Is this a moment of sanity? No. The blood rushes up, and beyond recall he cries, 'Come on, [Śakuni], with the lovely Draupadī I cast my throw!' This is not the language of someone forced to play ritually. At his words, there is consternation in the assembly hall. 'Fie! Fie!' cry the elders. The hearts of Bhīṣma, Vidura and other observers quail. Duryodhana's cronies rejoice. Dhṛtarāṣṭra, thrilled, unable to control himself, asks repeatedly, 'Has he won?'[4] But

Śakuni deliberates and flushed with anticipated victory, handles the dice one last time. 'Won!' he screeches, as the die is cast.

This is the moment that Duryodhana has been waiting for. Now he has the Pāṇḍavas in his grasp; he can humiliate them as he pleases. At once he sends for Draupadī. 'Fetch her' he tells Vidura, 'Let her sweep the place and run errands. Let's enjoy it!' (2.59.1). Vidura will have none of it. He responds by warning Duryodhana at length of the folly of his intentions. This will lead to a deadly feud between the Pāṇḍavas and the Kauravas, to Duryodhana's and his house's ultimate destruction. But in the process he raises a crucial point. 'I don't think [Draupadī's] come to slavery yet. For she was staked by the king when he was not his own master.' Indeed, Draupadī had been staked *after* Yudhiṣṭhira had wagered himself and lost. Was she legitimately staked at all? What follows pivots on this question.

Duryodhana is in no mood for doubts, however. With a curse on Vidura, he despatches an attendant to summon Draupadī all the same. 'You have nothing to fear from the Pāṇḍavas', he tells him. When apprised of the situation, Draupadī in turn sends the servant back to the hall to publicly ask her husband a question. 'Whom did you lose first, yourself or me?' Thus does the text emphasise the doubt first raised by Vidura. For the rest of the episode the question is associated with Draupadī, for she repeatedly seeks its answer. This is not just a doubt about the rules of a game. As is clear, the situation has grown far beyond that. Revenge, honour, humiliation, servitude, sovereignty, power, have all entered the picture. The conclusion of the dicing match is like the opening of Pandora's box. It is *dharma* that is at issue, as subsequent events will show increasingly clearly.

The messenger does as he is told. 'But Yudhiṣṭhira made no movement; he was as if senseless. He replied not a word to the servant, either good or bad' (2.60.9). Duryodhana sends the messenger back to Draupadī to summon her yet again. She must ask the question in the assembly herself. She says with touching faith, 'This is how the Disposer has now arranged it. He touches both the wise and the foolish. He has said that *dharma* alone is supreme in the world. When obeyed it will bring us peace' (2.60.13). She must go to the hall. Yudhiṣṭhira himself has summoned her to pose her question. Draupadī is in a bad way. Not only does she face dishonour before an all-male audience, but the situation is particularly humiliating for her because she is having her period, and according to the dharmic code she is to live secluded from men during this time, dressed in the prescribed fashion. 'With one garment, tied below, weeping and in her period, [Draupadī] went to the assembly hall and stood before her father-in-law.' She had put her faith in *dharma*. Will she be vindicated?

Now is the hour of trial of this woman whom again and again the text describes as devoted to *dharma* (see, e.g. 2.62.19; 2.63.25,33). At this point one of Duryodhana's brothers, Duḥśāsana, a willing stooge, takes a leading part. Duryodhana asks him to bring Draupadī before them. With a sneer he goes up to Draupadī. 'Come, come [Draupadī]', he says, 'you've been won. Look at Duryodhana without modesty now. You've been acquired according to *dharma* so come before the assembly' (2.60.20). Overwrought, she runs to the section reserved for the women of the court, hoping for protection. This is too much for Duḥśāsana. He grabs her by the hair (a particularly significant insult),[5] and drags her towards the venue of the match. She begs for restraint. 'I'm in my period', she says in a low voice, 'I've but one garment on. I cannot be taken like this to the assembly.' 'Period or no, clothed or naked, you'll come', replies her tormentor. 'You've been won at dice and you're now a slave. One can lust after slave-girls as one fancies.'

Draupadī now affirms her commitment to her *dharma*, and condemns the Kauravas for losing theirs. 'King [Yudhiṣṭhira] abides by *dharma*,' she says,

> and *dharma* is subtle, to be understood by experts. [So what Yudhiṣṭhira intends by allowing me to be dragged in this state to the assembly, I do not know.] But even at my husband's word, I do not wish to transgress in the slightest by abandoning what's proper to me.[6] . . . Shame! The *dharma* of the [Kauravas] is lost as is the practice of those who know how the noble behave, when all the Kurus in the assembly look on while the Kuru-*dharma* is transgressed.
>
> (2.60.31–3)

Indeed, none of the elders of the assembly, dismayed though they are by what is happening, seems able to intervene.

The respected Bhīṣma voices their hesitation in part when he says, 'Because *dharma* is subtle, my dear, I cannot rightly answer your question.' Then he poses the problem as he sees it: on the one hand, the man who has lost himself cannot stake what belongs to another; on the other hand, the wife falls under the husband's sway.[7] Again, Śakuni has no equal in dicing, yet he did not force Yudhiṣṭhira to play (so in theory Yudhiṣṭhira did have a choice in the matter). 'So I cannot answer your question' (2.60.40–2), concludes Bhīṣma, greatly distressed. During this impasse, Draupadī, like the good wife she is, tries pathetically to defend her husband Yudhiṣṭhira's actions. He was forced to respond to a challenge, she says, a challenge made by cheats. He did not suspect trickery; how could he be reckoned to have a choice in the matter? Finally, she demands an answer to her question.

The assembly must therefore strive to answer it. In fact, answering questions of *dharma* is one of the purposes of an assembly hall. The text indicates that there are three opinions on the issue. We have already heard what we may call the noncommittal view – that tendered by Bhīṣma. A second opinion is given by Vikarṇa, a very junior brother of Duryodhana. He reproaches the senior members of the assembly for not offering a view, reminding them of their responsibility to do so. Then he voices his own opinion:

> Draupadī was staked when [Yudhiṣṭhira], who was challenged by cheats, was acting in the throes of his passion. The blameless woman belongs to all the Pāṇḍavas; she was staked by this Pāṇḍava *after* he was won. Further, it was [Śakuni] who suggested Draupadī when he desired a stake. Considering all this, I do not think she has been won.
>
> (2.61.22–4).

Clearly, Vikarṇa does not accept that interpretation of *dharma* which requires that Yudhiṣṭhira must abide by his vow to accept a challenge even when it is dishonestly made. When Vikarṇa has finished, the assembly erupts in agreement. But as is so often the case in a debate, the matter does not end there.

We are now given the third and opposing view, and it is forcefully made by Karṇa, a sympathiser of Duryodhana's because he is an enemy of the Pāṇḍavas. Draupadī has been won according to *dharma*, he claims. Yudhiṣthira lost all he owned in the assembly, and 'Draupadī is part of all he owned'. Further, when Draupadī was clearly mentioned as a stake it was not contested by the Pāṇḍavas. Finally, as for summoning Draupadī in one garment before the assembly while she was having her period – only virtuous women deserve respect. But Draupadī is a slut. She submits to many men: she does not have one husband as is prescribed, but five, so no wrong has been done to her. 'She, a chattel of the Pāṇḍavas, and the Pāṇḍavas themselves, have all been won here by [Śakuni] in accordance with *dharma*' (2.61.31–7). As a fitting climax to his words and to make the Pāṇḍavas' humiliation complete, Karṇa demands that both they and Draupadī be publicly stripped.

Hearing no voice raised in protest and quite unnerved, the

Pāṇḍavas remove their upper garments. But Draupadī stands firm. Then Duḥśāsana, vile as ever, compounds his villainy by trying to strip Draupadī by force in full view. But, wonder of wonders, 'Draupadī's garment being removed, another just like it appeared time and again.' The assembly is in uproar. The enraged Bhīma who sees his wife thus manhandled utters a terrible curse against Duḥśāsana. He swears that he will rip the miscreant open on the battlefield and drink his blood. (In time he will fulfil his vow.) Frustrated and abashed, Duḥśāsana finally gives up: there is a pile of clothes on the floor and Draupadī remains covered. The Kauravas are condemned by the onlookers and an answer to Draupadī's question is demanded. Note, in passing, that whatever the solution to the riddle may be, the text implies that Draupadī as a righteous woman has not been righteously treated. Otherwise her final humiliation would not have been thwarted and her modesty miraculously preserved. This is a famous incident of the *Mahābhārata* and in popular versions Draupadī invokes Kṛṣṇa in the moment of her need and the coverings keep appearing by his grace.[8] Be that as it may, in the final analysis *dharma has* vindicated Draupadī. Her faith in *dharma* has not been void, although it has cost her dear.

Now Vidura speaks again. He has already declared his hand for which he has been accused of disloyalty, so he tries a different approach. The assembly must pronounce on Draupadī's question, he affirms, or it has failed in its duty. He tells the story of Virocana and Sudhanvān who staked their lives in a quarrel over a girl. The one not adjudged the better man would lose his life. They asked Virocana's father, Prahlāda, to judge between them. Prahlāda, who had no doubt in the matter, consulted the Sage Kaśyapa as to what would happen if he lied. Kaśyapa answered:

> When *dharma* pierced by *adharma* takes recourse to an assembly, then the assembly-members themselves are pierced [by *adharma*] if they do not remove (*dharma*'s) irritant . . . . They who would speak falsely to one asking about *dharma*, ruin their religious merit and seven generations of ancestors and descendants.
>
> (2.61.69,72)

Suitably warned, Prahlāda told the truth, even though it meant the loss of his son: Sudhanvān, not Virocana, was the better man. But Prahlāda had occasion to rejoice: because he respected *dharma* and told the truth, Sudhanvān rewarded him by not claiming his son's life. Thus, concludes Vidura, must *dharma* be honestly addressed in this assembly.

His message is indirect but clear: as the attempt at disrobing has shown, Draupadī is *dharma* afflicted by the *adharma* of her persecutors, and vindicated by *dharma*. She has taken recourse to the assembly; like Prahlāda, let the assembly in general and Dhṛtarāṣṭra in particular take Yudhiṣṭhira's side in this conflict and, disowning their own 'son' Duryodhana, adjudge Yudhiṣṭhira the better man. But even this appeal fails to elicit the desired response. The elders of the assembly remain silent, for, as the text says later, they were afraid to offend Duryodhana.[9] And so the drama continues.

Draupadī appeals to the better nature of those in the assembly. She recounts how she, a virtuous and noble woman, and now by marriage a member of the Kaurava family, so solicitously protected by the Pāṇḍavas in the past, has been humiliated in the sight of all. None, not even her husbands, have sought to defend her. She says:

> The Kurus allow – what perverse times! – their innocent daughter-in-law and daughter to be molested. Can there be greater shame than this that I a woman, pure, beautiful, now plunge into the middle of the assembly! Where is the *dharma* of you lords? We all know that one does not bring dharmic women before the assembly. That ancient, eternal *dharma* of the Kauravas is surely lost! . . . Tell me what you think, Kauravas, whether I've been won or not. I want an answer, and by that I'll abide.
>
> (2.62.7–9)

Bhīṣma's reply is telling. He still does not answer her question, but instead makes a somewhat cynical comment on *dharma*. *Dharma*, he avers, will triumph, but he repeats that it is hard to grasp. He goes on, 'What a powerful person sees as *dharma* in the world is accepted as *dharma* by others when *dharma* is at issue. I cannot speak to your question with certainty for this matter is subtle, obscure and serious' (2.62.14–16). *He* does not want to be accused of disloyalty, for he lives in Dhṛtarāṣṭra's court. But there is no doubt as to where his sympathies lie. 'Before long this line will come to an end' he continues, 'for all the Kurus are set on greed and delusion . . . whereas you, [Draupadī], though you have suffered much, have regard only for *dharma*' (2.62.17,19). In short, the Kaurava protagonists of this terrible affair are manipulating *dharma* to suit themselves, but you are the righteous one, Draupadī, though I cannot say it in so many words. Then, in time-honoured fashion, Bhīsma throws the ball into someone else's court. 'I believe Yudhiṣṭhira has the measure (*pramāṇa*) to answer this question. He himself is quite competent to declare whether you have been won or not.'

However, Duryodhana seizes on this suggestion to initiate new devilry. Let the four younger Pāṇḍavas declare that Yudhiṣṭhira had no right to wager Draupadī, he says, and she may go free. Or failing that, let Yudhiṣṭhira pronounce on the issue himself. Now Yudhiṣṭhira had a great reputation for being a man of his word and devoted to the truth. In fact, as an indication of this one of his names was 'Dharmarāja' or 'King Dharma'.[10] Duryodhana thereby confronts the Pāṇḍavas with a vicious dilemma. If the four younger brothers say that Yudhiṣṭhira spoke falsely when he wagered Draupadī – because, having lost himself he had no right to stake Draupadī, who was their common wife anyway – then Draupadī goes free. But then Yudhiṣṭhira will be dishonoured as a liar. In short, it is a choice between their eldest brother's (and their king's) reputation or their wife's freedom. On the other hand, if *Yudhiṣṭhira* pronounces on the matter, his dilemma is this: either he stands by his deed and the word it involved that he *was* entitled to wager Draupadī – in which case his (and his brothers') wife must submit to servitude at Duryodhana's hands – or he must admit that he spoke and acted falsely when Draupadī was staked. In the latter event everyone will be released, but Yudhiṣṭhira and his party will be publicly disgraced: a devilish conundrum.

Again there was uproar in the assembly hall. Some cheered, some lamented, then there was an expectant hush as everyone looked at the Paṇḍavas. How would they react? The two-pronged riddle was quickly reduced to a single barb. Speaking on behalf of the four younger brothers, Bhīma submits to Yudhiṣṭhira's authority; Yudhiṣṭhira will decide the issue. Bhīma says: 'If Yudhiṣṭhira, King Dharma, were not our guru, the head of our family, we would not have suffered. But he is master of our merits and austerities, lord of our lives. If he considers himself won (*jita*), then we are lost (*vijita*[11])' (2.62. 32–3). Bhima can do nothing; he feels he is 'bound by the noose of *dharma*'.

How does Yudhiṣṭhira respond – the head of the family, the master of his brothers' lives? In the same curious manner as before. He sits 'silent and mindless' (2.63.8), as passive as ever. Emboldened, it is Duryodhana now who grievously insults Draupadī. In full view, he bares his left thigh at her – a highly obscene gesture of the time.[12] Bhīma, enraged, makes another vow. He will smash that thigh with his mace in a great battle (he is to keep this vow too).

Then, just when it seems that an impasse has been reached in which the Pāṇḍavas' enemies have the upper hand, the Pāṇḍavas are saved by the bell (or its cultural equivalent). A jackal howls during the solemn *agnihotra* sacrifice being conducted on behalf of Dhṛtarāṣṭra's household, and this is followed by other inauspicious signs. Informed of this, the blind king Dhṛtarāṣṭra, blind for so long to what has been going on and the one person who has undisputed authority to resolve the whole matter, comes to his senses. He reprimands Duryodhana for mistreating Draupadī whom he calls a '*dharma*- wife' (*dharma-patnī*, i.e. either 'a dharmic wife' or 'the wife of *Dharma*, i.e. Yudhiṣṭhira'; in any case, he repudiates Karṇa's charge that she is a loose woman). Then he offers Draupadī a boon.

Draupadī asks for the freedom of her most senior husband, Yudhiṣṭhira. It is granted. Dhṛtarāṣṭra offers her a second boon. Draupadī requests the freedom of her other four husbands. This too is granted. Then Dhṛtarāṣṭra says, 'Choose a third; two boons don't do you justice. For, of all my daughters-in-law you are the best, for you live by *dharma* (*dharmacāriṇī*)' (2.63.33). Well, Draupadī could now choose anything. A suitable punishment for Duryodhana perhaps, or double the wealth that her husband lost. But again she abides by *dharma*. 'Greed makes for the destruction of *dharma*' she replies, 'I am not worthy to receive a third boon. . . . They say that . . . a Kṣatriya woman can have two boons', and she has had her two. She will ask for no more. Who or what, we may ask, came to the Pāṇḍavas' rescue when the jackal howled? Fate? The gods? *Dharma*? The question remains open.

Our story is nearly ended, although Karṇa did not want to let things pass without a final swipe at the Pāṇḍavas. Whoever heard of such a thing? he asks. 'Draupadī has become the haven here of Pāṇḍu's sons. When they had fallen into the deep, sinking without a ship to support them, [Draupadī] became the boat to bring them ashore!' (2.64.2–3). However, by and large the matter had ended. No one could gainsay Dhṛtarāṣṭra's decision. He gives the Pāṇḍavas leave to return to their kingdom in peace and restores all that had been lost in that 'friendly game' of dice, appealing to Yudhiṣṭhira not to bear ill will against Duryodhana. 'I intended this game just for fun (*prekṣāpūrva*)', says the king, 'I wanted to see my friends (the Pāṇḍavas) and how my sons would square up to them'. So much then for a friendly game of dice.

There is a sequel to this episode. While the Pāṇḍavas are still on their way home, Duryodhana and his followers once more persuade the old king to summon his nephews to a final throw of dice (that twentieth throw). Their plan is simple. This time they will play for the following stake: the losers will spend twelve years in exile in the forest and a thirteenth year trying to live incognito among the people.

If their disguise is penetrated during this year, they are to spend another twelve years in the forest. Śakuni will cheat again, win the throw, and in this way the Kauravas will rid themselves of their rivals once and for all. Dhṛtarāṣṭra agrees once more, and for the same reason (his love for his son). The game is played and Yudhiṣṭhira loses (he is as fatalistic as ever). The Pāṇḍavas and Draupadī go off into exile and make it possible for the epic tale to continue.[13]

We will pass the sequel by. The first dicing game will serve our purposes. Although it has been considered at some length, it has still been appreciably condensed. As we shall see, there is more than one reason for dwelling on this episode. To begin with, through it we catch a glimpse not only of the world of the *Mahābhārata* but also of the high drama of Hindu story-telling. We have the ingredients here of any modern blockbuster: family rivalry, hunger for power, unbridled ambition, treachery, deceit, glamour, sex, dastardly behaviour, passion and addiction, humiliation and rescue, and so on. But above all, the context is religious: the Pāṇḍavas are friends of the Lord Kṛṣṇa, and it is he, in the popular tellings, who rescues Draupadī, and it is he who just before the great battle will reveal himself so fully for the consolation of his devotees as the supreme Being. Perhaps now it is clearer why narrative *pāṭha* is so popular. The tellings and re-tellings in their various forms with their modern glosses keep the characters and the faith alive, and comfort and encourage the listeners through the vicissitudes of life.

II

Dharma*: an ambivalent concept as both descriptive and prescriptive. The moral component. The ambivalence extended: 'good/bad', 'right/wrong' in the tradition – their naturalistic and moral connotations. Challenging a notable confusion. Contemporary usage. Further examples.* Vidyā *not* gnosis. *Historical roots of the ambivalence. A modern sense of* dharma. *The analysis continues:* dharma *as deliberative.* Sanātana-dharma *and* sva-dharma. *The Gītā's contribution.*

Let us now consider the story in the context of our treatment of *dharma*. Both the tensions mentioned before are apparent, so that *dharma* emerges as a complex concept, functioning at different levels and in different ways. We will deal first with the tension between disorder and order.

Dharma is order, natural and imposed, in the midst of threatened or apparent disorder. When Draupadī protests to Duḥśāsana that she does not wish to transgress 'qualities proper to her' (*svaguṇān*), she implies both kinds of dharmic order: (i) the natural order – the role of a woman as a faithful wife is a natural one – and (ii) order imposed first, socially, e.g. a respectable woman should not appear before the (all-male) assembly, especially during her period (which indeed is a time of 'natural impurity' for a woman), and second, morally: a virtuous woman should not *want* to have sex with anyone not entitled to have sex with her (for Duḥśāsana was suggesting that as a slave she could bestow her sexual favours on her masters). She puts her faith in *dharma* thus understood, and is vindicated when Duḥśāsana tries to strip her. If he had succeeded, *dharma* would have been violated in both senses. Stripping Draupadī naked before strange men would have defiled her natural integrity as a woman. Bhīma, who generally sees issues in black and white, implies as much after Dhṛtarāṣṭra has granted Draupadī her boons, and the Pāṇḍavas, now free, are preparing to leave the king's presence. He says to Arjuna, 'Our lustre has been dimmed because our wife's been defiled. How can one have a defiled child?' (2.64.7). Arjuna replies to the effect that they should know their own worth which exceeds that of Duḥśāsana (i.e. that perhaps their worth will make up for their wife's defilement). But Draupadī's exposure would also have violated *dharma* in the moral sense, for it would have excited the lust of onlookers. At it is, the extraordinary 'cover-up' that happened frustrated both kinds of transgression.

Again, in advising Duryodhana to abide by his own *dharma*, it is *dharma* as natural order that Dhṛtarāṣṭra has largely in mind. Duryodhana is born to the calling of a Kṣatriya. The goal of a Kṣatriya is to behave and fight honourably, not to pursue wealth. Duryodhana turns the argument on its head to suit his lust for power and revenge. The calling of a Kṣatriya, he contends, is to win at all costs, irrespective of the morality of the situation. He will follow natural not moral *dharma*, but it is *his* (forced) interpretation of Kṣatriya-*dharma* that he will follow, which he bolsters later by appealing to tendencies in his nature formed in the womb by the 'one Guide' (2.57.8). Who is this Guide? Nature? Anyway, he will follow these tendencies, wherever they may lead.

It is clear that the text regards this one-sided naturalistic interpretation of Kṣatriya-*dharma* as wrong. Duryodhana is censured unequivocally more than once during the episode, and the thwarted attempt to disrobe Draupadī and his father's final reprimand endorse this condemnation. Indeed, Draupadī's *dharma* overcomes Duryodhana's *(a)dharma*. For Hindus, human *dharma* has always had a strong moral component.

In the context of the concept of *dharma*, let us now examine what Hindus mean by good and bad, right and wrong. A number of terms, both Sanskrit and vernacular (including *dharma* and *adharma*), measure up more or less adequately to these pairs. Generally each (Indian) term of a pair has both a naturalistic and a moral connotation. That is, positively or negatively, the same term is used to express both natural and moral goodness or evil respectively. For example, consider in its traditional context, the Sanskrit word *pāpa*, often translated as 'evil'. *Pāpa* can mean 'natural evil' or 'moral evil', or both simultaneously, depending on context, while its positive counterpart *puṇya* can mean 'merit', 'holy' and 'ritually pure'. Thus in *Gītā* 9.32, where women, Vaiśyas and Śūdras are described as '*pāpa-yonayaḥ*' or 'those with *pāpa-* origins', both naturalistic and moral connotations seem to be implied. In other words, all of the following interpretations of '*pāpa-yonayaḥ*' are applicable: (i) these individuals are 'evil-born' because they have been born in an undesirable state (as either women or low-castes) owing to demerit acquired in previous lives; or (ii) they are 'sources of evil' or ritual impurity according to the conventional code; or (iii) they are 'sources leading to wrongdoing/sin' in others. Naturalistic meanings predominate here, but there is also a moral connotation.

This bivalency of terms for 'good' and 'bad' can lead to serious misunderstanding of Hindu morality if careful distinctions are not drawn. Here is an example. In his book *Our Savage God*, R.C. Zaehner (1974) is at pains to analyse a *cause célèbre* of the late 1960s in which an American cult leader and some of his followers were convicted of a mass murder. Zaehner contends that the thinking behind the killings was similar to if not derived from a major teaching of the classical Upaniṣads, namely that the enlightened individual transcends the conventional morality of right and wrong, according to which, for instance, alms giving is good and murder bad. Zaehner asks,

> Can we, then, be surprised if the sage, fully liberated from the bonds of space and time and therefore from the whole world of 'appearance' in which alone the opposites of good and evil have any validity, should act out his life in accordance with either the good or the evil aspect of God since, when all is said and done, they are the *same*? . . (for) Hindus postulate wrong at the very heart of Truth.
>
> (Zaehner 1974: 97–8)

However, there is a profound confusion here, not only with respect to a Hindu conception of God, but also as regards Zaehner's understanding of the Upanishadic texts concerned. This confusion is based on a mistranslation, or rather a mis-contextualisation, of Sanskrit terms which Zaehner translates as 'good' and 'evil' in the western moral sense of virtue and vice. It is no wonder then that the Upaniṣads are supposed to teach that the enlightened person is not bound by everyday morality, especially if enlightenment is the transcending of this world of appearance. The terms in question are *puṇya* and *pāpa* and *sukṛta* and *duṣkṛta*. In context, these pairs do not mean 'virtue' and 'vice' in the western sense, but mainly the 'merit' (*puṇya/sukṛta*) and 'demerit' (*pāpa/duṣkṛta*) generated by good and bad observance of traditional ritualistic religion. The Upaniṣads teach innovatively that by the practice of a disinterested ethic, the enlightened individual must transcend this ritualistic, self-centred mentality. This is a very different teaching indeed. It does not mean that the Sage may commit murder or dismiss everyday morality with impunity, as the Vedāntins, for instance, interpreters of the classical Upaniṣads *par excellence*, have always been quick to point out. Zaehner's is a not uncommon (western) misunderstanding about Upanishadic morality, and one often resorted to for tendentious purposes.

In some vernaculars today the terms *pāp(a)* and *puṇya* are still commonly used in all sections of Hindu society, with both their naturalistic and moral connotations. Thus in traditional Bengali folk religion, *pāp* is used in the general sense of 'transgression'.[14] But among more educated circles of Bengali and Hindi speakers, for instance, the sense of 'moral wrongdoing' for *pāp* is increasingly being emphasised; in some contexts its meaning is equivalent to the western term 'sin'.[15] It is no accident that in the 1984 Bengali translation of the New Testament, highly acclaimed not least in reviews in the Bengali press, one finds *pāpī* for 'sinner'. In ethical contexts, *dharmik(a)* in the sense of 'righteous/virtuous (person)' is often used as an antonym of *pāpī* and *adharmik(a)*.[16]

Consider another example: the expression *durbuddhi*. Traditionally this is given naturalistic and moral connotations, and can mean both 'stupid, obtuse' and 'evil-minded, vicious'. The context determines which meaning should come to the fore, or whether both senses are to be given more or less equal emphasis. Duryodhana is often described as *durbuddhi* (usually in both senses). Because he is vicious he acts like a fool; again, his obtuseness compounds his viciousness. But the expression also has currency in some vernaculars, for example, in contemporary Bengali. Here again both senses can be implied. There is a further observation we must make: for Hindus, not only are terms meaning 'good' and 'bad', 'right' and 'wrong' bivalent in the way described, but a causal connection is often perceived to exist between their moral and naturalistic connotations. We can offer an explanation with reference to an important pair of words in Vedantic theology.

The words I have in mind are *vidyā* and *avidyā* (alternatively, *jñāna* and *ajñāna*) which may be translated as '(spiritual) knowledge' and '(spiritual) ignorance' respectively. One often encounters the view that Vedantic thought exalts 'gnosis' as a means to final liberation. This is an unfortunate translation for *vidyā* or *jñāna*. In Gnosticism, creation tends to be pathomorphic – a kind of sick effluence; it is not so in Vedantic theology which speaks of an Īśvara or God who produces the world deliberately, caringly and responsibly (see Chapters 10 and 11). In Gnosticism there is a fundamental contrastive dualism, ontologically and ethically, between God and the world. God is entirely transcendent and distant from the world of humans, and intermediary powers rule this world. Vedantic theology is not antithetically dualistic (quite the contrary). Here, God, for all his transcendence, is in direct saving contact with the world – through his agents and manifestations, his own inner presence, his grace, his *avatāra*s. In Gnosticism, the psychophysical realm, as opposed to the world of the inner spirit, is unrelievedly bad, lacking reliable footholds, epistemic or otherwise, for our spiritual ascent. As indicated in Chapter 7, this is certainly not the case for Hinduism in general or Vedānta in particular. Most Vedāntins tend to view the world – its experiences, images, realities – positively, as containing means and symbols of salvation.[17] In Gnosticism, the sole means of salvation is a kind of superior knowledge, revealed to initiates, tending towards an elaborate theory of things to be known as well as a *praxis* of arcane techniques and information (which includes 'maps' of post-mortem worlds leading to final liberation). Further, although the gnosis of Gnosticism is allied to a morality, in itself it has a strong *a*moral quality (evidenced by the fact that the morality of Gnosticism can be either libertine or ascetic). In Vedānta in general, devotion to the Lord is indispensable for salvation, and even the apparently uncompromising monism of Śaṃkara acknowledges the importance of the path of *bhakti* in the spiritual life, while the morality of Vedānta, anything but libertine, derives from its theology. Thus, although it may be the case that one can discern 'Gnostic elements' in aspects of Vedānta, there is on the whole more to separate the two traditions than to unite them. The point is that translating the *vidyā* of Vedānta by 'gnosis' is something of a non-starter. So what does *vidyā* mean?

To begin with, it has a naturalistic connotation; it entails right cognition about the nature of the world, the human being and *Brahman*, including the relationships between them. This is important. Someone who lacks this knowledge, or who is mistaken about these realities, cannot be spiritually advanced. (Each school of Vedānta naturally invests this knowledge with different content, ranging from monism to strong dualism; otherwise there would not be different Vedantic traditions.) But this knowledge is also experiential; it has a personal, practical side to it. It must be internalised; this is where *bhakti* comes in – *bhakti* to the guru, to God. The whole person must be caught up in *vidyā*: intellect, will, emotions. And from such a commitment, which entails a growing enlightenment, flows a morality which is sensitive to the distinction between virtue and vice, good and bad, requiring at all times the pursuit of the one and the rejection of the other.

In the *Kaṭha* Upaniṣad, an important text of the scriptural corpus from which Vedantic theology derives inspiration, we find a statement about the relationship between *vidyā/avidyā* and the good and not-so-good in the context of moral striving. Yama, the Lord of Death, is discoursing with Naciketas, a youth who seeks the secret of eternal life. A person can follow either of two paths in life, says Yama: the better way (*śreyas*) or the path of pleasure (*preyas*). The path of pleasure is the path of self-indulgence; it is the way of ignorance (*avidyā*) trod by the fool to whom 'the Beyond does not shine', who thinks: 'There is only this life; there is no other.' 'Again and again such a one falls into my power', says the Lord of Death. The better way, however (by implication the way of non-covetousness) is the way of wisdom (*vidyā*) which leads to immortality and to that which is beyond Yama's grasp (I.2.1–9). Thus for Vedāntins, and a great many other Hindus influenced by Upanishadic ideas, *vidyā* and *avidyā* are not only cognitive terms, denoting what is good and bad epistemically, but also words with moral content – value terms – referring to the moral condition of the knower and to moral goals. The two kinds of meaning are interrelated.

Vidyā is wisdom which implies purity of the mind (likened to a mirror) and purity of soul; the one sustains and enhances the other. (It is not an accident that white light and the reflection of light are common symbols of *vidyā* and the knowing process respectively.) *Avidyā* is spiritual ignorance (symbolised by darkness); in this condition *tamas*, a natural 'staining' constituent of the mind, dominates the knowing mechanism. In Hinduism the immoral person tends to be confused, the Sage to have a 'clear' mind. According to

Vedānta, the ordinary person is born in a state of *avidyā*, congenitally ignorant of his or her true spiritual condition and ultimate destiny: *avidyā* is a sort of 'original sin'. By various means one can pass from a state of *avidyā* to *vidyā*. What these means are depends on the distinctive teaching of each school, and in most Vedantic schools the way of *vidyā* necessarily involves action (*karman*) in this world and devotion (*bhakti*), first to the Lord and then to his representatives and creation. Thus *vidyā* is not simply a bloodless 'gnosis'.

The tendency to use the same terms to signify 'good/right' or 'bad/wrong' bivalently dates back to earliest times in the subcontinent. A good example is the dyad *ṛta* and *anṛta*, which was gradually superseded by *dharma* and *adharma*. Establishing *ṛta* (order, right) was the function particularly ascribed to the god Varuṇa (with whom Mitra was sometimes associated in this role). Consider the use of ṛta in the following verses of the *Ṛg* Veda. 'The rivers flow by the order (*ṛtam*) of Varuṇa' (2.28.4); 'I call upon Mitra and Varuṇa, the Lords of *ṛta*, of light, who foster *ṛta* with *ṛta*' (1.23.5). Note the juxtaposition of 'light' and *ṛta*. Light establishes order out of the chaos of darkness; as such, light *is* order. But light is also the symbol of moral order. This emerges in the following verse: 'Do not smite us, Varuṇa, with shafts that strike the transgressor at your command. Do not let us pass from light to darkness' (2.28.7). Varuṇa is the Lord of *ṛta*, the punisher of transgression (*enas*), of unright (*anṛta*) which clings to one even involuntarily. A *Ṛg* Vedic hymn to Varuṇa says: 'Release us from the offences of our forefathers, from offences we have ourselves committed. . . . Going astray was not intended, Varuṇa. . . . Even sleep does not drive unright (*anṛta*) away' (7.86.5–6). Here, in the same breath, evil or *anṛta* is spoken of as being received involuntarily (a burden passed down) and as being committed; it is endemic to the human condition.

When educated Hindus of the nineteenth century needed to translate the western concept of 'religion', the word *dharma*, with its central place in traditional Hindu usage and its connotations of a code of practice, a way of life, personal responsibility and duty, and socio-religious order, came readily to mind. Its naturalistic nuances either weakened or became somewhat divorced in a separate usage of the term. Today in Indian languages, *dharma* commonly means, or is a common translation of, 'religion'. This is not too procrustean a development by any means. In fact, centuries ago, in the Introduction to his commentary on the *Gītā*, Śaṃkara uses the term in a not dissimilar sense. He says:

> The Lord, having produced this world and desiring its stability (*sthiti*), first made the supervisors Marici etc. and propagated the *dharma* of involvement with the world (*pravṛtti-dharma*), called the Veda.[18] Then, producing others . . . he propagated the *dharma* of disinterestedness (*nivṛtti-dharma*), characterised by knowledge (*jñāna*) and renunciation (*vairāgya*). Thus Vedic *dharma* is twofold, pravrittic and nivrittic, which is the cause of the stability of the world.

Without straining its sense too much, *dharma* in this passage may be translated as 'religion', and a well-known nineteenth-century English translation of Śaṃkara's *Gītā*-commentary, still regularly used, renders *pravṛtti-dharma* and *nivṛtti-dharma* as 'the Religion of Works' and 'the Religion of Renunciation' respectively.[19] Thus today people talk of the Christian *dharma*, the Hindu *dharma*, the Buddhist *dharma*, and so on.

In our continuing exploration of the proliferating concept of *dharma* (which itself is something like the banyan), let us return to the story of the dicing match. I will try to show that in the Sanskritic tradition this action concept has generally implied the exercise of responsible choice. In other words, generally in the 'high' Hindu understanding of *dharma* the exercise of deliberation is ideally not subject to deterministic forces. This brings us to the second tension inherent in *dharma*. Consider Yudhiṣṭhira's predicament. The story places him at the centre of a range of centrifugal dharmic pulls. As the patron of the *rājasūya* sacrifice he must attend to the *dharma* of the sacrifice which, van Buitenen has pointed out, requires the ritual enactment of a dicing match. But for Yudhiṣṭhira this ritual demand is no more than an excuse to indulge his passion, as it is a literary device to shape the form of the story. How responsibly did Yudhiṣṭhira play, at the beginning, in the middle and at the end? More than once, and in different ways, the text raises this question, and leaves the answer open.

This is where fate (*daiva*) which represents both chance and necessity – powers which we cannot control – comes in. Throughout the story there is an interplay between fate and free will, and Yudhiṣṭhira is the central symbol of this interplay. In agreeing to enact the ritual of the dicing game his freedom was constrained up to a point by, for example, his passion for the sport and the summons of Dhṛtarāṣṭra, the head of his clan. However, Yudhiṣṭhira was certainly not a *pawn* of fate at crucial phases of the game, as the text makes clear. First of all, fate did not control the match as it might have if the match were played according to the rules. Śakuni controlled the game and Yudhiṣṭhira suspected as much, but he began his little speech before the contest by warning Śakuni to play fair, thereby indicating that he tried to allay this suspicion. Perhaps Yudhiṣṭhira believed that he was more skilled at dice than Śakuni. Yudhiṣṭhira, like Dhṛtarāṣṭra, used fate as a cover-up for his passion. But he was not *forced* to play by or against Śakuni. Before the game began Śakuni offered to let him pull out, but in such a way that withdrawal was difficult.

At every turn Yudhiṣṭhira had to struggle against constraints, some of which were more self-inflicted than genuine: his vow always to accept a challenge (even a trumped-up one?); Śakuni's barbed offer to allow him to withdraw (as a Kṣatriya, was he afraid to enter the contest, especially in the assembly hall of a rival?); his passion for the game (but as Bhīṣma's statement implies, it was not an overwhelming passion).[20] Some constraints were more or less genuine. These can be described as dharmic responsibilities or pulls. We have already noted one, the ritual demand of the sacrifice. There were others, especially poignant in the context of a person like Yudhiṣṭhira. Bhīma intimated a few. Yudhiṣṭhira was their king: as such he had a dharmic responsibility to see to their welfare. He was their elder brother; there is a *dharma* of the elder brother to protect his younger brother(s). He was Draupadī's husband: he had a responsibility to protect her, a responsibility compounded by the fact that Draupadī was the co-wife of his younger brothers who also had rights in the matter. Yudhiṣṭhira was a Kṣatriya: he had a duty to Kṣatriya-*dharma*, to fight a contest fairly and to treat his opponent honourably, giving him the benefit of any doubt; not to let his side down; to stick to his word, to abide by his stake (a genuine stake; was Draupadī staked genuinely, his brothers wagered honourably?). Doubt, conflict, constraint confront us at every turn.

It is no wonder that at the end Yudhiṣṭhira is described as being 'mindless' and 'silent'. At this point he symbolises each of us trapped by 'the noose of *dharma*' amid the complexity of life, at the centre of an array of conflicting, multivalent dharmic pulls. But we must decide, just as Yudhiṣṭhira had to decide once all the dharmic responsibilities confronting him had built up. Now what does the text do? It doesn't come up with a master solution which resolves the whole affair, but quite artificially cuts the Gordian knot by the literary device of making Dhṛtarāṣṭra undo all that has gone before at one stroke, by offering Draupadī her boons. *Solutio ex machina*.

In effect, the text teaches that *dharma* cannot be absolutised. It is pointed out more than once that *dharma* is subtle, obscure, hard to fathom. There is no universal master solution which can be taken off the shelf and applied to one's particular circumstances; each person must work out his or her own *dharma* in the context of the dharmic pulls and other constraints of his or her own situation, based on counsel and the responsible use of reason. Implementing *dharma* is a *rational* process. If it were not, Draupadī would not have pressed her question so persistently. She demanded an answer based on a careful assessment of the whole situation. The text leaves the answer open, as if intimating that Draupadī's unanswered question symbolises a question mark over our own lives as we seek ceaselessly to determine and implement our own *dharma* at any particular time.[21]

We will now consider a longstanding distinction which has important contemporary relevance. This is the distinction between *sanātana-dharma* (everlasting *dharma*) and *sva-dharma* (one's own *dharma*). Radhakrishnan for one – Hindu apologist *par excellence* – has made much of *sanātana-dharma*. Hinduism apparently teaches a *sanātana dharma* equivalent to a kind of *philosophia perennis*; this eternal *dharma* or way of life is made to coincide with Radhakrishnan's own interpretation of Advaita Vedānta. *Sva-dharma* then becomes the personal implementation (in Radhakrishnan's understanding) of the Advaitic vision.[22] Radhakrishnan goes on to tell us the whereabouts of the seeds of this Advaita in the major religions of the world and how these seeds may come to fruition.[23]

Then there are those who call themselves 'sanātanists' and who claim to follow some version of *sanātana-dharma*. Sometimes, being a sanātanist is meant to set one apart from reformed Hinduism (the unspoken assumption being that *sanātana* Hinduism is 'pure'/'true' Hinduism, whereas reformed Hinduism – 'reformed' from whose point of view? – is somehow unauthentic). Sometimes being a sanātanist is meant to set one apart from 'non-Hindus' (see Chapter 1; this too is not an uncontentious notion), the unspoken assumption here being that there are first-class citizens (the sanātanists) and second-class citizens (the non-sanātanists).

I have no objection to the use of '*sanātana-dharma*'. It is an ancient expression; the *Gītā* itself uses it. In 1.40, Arjuna tells Kṛṣṇa that 'when the clan is vitiated, the *sanātana-dharma*s [plural] of the clan are destroyed' (a similar expression was used by Draupadī when the onlookers did not speak up on her behalf). In this context, *sanātana-dharma* means the age-old code of conduct of the clan/family; it does not mean what either Radhakrishnan or sanātanists tend to mean by it. In fact, I have yet to discover a Hindu *sanātana-dharma* in the sense of some universally recognised philosophy, teaching or code of practice. Indeed there can be no such thing, for it presupposes that Hinduism is a monolithic tradition in which there is agreement about some static, universal doctrine. But the whole tenor of this book has been to intimate that Hinduism is a pluriform phenomenon in which there are many dynamic centres of religious belief and practice.

Thus *sanātana-dharma* can properly only mean an ancient and continuing guideline for an orientation in the world which may draw on the ancient codes of *varṇāśrama dharma*, and so on, but which is relative to one's group circumstances and status and which is flexible enough to require a deliberative response appropriate to the situation. *Sva-dharma* is the personal implementing of this guideline, part of the pursuit of 'one's truth' as described in Chapter 7. This appears to be one of the teachings of the story of the dicing match.

We can give further proof that the understanding of *dharma* has traditionally required a deliberative response to life. Jaimini's *Mīmāṃsā* Sūtras provides a classic definition of *dharma*, as the starting point of an enquiry into its meaning noted for its authoritative standing in the high tradition. The definition is as follows: '*codanā lakṣaṇo'rtho dharmaḥ*', i.e. 'Dharma concerns some directive' (1.1.2). At the time, this directive no doubt centred on the Vedic ritual. The point is, however, that according to this definition dharmic behaviour has to do with a *recommended* course or stay of action. Such a directive/recommendation would classically be expressed in the optative mood in Sanskrit (*vidhi-liṅ*), namely, 'One should/may [not] do so-and-so'. This makes no sense unless it is assumed that the subject of the directive has free will. Further, different kinds of dharmic recommendations obtained. Some were continually obligatory (during certain stages of life), others were occasionally obligatory, and still others were entirely optional. This implies duty and moral choice and the ability to implement both. Finally, it was well known that many directives seemed unclear or mutually at odds, so that deliberation and counsel were required to follow the right course of action. In other words, the pursuit of *dharma* was a rational process.

The Law Codes, the epics and other sources extended and confirmed this understanding. We have already noted that one of the primary concerns of the epics is the meaning of *dharma*. The story of the dicing match illustrates this well. Further, a key role was played by the *Bhagavadgītā*, traditionally a part of the Mbh, in emphasising *intention* as a pivot of Hindu morality. It does this, no doubt under Buddhist influence, by revalorising the concept of *karman* (action). Hitherto, *karman*'s paradigm meaning was 'ritually prescribed action'. Without entirely doing away with this sense, the *Gītā* revalorises this term to mean especially 'morally purposeful action'. This semantic transition takes place through a principal teaching of the text, namely that authentic human action (including sacrificial action) is consciously goal-oriented, and that action which is performed for its personal 'fruit' (*phala*) or gratification results in physical rebirth. Action, however, performed selflessly, preferably out of love for the Lord, engenders liberation from the cycle of rebirth. Self-centred and disinterested action may appear the same behaviourally; it is the intention that makes the difference. Thus the impassioned Rāmānuja could write, even a thousand years later, in his commentary on the *Gītā*:

> Behold this great difference! that with respect to those who perform the very same action (behaviourally), it is *by difference of intention alone* that there are some who, partaking even a little bit of [that action's self-centred] fruit, fall naturally [into the cycle of rebirth], whereas there are others who, partaking of that fruit whose nature it is to attain the supreme Person of unlimited and unparalleled bliss, never return [to this existence].[24]

Throughout history, the moral influence of the *Gītā* has been profound on religious Hindus, from the deliberations of a Gandhi to the quiet reflections of ordinary folk who continue to find the time to read regularly from the text. We will continue this discussion on the Hindu understanding of *dharma* and its implications in Chapter 9.

9 Morality and the person

Analysis of dharma *continued:* sādhāraṇa-dharma *and* sva-dharma: *their relationship illustrated through the practice of non-injury (*ahiṃsā*). Various understandings and forms of* ahiṃsā. Dharma *and fate (as illustrated by the story). The doctrine of karma and rebirth considered: roots, content, and uses (traditional and modern), scope. Karma and fate. Means of removing karma: transfer,* śrāddha, bhakti, jñāna. *The basic traditional model of the human person: spirit (*puruṣa/ātman*) and matter (*prakṛti*). Personal identity. Spirit as valorising, body as valorised. Ethical implications of karmic action.*

Manu comments on *dharma* in several places. 'Understand the *dharma*', says 2.1 'which is followed by the wise and recognised by the heart by the virtuous who are ever free from ill-will and anger'. There is an intriguing phrase or two here. Who are the 'wise' and the 'virtuous', and what does 'recognised by the heart' mean? B. K. Matilal, in an article entitled 'Dharma and rationality'[1] has pointed out that traditional commentators have glossed over these expressions in different ways. At the time the 'wise' and 'virtuous' would ideally have acknowledged the *dharma* of Vedic ritual, not to mention the *varṇāśrama dharma* of normative orthodoxy. But the matter does not end here. We have already pointed out that there was scope for conflict, doubt and exceptions in the implementation of such dharmic recommendations, many of which were optional. Resolution of one's dharmic uncertainties required guidance and deliberation.

Further, also exerting a strong influence on how one was to behave morally was what may be called *sādhāraṇa dharma*, namely, general morality (as opposed to *svadharma*). The Law Codes also imply or speak of a general morality. We read in Manu: 'Non-injury (*ahiṃsā*), truth (*satya*), not stealing (*asteya*), purity (*śauca*), control of the senses (*indriyanigraha*) – Manu has declared this to summarise *dharma* for the four castes' (10.63). The *Vāsiṣṭha* Law Code says: 'Avoiding backbiting, envy, pride, egoism, unbelief, guile, boasting, insulting others, hypocrisy, greed, infatuation, anger and discontent is approved *dharma* for all the stages of life'.[2] This would have been directed first at the 'twice-born', but it was to apply to all within the pale of 'Hindu' *dharma*, women, low castes and untouchables as well. This application would not be straightforward, but required careful attention to circumstances. We may illustrate this by reference to the virtue of non-injury (*ahiṃsā*).

Manu includes *ahiṃsā* (which means non-injury to all living beings) as a representative virtue of general *dharma*, so obviously practising *ahiṃsā* was regarded as of great importance to morality. But what about Kṣatriyas, whose caste duty it was to defend and protect, even at the cost of killing and being killed? It was understood that, in the line of duty, they were exempt from the injunction not to injure. In fact, a number of exceptions were made to the general *dharma* not to harm living beings. Consider the case of many Vedic rituals which involved not only injury to vegetative life, namely, plants, trees, etc. (for the making of sacrificial implements and so on) but also animal sacrifice. There were recommendations to perform such sacrifices as also to practise *ahiṃsā*. How to resolve this clash? Manu has a ready answer: 'One may regard the Veda-prescribed injury to moving and non-moving things as *ahiṃsā*, for *dharma* itself has arisen from the Veda' (5.44). Thus such injury can be reckoned as non-injury, or at least permissible injury. There are a number of Puranic texts which say that one may practise animal sacrifice at sacred places (*tīrthas*) only. Indeed, a number of dharmic authorities have declared that the quietus of animal sacrifice is quite deceptive; after all, the animal thus despatched attains heaven (exactly how we are not told). Another example is the animal sacrifice (*bali*) recommended in some forms of Tantric ritual. There were some Tantric sects which even practised human sacrifice. As in the case of Vedic animal sacrifice, Tantric sacrifice (which can be performed not only actually but also symbolically) was a highly ritualised act, on occasion taking many months to enact from the selection of the victim to its slaughter and disposal. However, this was regarded as either permissible violence or as non-violence.[3] Under Tantric influence, animal sacrifice (the victims often being goats and chickens) is common today in Śākta shrines.[4] The famous Kālī temple of Calcutta is one such place.

Let us also consider the recommendation to practise suttee, a suicidal form of self-injury. According to some authorities this was generally a good thing for wives just widowed, but exceptions were made. Thus the *Mitākṣara*, the most authoritative and well-known commentary (eleventh to twelfth century) on the *Yājñavalkyasmṛti* (see Chapter 4), recommends, but does not enforce, suttee on all wives, including the Caṇḍāla (one of the most despised castes; '*ā caṇḍālam*', says the text) *provided that* they are not pregnant or have young children to look after (1.86). Thus suttee overrides the directive to practise *ahiṃsā*, but the value accorded to new and vulnerable life outweighs the directive to practise suttee. Note that the text includes the Caṇḍāla within the scope of this dharmic injunction; the Caṇḍāla wife is enjoined both to commit suttee and to desist, depending on circumstances. So the conflict between *sādhāraṇa dharma* and *svadharma*, and the need to resolve it, apply to her no less than to the twice-born. *Dharma* was an all-embracing concept. The text mentioned actually says that it is the 'general *dharma*' (*sādhāraṇa dharma*) of wives to act in the manner described. Thus *sādhāraṇa dharma* is also a relative concept – relative to place, time, sex, and so on.

In fact, where *ahiṃsā* is concerned, it has been pointed out that there were conflicting views within Hindu theory and practice.[5] In certain circumstances injury to living things was permitted, even recommended (in which case, as we have seen, it might be interpreted as 'non-injury'). For example, the whole of the *Gītā* is based on the view that taking part in a bloody, internecine war is perfectly acceptable provided it can be interpreted as one's *svadharma*. Lord Kṛṣṇa tells his friend and devotee Arjuna that as a Kṣatriya it is his (Arjuna's) duty and natural role to fight in a just war, and that the best possible reason for doing this is not personal gain but the disinterested pursuit of (*sva-*)*dharma*, motivated by wholehearted love for Kṛṣṇa as God. There is a very robust and dominant strand in Hindu tradition of the appreciation of the need for (legitimate) violence, and violent action of one sort or another is almost the norm of the epics and other popular stories, both in the vernacular and in Sanskrit. In view of this fact, it is quite remarkable (partly to be explained by disorganisation, disunity, and mutual rivalry among Indians) that there was so little (physical) violence against colonial rule during the struggle for Independence. This is not to say that most Hindus would resort in the first instance to physical violence, of course, but it is also not to say that Hindus have no tradition of it or of thinking about it in moral terms.

This brings us to the view opposing violence in the tradition. This is also very strong and ancient, and may well have been stimulated by the early Buddhist and Jain critique not so much of war but of the high profile given to animal sacrifice in Vedic religion.[6] This has been called the view of the ascetic (viz. *Śramaṇa*) tradition.[7] There is no doubt that even in Vedic Hinduism general non-violence is the recommended practice for those embarking on stages of life after that of the householder. For such, the *dharma* of sacrificial and other ritual, of war and so on, are to be left behind. Texts specifically for those who wish to develop an ascetic way of life (and incorporating ways of thinking which may have originated as reactions to the sacrificial cult but which in time were absorbed into the general orthodoxy) generally laud non-violence as a supreme virtue. For example, the *Yoga Sūtra* of Patañjali,[8] an ancient and authoritative ascetical text – not least for many Tantric schools – says under 2.30–1: 'Non-injury (*ahiṃsā*), truth(fulness), not stealing, celibacy, and non-covetousness are the restraints. They apply at all levels irrespective of caste, place, time and circumstance'.

But we must not jump to conclusions. All ascetics, or so-called ascetics, have not necessarily felt bound by such dictates. From Moghul times, i.e. from about the fifteenth century, bands of armed ascetics began to assert themselves mainly in the northern half of the subcontinent. It seems that originally the idea was to resist attacks by various Muslim groups, but the ascetics soon developed bloody rivalries among themselves; from this it was a small step to preying on the general populace and/or enlisting as mercenaries or soldiers in the armies of the various rajas around. These were ascetics of a kind. They belonged to different sects, both Vaiṣṇava and Śaiva, and some were even Brahmins. They often went about naked or wearing only a minimal loincloth, hair matted, sectarian marks about their persons, bodies smeared with ash. They had their own codes and vows (to some of which they tended to adhere very lightly indeed, notably the vows of celibacy and abstention from covetousness and intoxicants). The most striking perhaps were the 'Kānphaṭās' (the 'Split-Ears'), of whom mention has been made in Chapter 1; they got their name from the heavy objects of stone or metal hung from their ears, and appear on the scene with a long and colourful history behind them.[9] Here is a description of the martial aspect, until fairly recent times, of the armed ascetics of which we speak:

> The generic name for this whole class of ascetic warriors was 'Naga', from the Sanskrit word *nagna*, meaning 'naked'. The Nagas were so called from their custom of going into battle naked, or with only a strip of cloth bound round the loins. They wore

> their beards parted in the middle and brushed up over the cheeks, to add to the fierceness of their appearance. Their bodies were smeared with ashes, and their foreheads and limbs painted with their respective sect-marks. Their weapons were the bow and arrow (later replaced by the matchlock), the shield, the spear and the murderous 'discuss' – the last worn, one above the other, like a ruff round the neck. Other weapons were a short sword or dagger; the 'rocket', a kind of glorified jumping cracker composed of a strong metal cylinder to which knives were attached; and the 'umbrella', consisting of a circle of iron balls suspended from a central rod, like a maypole, which when skilfully handled was said to be as impenetrable as a coat of mail, in addition to being a deadly weapon of offence. . . .
>
> The Nagas . . . made free use of bhang, opium, and intoxicating liquors. . . . In addition to being excellent swordsmen the Nagas were also skilled wrestlers, always eager to get to hand-to-hand grips with their antagonists. Their bodies were kept hard by severe physical exercises.[10]

The Kānphaṭās' numbers and activities declined drastically during British rule, but their memory lived on in the popular imagination. In 1882, Bankim Chandra Chatterjee, a Bengali intellectual, published a famous novel in Bengali entitled *Ānandamaṭh* ('Monastery of Bliss'). This was a glorified and fictional account of armed ascetics rising up against oppressors of the populace, the parallel with British rule being obvious. The novel popularised a stirring Sanskrit hymn entitled '*Vande Mātaram*' ('[I] Hail Mother [India]'), which inspired Bengalis, then in the vanguard of the nationalist movement.[11] *Bande Mātaram*, the Bengali pronunciation of this title, is regularly chanted in Bengal today during celebrations of national independence. Hindus have a long history of regarding the land in terms of female imagery,[12] so it was natural to address the country as the 'Motherland', not 'Fatherland'. In 1957, not long after Independence, there was a well-known remake of a classic pre-Independence (Indian) film called *Mother India*. In Benares,

> there is a modern temple called Bhārat Mātā, 'Mother India', containing no ordinary image in its sanctum, but rather a large relief map of India, with its mountains, rivers, and sacred *tīrthas* carefully marked. It is a popular temple with today's pilgrims, who circumambulate the whole map and then climb to the second-floor balcony for the *darshana* of the whole.[13]

Indeed, it was common for Bengalis and others during the nationalist movement to rouse themselves patriotically by using the mother Goddess in her terrible form (usually as Kālī) as a symbol of the nation.[14]

The Nāgas are not entirely a phenomenon of the past. Almost magically, they seem to materialise in their hundreds during the great gatherings of certain religious festivals. The 'Full' Kumbha Melā, a festival held every twelve years (see Chapter 12), is a good example. Nāgas of different sects turn up in large squads ('*ākhaḍās*'), most completely naked, bodies rubbed with ash. The weaponry is much reduced, though stout staves, swords and tridents are still in evidence. The ancient rivalry between various groups can still be strong, and members are not above cracking a pate or two when they see fit. One still hears of violent clashes between squads or disagreements of precedence in the processions that take place at the festival. Policing these occasions continues to be a sensitive issue. So much for the 'ascetic view' of *ahiṃsā*. In Hinduism, expect the improbable and do not rule out the impossible.

During the nineteenth century, in the aftermath of Ram Mohan Roy and others, the concept of *sādhāraṇa dharma*, mainly among the westernised, became valorised in terms of a universal, more or less egalitarian ethic embracing women and untouchables. (At least in theory; its practice was a somewhat different matter.) *Sva-dharma* then meant implementing this universal ethic in the circumstances of one's own life. For some, sensitised by emergent sociological and other understandings to the undoubted violence of caste and sexual discrimination in Indian society, the precept of *ahiṃsā* became an important part of this universal ethic. The most notable of such moralists was Gandhi. Gandhi made his own exacting understanding of non-injury in various spheres a central feature of his philosophy of life, and this has had an appreciable impact both nationally and internationally. But it is important to contextualise it historically. *Ahiṃsā* in Hindu tradition has always lived uneasily and ambivalently with *hiṃsā*.

It was the strong, traditional rational element inherent in articulating *dharma* that enabled creative minds like Ram Mohan Roy, Dayananda, Aurobindo and Gandhi to come up with new understandings of *dharma*. For their followers, such luminaries have become the new 'wise' and 'virtuous' of a reconstructed ethic, to be 'recognised by the heart' (see Manu's definition). At its best, 'recognition by the heart' entails a role for deliberation. This is quite in keeping with Manu's own understanding of the phrase, for as

Matilal points out in the article cited, according to Manu, *dharma's* authority is multi-rooted,[15] consequential dharmic decisions requiring on occasion a small council of deliberators to arrive at a conclusion.[16] Such deliberations would have taken into account the local time-honoured practices and conventions (*deśācāra*) of the community concerned, a consideration which plays an important part even today in the working out of social and personal *dharma*.

Thus *dharma* requires rationality, responsibility and free will. But the exercise of these criteria entails awareness of and allowance for 'cosmic' forces beyond one's control, represented by fate (*daiva*). Let us return to the story. Those who used fate as a cover-up in the name of *dharma* – Dhṛtarāṣṭra, Yudhiṣṭhira (up to a point) and Duryodhana – had in one way or other to bow to 'fate': Dhṛtarāṣṭra by the inauspicious signs at his household sacrifice which forced him to his senses; Duryodhana by the miraculous covering-up of Draupadī and by his father's fate-impelled nullifying of the dicing match, Yudhiṣṭhira through the consequences of his addiction (various humiliations, and being saved by a woman). But when *dharma* was respected, fate stepped in as an ally: miraculously, Draupadī did not suffer the ultimate shame. Out of the blue, she received the boons which were the Pāṇḍavas' deliverance. Thus fate protects those who attend to *dharma*, but sometimes at serious cost. This is a philosophy of fatalism at bay, not of fatalism rampant.

From very early times Hindus have struggled to divine the role of fate in this sense in their lives. The opening verses of the *Svetāśvatara* Upaniṣad raise this issue:

> The discoursers on *Brahman* say: 'Is *Brahman* the cause (i.e. explanation of things)? Whence are we born? By what do we live? And whither do we go (in the end)? Based on what, O knowers of *Brahman*, do we live out our lives in pleasure and its opposite'? Are we to think (that the cause) is time, nature, necessity, chance, the elements, the womb, the (contribution of the) male (to our make-up)? Or a combination of these? No. Then (does the explanation derive) from the being of the spiritual self? Even the spiritual self is subject to the purposes of pleasure and pain. (1.1–2)

This theistic Upaniṣad goes on to say that it is the Lord who rules over all these secondary causes. Once again, blind, impersonal forces do not have the upper hand.

Time, nature, necessity, chance, the womb, the individual: this list contains the ingredients of what is often regarded as a central belief of Hinduism in the influence of cosmic and determining forces, namely, that of karma and rebirth. There are two sides to this belief: that of karma teaches that certain kinds of action invariably produce good and bad 'fruit' or recompense; that of rebirth generally teaches that this recompense must be experienced by the agent of the actions in some *non-eschatological* existence (which may well include a return to this world), that is, in a form of life which does not necessarily – like the Christian purgatory – lead to ultimate fulfilment. This is the general teaching of the rebirth doctrine (there is an exceptional variant which we will discuss later). We must now examine the content and scope of the belief in karma and rebirth.

This is a very old teaching, but one seemingly not part of the original tradition of the Vedic Indians. There is no clear reference to it in the Saṃhitās,[17] although the Saṃhitās clearly speak of a belief in eschatological existences, good and bad, *merited* by certain actions in this life.[18] Generally in the Saṃhitās one lives on (metaphorically) in this world through one's progeny.[19] Glimpses of a perhaps germinating form of belief of rebirth seem to appear, however, in the Brāhmaṇas, which occasionally speak of *punar-mṛtyu*, 'repeated death'.

It is in the Upaniṣads that we have evidence that the belief in karma and rebirth was taking developed form, though even here, in early references, the teaching is shrouded in an air of mystery and secrecy. This is well-exemplified in the famous conversation (in BĀUp III.2.13) between the Sage Yājñavalkya and the scholar Ārtabhāga. The occasion is the great debate between Yājñavalkya and other pundits sponsored by King Janaka of Videha and mentioned earlier in the book. During his round with Yājñavalkya, Ārtabhāga is not doing too well and eventually challenges the Sage to tell the assembly what happens to the individual after bodily dissolution at death. 'What finally becomes of this person?' he asks.

> Yājñavalkya replied, 'Ārtabhāga, take my hand, friend, only we two shall know of this; this is not for us to make public'. The two went apart and conversed. What they spoke of and celebrated was action (*karman*). (The dead person) becomes good (*puṇya*) by good action and bad (*pāpa*) by bad action. Then Jāratkārava Ārtabhāga held his peace.

Explicit mention is made here of the doctrine of karma; rebirth may be only implied. But the *Chāndogya* Upaniṣad, for instance, speaks clearly of both aspects of the teaching. Under v. 10 three post-mortem paths for the soul are mentioned. Enlightened souls move along the 'path of the gods' via heavenly stations, eventually reaching the world of *Brahman* (or Brahmā?). These souls have transcended the cycle of rebirth. There are others who live morally mixed lives, on the one hand seeking by good works to build up merit for themselves rather than trying to dissolve the ego, on the other hand failing to avoid demerit through various transgressions. These travel the 'way of the fathers' after death, eventually returning by a complicated process to rebirth in various forms of life in this world, including (apparently edible) vegetation. The text is not clear, but it seems that residual merit (i.e. 'karmic residue') determines the kind of birth awaiting one. Where non-vegetative life is concerned, those of good conduct in this world attain a 'good womb', e.g. of a Brahmin, Kṣatriya or Vaiśya, but those of bad conduct attain a bad womb, e.g. of a dog, pig or Caṇḍāla. There is still a third post-mortem path, reserved apparently for the entirely lawless. These are reborn as tiny creatures, living and dying with seemingly no chance of breaking the cycle (*asakṛd-āvartīni*, the suggestion being made earlier that rebirth as edible vegetation, while not particularly attractive, at least enables one to move up the chain of existence towards eventual liberation: one assumes the same nature as the ingester of one's vegetative form, taking on the appropriate embodiment after being emitted through the semen in copulation. No such prospect for those reborn as tiny creatures).

Note that in its early forms, belief in the transmigratory cycle encompassed non-human forms of existence. This is a common feature of the belief in karma and rebirth even today. I have often heard both educated and non-educated Hindus say that one may be reborn as animals and even as insects. Some then go on to draw various conclusions from this, e.g. that one should respect all life, that one should eat only vegetarian food (in this case, the belief that one can be reborn as vegetative life is often absent). There are others who reject the idea that one can be reborn in sub-human life-forms, interpreting texts like those of the *Chāndogya* symbolically, i.e. being born as a tiger, insect or hog means being reborn as a human with either rapacious or backbiting tendencies or in a ritually impure condition, and so on.

In the course of time, belief in karma and rebirth developed and became more and more pervasive among Hindus. But this took time. Thus, interestingly, there is little if any reference to the teaching in the story of the dicing match. The belief could have played a major part in the story. The fact that it does not indicates that the episode of the dicing match was an integral part of the original story-line at a time when the belief in karma and rebirth was not widespread. Even in a more or less developed form, from about the time of Manu and the *Gītā*, there was no single dominant version of the doctrine. This situation continues to the present day; one can say glibly that there are as many versions of the belief as there are believers. We shall now review some of the chief features of the karma doctrine.

The teaching about karma itself indicates that the belief developed in an attempt to wrestle with the relationship between moral striving and the attainment of 'salvation', namely, absolute freedom from and sovereignty over the conditioned nature of worldly existence. Only the unattached, the non-egoistic, could attain this state. Yet the performance of action, especially sacrificial action, entailed a self-centred, calculating mentality. The individual had to be weaned from this mentality. It was thought that one life was not enough for this. Further, it is distinctively Hindu not to reject outright previous teaching if one can help it, but to assimilate this teaching in a new synthesis. We have already considered this tendency in our analysis of the attitude that Hindus have to truth. Therefore, the sacrificial or 'karmic' mentality was acceptable if one had no more than enjoyable post-mortem existences in sight. For true immortality the soul was still not purified enough. It was thought that after one has enjoyed the fruit merited by the performance of the ritual, one must return to this life, for there is nowhere else to go. True immortality, i.e. transcending worldly existence which is characterised by the calculating, 'commercial' ethic, has still not been achieved.

On the other hand, those who lived an un-Vedic, lawless existence, despising even the meritocratic if limited ethic of the ritualist mentality – an ethic which nevertheless maintained basic socio-religious order (*dharma*) in the world – would equally have to return, this time to expiate the demerit incurred by their contempt for the traditional, but useful, meritocracy. Better an ethic of meritocracy, rooted in the recommended practices of the past, than no such ethic; best, however, a selfless morality, based on such basic virtues as non-injury, liberality, general benevolence, control of the senses, respect for others and their property, etc., which leads to what traditional and indeed modern religious Hinduism has always set up as the supreme goal: ultimate liberation from conditioned existence. This ethic of non-attachment is a distinctive feature of the Upaniṣads which record a moral reaction to the mentality of the earlier sacrificial cult. It is no accident, I believe, that the belief in karma and rebirth first begins to assert itself in the Upaniṣads.

With the passage of time, the theorists developed the belief still further. It was made more individualistic, but not entirely so. That is, the belief in karma and rebirth became a belief governing one's personal morality. Every moral action, i.e. every conscious deed (including mental acts) with a sense of 'ought/may' or 'ought not/may not' to it (including, of course, but not exclusively, the realm of varṇāśramic action), incurs recompense which must be experienced by the doer. Such action does not incur recompense if it is an action one ought to do or may do but which is done disinterestedly, i.e. without the desire for self-gratifying recompense or its 'fruit' (*phala*). This recompense is called 'karma' (derived from the Sanskrit word for action, namely, *karman*) which is the merit or demerit (*puṇya or pāpa*) stored up as a result of self-centred moral action. Since karma cannot hang void but must be attached to some agent, it must be experienced. It can be experienced in another life requiring embodiment (an idea derived from the traditional view of the sacrifice; many sacrifices were performed for results to be obtained in a future existence). So the belief in rebirth became a corollary to the belief in karma.

This composite belief was extended and regularised to explain a number of things. One of these was one's situation in life; this included one's sex, caste, dispositions, and even various desirable and undesirable experiences. For example, we have seen that it was traditionally reckoned a disadvantage to be born a woman or an outcaste, so one must have acquired bad karma in a previous life to be born in this condition. On the other hand, being a male member of a twice-born caste is a good thing: this must be the result of past good karma. Again, being born poor or handicapped in some way is undesirable, while experiencing a windfall or a lucky escape is desirable. Both kinds of situation can be explained by the maturing of karma accumulated in a previous existence. Why only *one* previous existence? If karma and rebirth are a process, logically there is no cogent reason why they must have a beginning, so generally in the normative texts the process of *saṃsāra*, the flow or cycle of karma and rebirth, is without beginning (*anādi*).

Indeed, it is common for Hindus today to appeal to the doctrine as *the* Hindu solution to the problem of suffering and evil in the world. Why do good folk, the morally innocent, suffer oppression, ill luck and grief of one sort or another? Why do evil people prosper variously, and continue regardless in their wickedness? The answer is karma.[20] Evil deeds, if they do not find a recompense in this life, will do so in a future existence; virtuous actions, though they may not get their due now, will receive appropriate post-mortem reward too.[21] And so the idea of various heavens and hells, as part of the samsaric cycle, developed from fairly early times (since the beginning of the Common Era), replacing or co-existing with – in Hindu minds – the kind of post-mortem programme described in the *Chāndogya* Upaniṣad.

There are lurid descriptions in the Purāṇas of hells in which the punishment is made to fit the crime. The *Bhāgavata Purāṇa*, for example, waxes strong on this.[22] It declares that those who in this life cook animals and birds alive are thrown into a hell called Kumbhīpāka where *they* are cooked in boiling oil; a person who indulges in illicit sex receives the hellish recompense of having to embrace red-hot models of men or women (as appropriate); rulers or their officials who extort what is not their due are consigned to a suitable hell where 720 dogs with teeth like thunderbolts get to work on them, and so on. Alternatively, good karma can propel one into the appropriate heaven (there are numerous grades of heaven or *svarga*) where suitable reward is experienced in the form of heightened earthly pleasures in the company of the gods. After one's karmic recompense has been meted out in heaven or hell one is reborn again in the appropriate sphere of existence. The gods in this belief are often no more than 'firsts among equals' – holders of the different godly offices or names, who themselves, when their good karma is expended, will have to abandon their positions to a successor and be reborn in the manner that their freshly maturing karma dictates.

From these currently still widespread beliefs in karmic heavens and hells, we note that the samsaric cycle is three-tiered (heaven, earth and hell); that neither heaven nor hell in this conception is a permanent state – heaven or *svarga* here is not to be confused with final liberation (*mokṣa*; see Chapter 12); that liberation from *saṃsāra* is attained only by a self*less* morality rather than by the karmic ethic of reward and punishment; and that embodiment of one sort or another is a feature of the whole samsaric cycle.[23]

In fact, the belief in karmic heavens and hells is an attempt to articulate the doctrine of karma and rebirth as an expression of a cosmic moral law, valid for all human beings. Modern believers in the doctrine, including the learned, can make much of this. The philosopher Aurobindo Ghose has written:

> To be assured that there is an all-pervading mental law and an all-pervading moral law, is a great gain, a supporting foundation. That in the mental and moral as in the physical world what I sow in the proper soil, I shall assuredly reap, is a guarantee of divine government, or equilibrium, of cosmos; it not only grounds life

> upon an adamant underbase of law, but by removing anarchy opens the way to a greater liberty.[24]

Modern surveys show that people believe in karma and rebirth because they think the process expresses what should be the case, namely a law of causation operating in the moral world in as invariable and inviolable a manner as it does in the physical world.[25] But there is a complication. The moral force of the doctrine can be diluted by another, not unpopular, belief in the outworking of karma. This is the belief that one can receive karmic recompense for actions performed inadvertently, rashly or mistakenly. For example, it is not uncommon for people to believe that an honest mistake, say in punishing or censuring someone, will nevertheless yield undesirable karmic fruit. There is thus a mechanical aspect to this view of karma which militates against its moral rationale.

Aurobindo's words give us a clue to another popular reason for recourse to the doctrine: it allows one to believe that personal and spiritual growth, or at least progress up the scale of the human condition, can take place. This is an ancient facet of the teaching. We find it expressed in the *Gītā*. 6.45 says: 'But the aspirant (*yogī*), cleansed of stain, with mind controlled through much effort, is perfected after many births and thence treads the highest way'. We have already seen that this idea can also be used tendentiously. Manu declares (see Chapter 4, n. 24) that if the Śūdra behaves himself he will be rewarded with rebirth in a higher caste. Aurobindo, in his modern interpretation of the belief, has gone so far as to say: 'The true foundation of the theory of rebirth is the evolution of the soul, or rather its efflorescence out of the veil of Matter and its gradual self-finding'.[26] Since the closing decades of the nineteenth century it has been popular among educated believers of the doctrine to claim that it accords with or is an expression of the scientific theory of evolution. Justifying this claim is another matter, of course.[27] Scientifically acceptable or not, the teaching at least enables people to hope that they have a chance of improving their lot, if not in this life then in some future existence, especially if they feel weighed down by what seem to be circumstances beyond their control. Sometimes this hope is contrasted morally with the doctrine that we have only this life, to be followed by the judgement of eternity. On this, Aurobindo says:

> The difficulty [with the one-life doctrine] is that this soul inherits a past for which it is in no way responsible, or is burdened with mastering propensities imposed on it not by its own act . . . . We

> are made helplessly what we are and are yet responsible for what we are – or at least for what we shall be hereafter, which is inevitably determined to a large extent by what we are originally. And we have only this one chance. . . . The fortunate child of saints . . . and the born and trained criminal plunged from beginning to end in the lowest fetid corruption of a great modern city have equally to create by the action or belief of this unequal life all their eternal future. This is a paradox which offends both the soul and the reason, the ethical sense and the spiritual intuition.
> (Aurobindo, op. cit.: 110)

As this extract intimates, for Hindu adherents of the belief in karma and rebirth the notion of a life-span contains a distinctive perspective, one which accommodates not only the potential for spiritual development in successive births but also the realisation that this life is not a guillotine. No doubt the prospect of an indefinite series of future lives may and often does lead to apathy in the face of personal hardship for self and others. The stimulus for action to alleviate one's own lot and that of other people in the here and now is thus dampened. But from early times there has been a strong current in the literature to counter this negative reaction. It is based on the supposition that it is only as a human being that one may work for and attain salvation.[28] Thus life in non-human forms (whether on earth or in heavens and hells) is only for expending good or bad karma, not for creating a fresh supply.[29] From ancient times to the present, religious Hindus have usually accorded a uniquely irreducible value to human existence, even though the dualistic conception which has dominated their understanding of the nature of the human person may suggest otherwise (e.g. by allowing for traffic in rebirth between human and non-human forms of being).[30] We will consider this dominant Hindu model of human personhood later.

Aurobindo's words in particular imply that the doctrine of karma and rebirth enables one to reconcile belief in free will and in deterministic forces or 'fate'. On the deterministic side we have the accumulated karma of a beginningless chain of previous existences. The maturing of this karma can be resorted to to explain various factors that the individual cannot control, e.g. his or her sex, genetic make-up, status and situation at birth, various experiences or circumstances that life deals out. One's accumulated karma tends to be pictured as a 'bank' or store, consisting of good and bad stock which combine to mature partially in particular ways in one's life which cannot be predicted, though there is evidence to show that it has always been a popular belief that certain deeds receive quick and/or corresponding recompense (e.g. parricide results in speedy retribution, liberality results in a life of plenty or at least in a much-needed windfall, and so on). Further, in the tradition, one's karmic bank has been distinguished as consisting of three types of karma. These are as follows:

1 *Prārabdha* karma. This is the karma that has begun to mature in one's life. One can do nothing about this, whether the karma be good or bad; one must experience it. This concept has been invoked to explain how it is that even a manifest saint can suffer pain or oppression acutely, and how a villain of the first order can prosper.
2 *Kriyamāṇa* karma. This is karma in-the-making, the residue of merit or demerit that one is freshly storing up.
3 *Saṃcita* karma. This is already accumulated karma which is not being activated. When or how the combination of (ii) and (iii) will mature is not easily predictable.

Free will has a role to play in the context of all three kinds of karma. Thus it is up to the individual to decide how to cope with one's *prārabdha* karma, whether this will be attempted dharmically or not. True, one cannot control one's genetic make-up and other determinants of life, but generally one has a decisive say in what one makes of life. For Hindus it is a question of balancing deterministic forces and the strength of free will (informed by God's grace in theistic conceptions), and, in weighing up the scales some give more weight to one side, some to the other. In the case of *kriyamāṇa* karma, the exercise of free will can be given much significance. One can strive to integrate factors beyond one's control in building up one's life or paradoxically one can 'choose' to be overwhelmed by them. And in the case of *saṃcita* karma one is given the option of seeking to wipe it out. This brings us to the next point.

In Hindu teaching the process of *saṃsāra* is without beginning, as has been mentioned, but it is not necessarily endless. We have already noted that action (including mental action) which is not motivated by personal gratification of some kind, namely, action which is disinterested or non-egoistic, does not generate karma. Such action is called *niṣ-kāma*, i.e. non-covetous. Hindus believe that the *niṣ-kāma* individual need not be lacking in personality; he or she need not come across as a sort of bland, dried-up cypher from whom life's emotional sap has been squeezed out. Far from it, if the lives of acknowledged saints and gurus are anything to go by. In fact, the dissolution of self-centredness, consisting of those tight little knots (*granthinaḥ*) of selfishness which make up the covetous ego (as some texts put it), allows the individual to be truly himself or herself in an expansion of the personality which enables it to retain its charm while expressing a full measure of compassion and benevolence. Ramakrishna, widely regarded as a liberated soul, was partial to mangoes all his life, while Ramana Maharashi, enlightened Sage in the eyes of many, was noted for his gentle humour and bright-eyed smile. Besides, the karmic dross of the foibles and peccadilloes which are the inevitable mark of daily existence even for the saintly, is continually consumed in the self-effacing fires of enlightened living. But what about the soul's, even the newly enlightened soul's, vast burden of karma already accumulated (*saṃcita*) over a beginningless series of previous lives and waiting to be activated in future existences? Can this be done away with?

It is generally believed that it can, though different methods to effect this have been proposed. I noted earlier that the karma belief became gradually more individualistic, but 'not entirely so'. In other words, the doctrine was increasingly perceived as an expression of a cosmic law of personal morality, namely, 'As one sows, so one reaps', but even from very early times one encounters loopholes or perhaps inconsistencies in the application of this law. Thus there has always been a place in the Hindu mind for the notion of the transfer of merit (and demerit) or some suspension of the law of karma. For example, there are passages in the Upaniṣads which speak of the store of one's good and/or bad deeds being passed on either to one's son or to relatives,[31] or of one being deprived of merit accumulated.[32] Again, in the context of Pāśupata ascetic practice,

> restricted to brahmin males who had passed through the orthodox rite of investiture (*upanayana*) . . . in the second stage [of his practice, the ascetic] left the temple. Throwing off all the outward signs of his observance he moved about in public pretending to be crippled, deranged, mentally deficient or indecent. Passers-by being unaware that these defects were feigned spoke ill of him. By this means the Pāśupata provoked an exchange in which his demerits passed to his detractors and their merits to him. . . . Purified by this period of *karma*-exchange, the Pāśupata withdrew in the third stage to a remote cave or deserted building to practise meditation.[33]

Or consider beliefs associated with the common practice of performing commemorative rites (*śrāddha*) for one's dead. It is generally believed that by these rites the *preta*, i.e. the soul of the departed awaiting a resolution of its post-mortem fate, is in some manner given a ghostly body and fed and/or set at peace. By a transaction of karma (e.g. the accruing or transfer of merit, the annulment of demerit) accomplished by the *śrāddha*, the departed ceases to be a *preta*. A great many Hindus from all walks of life still believe that it is very important to perform the rites for the dead (for both their own peace and that of the *preta*). It is quite undesirable to have *pretas* wandering about; they tend to cause trouble in the human world, especially for their relatives.

But there is no generally accepted explanation as to *why* the law of karmic embodiment either in this world or in another fails to take over in the case of unsatisfied *pretas*, or as to what is the karmic link between satisfied souls of the departed and their rebirth. This is a grey spot in the logic of the doctrine of transmigration. Yet it does not stop people believing both in *pretas* and the need for the *śrāddha* rites, *and* in the law of karma and rebirth. Often in popular Hinduism apparently inconsistent or conflicting beliefs are happy bedfellows, awaiting implementation separately or in combination as and when occasion demands. Many practical anxieties are thus resolved, even if often undetected intellectual tensions remain.

Thus, for some, *śrāddha* rites are one way of doing away with past karma. There are also other ways which are believed to exert joint or independent efficacy. Often, in theistic world views, God is now brought into the picture. Generally in *bhakti* traditions it is believed that selfless devotion to God nullifies one's *saṃcita* karma. Love of God (in both the objective and subjective senses of the phrase) overcomes all, even the vice-like grip of one's past karma. It is sometimes believed that this love of God may be coupled with specific rituals which can destroy past karma without at the same time building up a fresh supply.[34] In so far as sufficiently selfless love of God has not been attained, however, and one lives a self-centred morality (i.e. importuning God in order to achieve success in various ventures, good health, long life, etc.) the law of karma and rebirth may be perceived as an expression of the divine justice and mercy: divine justice because it is God who sanctions ethical reward and punishment, and divine mercy because a purified love of God results in the annulment ('forgiveness') of past karma. For some Hindus, it is the fire of self-realisation (*jñāna, vidyā*) which consumes the burden of one's *saṃcita* karma. So, one way or another, one need not be cowed by the apparently inexorable outworking of the law. Fate in the form of karma does not necessarily reign supreme.

In fact, in the transports of their devotion, some Hindus have expressed a desire for rebirth precisely because one can then continue to hanker after the Lord. This is a mark of a certain kind of *bhakti* symbolised by the intense yearning of separated lovers (see Chapter 12). But generally rebirth is never presented as something desirable out of love for life in the world. On the contrary, for all its positive features and pleasures, life in *saṃsāra* is generally characterised as inherently sorrowful and, as such, undesirable. One's goal should be liberation (however this may then be described) from the seductive thrall of this world. The *Gītā* says that this world is 'the abode of sorrow' (8.15); Ramana Maharshi has described it as a 'wild and terrible forest' and a 'prison'. The wise person realises that even our earthly pleasures contain the seeds of their own decay, for as soon as we are gratified boredom sets in or we grow anxious that something will snatch the cause of our gratification from us. In short, like Tweedledum and Tweedledee, *sukha* or pleasure and *duḥkha* or pain are inseparable, with *duḥkha* dominating the relationship. True happiness (*ānanda*), on the other hand, is self-sustaining; it is the mark not of gratification but of selfless living.

The sorrowful nature of *saṃsāra* does not mean, according to Hindu teaching, that we are entitled to seek to manipulate our karma to shorten our existence for selfish reasons. Thus suicide to escape adverse circumstances is generally regarded as highly reprehensible (though there may be strong reasons to mitigate censure of the act and its karmic recompense). Suicide, however, in a dharmic cause (an act of rescue, war, suttee) has been regarded as praiseworthy. For Hindus there is such a thing as timely and untimely death. In this connection we must respect our own and others' maturing karma and seek to overcome undesirable aspects of it only by dharmic means. It is not permissible to perform undharmic actions in the name of fate or karma. Such decrees do not override human responsibility, as for instance, the *Caraka Saṃhitā*, a fairly early authoritative medical text (200–600 CE), declares:

> If all life-spans were fixed [by the decrees of karma/fate, irrespective of human acts like suicide, murder, abortion etc.], then in search of good health none would employ efficacious remedies or verses, herbs . . . oblations . . . fasting. . . . There would be no . . . anxiety about falling from mountains or [into] rough, impassable waters; and none whose minds were [considered] negligent . . . no violent acts, no actions out of place or untimely. . . . For the occurrence of these and the like would not cause death if the

> term of all life were fixed and predetermined. . . . Undertaking to employ the stories and thoughts of the great seers regarding the prolongation of life would be senseless. Even Indra could not slay with his thunderbolt an enemy whose life-span was fixed.[35]

The decrees of karma and the freedoms of *dharma* are thus not necessarily regarded as incompatible.

It is now time to consider a basic presupposition of the doctrine of karma and rebirth: that of the dualistic nature of the human person. We will thus gain a deeper appreciation not only of the ramifications of the belief in rebirth but also of a central and widespread teaching of traditional religious Hinduism.

According to this teaching, the human person is a composite of two distinct principles: spirit (*ātman, puruṣa*) and the stuff from which psychophysical being arises (*prakṛti*, often called 'matter', but not too felicitously for reasons given below). This is a very ancient understanding reaching back to early Upaniṣadic times. It is not clear if the *Ṛg* Vedic conception of human personhood was dualistic. Certainly, according to this conception, the individual had what was variously characterised as an animating principle (*asu*), a life-essence (*ātman*), a life-force (*prāṇa*), which did not perish at death. This principle seems to have derived from an underlying cosmic life principle in some way. The human individual had a subtle and a gross aspect to his or her being; at death the gross part dissolved into elemental constituents but the subtle part endured. Cremation seems to have been the usual way of disposing of the dead. Agni, the 'god' of fire, was invoked to send on the subtle *persona* of the righteous to the next world. There are texts to indicate that the unrighteous were consigned to a realm of darkness;[36] whether this was meant to represent annihilation is doubtful. Early Vedic conceptions of the next life for the righteous are vague. However, it seems that this was a state of heightened happiness entailing a human 'glorified' body in the company of loved ones and the ancestors and gods. It was a condition of 'immortality', but whether this meant an indefinitely long existence or true never-endingness (or both with respect to different individuals) is left unclear.

In the classical Upaniṣads a clearer dualistic conception of the human person emerges. The metaphor of the chariot quoted from the *Kaṭha* Upaniṣad (fifth to fourth century BCE) in Chapter 7 demonstrates this. The terminology of the metaphor is derived from concepts associated with the Sāṃkhya system of thought which attained its classical formulation in Īśvarakṛṣṇa's *Sāṃkhya Kārikā* (second to fourth century CE), and it is the Sāṃkhya model which has dominated the philosophical understanding of the nature of the human person in Hinduism to the present day. Much of the traditional terminology may be in disuse or unknown to most latter-day Hindus, but the basic dualistic conception of the association of spirit (for which *ātman* has become the more popular term) and psychophysical matter (*prakṛti*) endures.

According to the basic model, the nature of *ātman* is to be the locus of blissful consciousness. The relationship of such consciousness (*jñāna, vidyā*) to the spirit (or *ātman*, sometimes rather misleadingly translated as 'the self') may be explained in various ways. Thus for Nyāya Vaiśeṣika the *ātman*, not being conscious in itself, possesses consciousness as an attribute, whereas in Vedānta and in most other systems of religious Hinduism the spirit is inherently self-conscious. No matter, the home or locus of consciousness is generally the *ātman*. The individual is regarded as an expression of a particular relationship between spirit and *prakṛti*. We have called *prakṛti* 'the source of psychophysical being' and now we shall explain why. *Prakṛti* is a basic principle of being, made up of three *guṇa*s ('strands') known as *sattva*, *rajas* and *tamas*. These three *guṇa*s exist only in combination; none can exist separately. Though each has different attributes, they share the common characteristic of being inherently non-conscious (*prakṛti*).

In a cosmological context, *prakṛti* exists at first in a subtle, unevolved state. By power of or association with spirit (spirit's initiatory role is explained differently in different systems of thought) *prakṛti* begins to evolve into the differentiated, material world that we experience. In effect, this means that the *guṇa*s undergo modifications (*vṛttis*) to produce distinctive characteristics of empirical experience. On the physical side, *sattva* gives rise to brightness, lightness and related material properties and is associated with the colour white; *rajas* is responsible for mobility of various kinds and is associated with the colour red, while *tamas*, which is associated with the colour black, produces darkness, inertia, decay and related phenomena. When combined in various strengths, the three *guṇa*s produce the experienceable physical universe in which we live. This is the traditional Hindu cosmological picture of material being. It is interesting to note that some modern thinkers have sought to relate these basic metaphysical principles of *prakṛti* to contemporary scientific data. Thus the luminosity and visibility of light is a particular manifestation of *sattva*, sub-atomic particles, which display extreme transience and mobility, manifest to a high degree *rajas*' distinctive nature, *tamas* is distinctively expressed in the law of gravity, and so on.

However, it is important to keep in mind that according to the traditional conception our experience of moral and mental activity also derives from the *guṇa*s. Not only does *sattva* give rise to certain physical phenomena, but at the level of the individual it undergoes modifications so as to produce experiences and dispositions which we characterise as serenity, peace, compassion, benevolence, kindness, forgiveness, awareness, intelligence, insight, clarity of mind, etc. Likewise, *rajas* produces passionate mental and moral activity (a mercurial temperament, volubility, wrath, lust, etc.) including the experience of pleasure and pain of different kinds (joy, sorrow, anxiety), while the modifications of *tamas* give rise to such things as sloth, stupidity, mental confusion, cowardice, and so on.[37]

The point is that *prakṛti* in the form of the modifications of the *guṇa*s acting in combination, is the stuff which gives rise not only to material being but also to mental experience as we know it. In other words, in this conception the difference between mental and material being is one of degree, subtle forms of the former (conceptualisation, 'intuition', for example) and gross aspects of the latter (inanimate bodies, perhaps) being at opposite ends of a continuum. This is why we have called *prakṛti* not 'matter' or 'energy', but 'the source of psychophysical being', the stuff from which such being arises. Further, as *prakṛti* is inherently non-conscious, human mental activity is not an expression of 'real' consciousness, for only the spirit possesses true consciousness – which leads us on to the next point.

The experience of awareness, and of personal identity for that matter, arises at the interface of the association between spirit and *prakṛti* which constitutes the individual. This association is an intimate one, the spirit in effect pervading the whole psychophysical organism ('bird-in-a-cage' models of the relationship being quite inappropriate). Mental activity appears as conscious and has the *semblance* of true consciousness, because in its variegated forms it is the reflection (perhaps better, refraction) of the consciousness of spirit that informs the psychophysical being. This reflection takes place in the *buddhi*, the faculty of deciding and discerning and the most subtle aspect of *prakṛti* in the individual, consisting predominantly of *sattva*.[38] Through discriminative thought we may have an idea of the true nature of spirit, which in most philosophical–theological systems of Hinduism essentially transcends the grasp of empirical concepts.

For most religious Hindus, the centre of gravity of human personhood lies squarely in spirit, not in the psychophysical part of our being. It is spirit which gives the human being its intrinsic worth, which sustains the body, and which is destined for ultimate immortality. Hence our usual awareness of personal identity, which may be expressed in such statements as 'My name is so-and-so', 'I am tall/short, fair/dark, male/female', 'I come from such-and-such a family/village/city', 'I have such-and-such memory experiences', 'These are my hopes, fears, expectations, relationships', etc. – in other words, our self-image as the psychophysical ego – is to a large extent a false centre of consciousness. This is because it is located mainly in *prakṛti*; as such it is changeable and changing, provisional and transient and not the basis of our ultimate fulfilment. The prakritic complement of our beings has a borrowed value, a value derived from the sustaining and essentially unchanging transcendent spirit within. The psychophysical ego is not entirely a false centre of consciousness because in experiencing it we also experience – though for all but enlightened souls this is more or less a confused, unrealised experience – our 'true self', namely, the sustaining *ātman* within. Only enlightened souls have attained a state of discrimination between the real centre of their beings which is spirit, and the construct, which is the psychophysical ego. As such they live not through the ego, which normally grows through self-centred desire (*tṛṣṇā*) by assimilating everything and everybody to itself, but through the expansive, egoless nature of spirit. For the enlightened, the ego – a necessary pivot for everyday living – becomes a more or less transparent focus for the presence of the spirit within. Every selfless act is a spiritual act, every selfish act is unspiritual. As we have seen, salvation is attained by selfless action (*niṣkāma karma*).

To say that spirit is the valorising principle, the centre of gravity of human personhood, does not mean necessarily that matter and the body are to be unilaterally despised. No doubt there is a strong ascetic current especially in traditional, post-Saṃhitā, Sanskritic Hinduism, in which materiality has been devalued (see Chapter 7). But both in Hindu theology and on a more popular basis, there have been counter-currents. Sometimes these popular currents have been on the margins of the Sanskritic tradition (e.g. some Tantric cults which ritually use bodily products and processes in unconventional contexts as a means to spiritual fulfilment), sometimes within it. As to theology, within the Vedantic tradition, Rāmānuja's thought provides a famous example of an attempt to rehabilitate to a significant extent the Advaita Vedantic denigration of the body. A pivotal idea in Rāmānuja's theology is that the world is *Brahman's* 'body' understood in the special sense of something that the deity fully sustains and controls and which serves the divine ends.[39] On the whole, however, the Hindu attitude to the body is ambivalent, and it is the (human) female body which usually best symbolises this ambivalence. On the one hand, woman's body can symbolise creativity, service in a higher cause, fertility, fidelity, power, protectiveness, nourishment, and so on. These positive connotations are usually expressed in the context of either the chaste wife or the Goddess as subordinate to her divine consort. But the female body also symbolises destructiveness, lustfulness, deceit, spiritual delusion, the doorway to suffering and death – negative connotations separately or collectively usually associated with the unmarried woman or sometimes with the Goddess as dominating her divine consort. This ambivalence naturally has repercussions for the status of woman in Hinduism and it remains for Hindus to tackle this issue in a concerted and egalitarian manner. Finally, we note in passing that in the popular imagination, not least in popular *bhajans* etc., the body is often regarded as an instrument, or an enfolding garment, which is spun out at each new birth and folded away at death.[40]

Now we may ask, who or what is the agent of karma in the context of this dualistic model of the person? Is it spirit acting through the ego, or is it the psychophysical ego itself? Broadly speaking, two kinds of answers are given in the different schools. In monistic traditions (e.g. Samkarite Advaita, Kashmiri Saivism), according to which there is but one ultimate spiritual reality and an indefinite number of provisionally real egos associated with it, only the ego is responsible for the production of karma. Salvation means the dissolution of the ego, which leaves the underlying spirit to continue its unchanging existence. In dualistic traditions (e.g. Ramanujist Vedānta, Southern Śaiva Siddhānta), according to which each conscious being is a conjunction of a separate *ātman* and ego, spirit acting through ego is the agent of moral action.

For either answer, however, note that death entails the destruction not only of the visible body but also of the mental ego, i.e. of our particular sense of 'I'. What endures each death in the chain of rebirth is spirit conjoined to what is called the subtle body (*liṅga śarīra*). It is the subtle body of each individual which identifies his or her particular series of existences, linking one birth with the next. As such, the subtle body is an entirely prakritic substrate (not susceptible to ordinary sense experience), the repository of the memory traces and accumulating karma of a particular karmic chain.

In the case of an impending birth into this world, it is claimed, an individual's subtle body finds a suitable couple through whose reproductive union its maturing karma will find appropriate corporeal expression. The growth of a new human individual involves the development of a new psychophysical ego, a new sense of 'I'.

If this is the case, in what sense may a particular individual be said to be responsible for the past karma of its karmic chain? Philosophically and morally at any rate, it seems in a very tenuous sense indeed. For the ego of this life, which, it may reasonably be argued, whether in association with spirit or not, is crucial for the notion of moral accountability, is not the ego of a previous life, nor will it be the ego of a future existence. Perhaps this is why it seems that for Hindus the doctrine of karma and rebirth is largely a 'gut-belief', absorbed uncritically through the culture, resorted to in order to plug holes in a basically rational understanding of the universe. 'Why is this happening to me?' When no obviously rational explanation is available, fate/karma steps in as the answer.

Let us consider the following explanation. Somebody has cursed or blessed me (Sanskrit and vernacular literature is full of cursings and blessings and their inevitable consequences) or cast a spell on me (i.e. this is why this is happening to me). Many Hindus have traditionally found such explanations convincing. But for the believer in karma these are what we may call 'penultimate explanations' of otherwise obscure happenings, which can easily be fitted into the more ultimate explanation of the karma doctrine. Again, what will happen to me if I behave in a particular way? I cannot foresee, so fate/karma will take care of it. How to explain the anomalies of this existence, the obviously unmerited sufferings of the innocent or fortunes of the villainous, the structure and kind of world in which we live? Fate/karma steps in: at the beginning of a new cosmic cycle, the accumulated karma of the previous dissolved world's inhabitants, in most theistic conceptions under the guidance of God, shapes the kind of world freshly coming into being. In short, the doctrine of karma and rebirth – with or without the aegis of divine providence – is a distinctive Hindu way of papering over the cracks in a rational appraisal of existence. This is why, for practical purposes, it is a doctrine and not a theory, although philosophical minds have attempted to make a theory of it.[41]

It is a common fallacy that belief in karma and rebirth is wellnigh universal among Hindus (even religious Hindus). This is an important reason why in Chapter 1 we did not use it as a distinguishing criterion of what it means to be a religious Hindu. It is certainly a widespread and deeply entrenched belief, but it is not a universal one by any means. Thus the two surveys cited in n. 25 indicate that an appreciable minority of at least some sections of (urban) Hindu society in general and of religious Hindus in particular find the belief in karmic recompense and/or rebirth (of which a number of variants are mentioned) unconvincing or doubtful. It is significant, I think, that these doubters were exposed to at least some degree of western education. Further, studies show that there are appreciable strands of folk Hinduism in which belief in a causal relationship between karma and rebirth is largely absent, or plays only a minimal role. In these strands recompense for good or bad deeds is often meted out in the present life. In the *Manasā Maṅgal*, for instance, this view prevails, although there is also recourse to the rebirth doctrine.

A number of Hindus attribute a symbolic significance to the belief in karma and rebirth. Thus, they say, it may not be literally true that rebirth takes place in order to expend accumulated karma, but this is a potent way of symbolising the responsibilities that one generation of human beings bears in respect of succeeding generations. Current ecological sensitivities give point to this perception. The child is father of the man in a new sense: are we not reborn in our children who will have to face the consequences of our physical, social and environmental decisions – the 'karma' we have created – in the lives and world that they inherit from us?

Part III

Images of time, space and eternity

10 Modes of reckoning time and 'progress'

Conceptions of time in Sanskritic tradition: the yuga-*view. Time and freedom:* līlā *and* māyā. *Implications of time in the Kali-age. Time as 'progressive': exemplified by the* āśramas, tapas *(illustrated through a story), the* puruṣārthas, *the* saṃskāras, *including observations on modern practice. Time and the understanding of history in Hinduism.*

It is often said that traditional Hinduism, religious or otherwise, is entirely lacking in the groundwork for a concept of history in the modern sense. This is attributed to the supposed Hindu tendency to view time as an endlessly repetitive sequence of events, in the context of which the concept of real socio-religious progress for a community or true religio-moral growth for an individual cannot consistently be accommodated. There is more than a semblance of truth to this claim; nevertheless, it is a gross over-simplification. The reality is far more subtle. To appreciate why, we must first examine the classical Hindu view of time and its passage.

In traditional Hindu philosophy there are a number of different views about the nature of time (*kāla*). Thus according to Nyāya-Vaiśeṣika time is a real substance with properties, but for the Advaitic tradition time is a condition of, and of a piece with, empirical reality which, compared to the ultimate and lasting reality of *Brahman*, is neither real nor unreal; it is of the nature of appearance.[1] The traditional popular conception of time, however, is of something quite real. Scholars have derived *kāla* from the root *kal*, meaning to count, to bring about. Time is the great reckoner; it presides over the coming-to-be and the destruction of worldly being. In the *Gītā* (11.32), Kṛṣṇa identifies himself with time. 'I am Time, bringing about the destruction of the world.'

It is interesting to note that in this capacity time is often regarded as the devourer of all. Hindus have a tendency to link temporal transitions with a devouring of some kind and the act of devouring/consuming/swallowing with experiencing the vicissitudes of this life. In traditional mythology, eclipses of the sun and moon are attributed to Rāhu, 'the seizer'. The story goes that in the beginning of time the gods and anti-gods used the cosmic serpent and mountain as a rope and rod to churn the elixir of immortality (*amṛta*) from the primeval waters. As the *amṛta* appeared, Rāhu, an anti-god, disguised himself as a *deva* and swallowed some of the elixir. But the sun and moon exposed his disguise and his head was chopped off by Viṣṇu. Thus since the beginning of time the vengeful Rāhu has been periodically swallowing his detectors, who in due course emerge from his severed throat. Here the temporal phenomenon of an eclipse is linked to the act of devouring. Again, it is common for Hindus to describe the experiencing of life's woes as a 'swallowing' (e.g. the Bengali idiom of 'eating' a beating or insults).[2] This echoes the classical Hindu notion of mundane existence as *saṃsāra*, the stream of life in which the ordinary human being struggles to keep head above water.

In the traditional popular conception time unfolds in the form of cycles of four ages or *yuga*s which start with an age of perfection and end, through progressive decline, with an age of degeneration. But what declines in this process? We shall get an idea if we briefly review the character of the four ages. In the first age or *satya yuga* (also called the *kṛta yuga*), *dharma* or the socio-religious order, likened sometimes to a sacred cow, is firmly established on four legs.[3] Human passions are generally kept at bay in this age, the rules of the caste hierarchy are respected, and even human sensibilities and capacities are heightened (e.g. the span of life is much longer than at present, and so on). This is the golden age, the longest *yuga*, where the veil between mundane existence and the transcendent is transparent. The *Viṣṇudharmottara*, a Purāṇa-like text,[4] says that in the *satya yuga* the deities are worshipped in their visible form (i.e. by *pratyakṣa-pūjā*). There is no need for images or temples.[5]

But there is an inexorable decline of *dharma*. This is the result of human beings allowing their passions to get out of control. Goodness, in its naturalistic and moral senses, progressively declines, and the world becomes more prone to disorder. We are in the shorter *treta yuga* in which the sacred cow of *dharma* is more or less steady on three legs. In due course the proportionally shorter *dvāpara yuga* begins, where *dharma* balances on two legs. As human sensibilities (and life-spans) wane the deities are worshipped in their visible form less and less, and through fashioned images more and more. The veil between mundane existence and the transcendent is darkening. Finally, the *kali yuga* sets in, characterised by the *Viṣṇu* Purāṇa as follows:

> [It is the age] when society reaches a stage where property confers rank, wealth becomes the only source of virtue, passion the sole bond of union between husband and wife, falsehood the source of success in life, sex the only means of enjoyment, and when outer trappings are confused with inner religion.[6]

This is proportionally the shortest age, *dharma* wobbling on one leg only. Worship through images is rife; the deities cease to be visible. *Avidyā* or spiritual obtuseness clouds the mind. According to Hindu reckoning this is the age in which humankind lives today, and it has hardly begun. When it has run its course it will be brought to an end by conflagrations or floods (or both), and the cosmos will be reabsorbed progressively into its prakritic source. Human and other souls will exist in a state of suspended animation. Everything is absorbed into the *deva* Brahmā, who presides over the process. Then a new *satya* age begins, worlds being emitted from Brahmā. And so the *yuga*-cycles, folding and unfolding, run on. Each series of four ages or *yugas*, from *satya* to *kali*, is called a *mahā-yuga*. One thousand cycles (called one *kalpa*) of world projection and dissolution are usually regarded as a Brahmā-day, at the end of which there is an equally long Brahmā-night. After a hundred Brahmā-*years* of this process even Brahmā himself is absorbed into the bosom of the Absolute and there is creational quiescence for an equally long period. Then the productive cycle begins again. And the process continues indefinitely. This is the traditional and pervasive mythic conception of time of Brahminic Hinduism.

It may well seem that in this conception there is insufficient basis to construct a modern concept of history, of true contingency and of real progress. But on scrutiny this impression is misleading. The mythic account has a number of inbuilt inconsistencies and hiatuses which can be (and have been) exploited in the tradition to accommodate historical and progressivist consciousness on popular and learned levels. In the first place, there is little if any support for the view that each succeeding cycle is a replica, so far as individual lives and events are concerned, of the preceding one. Certain things are duplicated with the cyclical passage of time, e.g. the basic structure of the universe, certain 'offices' (e.g. that of Brahmā), the form of the Vedas, and so on. But usually in each cycle human beings retain a basic freedom to shape their lives and worlds as they see fit.

In this connection, note the following anomaly. On the one hand the cyclical process is presumed to be inherently degenerative; on the other hand decline is invariably if implicitly attributed to voluntarily allowing the passions to get out of control. Thus logically, decline *need not* have taken place. But because human beings – and even the gods in the mythic account (there are many myths to illustrate this) – exist, even in the *satya yuga*, as essentially imperfect with the capacity for baser instincts, things can and do go wrong. Thus from the beginning the element of contingency is introduced as a real possibility into the mythic account of the passage of time. There is room for the exercise of free will (and reason) and consequently for real progress (and decline) in the development of human affairs both communal and individual. In earlier chapters, in our analysis of the concepts of *dharma*, rationality, karma and fate, we have seen how this is affirmed in the tradition.

Generally theologically too, as opposed to mythologically, the freedom of the Godhead to produce the world is invariably affirmed in a context in which human freedom reflects the divine freedom. Thus Rāmānuja argues that the divine production of the world is a free act since it is based on prior consideration (i.e. it is *buddhi-pūrvaka*). He appeals to the scriptural passage, 'It thought, "May I be many, may I bring forth" ' (e.g. *ChāndUp* VI.2.3) as illuminating the creative act. Rāmānuja interprets this statement as implying God's freedom to produce the world.[7] Madhva also stresses the divine sovereignty. In fact for Madhva this is the chief distinctive characteristic of the supreme Being.[8] In these views the divine production of the world does not entail a deterministic providence so far as human action or events are concerned. Again, in the context of Tantra, Abhinavagupta insists that the progressive manifestation of dependent reality, whether subjective or objective, word or object, depends entirely on Śiva's sovereign will to initiate and sustain the whole process. Thus a blanket determinism in the development of world affairs, whether on the part of the deity or of human beings, has no philosophical underpinning in traditional Hinduism.

At this point it would be relevant to consider an important concept of traditional Hindu thought which is often expressed, even today. This is the concept of *līlā*, usually translated as 'play' or 'sport' with reference to the supreme Being's production of or involvement with the world. Thus Hindus characteristically say that the production of this world or some event or sequence of events is an expression of the deity's *līlā*. No doubt on a personal, spontaneous level this may express different mental states, e.g. a sense of frustration or resentment that things are not going one's way perhaps, bafflement or wonder at the divine will over something, etc. On a more considered level, Hinduism has sometimes been criticised because the concept of divine *līlā* intimates that God does not take the world or human affairs seriously, and that the world is not an arena for responsible divine action. This charge is quite misdirected, and has no philosophical–theological backing in the major strands of Hinduism.

Here *līlā* invariably signifies that there is neither intrinsic nor extrinsic *physical* necessity on the deity's part to perform any action with regard to the world, whether this concerns bringing the world into being or presiding over its affairs and destiny. The deity is not constrained by his or her nature to produce the world in the first place. Theologians have posited a *moral* necessity in God to act in certain ways consequent upon the sovereign decision to produce the world, ranging from manifesting certain scriptures to upholding the law of karma as an expression of the divine justice, to reaching out in salvific love to the devotee. But all this indicates nothing if not responsible divine action, and refutes the interpretation of divine *līlā* as toying with humankind. On the contrary, *līlā* signifies the deity's freedom to produce and govern the world without an ulterior motive of any kind. That God cares for the world is shown in various ways: the production of a structured universe with stable physical and moral laws, the bestowal of salvific scriptures and rituals, the divine descent in various forms to teach and to save, etc.

However, in some traditions *līlā* has an extended meaning. It points to the sovereignty of action, the spontaneity, the existential thrill of the Lord during his *avatāra*s into the world. This comes out especially in the Vaiṣṇava *bhakti* traditions with reference to the pastimes of Kṛṣṇa. We have referred to accounts of the youthful Kṛṣṇa engaging in amorous exploits with the *gopīs* or cowherdesses in the idyllic setting of Vṛndāban on the banks of the Yamunā river. Kṛṣṇa pilfers butter, gets up to mischievous pranks with his friends, teases and makes love to the *gopīs*, and dances in abandoned delight with them under the moonlight in a whirling ring in such a way that each *gopī* believes that he dances with her and has eyes for her alone (the famous *Rāsa* dance). This is *līlā*.

Besides enjoying the narrative, the religious mind can see an underlying theology here. Kṛṣṇa's love-sports with the *gopīs* symbolise the adorable Lord's passionate and unique love for each soul and his refusal to subject himself to human conventions and expectations.

This is the Lord's *līlā*.[9] Theologically, it is the image of a smile playing about the Lord's lips that lingers; unlike Christ, he is not 'a man of sorrows'. The Lord is invariably in command of the situation, his divine sovereignty barely masked. Thus we may say that *līlā* is an anti-deterministic notion.[10]

The idea of *līlā* is connected to another important concept which we have encountered already – that of *māyā*. Here let it suffice to say that *māyā* has philosophical and popular meanings. Philosophically, it refers to the bewildering power of appearance in two ways. (i) The term can signify that the world is only provisionally or deceptively real as a masking projection of the divine power. *Māyā* is made much of in this sense in non-dualist traditions of Vedānta and Tantra. In these traditions there is only one permanent underlying reality (e.g. *Brahman*), essentially distinctionless and of the nature of pure consciousness and bliss. But this nature is masked by the provisional world of differentiation of which we are a part. As such the world or worldly experience is sometimes described as the Absolute's *māyā*. Our religious goal is to pierce the veil of *māyā* by a disclipined scriptural, ritual and ethical path (*sādhana*) and to experience our essential spiritual identity with the Absolute. But (ii) *māyā* can also be used philosophically in a strongly *realist* sense to signify this world or worldly phenomena as expressing the deity's wondrous and bewildering power. The world or its phenomena are real enough, but they can take on a dazzling quality either as manifesting or as masking the divine action. Rāmānuja, for one, uses *māyā* in both nuances of this second sense.

In its popular meanings *māyā* retains the connotations of dazzlement and deceptiveness with respect to the divine activity. In Chapter 7 we gave an example of this usage. In all of these meanings, *māyā* can be seen to have semantic links with *līlā*. The Absolute's untrammelled and spontaneous sovereignty dazzles, bewitches and captivates mortal eyes. In short, the concepts of both *līlā* and *māyā*, which revolve on the ideas of freedom and sovereignty, seem actively to support the possibility of contingency and progress in the development of human affairs.

We now return to the classical account of the degenerative passage of time. This has been exploited both psychologically and religiously. In the nineteenth century, especially among the Bengali intellectuals who helped form the modern Indian mind, the idea of a golden cultural age in ancient India (an idea first implanted by the researches of western orientalists) played an important role in raising self-esteem and nationalist consciousness. This idea could only have been consciously or subconsciously reinforced by the traditional conception of degenerative time. But it also inspired various movements for both socio-religious reform and revivalism – a process which continues apace. Aspects of these movements have been considered at various points in this book.

Today it is not uncommon for religious Hindus in various walks of life to account for something they deplore as an expression of life in the *kali yuga*. 'Can you expect anything better in this *kali* age?' they may say of some undesirable event or trend. But religiously there is also a consoling side to living in this dark age. It has long been used to justify the simplification or reform of religious practices. According to this way of thinking, the decline of human capacities in the *kali yuga* must inevitably result in concessionary forms of religious practice. We are not equal to what was required religiously of the inhabitants of the preceding ages – the mores, the meditative techniques, austerities, etc. So in our age salvation is made easy. This way of thinking has been characteristic of *bhakti* religions. Here is an example from the religious teaching attributed to Caitanya (thought to have lived from 1486–1533).

Caitanya[11] was born in a Vaiṣṇava Brahmin family in the town of Nadia in Muslim-ruled Bengal. From early manhood he became intoxicated with love for Kṛṣṇa and was known for leading processions of male devotees through the streets of Nadia ecstatically singing to Kṛṣṇa and chanting his name. This singing and chanting, called *kīrtana*, became an important devotional practice among his followers in the cult of Gauḍīya Vaiṣṇavism, and continues to this day in wider context. Thus in the last century, the Brahmo reformer Keshab Chandra Sen led similar processions through the streets of Calcutta as a feature of his brand of devotional Hinduism. The members of the Hare Krishna movement, who look to Caitanya as a seminal source of their faith, consider *kīrtana* (in which women participate) to be an essential part of their religious practice. This communal singing and chanting can sometimes last for hours, leading to heights of emotional transport. In 1516, Caitanya, who had renounced worldly ties some years earlier, settled in the holy temple town of Puri in Orissa and worshipped Kṛṣṇa in the form of Jagannātha, the temple deity. He based his teachings on the *Bhāgavata* Purāṇa where the highest form of the Godhead is personal (*Bhagavān*, the Adorable One) and followed a form of devotion which derived its poignancy from feeling the absence of the Lord through the persona of the Lord's divine lover, Rādhā. This kind of *bhakti* is called *viraha bhakti*, namely, the *bhakti* of separation.

According to Caitanyaism human beings exist in an unfathomable relationship of identity and difference with respect to the Lord (called *acintya-bhedābheda*) and undergo rebirth in accordance with the law of karma until they realise that they exist to serve and love Kṛṣṇa alone. Once one's eyes have been opened by faith, loving service of the Lord is enacted through the roles of his associates: his parents, friends, lovers, etc. In the past, complex religious duties and practices were required for liberation, but in this *kali* age simple, whole-hearted devotion to Kṛṣṇa is enough to wash away past karma and attain salvation. In time Caitanya came to be regarded by his followers as the embodiment of the divine pair, Rādhā and Kṛṣṇa, and he is an important religious figure even today. Many other examples of 'concessionary religion' for the *kali yuga* can be cited.

The notion of living in the *kali yuga* has also given rise to the concept of *kali-varjya*, namely, what is to be avoided (*varjya*) in the Kali age. This is the converse of the idea of concessionary religion, and it also has much expediency value. Here is a topical example. There is not the slightest doubt that in ancient India (at least until about the beginning of the Common Era), meat-eating and the slaughter of cattle were tolerated, on occasion even endorsed by Vedic *dharma*. Killing a cow in order to feed honoured guests was expected; and killing a cow as part of the marriage rite and for similar reasons was recommended. A number of the early Codes were precise about which meats could be eaten and the list included beef.[12] But in time, for various reasons (some of which have been mentioned already) culminating, no doubt, in the desire of the orthodox to recoil collectively from the characteristic Muslim practice of beef-eating especially on religiously festive occasions, the killing of cows became unacceptable. A way had to be found for reinterpreting the permissions of the Law Codes, and for this the concept of *kali-varjya* was convenient. So the Purāṇas teach that although meat-eating and/or the slaughter of cattle may have been permitted in the preceding ages for one reason or another, it is now *kali-varjya* – so much so that it came to be abhorred as a practice which *symbolises* our degenerate times. Today, somewhat ironically from a historical perspective, opposing the slaughter of cattle has become a necessary element of Hindutva in some circles. Many other examples can be given of using the concept of *kali-varjya* as an expedient.

There are a number of significant concepts in traditional Hinduism which subtly modulate if not counteract the classical conception of degenerative time. Take for example the idea of the four *āśramas*. There is a sense of progression to the spiritual life here: in theory one may pass from the stage of the student in which one is formally initiated into religion to that of the householder and then on to the stages of the forest dweller and renouncer. But as intimated in Chapter 4, the progression here is not straightforward in any obvious sense. Stages can be bypassed; studentship which is a phase of renunciation and celibacy can lead to what must be regulated enjoyment of sex and prosperity in the householder stage. This in turn can lead to the renunciation of sexual pleasure and wealth as a 'forest dweller' (i.e. one who withdraws from the world) and the ultimate severing of worldly ties in *saṃnyāsa*. Spiritual progress (ideally for men) is envisaged here, but a progress which consolidates the growth of the past and which, rather than necessarily intensifying a line of development (e.g. a more and more socially exclusivist practice of celibacy), encourages a rounded experience of life, inclusive of sex, in which the preceding stage is integrated into the succeeding. In other words, the ideal of the renouncer – an integrated ideal – overarches and in a way permeates the stages leading up to it. The final goal is represented in some way at every stage leading towards it, and every such stage contributes something towards that final goal. Theoretically, this notion of progression is distinctive of the Hindu family of religions.

Practically, too, it lives on in modern adaptations of the classical ashramic ideal. Among the middle and upper classes at any rate, there is a general feeling that one's passage through school and university should be a celibate state. The open cohabiting of university students, for example, would hardly be tolerated, though clandestine affairs are not uncommon. Especially for males, it is only after a job has been found that marriage is contemplated. In the Indian situation this no doubt makes economic sense, but it also expresses a sense of priority and progression – there is a proper time in life for marital experience. As old age sets in and children are married off, many religious Hindus would ideally like to project a personal image of withdrawing from the maelstrom of life, including sexual activity. There is a tendency to become more involved in such religious activities as attending religious addresses or regular prayer meetings, practising yoga, and engaging in private devotional practices. Some are formally initiated by a guru or family priest (*purohita*) into a religious way of life which can be followed from the home. In general, the aim is to allow the younger married couple(s) of a joint family to get on with their lives while their elders stand back, and help and advise in the raising of the children. Human nature being what it is, however, the reality does not always mirror this ideal, the proverbial obstacle to the latter's realisation being the reluctance of the mother-in-law to relinquish control over household affairs and the allegiance of her son's affections.[13] The modern form of withdrawing from the world described here may be regarded as the equivalent of the classical ideal of retiring to the forest (*vānaprasthya*), if not of total renunciation (*saṃnyāsa*). Those who actually seek to adopt a life of renunciation by leaving home are few and far between, of course, and, for social reasons being generally male, usually enter a monastery or become a wandering mendicant.

The idea of the renouncer in the traditional mould is generally still highly regarded in Hindu India among villagers and urbanites alike.[14] We will examine briefly an important idea underlying the practice of renunciation, both in its traditional and modern forms, which has an interesting temporal dimension. The idea we have in mind is that of *tapas* or spiritual energy. Renunciation builds up *tapas*. Renunciation means not only giving up certain things (e.g. sense-gratification, desire for wealth, worldly ambition, and so on) but equally importantly, doing certain things (cultivating an attitude of mind benevolent to all life, practising physical and mental austerities, etc.). In short, renunciation is a state of being, a way of life, a form of interiorisation. Thus it is said that the possession of wealth in itself is not unspiritual but the spirit of acquisitiveness is. In this sense a king may be renunciant while a pauper or monk may be a wanton. Hindu tradition, high and low, is full of tales of renouncers building up a large store of *tapas* over many years by lives of single-minded and sometimes spectacular austerity. There is a sense of linear progression here, for *tapas* is likened in the tradition to a physical substance which increases by accumulation. Classically it is expended in two ways: (i) gainfully, by first, consuming the *tapas*-maker's outstanding karma (thereby enabling him or her to draw closer to salvation), and second, in the realisation of a curse or blessing willed by the *tapas*-maker; and (ii) uselessly, by self-indulgence especially through outbursts of anger and by sexual activity, in particular, orgasm. The classic symbol of the loss of *tapas* is the discharge of semen. The tradition abounds in stories of awesome ascetics being seduced by nubile maidens with a resulting loss of their power to influence events by issuing imprecations or blessings.

We note here another example of the ambivalent religio-moral status of women in Hinduism. The typical seducer and symbol of obstacles to spiritual development (which itself is often symbolised by the increase of *tapas*) is the sexually attractive, unmarried female. Such women are spiritual hazards but they are also reckoned as expressions of divine power (*śakti*) in their own right, dangerously unstable for good or ill. This power is brought under control when it is literally domesticated, that is, when nubile female is transformed into wife or mother. What is envisaged in the classical conception of renunciation or its modern adaptations is the accumulation of *tapas* for spiritual ends, namely, salvation or the exercise of power. The renouncer (house-dweller or ascetic), by the increase of personal *tapas* acquired through the linear passage of time, ideally attains a state in which he or she can overcome the effects of time by directing *tapas* to accomplish atemporal ends, e.g. nullifying karma or manipulating it by attracting 'good luck' or warding off calamities (personally or for the family).[15] The women of the family have always had an important role to play in this regard. In Sanskritic and vernacular sources many examples are given of devoted wives, mothers, etc. undergoing rigorous vows or *vratas* in the form of fasts, pilgrimages and other austerities so as to bring a blessing on their menfolk or their families or to liberate someone from a curse. Here is a classic example. It is taken from a story in the third book, the Forest Book or *Araṇya Parvan*, of the *Mahābhārata*.[16] The gist of the story is as follows.

Aśvapati, a virtuous and austere king, was childless and advancing in age; the kingdom had no heir. So for eighteen years he fasted and sacrificed, uttering the *sāvitrī* mantra, until the goddess Sāvitrī granted him the boon of fathering a child. A girl was born, and she was called Sāvitrī in honour of the goddess. The king's daughter grew up to be beautiful and virtuous, but so intimidating was her splendour that no suitor came forward to ask for her hand. So, instructed by Aśvapati to look for a husband, she toured the land. In due course she returned and reported that she had fallen in love with Satyavat, the son of a king who had become blind and whose kingdom had been usurped in consequence. Together with his wife, the king had brought up his son in the community of a forest hermitage. The Sage Nārada who was present when Sāvitrī returned knew all about Satyavat. He praised the boy's character and looks, but also revealed that he would die in a year to the day. But Sāvitrī would not be moved; she had set her heart on marrying Satyavat.

So they got married, and Sāvitrī lived happily with Satyavat and his parents in the forest according to the austere hermitage rules, which seem to have implied celibacy. As the year went by Satyavat's impending death (which she kept to herself) weighed heavily on Sāvitrī's mind. Three days before the fateful day, Sāvitrī undertook a rigorous vow to fast and remain standing the whole time (including the nights); and this she kept. On the appointed day she accompanied Satyavat on an errand into the forest to cut wood for the ritual. While he was engaged in this task a fit of weariness overcame him and he lay down to rest with his head in Sāvitrī's lap. To his wife's great anguish, his time had come.

As Satyavat lay unconscious, Sāvitrī saw the awesome figure of Yama himself come to claim her husband's soul. This he extracted with his noose from Satyavat's body in the shape of an individual the size of a thumb and began to lead him off to his realm. Sāvitrī, who had gently placed her husband's head on the ground, followed. Her place was by her husband's side, she said. Yama was touched; he granted her any boon except Satyavat's life. Sāvitrī asked that her father-in-law regain his sight. It was granted. Yama continued on his way and still Sāvitrī would not leave her husband's soul. Impressed, Yama granted her another boon on the same condition. Sāvitrī asked that her father-in-law regain his kingdom. This too was granted. Yama told her that she must now return. Sāvitrī refused; she would stay by her spouse, but since she realised that Yama was acting according to the law of nature she bore him no ill will. Greatly impressed, Yama offered her a third boon provided she would not ask for Satyavat's life. This time Sāvitrī requested that her own father produce a hundred sons to continue his line. This too was granted. Yama went on and Sāvitrī followed, telling Yama that love and a sense of duty impelled her. Choose a fourth boon, said the lord of death, but do not ask for Satyavat's life. So Sāvitrī obeyed this instruction to the letter. She asked that she might have a hundred sons by Satyavat. Unmindful of its implication, Yama granted the boon. After more fine words, Sāvitrī spelled out her request. 'Deprived of my husband. I want no happiness. Deprived of my husband, I don't want heaven. Deprived of my husband, I want no wealth. Without my husband, I don't want to live' (3.281.62). So Yama released Satyavat's soul, which returned with Sāvitrī to the corpse. Sāvitrī once more took her husband's head in her lap and he regained consciousness, safe and well. Meanwhile, Satyavat's parents had grown frantic at their absence so that there was great rejoicing when they returned. Two of the other boons had also started to materialise, and everyone lived happily ever after.

Sāvitrī has always been held as a model of wifely devotion and resolution.[17] But it was her practice of austerities and accumulation of *tapas* which enabled her to convert these virtues into success. The text clearly implies that *tapas* is a lever of power. Aśvapati obtained Sāvitrī through rigorous austerity, and Sāvitrī won her boons in the same way. Thus as Yama unbends towards Sāvitrī at the beginning of their meeting, he calls her 'a devoted wife' (*pativratā*) 'having (the power of) *tapas*' (*taponvitā*; 3.281.12). When the sages are trying to comfort the parents in the absence of their son and daughter-in-law, one says: 'Because his wife Sāvitrī possesses *tapas* and self-control, and is of good conduct, Satyavat lives!' (3.282.10). And at the end, the story-teller concludes by saying: 'Thus by mortification (*kṛcchrāt*) Sāvitrī saved all – herself, her father, her mother, her mother-in-law and father-in-law, and her husband's line' (3.283.14). By duly accumulating *tapas* in time, Sāvitrī overcomes what symbolises the irrevocable passing of time: old age (a hundred sons for her aging father) and death. Something similar happens in the vernacular traditions, many of which arise from (semi-Hinduised) folk culture. In the Bengali *maṅgals*, for instance, goddesses like Manasā and Caṇḍī are placated by the observance of rigorous *vratas* by women for the welfare of their loved ones.[18]

For Hindus generally, a key means to acquire *tapas* is sexual restraint. It is remarkable how widespread and deep-rooted the belief is, even among educated people, that sexual activity results in loss of spiritual and even physical power to accomplish things.[19] Even in those Tantric traditions in which sexual intercourse not only symbolises but is also envisaged as actually bringing about spiritual fulfilment, it is only intercourse as part of a strictly controlled ritual that is endorsed.[20]

The traditional significance of *tapas*, with special reference to sexual restraint, was clearly in evidence during the nationalist movement. It accounts for much of Gandhi's views on sex and personal stress on ascesis. It is no accident that a number of early nationalist leaders advocated an ascetic or restrained life-style (which on occasion they exemplified personally by observing celibacy) as a means to bring about *svarāj*, i.e. 'self-rule', interpreted as personal, spiritual self-control which would ground political sovereignty. In this context, *tapas* acquired could be directed through appropriate action (social, educational, political, religious) to the wholistic liberating of the body politic, first in the individual who would shake off his or her slavish mentality (to the passions, to deracinating forms of behaviour, government, etc.) and then to the transformed community in which the newly-formed free mentality would find expression politically, socially, and so on. This view of the temporal acquisition and expenditure of *tapas* was instrumental in creating a new historical perspective in which one kind of past – that of fragmentation and alienation – would be transformed into a qualitatively different kind of future, one of national unity and cultural integration.

The ethic of the *puruṣārthas* may be regarded as the pursuit of *artha, kāma* and/or *dharma* (understood as ritual purity in terms of one's caste avocation) against a horizon of seeking *mokṣa* or spiritual emancipation. Ideally, the first three *puruṣārthas* could be cultivated only with liberation in view. Here again there is a progressive understanding of time at work. The timeless quality of liberation and its atemporal ethic of non-violence, benevolence, truth-telling, and so on – 'atemporal' because it applies to all, in all circumstances and in all stages of life – must inform the time-conditioned ethic of the other *puruṣārthas*, governed as it is by considerations about particularities of sex, caste, occupation, period of life, etc. In the modern context this means that in the pursuit of *artha* (wealth), say, dealings must be honest, employment considerate, wages just, competition not ruinous, advertising sensitive and fair, and so on. In this way, the accumulation of wealth is not time-serving; it neither kills the spirit nor becomes an end in itself.

Let us consider one more example of temporality in Hinduism – that of the rites of passage or *saṃskāras.* A *saṃskāra* is a ritual intended to purify and transform the individual at particular phases of life's journey. The word derives from the root *saṃs-kṛ*, meaning to cleanse and perfect.[21] By the action of the *saṃskāras*, the individual is progressively and cumulatively protected from hostile influences and made whole. In so far as Vedic utterances are used, the *saṃskāras* are intended ideally for the twice-born male. This must be kept in mind in the following discussion. But the female, either as child or adult, was also included in their scope in various ways, namely, as the recipient, or partner, or condition for implementation. Thus the texts make a distinction between *garbha-saṃskāra* and *kṣetra-saṃskāra*; the former kind focuses on the embryo (*garbha*), the latter on the 'field' (*kṣetra*) in which the seed is sown and nurtured, i.e. the woman. But the texts also indicate that even Śūdras could receive some *saṃskāras* (at marriage and death, for instance) though not with Vedic utterances (other purifying *mantras* were to be used). Many low-caste groups have evolved their own rites of passage administered by their own priests. However, today it is by no means unknown for Brahmin priests (discreetly) to apply the Veda for Śūdra clients, in which case they tend to distinguish between touchable and untouchable Śūdras, and minister to the former. The *Gṛhya* Sūtras contain the earliest formal descriptions of at least the major *saṃskāras*, though the Law Codes, Purāṇas and other ancient sources also deal with this topic.

There is no unanimity in the śāstras concerning the number of *saṃskāras*. As society changed the number was added to and the rites elaborated, not least in the endless chain of local *paddhatis* or manuals. It is also worth remembering that the calendar in use in administering the *saṃskāras* – for the fixing of auspicious days and times – is generally the lunar calendar, as in the case of other religious observances such as celebrating festivals, undertaking pilgrimages, building a temple, etc. Finally, a *saṃskāra* usually has variant forms, depending on *deśācāra* (regional practice), *jātyācāra* (caste-practice), *kulācāra* (family practice), and so on. Such modifications were recognised as legitimate. We will discuss sixteen *saṃskāras*.[22]

The first three *saṃskāras* are scarcely used, and the ancient authorities disagree on whether they are to be implemented at the first pregnancy only or at subsequent pregnancies. They are (i) *garbhādhāna* or impregnation. Intercourse, which was to take place during the wife's fertile period, reckoned to occur from the fourth to the sixteenth day after menstruation, was to be rendered efficacious by the husband's invocation of certain Vedic deities (later this procedure was elaborated). Ideally, the first-born would be a son. The aim of (ii) *puṃsavana*, performed in the fourth month, was to ensure that the child would be a male. This was followed by (iii) *sīmantonnayana* or the ceremonial parting of the mother's hair (recommended generally from the fifth to the eighth month). By the performance of this *saṃskāra*, various good effects were supposed to arise: protection of both mother and child from evil spirits, health and prosperity, the contentment of the mother, etc. (The hair, especially of women, and its grooming, is traditionally a symbol of well-being in Hindu culture.)

Today, *saṃskāras* tend to be more practised from (iv) *jātakarma*, understood loosely as the rites performed in connection with the imminent birth. These are meant to prepare the mother and the household for the child's coming, to ensure a smooth delivery and to celebrate a successful birth. Strictly speaking, this *saṃskāra* is begun just before the severing of the umbilical cord and includes rites seeking the mental and physical welfare of the child. The time of birth is important for the preparing of the infant's horoscope, which will have an important role to play in later life. (v) The formal name-giving or *nāmakaraṇa* is quite popular in many circles. The texts give rules as to how and what a child is to be named, even in some cases to the extent of the number of syllables allowed. Even today, Hindu personal names are not just sounds but invariably and obviously mean something, often in commemoration of or in connection with some deity.[23] This rite is usually completed within six months of birth.

(vi) *Niṣkramaṇa* is the first formal outing of the infant, its first exposure to the outside world, to be performed during the day (so that the life-giving sun can be seen) and before the sixth month. As a *saṃskāra* it is virtually defunct. (vii) *Annaprāśana*, or the weaning, is more common. In non-westernised households even today, breast-feeding can continue for a year-and-a-half or more. This is an ancient custom, so it made sense to introduce the child to solid food at a reasonably early date. The recommended time for this rite is in the sixth or seventh month. (viii) *Cūḍākaraṇa* or tonsuring, also called *muṇḍana* (and only for males, of course) was intended to prolong life. The body is likened to a tree or plant, and the rite was thought to have a 'pruning' effect. It is still practised and should be performed by about the seventh year. (ix) *Karṇavedha* or the ceremonial piercing of the ear(s) is of late origin. It was originally intended, no doubt, to ratify the already popular practice, among both women and men, of boring the ear-lobe for ornamental purposes. Making an aperture in the body could be threatening (either from disease or in other ways), so the individual needed protection. Incidentally, earrings worn by men differed in style from those worn by women and this difference was made use of iconographically. Thus you will notice that the figure of Śiva in his famous pose as Lord of the Dance bears a masculine earring in the right ear and a feminine earring in the left. This symbolises the union of complements in the deity. *Karṇavedha* is little used today,[24] though the wearing of earrings by girls and women is popular in all sections of Hindu society.

(x) *Vidyārambha*, another late rite, marks the beginning of secular learning and is still sometimes practised. It should take place in about the fifth year, usually with the priest in the role of teacher helping the child to trace mystic syllables and/or letters of the alphabet on the ground. (xi) The *upanayana* ceremony is, as we have already seen, regarded as crucial: it is the rite initiating into second birth. As such it is still an important ceremony, socially if not always religiously. Today it is usually combined with the investiture of the sacred thread or *yajñopavīta* and is sometimes called simply by this name. This has become a greatly contracted and only symbolic ceremony, in contrast to the ancient and more lengthy performance of the rite.

On an auspicious day determined by the family priest, the young boy, sometimes after first having had his head shaved (a purifying ritual), is bathed and dressed in clean cloth (the style, which should be traditional, varies). An altar or *vedi* is constructed for the sacred domestic fire; another may be built for the *navagraha*, a group of nine heavenly bodies which includes some of the planets. The candidate, with family and well-wishers in attendance, sits on a mat in front of the *vedi*(s) and Vedic mantras are recited enjoining him to live a chaste life devoted to Vedic study and to be obedient to his elders. He is sprinkled with Ganges water to purify him. The *navagraha* and Gaṇeśa, the elephant-headed deity, may be invoked for blessings and success. The youth is invested with the sacred thread in which the gods are asked to dwell to strengthen him, and the *Gāyatrī* mantra is repeated in his right ear. He may be given a staff – the sign of the mendicant and the mark of the traveller on the road of spiritual knowledge; then he ceremonially begs from his relations so that what he receives may be offered to his 'guru', namely the priest who has initiated him. A fee (*dakṣiṇā*) is also given to the priest. Moral advice on how to live a good life may then be given by the priest and this is usually rounded off by a festive meal or the offering of food to those present. We have described but the gist of the ceremony.

(xii) As a *saṃskāra*, *Vedārambha* or the formal beginning of Vedic study is of later origin than (xiii) *keśānta* or the first shaving of the beard (usually at the age of about 16). *Keśānta* was meant to mark the end of puberty. (xiv) *Samāvartana*, as we have seen (Chapter 4), formally marked the end of *brahmacarya* or the state of celibate studentship under the teacher (*ācārya*). It is also called *snāna* after the ritual bath taken to complete this stage. Today it tends to be incorporated into the *upanayana* ceremony or sometimes into the next *saṃskāra*.

(xv) This is marriage or *vivāha*, one of the most important *saṃskāra*s for all four *varṇa*s. Tradition recognises eight kinds of marriage as religiously licit, provided that prescribed forms of ritual were carried out in due course (inter-caste marriage in this context would be a complication[25]). Each kind of marriage is described from the point of view of the husband. For reasons that will become clear, to say that these forms of union could be religiously valid does not mean that all were socially encouraged. The *paiśāca* or 'demonic' form of marriage was based on sexual intercourse resulting from deception of some kind, the female partner being not fully aware of the situation because she was either drugged, intoxicated, duped or out of her senses at the time. This is technically rape, which is condemned. But a marriage recognised as valid could be formed out of this, provided that the prescribed ritual was enacted and both parties consented. As in the case of the *rākṣasa* or 'ogrish' form of marriage, which was based on abduction by force (the female partner being aware of what was happening), this was a traditionally patriarchal society's way of making the best of a bad job especially from the hapless woman's point of view, and of legitimating unions that had originated in undesirable circumstances so that both wife and offspring could have social and legal recognition. As in other ancient cultures, women, especially the unmarried, who were known to have experienced extra-marital sex were virtually depersonalised socially (not to mention any resulting offspring) unless ways were found to rehabilitate them. This leads us to the *gāndharva* or 'Cupid's' form of marriage which originated in mutual desire. The couple had had sexual intercourse or were cohabiting and wished to ratify their union. This has a modern ring to it, but this kind of marriage was not encouraged. For most of the history of Hinduism, premarital virginity, especially on the part of the bride, was the ideal – as it is today. Further, it has always been the Hindu view that desire (*kāma*) should not be the leading motive for marriage. *Kāma* must be tempered by *dharma*, as we have seen, and *dharma* traditionally ruled out extra-marital sex (especially for women).

Both of the forms of marriage called *āsura* ('anti-godly') and *prājāpatya* ('procreative') have this in common that they are based on a mutual contract between the marrying parties, except that in *āsura* a dowry or bride-price of some kind was exacted by the groom's side as a necessary condition. Traditionally, *āsura* marriage was tolerated but not encouraged. Today, in spite of legislation to discourage it, the exacting of dowries is still widely practised at all levels of society. Sometimes dowries are not made over at a stroke, but continue to be paid even after the marriage. They can result in intolerable financial strain on the bride's party and persecution (on occasion to the point of murder) for the bride by disgruntled in-laws. The deity Prajāpati ('lord of creatures') symbolises a contract so that *prājāpatya* was a purely contractual form of union for the performance of marital *dharma* and the procreation of children (especially a male heir).

The last three kinds of marriage were the most approved of, in ascending order of approval. The *ārṣa* or 'seer's' form of marriage was undertaken with the groom in the role of patron of a sacrifice. To this end he gave his prospective father-in-law a gift (usually two cows) as a bond or fee, so that the sacrifice could be performed. After all, the solemn sacrifice had to be enacted and compelling incentives found. Later, by the beginning of the Common Era, this form of marriage was criticised in the Codes as based on a kind of purchase of the bride. In the 'godly' or *daiva* form of marriage, the girl herself was offered to a priest as the fee (*dakṣiṇā*) for a sacrifice of which her father was the patron – ancient India's equivalent of a Mass stipend. This was supposed to be a meritorious thing to do, and could only have been practised by the twice-born. Finally, the ideal form of marriage was the *brāhma* or 'Brahminic', in which the girl (*kanyā*) was given as a free gift (*kanyā-dāna*) by the father to a suitable groom. 'The Smṛtis regard it as the most honourable type of marriage as it was [supposedly] free from physical force, carnal appetite, imposition of conditions and lure of money' (Pandey 1969:169). No one cares to mention whether the bride was content to be viewed as a free gift, nor whether her views about the match were formally taken into account.[26] We have noted elsewhere that ancient authorities permit polygamy but not the taking of more than one husband (the case of Draupadī and the Pāṇḍavas is the exception that proves the rule). The senior wife, the wife who 'completed' the man in the context of the performance of prescribed ritual, was formally called the *patnī*; she was his *sahadharmiṇī* or partner in *dharma*. The practice of taking more than one wife persisted till not so long ago. But in India today, having more than one wife is legally prohibited to Hindus.

In India today, many old ideas about marriage remain unchanged among village people and traditionalists. 'Love-marriages', i.e. marriages based on prior mutual attraction (if not pre-marital sex), are still generally taboo; arranged marriages are the order of the day. All the more so among many village communities, where betrothal and often marriage take place when the couple are still young children (though they only come together after puberty). A number of reasons for this practice may be in force: custom, localised śāstraic injunction, parental need to earmark, in an unpredictable market, a suitable spouse for their child within the constraints of caste-parameters, advance warning of economic security or liability (in the form of dowry), and so on. In this context, child widowhood, and all that this implies in a traditionalist milieu, are still in evidence.

Among the more westernised, although 'love-marriages' are certainly not unknown, arranged marriage is still common, but in ways adapted to modern living. Here is what is likely to happen in average Bengali, urban, middle-class practice. Girls tend not to be married off before they have completed an undergraduate degree and boys before they have found a job. College friendships, provided that they do not infringe acceptable limits of consanguinity (at present, generally those who are related in the same *gotra* or clan up to seven generations cannot marry) and caste (the three top castes tend to intermarry), may well be the basis for parents to agree to a match.

But living together or even openly courting in public is unacceptable. If there is no earlier friendship to consider, parents of either boy or girl seek out what seems to be a suitable match for their child. Sometimes the services of a marriage broker are used. If preliminary soundings are satisfactory (family and personal background, financial situation, health, etc.), photographs of the prospective couple are exchanged. Often either partner has much latitude at this point as to whether to proceed. If the go-ahead is given, the couple meet, usually more than once, in a friend's or relative's house to establish personal contact. If no problems arise, serious parental negotiations ensue about wedding arrangements, etc.; in this context the distinction between dowry and trousseau is often blurred. If the negotiations are satisfactorily concluded, an auspicious day is set for the wedding.

In the present social climate, such arranged marriages – which may be quite happy – usually last for life, though divorce is becoming increasingly common. It is fair to say that middle-class Hindu society in general still views with horror the divorce statistics and broken homes of 'the West', which are regarded as a natural outcome of 'love-marriage' and permissive sexuality. It is also important to mention that even now for the overwhelming majority of Hindus in all walks of life, one's natal horoscope plays a vital role in regulating a match. It is drawn up by a professional astrologer and interpreted by another professional (a priest or astrologer). Sometimes horoscopes are interpreted to conveniently endorse a much-desired match. Horoscopes still exert a great influence in Hindu minds, westernised or otherwise. I have often heard educated Hindus claim how personal events such as marriages, deaths, jobs, sickness, travel, etc., 'predicted' by horoscopes, and professedly not believed in before the event, were supposed to have materialised.

Local customs apart, there are certain basic features of a traditional Hindu wedding. We need not describe them all. Before the ceremony, various purificatory and auspicious rites (e.g. a ritual bath, smearing the body with turmeric paste) are performed by the prospective bride and/or groom. On the day of the wedding, the groom and his party go to the wife's home (or the location appointed by the bride's side). The groom travels in style, usually by horse or horse-power (either being richly decorated), in the first case often to the accompaniment of a vigorous band. In Bengal, the wife's wedding sari is usually red or some variant (e.g. deep pink or purple). This is the colour of the goddess Lakṣmī, who bestows prosperity. Traditionally, though the groom is feted, this is the bride's special day – the day that she will acquire status as wife and potential mother.

During the wedding there are rites, some supported by Vedic utterances, which symbolise fertility, bonding, fidelity, long life, steadfastness, and other aspects of a successful union. These rites include the knotting together of a garment of the bride and groom, the *pāṇi-grahaṇa* or grasping of the bride's hand by the groom, various *homa*s or fire-sacrifices, circling the fire, and perhaps most important, the *sapta-padi* or seven steps made by the groom with the bride in tow, each step symbolising some aspect of fertility or prosperity.[27] Throughout, the sacred fire – personified as the *deva* Agni – plays a central role as witness and bridge between earth and heaven, temporality and eternity. During or after the ceremony the guests are fed as lavishly as the parental purse(s) will allow. The wedding ceremony, which can run for hours from start to finish, is treated as a *festive* occasion, with a high social profile. During the elaborate ritual, guests, including children, may crowd round the participants, at suitable moments exchanging banter with them and each other. Solemnity is put in its place, and a good time is had by all. This underscores a salient feature of the *saṃskāras*: their marked *social* dimension.

Finally, we come to (xvi) *antyeṣṭi* or the death rites. Some ancient texts describe a deathbed rite or two, but we do not know how widely this was practised. It is at death and after that rites for the dead have widespread currency. It is generally believed that religious Hindus always cremate their dead, but this is not so. There is no doubt that cremation is an ancient and pervasive custom in Hinduism. The earliest texts indicate, however, that burial was at least sometimes an alternative. Before long cremation became the standard practice. Traditionally, however, in society regulated by Brahminic norms, neither very young children (up to about 7 years of age) nor renouncers have been cremated. This stems from the Vedic belief that by cremation Agni the purifier consumed the dead person's physical and mental impurities caused by the appetites of the flesh, enabling the soul to ascend to heaven and assume a glorious, pure body (*tanu*). Young children and renouncers, however, are supposed not to be defiled by carnal appetites so that they do not need to be cremated. This does not mean that they may not have to expend accumulated karma in a subsequent birth; the belief in karma came later, so that these two beliefs coexist uneasily in logic. The bodies of young children or renouncers are usually either buried or immersed in rivers, mother earth and water being purifying agents anyway. Further, it may come as a surprise to learn that in some low-caste communities, burial rather than cremation is the standard way to dispose of the dead. You cannot generalise about Hinduism with impunity.

The basic purpose of the *antyeṣṭi saṃskāra* is to purify and to console – both the individual who has died and the bereaved. As we have seen, it is a tenet of religious Hinduism that the soul survives death. So by various rites, e.g. a ritual bath, the sprinkling of Ganges water, covering with new cloths, daubing parts of the body with clarified butter, Vedic utterances for the twice-born, etc., the deceased person is purified and strengthened for the post-mortem journey and the bereaved derive satisfaction from this send-off. Low-caste, including untouchable communities, have evolved their own, local rites but the basic rationale of these is the same. Nowadays, arriving at the place of cremation, and its method, are matters of circumstance and preference. The more well-to-do generally use motorised transport to get to the crematorium; the less well-to-do (and more traditional) practice is to process at a brisk pace to the cremation ground (with the body borne on a bed, charpoy, or litter) from time to time loudly invoking the deity. The body is then duly burnt on the pyre, the ashes and unconsumed fragments of bone being either buried later or more usually thrown into a river – the holier the river's reputation the better. In general it is still ritually important for the son of the deceased to light the pyre, although the actual preparation of the pile is done by individuals of specific low or untouchable castes. The ashes may be kept until a close relative can journey to a pilgrimage centre on the banks of a particularly sacred river like the Ganges and immerse them. Such immersions are believed to be of great benefit to the souls of the dead. It is also not uncommon for Hindus, as death approaches or in fairly advanced old age, to take up residence in those sacred sites (usually on river banks) from where it is believed that at death salvation can be immediately attained. The sight of smoke curling from funeral pyres at holy river sites such as Benares is a familiar one; it has even become something of a macabre tourist attraction.

The period of impurity for the close relatives of the dead lasts anywhere from eleven to seventeen days from the day of the death. During this time rites are conducted to build up and feed a (supposed) tiny, temporary, attenuated body of the soul of the deceased, who is now called a *preta* or ghost. We pointed out in Chapter 8 that it is considered very important to appease the *preta* by rites and offerings of food (*piṇḍa*) and even clothes, for unappeased *pretas* can turn quite nasty towards humans, especially their neglectful relatives, even possessing people on occasion. In many traditional-minded and low-caste circles possession by *preta* is commonly believed to occur. The rites to satisfy the *preta* are called *śrāddha* rites and are believed to effect transfer of merit to the *preta*. The popular belief is that it takes a year before the *preta* is judged and consigned by Yama, the Lord of the Dead, to a post-mortem fate merited by its karma. This is why the *śrāddha* performed on the first anniversary of the death is so important – it is the last chance of putting the *preta* in the best light before Yama's judgement.

It is hoped that during this description of the *saṃskāra*s useful comments have been made about changing Hindu mores and values. But we must not forget the temporal context in which the topic was raised. First, besides expressing characteristic Hindu obsessiveness with ritual purity and pollution, implementing and undergoing the *saṃskāra*s has been one important practical way in which Brahminic Hinduism has maintained a sense of, albeit changing, identity down the ages. It is interesting to speculate what future this mode of perpetuation has. But the succession of the *saṃskāra*s itself implies a sense of progression through life which is not simply linear. This is indicated by the fact that in some texts the description of the *saṃskāra*s is begun at marriage – the basis, so to speak, of the beginning and sanctification of human life. As we have indicated, in the context of the *saṃskāra*s and *āśrama*s (and the belief in karma and rebirth), human life is meant to be viewed as a purposive whole against the horizon of the transcendent. Thus from our discussion we see that in traditional religious Hindu consciousness time is not simply some cyclic or repetitive process but a framework for real development and growth in which free will has a central role to play. (This is not to say, of course, that there are not Hindus who subscribe to some 'replica view' of time).

There is the groundwork here for a distinctive historical and progressive consciousness – not necessarily western, but doubtless adaptive to western forms – which has been actualised in Indian secular history, e.g. in the way Hindu rulers have viewed, and have been encouraged by religious authority to view, their positions in temporal lines of succession, or in the way *guru-paraṃparā*s or 'lineages' have been reckoned.[28]

This groundwork also makes possible new kinds of historical reconstructions and interpretations of Hindu secular and religious tradition which we cannot go into here. For history is not simply chronology; it is an assessment of the past in the light of the present (and up to a point, of the present in the light of the past) in terms of cause and effect. Sacred history, as a division of history in general, shares in the latter's 'progressive' and teleological methodology. Christian sacred history, for instance, is not simply linear: to say that the religious history of the human race, past and future, is summed up and consummated in an Event – the 'Christ Event' – that took place about 2,000 years ago (reckoning chronologically) is not a simply linear way of assessing time. Hindu religious historical consciousness too need not be subject to some directly linear understanding of time.

We will not engage in a similar discussion of space, for in the Hindu understanding space is of a piece with time, the space–time continuum in which we live being an expression of *prakṛti*. Rather let us consider some important ways in which space and time converge in Hindu religious thought and practice in the context of 'salvation'. We will do this by focusing on objects of worship, on pilgrimage and festivals, and on paths of deliverance in Chapters 11 and 12.

11 The sacred and its forms

Time and space as assimilative concepts: some examples – myths, Kashi, the Ganges. The relationship between the sacred and the secular in the context of the Hindu temple: origins, purposes, construction, the icon, worship. Domestic worship. Features of Hindu iconography with reference to some examples (Viṣṇu, Śiva, Gaṇeśa, Kālī). A comment on the status of women in Śākta and Tantric worship. Animate and inanimate expressions of the sacred in Hindu religiousness. All (religious) Hindus not icon-worshippers, but most ritually-minded. Hymns and chanting as an aspect of worship; the Sahasranāma.

Many Hindus still live through a context of what we may call mythic space and time. We can illustrate this by an experience recounted by Roger Hooker in his *Themes in Hinduism and Christianity*.[1]

> Once, when out for a boating trip on the Ganges, I asked the boatman if he and his caste-fellows were well-treated by the higher castes. 'Of course,' he replied proudly. 'Was it not we who took Rāma across the river?' That laconic sentence contains a wealth of meaning . . . . In the incident to which our boatman referred, Rāma has arrived at the banks of the Ganges: he wants to get across [but] word has spread that the touch of his feet has turned a rock into a beautiful woman . . . . Rāma calls for a boat, but the boatman refuses to bring it. 'I know your hidden power,' he says. 'All say that the dust of your lotus feet is a kind of magic charm for making man. A rock touched it and became a beautiful woman; and wood is no harder than stone! If my boat becomes a hermit's wife, I shall lose my boat and my livelihood too! If, my lord, you really want to cross the river, then bid me wash your lotus feet.' Rāma agrees, and after washing his feet and then drinking the water, the boatman takes him across the river.
>
> (pp. 19–20)

With regard to caste-respect, there may be some wishful thinking here on the boatman's part, but in common with a great many other religious Hindus in all sections of society, in certain aspects of his life he lives in the borderlands of mythic time and real time, mythic space and real space. Though perhaps an increasing number are losing touch with it, most Hindus have the knack of being able to activate their mythic heritage so as to make life meaningful and bearable. Here is another way in which this is done. With reference to the holy city of Benares, Diana Eck has noted the tendency Hindus have of seeing particular focuses of the sacred, with their distinctive purificatory, salvific and other characteristics, as able to repeat themselves and their powers in various ways and contexts. We may characterise this as a variant of the *svarūpa–bahurūpa* relationship. It is common to view the intrinsic powers (*svarūpa*) of a particularly sacred pilgrimage site or ford (*tīrtha*) as focusing, as if through a lens, the sanctity of other holy places, and unifying the distinctive features of these other places under a common head, as if they were particular manifestations or forms (*bahurūpa*) of the radiating 'original'. This is the phenomenon of experiencing the macrocosm in the microcosm and the microcosm in the macrocosm. Eck describes it well with reference to the holy city of Benares or Kāśī (an archetype of the holy place) on the western bank of *the* sacred river of Hindu India, the Ganges:

> Among India's *tīrthas*, Kāshī is the most widely acclaimed. Pilgrims come from all over India to bathe in the Ganges at Kāshī and to visit her temples, and they come from all sectarian groups – Shaiva, Vaishnava, and Shākta alike. From one perspective, Kāshī is a single *tīrtha* among others. . . . At the same time, Kāshī is said to embody all the *tīrthas*. One may visit the far-off temple of Shiva, high in the Himālayas at Kedāra – right here in Kāshī. And one may travel to the far South to Rāmeshvaram . . . right here in Kāshī. And even if one does not visit the sites of these transposed *tīrthas* in Kāshī, the power of all these places has been assimilated into the power of this one place, and the pilgrims who visit Kāshī stand in a place empowered by the whole of India's sacred geography. . . .
>
> A place such as Kāshī is important, even supreme, without being unique. . . . To celebrate one god or one *tīrtha* need not mean to celebrate *only* one. Far from standing alone, Kāshī, like a crystal, gathers and refracts the light of other pilgrimage places. Not only are other *tīrthas* said to be present in Kāshī, but Kāshī is present elsewhere. In the Himālayas . . . on the way to the

> headwaters of the Ganges, the pilgrim will come to a place called the 'Northern Kāshī' . . . . This kind of 'transposition of place' is a common phenomenon in Indian sacred topography . . . the affirmation is that the place itself, with its sacred power, is present in more than one place. In addition to the northern Kāshī, there is a southern Kāshī and a Shiva Kāshī in the Tamil South . . . . In a similar way, the River Ganges is a prototype for other sacred waters, and her presence is seen in countless rivers and invoked into ritual waters all over India.
>
> (Eck 1983: 39–41)

The Ganges is invoked thus not only all over India, but also in other parts of the world. For example, there is a freshwater lake in the island of Mauritius, which is a pilgrimage centre for Hindus. Temples have been built around it and it is particularly crowded during religious festivals. According to secular geography, this lake and the original Ganges are thousands of miles apart. Yet the lake is holy because it is commonly believed that some Ganges water, brought from India, was mingled with the natural waters. The lake has an official name, but it is known locally to Hindus as 'Ganga Talab'. The purifying and sanctifying powers of the Ganges have been transferred to this lake, so in a way it *is* the Ganges.[2]

Under an overarching perspective, various times and spaces can be run together even in Hindu religious art. An example of this occurs in a magnificent depiction, sculpted from the living rock, of the myth of the descent of the Ganges at Mahabalipuram, south of Madras on the Coromandel coast. The gist of the story is as follows. King Bhagīratha needed the sacred waters of the Ganges, who dwelt in heaven, to purify the remains of a large group of his ancestors so as to get them to heaven. After he had performed arduous austerities for a thousand years, the Ganges agreed to descend to earth at the Himalayas, but she advised Bhagīratha that unless Śiva cushioned the impact of her torrential fall in his matted locks, the earth would be torn apart. More intense mortification followed, and Śiva consented to break the Ganges' descent as requested. So in the Himalayas, the Ganges, known as the daughter of the Himalayas, plunged from heaven towards earth, first crashing into Śiva's tangled hair and then meandering through so as to fall gently to earth. Bhagīratha led the all-powerful flow to where his ancestors lay so that they were purified, and thence to what is now called the Bay of Bengal so that the ocean's space could be filled. The world has benefited ever since.

In the Mahabalipuram relief, about 88 ft. by 30 ft. and belonging to the Pallava period (the seventh century), the eye focuses on a central cleft in the rock down which the Ganges is expected to flow to earth. Two serpent figures, the top half human with sinuous bottom halves, rise upwards. Their hooded heads meet and add to the fanning effect of the water cascading down from a cistern (no longer present) placed at the top. On either side of the cleft, animals and heavenly beings flock towards the centre, to witness the marvel of the descent. A disproportionately huge and impressive elephant family stands on the right as you look towards the relief, while on the left side Bhagīratha is seen as an ascetic, first in a pose winning the boon of the Ganges' descent, and then directly above in the presence of a giant Śiva agreeing to break the impact of the plunging river. Here we have the spaces of the heavenly and earthly worlds, and the times of Bhagīratha's first and second ascetic labours as well as their fruit, the descent of the Ganges – indeed the borderlands of myth and reality – meshed into one grand spectacle. It is well worth seeing.[3]

Sacred and secular times and spaces interrelate in other ways. Consider the temple. Early Vedic religion did not make use of temples. The place where the sacrificial ritual (*yajña*) was performed became (temporarily) sacred, and was sometimes referred to as the *nābhi* or navel – centre point – of the world. The time during which the *yajña* was performed became sacred time, opening the doors to immortality. The *yajña* was likened to a womb with the patron of the sacrifice (*yajamāna*) as the embryo. The sacrifice gave new birth to the *yajamāna*, and as such was the bridgehead to the transcendent. In time, as an alternative pattern of ritual became established – that of image worship, generically called *pūjā* – it was believed necessary to build 'residences' (*mandira, devālaya*) to house the objects of such worship. This alternative pattern would have started taking shape by about the fifth to fourth centuries BCE, perhaps prompted by assimilated Harappan practices.[4] From the beginning, natural features, such as caves and bowers, seem to have been perceived as significant contexts for image worship. This, and not only technological inexpertise, would explain why archaeological evidence for (stone) temple-building begins to mount up only at a comparatively late date, namely from about the fifth century CE, though earlier constructions from perishable materials have doubtless been lost. It also explains why the sanctuary of a temple resembles a cave, both in aspect and in its inaccessibility to sunlight. But there may also be a connection with the early Vedic ritual, for the sanctuary is called the *garbha-gṛha* or 'womb-house'. In the sacred confines of the temple the worshipper is to be transformed and reborn.

The Hindu temple embraces a host of religious paradoxes: a temporal dwelling for the timeless divine; a multiple focusing, by virtue of its many images, of one underlying divine source; a descent into the spiritual womb or cave of the heart in order to emerge into the light of divine grace and wisdom; an earthly mapping of divine celestial dwellings; an ideal microcosm of the macrocosm of the world; a pure and purifying locus of life's various pollutings. But it is more. It has always been a social centre for the worshipping community – though usually to the exclusion of untouchables who have had to establish their own places of worship – whether in village or urban centre. Great temples have been occasional and permanent employers with respect to innumerable occupations – of many priests involved in temple ritual, dancer-singers, musicians, builders, carpenters, sculptors, water-carriers and sprinklers, cleaners, and a host of other artisans and functionaries. These temples have also been charitable benefactors, especially in times of distress.[5] Hundreds of thousands of temples, some ancient, others quite recent, some tiny buildings, others complex structures covering an immense area, inhabit the Indian landscape. They remain instrumental in knitting together, sometimes not altogether desirably, old and new customs into the fabric of the present.

Although they have been built in many different styles, the construction of these temples, usually along an east–west axis, follows strict rules pertaining to proportion and material, laid down in iconometric and other texts, some of which are well over a thousand years old.[6] The whole process of temple-building is subject to what is determined as auspicious locating and timing. Temples or shrines are often erected on promontories, hills or in the mountains – in fact, temples are often built and viewed as symbolising mountains – often with long flights of steps leading up to them, the ascent signifying life's spiritual pilgrimage.[7] Climbing these steps is itself a purificatory and enlightening experience. The temple is a kind of *maṇḍala*, or structured pattern of sacralised space and time. It may be more or less complex, but at its heart, in the womb-house, is located the main deity honoured in the temple. Other deities and attendant figures may be present at various places and points of the compass. Here too, where image-making is concerned, there are time-honoured rules pertaining to material, design and proportion. Large temples often contain an artificial pond of considerable size. Such ponds symbolise fecundity, and water is always used in temple rituals of regeneration and purification. For this reason, there is often naturally flowing water in the temple environs. A flag impressed with the characteristic symbol for 'Om' may well flutter from a *śikhara*, indicating that the temple is a place of active worship – the deity is in residence.

The worshipper is meant to be prepared and purified progressively in his or her approach to the sanctuary. This can begin by passing through walled enclosures surrounding the temple and includes ablutions (perhaps a ritual bath) and circumambulations, usually clockwise, of secondary images, shrines, or even of the temple itself. Sometimes worshippers make circumambulations, called *pradakṣiṇas* or *parikramas*, lasting several days. (India itself can be circumambulated via strategically chosen holy places.) The functionaries and priests, often hereditary, connected with *pūjā* and pilgrimage are of different kinds and need not be Brahmins.[8] At a large centre like Benares,

> there are the *pandās*, who meet the pilgrims at the train station, arrange their rest houses, and oversee the entire pilgrimage. For many pilgrims, the *pandā* will be the same man or of the same family who has cared for their ancestors. There are the *karmakāndīs*, priests who assist in particular rites; the *ghātiās*, priests of a somewhat lower class who have proprietary rites along the *ghāts* [quays or steps leading to the water] and who tend to the needs of the bathers; the *pūjārīs*, who officiate in the temples; and the *mahāpātras*, who specialize in death rites.[9]

At pilgrimage centres and temples people may perform various specialised rituals, such as undergoing penance, making offerings, receiving instruction, hearing *pāṭhas*, expiating or undertaking vows, immersing ashes, bathing, undergoing *saṃskāras*, worshipping, giving alms, even dying and cremating. Specialised activities require specialist officiants. These we must distinguish from the *purohita* or domestic priest, who may also be hereditary and who administers the *saṃskāras*, gives advice, etc. at home.[10]

The image or 'icon'[11] (*mūrti, vigraha, pratimā, arcā*[12]) of the deity worshipped must be formally installed. This is called *prāṇa-pratiṣṭhā*, namely, animating the icon. The ceremony is elaborate, but once it is concluded the deity (Vaiṣṇava, Śaiva or Śākta) is believed to take up residence in the image. Sometimes a composite icon – male-female, or Vaiṣṇava-Śaiva, or Śaiva-Śākta – may be installed. This only serves to underline the point that in theory the deity is one but manifests in a pluriform way. The icon is taken over by the deity and becomes its temporary body. But the deity may thus reside in innumerable bodies in innumerable locations without being essentially exhausted in any way. Because the Godhead is invariably believed to be essentially spiritual and formless (though many traditions of Hinduism maintain that the deity *also* has a personal celestial, anthropomorphic form) it is an act of loving graciousness on the deity's part to become an accessible focus of human devotion in the icon. The invisible God/Goddess becomes visibly concrete, for our needs and salvation to his or her glory.

The main deity of the temple is treated like royalty. Three or four times a day – at dawn, midday, in the evening and at night – the image is ceremonially worshipped. Often a screen or door partitioning the main shrine is opened or closed at the appropriate times. The icon is awakened, glorified, fed, ritually bathed, garlanded, entertained, cooled by the smearing of sandal paste, allowed to rest in the heat of the afternoon, formally taken leave of at night, sometimes clothed or given a change of clothes; in short, it is treated as a living resident.[13] And indeed, it does live: in the minds and hearts of the worshipper, in the mythic tradition associated with the immanent deity, and in the divine grace that the latter bestows through the visits, fasts, prayers, vows, sufferings and joys of the worshipper's life. Secondary images may be treated similarly. I have heard devotees recount with implicit belief stories of how the temple image has mysteriously disappeared or 'walked away' to avoid desecration in times of great danger, only to reappear in due course in its familiar form.[14]

At certain times of the day, the image holds court with a priest or priests in attendance. This is when votaries can come forward to receive the deity's 'darshan', i.e. they look upon the image and savour the deity's presence. Offerings – money, fruit, sweetmeats or flowers – are made while a priest may perform an *ārati*, namely clockwise circular movements of an oil-lamp held in the right hand, in the gloom of the sanctuary before the icon. The priest usually holds a handbell in his left hand, which he rings continuously during the process. The whole scene – the position and form of the icon (sometimes ornately apparelled), the bells and incense, the flowers and offerings, the *ārati*, the priest usually with his *tilaka* or 'sect' marks in paste on his forehead (a V or vertical strokes for Vaiṣṇavas, horizontal strokes for Śaiva-Śākta) – is a study in sacred 'power-dressing'. The darshan is thus activated; direct contact between the divine focus and the worshipper is established. The gloom of earthly space and time is lit up in a moment of grace. At festivals, the main icon(s) may be taken in grand procession on special floats or carts (called '*rathas*' or 'chariots') through the local streets so that the saving darshan may be accessible to all, though in many cases separate processional images may be used. The rituals of temple worship are an instance of *smārta* rites because they are recorded in the *smṛti* or tradition of the community.

Domestic worship has its formal features, but it is individualistic and highly variable. In almost every religious Hindu's home there is a shrine for *pūjā* or at least sacred drawings or pictures to evoke an atmosphere. A cupboard, recess, or even a room, may be set aside for images or pictures of the deity. Sometimes the divine representations are highly eclectic (I have even seen a cast-off crucifix rescued and placed among the artifacts of the shrine), but the underlying belief is the same: the Godhead is one but manifests itself in various ways. Generally an *iṣṭadevatā* ('chosen deity') prevails. Yet this is not arbitrary. Usually it is the divine form or person worshipped in the family for generations, or recommended by the guru or by a particularly significant event in one's life or by some conversion experience. It is the concrete form in which the Godhead established contact with the worshipper. As such, it is a sign of divine election rather than the reverse.

It is usually the senior woman or women of the household who tend the domestic shrine and see to the *pūjā*. But they do this on behalf of all the family members. Anyone may worship and at any time, of course, as circumstances dictate, but as a rule specific days of the week and times are set apart for regular worship. This depends upon the deity worshipped, the religious traditon one belongs to, and local customs. Variations are legion, but in Bengal, where Śākta religion predominates, for many the Goddess in her form as Lakṣmī is specially worshipped on Thursdays; similarly Saturdays (and also Tuesdays) are special to Kālī, and Mondays and Fridays to Śiva. Traditionally, the worshipper (usually the woman or women) would fast, bathe and then perform worship. This could consist in *ālpanā* (making stylised drawings of various motifs with rice paste or powder on or about the shrine), ritually bathing the deity, *pāṭha*, offerings of sweetmeats, water, flowers, etc. At the end of the worship children and other members of the family may be given a morsel of the *prasāda*, i.e. the food offered to and returned by the deity with a blessing, to eat. This is a sign of communal participation in the benefits of the worship.[15]

It would be appropriate to comment here on some features of Hindu iconography. As noted, the icon does not exhaust the Godhead; it is 'not an object at which one's [spiritual] vision halts, but rather a lens through which one's vision is directed'.[16] When damaged or destroyed, it is disposed of ritually, usually by immersion, and another installed in its place. Nevertheless, it is still very important and, as noted, its stylised fashioning is subject to the directives of a long textual and/or local tradition. The image will usually depict a particular myth of the great, or a minor tradition, a particular manifestation or facet of the deity or member of its religious family, or a particular teaching, or indeed a combination of these, thus either particularising or diffusing one's spiritual focus as the case may be.

Let us consider a Vaiṣṇava image. It may be of Viṣṇu himself, the cult icon of a sect, distinguished by the sacred thread over the left shoulder, beautifully arranged hair, and a *cakra* or disc in one hand, symbolising the wheel of *dharma* or the orb of the sun, Viṣṇu and the sun sometimes being associated in the texts: Viṣṇu – the establishment figure, the god of order. Or it may be of Viṣṇu with one leg raised high, i.e. *Viṣṇu tri-vikrama* or *urugāya*, 'Viṣṇu of the three strides' or 'wide-striding', harking back to a motif of early strands of the Vedas. Or it may be of Viṣṇu as one of his *avatāras*: Narasiṃha, the 'Man-Lion' perhaps, with the anti-god Hiraṇyakaśipu being torn open on his lap – another well-known, but much later motif. Or the icon may be of Rāma, or of Kṛṣṇa dancing on the multi-hooded Kāliya, a serpent king whom the boy God subdued in a famous story of the *Bhāgavata* Purāṇa. It may be of Kṛṣṇa in the company of Rādhā, he dark and playing the flute, she fair, possibly demurely showing the *varada-mudrā* or boon-bestowing gesture to the devotee. The Rādhā-Kṛṣṇa icon may be 'Vaiṣṇava' for purposes of classification, yet in various devotional schools drawing inspiration from Caitanya, the pair are *the* conjoint Godhead, worshipped in their own right. Or as Vaiṣṇava the icon may be of Hanumān, Rāmā's monkey helper (see Chapter 5). Here, deity is focused through a beloved animal representation, often a cult object in its own right. While it is true that when it comes to icon worship there is often fierce sectarianism among Hindus (even within the same broad tradition), it is no less true that many Hindus, while perhaps having a favourite iconic form, may happily relate to a number of icons across sectarian divides at various times and circumstances so as to form a composite picture, perhaps by a kind of icon prioritisation, in their worship and approach to the divine. Although Viṣṇu was a significant focus of the transcendent already in the *Ṛg* Veda, the processes which led, increasingly from the first centuries of the Common Era, to his becoming the assimilative centre of worship for a great many Hindus, are far from clear.[17]

The situation is similar in the Śaiva context. Speaking historically, the Śiva of latter-day devotion is a composite figure, originating from various sources including the Vedic gods Agni and Rudra and perhaps Harappan religion.[18] On the basis of the *Śvetāśvatara* Upaniṣad, which seems to exalt Śiva, we may conjecture that by the beginning of the Common Era he was a monotheistic cult deity. In time, like Viṣṇu and the Goddess, he became the assimilative centre of a vast and many-faceted mythic tradition. Iconographically, we may have Śiva on his own, with trident and matted locks this time, one or more cobras draped about him and a tiger-skin around his loins: Śiva the ascetic, the unconventional, fertile, disruptive God. Yet matted locks notwithstanding, he may be depicted in his famous pose as Lord of the Dance – the cobra symbolising fertility entwined about him – four-armed, with one hand bearing the flame of wisdom in its palm, another the small double-faced drum of creative sound, a third displaying the *abhaya-mudrā* or gesture counselling not to fear, and the fourth pointing to an upraised foot inviting all to take refuge in the lotus feet which have trampled the snares of this world. Here we have a finely balanced combination of eros and asceticism. Or Śiva may be depicted in various seated postures, embracing Pārvatī, his wife, consort and lover in a synthesis of complements.

In the Śaiva context, let us consider the iconography of what to western tastes may be a bizarre focus of the divine – the elephant-headed Gaṇeśa.[19] Gaṇeśa is placed in Śiva's family; according to the dominant mythic theme, he was produced from rubbings off Pārvatī's body, decapitated in a fit of anger by Śiva (who was ignorant of his identity), and then restored to life with an elephant's head and adopted by a penitent Śiva. *Gaṇeśa* means 'Lord of the *gaṇa*s', Śiva's gnomish henchmen.[20] Gaṇeśa lost his own head in trying to guard his mother's privacy, and it is in the role of guardian and facilitator that he is generally worshipped. His main feast is celebrated on the *caturthī* or fourth day in the bright half of Bhadrapadā (August–September); the celebrations may last for up to ten days.[21] Gaṇeśa protects his devotee from danger and mishaps. As 'Lord of obstacles and Lord of beginnings', Gaṇeśa will be invoked by the pious Hindu (not only within Brahminic Hinduism) at the start of some enterprise, religious or otherwise: a journey, a building project, worship, examinations, a business venture, marriage, writing a letter, the working day, and so on. Otherwise the sinister streak in his make-up may assert itself and he may refuse to make situations easier. As lord of obstacles, not only can he remove them, he can also create them. Although history records a fairly minor tradition of Gaṇeśa as a central cult deity, today he generally plays his important but subordinate role within a larger theistic context.

So there he is, usually sitting or standing (very occasionally dancing on one leg) before you, sometimes many-armed, with his elephant-head and paunch. What to make of him? As in the case of myth, the Hindu relates to the icon on more than one level at the same time. There is the level of narrative and myth. He or she knows Gaṇeśa's religious role and how he came by his elephant's head and broke (or lost) a tusk. There is also the level of religious symbolism. The elephant symbolises sagacity and power and, when in rut, that unpredictability which is so dangerous. The trunk has phallic associations and hence stands for creativity and fertility; the ears are like winnowing-fans, sifting wisdom. The trunk, the tip curled around a sweetmeat, usually extends along the pot-belly and ends near a little jar full of the same sweets (Gaṇeśa, the symbol and giver of success). One hand may carry a hatchet which signifies 'the cutting away of . . . false teaching'; another often holds an elephant-goad representing 'the logic that cuts through illusion'. Yet a third may bear the noose with which wild elephants are roped, signifying the power to restrain worldly passions; or a hand or two may gesture reassurance and the giving of blessings.[22] For the Hindu devotee, the divine essence does not have many hands, but for the artist many hands can bear many objects signifying different things; it also symbolises the dynamism and power that the worshipper expects of God. When the deity is represented as serenely self-controlled – as in the case of Śiva, the meditating Yogī – only two relaxed hands are depicted.

So the featuring of many hands is a distinctive artistic device. It is a way of compacting a wealth of symbolic meaning which can be read off by even the most rustic votary. But one more feature deserves mention. Gaṇeśa is almost always accompanied by a rat, placed about or under his feet. This is known technically as his *vāhana* or animal supporter (in both senses). Most cult figures have their *vāhana*s; iconographically they help identify their icon. Śiva has Nandī his bull, Kṛṣṇa is sometimes accompanied by a cow, Viṣṇu has Garuḍa, the eagle and also the cosmic serpent Śeṣa or Ananta, the Goddess Durgā has a lion, the snake-devī Manasā a white goose, Kārttikeya, another son of Śiva, the peacock, Śītalā, a devī who protects from smallpox an ass, Brahmā (the demiurge) a swan, etc. Traditionally, the characteristics of the *vāhana* are sometimes identified with, sometimes overlap with, and sometimes complement those of its icon. Thus elephants and rats are supposed not to get on; juxtaposing Gaṇeśa and his rat signifies the overcoming of opposites in the deity. The elephant is large and powerful, the rat small and surreptitious. The two together symbolise transcendence and might, conjoined to immanence and perseverance in the religious context. Thus all in all, when properly understood, the Gaṇeśa icon is a powerfully meaningful representation. Does not the half-animal, half-human figure represent the divine in search of the human and the human (including animal creation) in search of the divine?

And now to the icon of Devī or the Goddess. As the Śākta tradition demonstrates most clearly, she is divine *śakti* or power personified. She has her benign form and her horrific form. Kālī is perhaps the best-known example of the latter. In Bengal, traditionally a stronghold of Śākta religion, Kālī's most popular image is of a young woman, jet black and naked but for a garland and short skirt of gory severed heads and hands respectively. She has very long, black, dishevelled hair and a vividly red, protruding, blood-smeared tongue. Dark and dynamic, she has her consort Śiva underfoot, recumbent and white in stark contrast. In some contexts, this symbolises the conjunction of *Prakṛti*, the ever-active female engaged in the dance of creation, activated, for the liberation of the pure, spiritual *Puruṣa*, by the presence alone of the *Puruṣa* within. Here *prakṛti* is the visible *śakti* of *puruṣa*. It is no accident that in our story of the dicing incident, it was Draupadī who actively encompassed the release of her rather supine male consorts, especially the strangely undemonstrative Yudhiṣṭhira. On the other hand, in some (especially Tantric) theological contexts, the Goddess, often herself called *Prakṛti*, is the spiritual power personified of the Godhead, the supreme *Puruṣa*.

Kālī is usually four-armed, wielding the sword of enlightening wisdom, a severed head, a bowl of plenty perhaps, with one or two hands in the boon-bestowing or reassuring gesture. A cobra may be draped about her neck. Sometimes a vertical eye in the middle of the forehead – the third eye of spiritual knowledge – is included. This may be a grisly image, but it speaks volumes to its votaries, and remarkably is psychologically comforting at the same time. For those who worship Kālī in socially acceptable ways, and they comprise the overwhelming majority, Kālī provides the opportunity to acknowledge and then sublimate the inevitably disruptive, violent and unruly in their lives. Kālī stands for disorder just about contained; the unpredictable dance of creation which carries the saving hope of one's final spiritual fulfilment.

However, there are some who worship the Goddess in ways unacceptable to the majority. This *sādhana* or spiritual discipline may make use of the so-called five Ms – *matsya* (fish), *māṃsa* (meat), *mada* (liquor), *mudrā* (grain) and *maithuna* (copulation) – or other techniques,[23] to ritually wrest salvation and wholesomeness, by a reverse logic so to speak, from contexts conventionally regarded as degrading and polluting. Salvation is achieved by 'transgressive' methods. It is important to note that in either case, Kālī is not terrifying to her votaries. On the contrary she is endearing, for her very grisliness intimates that she has overcome opposition and will indeed save her followers.

In the Śākta context, the Devī's perhaps most benign form may be exemplified by Durgā. Durgā's most well-known representation is of her as *mahiṣa-āsura-mardinī*, the slayer of the buffalo demon. The story is first told in the *Devī-māhātmya*, a eulogy on the Goddess forming a section of the *Mārkaṇḍeya* Purāṇa. It is dated to about the sixth century CE. After acquiring great *tapas*, the anti-god Mahiṣa received the boon that only a woman would be able to overcome him. He then made himself most unpopular with the gods. So all the gods having gathered, they concentrated their energies to form the Goddess and her weapons. Then, mounted on a lion-*vāhana*, she joined battle with Mahiṣa and slew him. Durgā Mahiṣāsuramardinī is the central icon of the greatest Bengali religious festival of the year, the Durgā Pūjā. We will come to this later.

Śākta religion has a long and geographically scattered tradition of human sacrifice to placate and win the favour of the Goddess.[24] There is evidence to show that until as recently as the early decades of the nineteenth century (when it was banned under British rule), there was regular human sacrifice in some of the main Śākta temples of Bengal. Although human sacrifice today is universally abominated by Hindus, Śāktas included, from time to time one still comes across newspaper reports of demented parents sacrificing a child to propitiate some devī or other. Animal sacrifice to the Goddess, however, continues unabated. As noted in an earlier context, this is not reckoned to be a reprehensible form of violence. The victim is invested with the power of the Goddess and its soul is instantly transported to her presence. Note that Durgā has her fearful aspects and Kālī her benign. The Śākta Goddess always combines the two, so that it is somewhat misleading to speak univocally of benign and fearsome forms in this context. For an entirely benign aspect of the Goddess one must look to, for example, the Goddess Śrī or Lakṣmī in Śrī-Vaiṣṇava worship in the South. The Hindu of the high tradition at any rate does not tend to dichotomise the different aspects of the Goddess. She is one, but manifests plurally, taking one form or other for different reasons not only mythologically but also in the context of religious worship. Religiously she is the universal Mother, bringing forth and nurturing or destroying as the case may be; she is the power of the Godhead, the womb of the bewildering play of creation, rescuing or deluding. In some contexts she is also the model wife and/or passionate lover of the male principle in the deity, symbolising by this role intimate divine union. Śākta religion often views woman as a manifestation or aspect of the Goddess. This is how the *Brahmavaivarta* Purāṇa puts it:

> All women are sprung from Prakṛti [here an aspect of Devī],
> the best, the worst, and the intermediate.
> The best are derived from the *sattva* portion; they are well-mannered and chaste.
> The intermediate are parts of *rajas*,
> Seeking pleasure and ever intent on their own ends.
> The worst are parts of *tamas*, of unknown ancestry,
> Bad-mouthed, unchaste, licentious, independent, fond of quarrel.
> Unchaste women on earth and the heavenly nymphs
> Are known as prostitutes, and are parts of *tamas*.

The author continues,

> Here we see that the three basic types of women are derived from the *guṇas* of Prakṛti [=Devī]. It is the *rājasī* and especially the *tāmasī* women who hinder men from attaining peace in the world and salvation hereafter. The *sāttvikī* women, on the other hand, help their husbands perform religious rites, free them from sin and *karma*, and even lead them to liberation.[25]

It is said sometimes that in contrast to how it may be in the rest of Hinduism, women in Śākta and Tantra religion are given a positive status. To begin with, the chief or most vital personification of deity is feminine – the Goddess. Further, Tantric and Śākta *sādhana* often requires the complementary ritual participation of women and men, as we have already noted. However, one must enquire further into what this positive status is supposed to be. If it is social status it would seem that in general the position of women is not significantly improved in these religions. They participate in the cult and consequently have an enhanced status, only in ritual contexts, while their everyday social standing is left largely untouched. Indeed, it has been pointed out that because of their religiously highly unconventional practices (e.g. ritual copulation often between married partners who may not be married to each other), the known followers of these cults are socially despised in places.[26] It may be then that women have a positive religious and theological status in such forms of religion. But even this is ambivalent. First, note that further distinctions concerning the female sex are often called for; thus it is usually the virgin girl or woman who is exalted in this context above her married counterparts. Second, it is difficult to escape the conclusion that though the Goddess herself may be deferred to as Supreme, her human embodiment is treated in the ritual in an instrumentalist fashion. For it is the men among the worshippers who have the leading role in the form and purpose of the ritual. Too much must not be made then of the so-called positive status of women in Tantra and Śākta religion.

Hindus have a way of seeing the sacred everywhere, and it can be signified by almost anything. We have already discussed Śiva's non-realistic (phallic) symbol, the *liṅga*, usually conjoined to the (also aniconic) symbol of the *yoni* or sexual organ of the Devī (see Chapter 7). But many other things, vegetative, animal and inanimate, have traditionally been invested with sacred significance. Mention may be made here again of the banyan and pipal trees (*ficus benghalensis* and *ficus religiosa* respectively). We can add Kuśa or Darbha grass (*desmostachya bipinnata*) which has a role in both *śrauta* and *smārta* ritual, and the basil or Tulasī/Tulsī plant (*ocimum sanctum*) which, among other qualities, is supposed to discourage Yama the lord of death from visiting. This plant is used in the funeral pyre and is grown in pots or in the yard in houses of the pious, where a daily ritual may be performed to it.

In various places and cults, a number of animals are also regarded as peculiarly significant in a religious context. We may single out the snake. In iconography it is usually the cobra which is depicted; it also represents the *nāga*, mythical half-human half-serpent beings which dwell in water. The cobra, which, among other things, stands for creativity and, by its coils, the unendingness of space and time, is associated with deities of all three major traditions: Vaiṣṇava, Śaiva and Śākta. It evokes a sense of dread and insinuates that however benign the deity may appear, there are elements in the divine make-up which cannot be taken for granted: the spiritual life is not without its hazards. The cobra is also a chthonic being, a creature of the soil, and symbolises the nurturing and fecundating qualities of the earth. For all these reasons, the cobra – or some other snake, depending on local tradition – is the object of religious veneration in many parts of India. There may be a marked reluctance to kill these snakes even if they intrude into places of human habitation. Many Hindus regularly place saucers of milk and other food in spots which the designated snake is expected to frequent, and around the country one comes across tablets of stone with snakes carved on them, to mark the religious veneration of the snake. These are often found beneath well-established trees. Particularly in eastern India, Manasā, the snake devī, is worshipped to protect from snake-bite. As we have seen in Chapter 5, this region has a tradition of *maṅgals* or verse-narratives in her name. Of the sacredness of the cow we have spoken in an earlier context (see Chapter 2). Although the cow is generally an object of veneration among Hindus, particular communities observe various special feasts in its honour. This may include gaudily decking out and feeding a cow as representative of its kind.

There are also natural inanimate objects which may elicit reverence or worship. Most common among such objects are stones or rocks which are deemed to bear the shape of the *liṅga* or *yoni*. A famous example occurs in the Lingaraj Mahaprabhu temple in Bhubaneswar, the capital of the state of Orissa.

> The temple houses a rough-hewn block of stone eight feet in diameter reputed . . . to have been found in a mango forest south of the Old Town. This stone is believed to possess particularly sacred powers as the *lingam* of the god Shiva and attracts many pilgrims from other parts of India. . . . Between the eleventh and fifteenth centuries, Vaishnava influences became so strong that the temple was renamed the Lingaraj Mahaprabhu Temple. Lingaraj (king of the Lingam) is an epithet of Shiva; Mahaprabhu (Most Powerful One) is an epithet of Vishnu-Krishna. The stone *lingam* itself is today called Harihara, a combination of Visnu (Hari) and Shiva (Hara). A natural cleavage in the *lingam* is said to manifest its dual Shaiva-Vaishnava character.[27]

Mention of mangoes brings to mind the following example, taken from a newspaper report, which illustrates well the Hindu's penchant for perceiving the sacred in unexpected places. The report tells of a mango being discovered, still on its tree, in what looked like human shape. People came from miles around to worship this chosen manifestation of the deity. In rural areas natural mounds of earth are sometimes designated as shrines of the local mother goddess. Here a simple form of worship may take place regularly. A pot of water is often placed near the mound (sometimes under a tree), with a coconut sitting on the mouth, holding flowers and leaves in place round the rim. The pot symbolises the (womb of the) goddess and corresponding ideas of fertility and fecundity. This is an aspect of what has been called folk religion and we will return to its theistic implications.

Again, the hill Arunacala at Tiruvannamalai in Tamil Nadu, is itself holy, a sort of *axis mundi* of devotion. It was especially dear to the sage Ramana Maharshi (see Chapter 7) who dwelt there, his presence a focus of its sanctity. Finally in this context we may mention the *śālagrāma*, a short, smooth, tubular stone, revered by Vaiṣṇavas as representing Viṣṇu.

> The sacredness of this . . . stone containing fossil ammonite seems to be comparatively ancient. A motive for it seems to be that several interior spiral grooves visible in the stone are considered by the people to be representations of Viṣṇu's discuss. Another interpretation . . . may, however, possibly be more original: a śālagrama can be of nine colours, and then represent the nine 'historic' avatāras of the god.[28]

The *śālagrāma* is wrapped in a clean cloth and usually bathed, the water after this ritual being drunk since it is believed to wash away sin and impurity. The beds of certain rivers are the prized locations for procuring *śālagrāma*s.

The rationale behind the worship/veneration of all these natural features is often the same, though it may be articulated more or less explicitly and with more or less sophistication. It is that the transcendent or the deity is present everywhere, immanent in all things. At any point in space and time this presence may burst through, and when it does it should be acknowledged, or at least the ubiquitous presence of the sacred should be marked in designated ways. This does not mean that even the so-called sophisticated are prone to seeing miracles at every turn; it means rather that every level of being is within the compass of the divine power, and may be made transparent to it. But I do not wish to imply that all instances of such veneration carry this underlying rationale, however dimly perceived. In fact Hindus can be very superstitious about the sacred or occult powers of different kinds of objects. Thus in his survey among the urbanised in Chirakkal, Ayrookuzhiel records that out of '187 interviewees, 108 believe in the *śakti* [power] of *nāgam* [here a particular species of snake]'. A further fifty-two expressed doubt in this regard, but wanted to take no chances; thus all were opposed to harming the snake. Further, exactly what its *śakti* implied and how this was thought to manifest varied.[29]

There are other instances of reverence for inanimate things, e.g. the use of amulets containing some *mantra* (often taken from the

Atharva Veda) tied around the upper arm, or finger-rings of various materials worn to ward off evil planetary and other influences. Thus coral is believed to be an auspicious substance and to protect against any possible malignant effect of Mars and the Sun. Many, from all walks of life, believe in spirit-possession, by some disgruntled *preta* perhaps, manifesting in hysteria, fainting-fits, illness, etc. The subjects of this phenomenon are usually women. Some of the possessed may be able to foretell the future, so this can be quite a profitable business. Belief in ghosts (*bhūta*) is also common. These spirits are usually malign and take up residence in a tree, house, or near a cemetery or on wasteland.[30] Exorcising with the help of *mantras* and rituals – from people possessed or before a house is newly occupied and so on – can be an important part of the bread-and-butter work of domestic priests. There is also the notion of the 'evil eye'. Not only envious human beings but even a local goddess may look with venom at someone and thereby cause them harm. Married, childless women in particular are careful not to praise a bonny baby in public, for fear of being accused of casting the evil eye; otherwise any subsequent illness or misfortune of the child is likely to be blamed on them. The eyes of infants are often heavily outlined with black pigment; besides being an attempt to prettify, it may also be intended to counter the evil eye. Of course, there are many Hindus who do not entertain such beliefs, yet such beliefs are surprisingly potent and pervasive in Hindu society and can exert great psychological influence. They may be used as instruments of vicious psychological warfare.

It must also be remembered that not all Hindus exalt icon-worship. There are – usually intellectualised – forms of religion in which this is discouraged or belittled. Advaita Vedānta is a case in point. Śaṃkara declared that worshipping the Supreme through symbols or icons (*pratīkopāsana*) was for the *alpa-medhaḥ* or religiously small-minded or undeveloped. *Brahman* is utterly pure and formless and identical with our inner spirit. Progress in the spiritual life dissolves the need for name and form as the object of worship. Most Hindus, unashamed icon-worshippers and devotees of a personal God, would reject this understanding of the supreme Being.

But this does not mean that followers of the Advaitic vision have no place for religious ritual. On the contrary; ritual is part of the Hindu way of life. Thus the monks of the Ramakrishna Order, who profess Advaita, have devised an elaborate ritual for their daily *ārati* services, which are frequented by lay supporters. In place of an icon there is usually a commemorative photograph or bust of Ramakrishna (in addition there may be photographs of one or more past heads of the particular centre at which the worship takes place). Certain constants remain: incense, the handbell rung continuously during the ceremony, flowers, oil lamps and other symbols (e.g. the shell symbolising water/infinity). But where required, the significance of these symbols is reinterpreted in an Advaitic context. Thus objects signifying the five traditional basic elements of prakritic being – a flower for earth, a shell for water, an oil-lamp for fire, a fly-whisk for air, and a folded napkin cupped in the hand (like the hood of a cobra) for space – may be successively and solemnly displayed, not as an offering to some godhead, but as signifying the fundamental unity of the microcosm (the individual person) and the macrocosm of being.

The singing of hymns is also usually a part of the ceremony, another ubiquitous item of collective Hindu worship. Such worship is variously called *kīrtan*, *satsaṅg* or *bhajan* (or the singing of *bhajans*). It arouses devotional fervour and bonds the worshippers, at least temporarily overcoming divisions of caste, sex and social status.[31] We may mention here the recitation of the *Sahasra-nāma*, the Thousand Names of the deity, which is often done collectively. There are well-known Vaiṣṇava, Śaiva and Śākta *sahasranāma* – lists culled from epic and Purāṇic literature and from the more sectarian scriptures or Āgamas. It has been a centuries-old custom for religious thinkers to write commentaries on each name of particular lists. This is how one modern translator of such literature comments on the *Viṣṇu-Sahasranāma*:

> The Vishnu Sahasranāma, containing 142 verses, is extracted from the Ānuśāsanika Parva . . . of the Mahābhārata, in the dialogue between Bhīshma and Yudhisthira.
>
> It is held in great veneration all over India, from Cape Comorin to the Himālayas and is recited by persons of all stations in life . . . on every occasion of joy or sorrow, fear or hope. Miraculous virtues are attributed to it. . . .
>
> The ancient custom, still observed in the village parts, especially of the South, is to repeat each name of the Sahasranāma, offering Tulasi petals or any available flowers of the season before the idol of Vishnu in his various incarnations of Rāma, Krishna, etc. This is done for the fulfilment of one's desires, or to ward off the evil influence of planets. Many merely repeat the whole book sitting before the idol with Bhasma (sacred ashes) in a plate by their side, which is afterwards distributed among the village people. Sometimes some wealthy householder, in celebrating the thread or

> initiation ceremony of his son, feeds one thousand virtuous Brahmins repeating each [name] before a Brahmin.[32]

Perhaps these claims are somewhat exaggerated, and times have changed (this was written in 1926). But the devotional practice is still current, not least in the South. The Names of the *Viṣṇu-sahasranāma* are of various kinds, either theological – 'the supporter of being', *bhūta-bhṛt*, No. 5; 'self-existent', *svayaṃbhū*, No. 38; 'formless', *amūrti*, No. 830; or 'mythic' – 'embodied as the Man-Lion', *narasiṃha-vapu*, an avatar of Viṣṇu, No. 21; 'The Monkey-Chief', *kapīndra*, i.e. in the form of Rāma, No. 501; 'Three-stepping', *trivikrama*, which refers to the story of Viṣṇu appropriating the universe (see Chapter 12), No. 530; or attributive – 'golden-naveled', *hiraṇyanābha* (the navel representing the centre of the universe) No. 194; 'thousand-eyed', *sahasrākṣa*, No. 226; 'the great devourer', *mahāśana* (as time) No. 303; 'lovely-limbed', *svaṅga*, No. 616; 'Cooling dew', *śiśira* (because he removes the fever of sin and suffering) No. 913; 'bearer of the club', *gadādhara*, No. 997, etc. The Names of Śiva and the Goddess are similar. The idea underlying this practice of chanting or repeating the divine Name has much in common with the Sant view that the divine Name has a saving power in its own right. The Name is like a *mantra*, or rather it is a *mantra*, thought to empower the utterer in various ways. For those who seek only to love God, it can be an ecstatic way of uniting intimately with the Beloved.

12 Means, ways and ends

I

Religious festivals as exemplified by Dīwālī, the Pūrṇa Kumbha Melā and Durgā Pūjā. The way as yoga *or integral union. The* yoga *of* bhakti*: its Vedic roots. Levels of* bhakti.

Let us now examine the way Hindus celebrate religious festivals in order to gain further insight into how space and time co-ordinate in worship. We will briefly consider three different kinds of festivals, exemplified respectively by: (i) Dīwālī, which is annual and virtually pan-Indian; (ii) the Pūrṇa Kumbha Melā, which is occasional and localised but the cynosure of enormous interest; and (iii) the yearly Durgā Pūjā, special to its heartland, Bengal.

Dīwālī

Dīwālī has been known in the tradition by various names, the most well-known alternative being Dīpāvali, i.e. 'a row of (oil-)lamps'. Thus Dīwālī is a festival of illumination. It may continue for about five days, though the core of the festival lasts for three days. These fall at the juncture of the lunar months of Āśvina and Kārttika (in the month of October) when the moon has completely waned at the end of the dark half of Āśvina; the day of the new moon (called *amāvāsyā*), and the first day of the bright half of Kārttika are included. Thus the darkness of *amāvāsyā* sets the scene for the illuminations of the festival.

Traditionally, the feast of Dīwālī does not have a single religious focus; rather, it is a feast of renewal. Although there are regional variations, the celebration of Viṣṇu's or Kṛṣṇa's victory over the anti-god Naraka is the dominant idea of the first core-day. Naraka means 'hell' or 'nether-world'. Thus the divine power has overcome the darkness of the underworld. This theme, symbolised by light, runs through the feast. Central to new-moon day is the worship of the goddess, Lakṣmī, who bestows prosperity. The business community in particular, from the exalted to the lowly, start their financial year on this day; old books are closed and new opened. The season is appropriate; the rains have passed, crops have been harvested, new winter seed is being sown. One can see why Lakṣmī is invoked. On the third core-day, the first of the bright half of Kārttika, the dominant celebration is that of the myth of Viṣṇu overcoming the anti-god, Bali. Bali was a great and generous king who, to increase his sovereignty in the world, began the *aśvamedha* sacrifice. Viṣṇu approached him in the form of a dwarf and asked to be given as much territory as he could cover in three strides. Bali agreed. Viṣṇu then began to expand; with his first stride he covered the earth and with his second the heavens. With his third he pushed the submissive Bali into the nether-world (Bali was rewarded with the promise of future greatness). Thus, by timing and motif, the feast of Dīwālī cumulatively exalts the divine sovereignty over space, time and the powers of darkness (represented by the underworld) as also the divine power to manifest in space and time.

Hindus characteristically mark Dīwālī's theme of illumination and renewal by letting off fireworks at night (almost every house that can afford it has its own display) and by decorating balconies, window-sills, etc. with rows of candles, and so on. There is also the belief that these lights show wandering spirits (especially those of one's forefathers) the way to their next world. In northern India, especially around Mathura and Vrindaban, places sacred to the boy Kṛṣṇa, cows and bulls are decked and venerated as symbols of Kṛṣṇa and prosperity.[1]

The Pūrṇa Kumbha Melā

This offers one of the most impressive spectacles among Hindu religious festivals and celebrates the spilling of the jar (*kumbha*) of the nectar of immortality (*amṛta*). First the background story: the primeval waters were being churned by the 'gods' and the anti-gods in order to extract the *amṛta*. In due course it emerged in a jar borne by the divine physician Dhanvantari. Viṣṇu, in the guise of the siren Mohinī, was asked to apportion it between the two rival sides but the inevitable dispute broke out and in the ensuing melée the *kumbha* was spirited away to the world of the 'gods'. The *kumbha* took twelve (human) years to reach its destination; every three years one drop of *amṛta* fell to earth – at Hardwar, Nasik, Ujjain and Prayaga (modern Allahabad) – four drops in all. So every three years consecutively the festival is celebrated in these places. The grandest celebration, the so-called 'Full Kumbha Gathering' (*pūrṇa kumbha melā*), is held at Prayaga once every twelve years. Prayaga has this distinction because it is situated at what is traditionally regarded as one of the holiest places of religious Hinduism: the confluence (*saṃgama*) of the Yamuna and Ganges rivers. Conjunctions of all kinds – of the day and night, of the *yuga*s, of rivers – are regarded as specially charged religiously. They must be handled with care. The exact period of the festival is reckoned by a particular conjunction of Jupiter, the sun and the moon. The last Kumbha gathering at Prayaga was in 1989, from 14 January to 10 February, when the sun and moon were in Capricorn and Jupiter was in Taurus. It was an especially sacred occasion because there was a lunar eclipse at the time (another conjunction). A dip in the waters at the high point of the festival is equivalent to performing innumerable *aśvamedha* sacrifices and circumambulations of the motherland: sins and impurities are washed away and the merit attained is incalculable. Indeed, if the conditions are right, one might even be within reach of or attain *mokṣa*.

Pilgrims, not only from India but from around the world, start arriving weeks beforehand. As the climax of the festival approaches, they pour in, wave upon wave, from every walk of life, caste and sub-caste: rich and poor, young and old, Brahmin and untouchable, male and female ascetics, religious leaders and gurus of countless sects – Vaiṣṇava, Śaiva and Śākta and many other allegiances. The currents of people streaming in are continuous; most carry little bundles of possessions, some their very young in their arms or their very old on their backs, the immense ebb and flow of this human tide a fitting image of the great stream of *saṃsāra*. (It was estimated that at the high point of the 1989 Melā between fifteen and twenty million people were present. Religious Hinduism is alive and well!) The journey itself to the site is a pilgrimage, gaining merit and expending sin and bad karma for the pilgrim.

Slowly, in the bustle along the river bank, a city of tents takes shape. Some shelters are grand affairs, others barely adequate to protect from the shifting, choking dust and the bitter cold of the northern winter nights. Little smoke-streaked fires and stoves spring to life. The smell of cooking, here and there a subtle blend of regional specialities, fills the air. But in certain places the stench of the thousands of state-built provisional latrines constantly in use is overpowering. Itinerant hawkers and rows of makeshift shops ply their trade, selling cheap toys and trinkets, shawls and blankets, flowers and garlands (especially of marigolds for offerings, etc.), sweetmeats, savoury snacks, fruits and vegetables, different kinds of shells and coloured powders (these have their religious uses), bead and berry necklaces (the first ornamental, the second a sacred symbol), peacock plumes, plastic water-containers, and a host of other desirables for the captive crowds. In the cramped conditions everyday contact is indiscriminate, a far cry from the studied distinctions of life in the outside world. Everywhere the tramp of feet, the stifling dust, the colours and hubbub of the immense, congested human mosaic, overwhelm the senses. This will last for days.

Pilgrims cluster round various naked or ochre-robed holy men (*sādhus*), seeking their darshan or a blessing or a word of advice, and making offerings of food or money. Some of these *sādhus* are in the throes of extraordinary mortifications, undertaken to build up *tapas* or remove karma. One man, in the seventh year of a vow not to sit or lie down for twelve years, rests on one foot, suspended by a rope around his waist; another has remained with right arm upraised continuously for years (the muscles have atrophied); a third has nearly completed a vow not to speak for ten years (his white-daubed face communicates by whistles, grunts and vivid expression), and so on; their acolytes eagerly sing their praises. The pilgrims see that the age-old ascetic ideals of their faith are alive and that some souls are on the threshold if not in the embrace of enlightenment, and are encouraged and comforted in their own spiritual endeavours.

For the more articulate, religious lectures and discussions, private and public, are freely available, the medley of ideas on offer sometimes reinforcing, sometimes challenging, traditional wisdom. Groups of minstrels wander from camp to camp, singing rousing devotional songs and receiving money and food in return. Rich businessmen distribute food, money and clothing to holy men and women in order 'to purify their mind and wealth'.

The processions of the different sects and religious bands – arriving, departing, taking up positions, proceeding to the river's edge – are an outstanding feature of the festival. Here, the powder-painted, richly caparisoned elephant of a holy man in saffron, who sways on his festooned howdah-perch, an attendant flicking a fly-whisk over him, his devotees filing in front and behind;[2] there, the column of a female guru enthroned on a crowded float pulled by a tractor. Some processions boast noisy brass bands, in others loudspeakers broadcast deafening music which is often an incongruous mix of the sacred and profane. But is anything profane in this milieu? Particularly impressive to the spectators are the ranks of nāgas or naked ascetics, processing in their separate ākhaḍās (traditional sectarian bands), their perfectly nude or G-string clad bodies smeared with whitish ash (symbolising that they are dead to the world), with garlands of marigolds around their necks or incongruously twined in their dishevelled hair. Some sport staves, others tridents, lances and swords: a reminder that some of these bands have a martial history stretching back to medieval times (see Chapter 9). In the wake of these processions, some pilgrims, usually women, prostrate themselves on the ground or gather into little jars the sanctified dust trampled underfoot. These will be souvenirs of the Melā, or some may be sold. Ritual observances – worship at temples on site, prayer meetings, discourses, darshans, dips in the sacred river – continue into the night; on special days and at the end of the festival there will be evening illuminations and festivities. Hindu religious festivals are inevitably as much social occasions – a chance to enjoy life – as opportunities to improve life's spiritual prospects.

Crowds bathe ritually in the holy waters daily. But on the most auspicious day, that of *amāvāsyā* or the new moon, everyone wants to take a sacred dip. This is the time all have been waiting for. From dawn, seething masses of people heave towards the river's edge. First to enter will be ascetics of various sects and bands, in a pre-arranged sequence (lest quarrels break out). They process noisily towards the river's edge, many naked in spite of the morning chill, some blowing blasts from serpentine trumpets, others chanting, still others waving lances and tridents or flashing ceremonial swords. They rush into the cold waters, gasping and splashing joyfully. Then the ordinary folk, from babes in arms to the very old, surge into the water, fulfilling the observance for which so many have travelled so arduously across the land. For most of the day along the banks, hardly a square inch of ground is visible under the teeming crowds. Now spiritually uplifted and satisfied, the great mass of humanity – impressive in its commitment, touching in its faith – slowly disperses over the next few days. In a brief compass of sacred space and time, across the everyday barriers of caste, sex and sect, we have caught an elusive glimpse of the tenuous unity of the great family tree of religious Hinduism.

Durgā Pūjā

This is the great autumnal festival of Bengal – Bengal's counterpart to Daśahrā. The festival celebrates Durgā as Mahiṣāsuramardinī, slayer of the buffalo demon, as noted earlier, though in the popular imagination it is the occasion for celebrating Durgā's ten-day holiday to her parental home, leaving her husband Śiva and their married abode behind. These are the first ten days of the bright half of *Āśvina* (September to October). Though similar ideas of renewal and prosperity to those of Dīwālī are interwoven into the significance of the celebrations (because of the season), the main emphasis is on the triumph of the power (*śakti*) of the Goddess over evil and chaos, celebrated in a joyous atmosphere. After all has not Durgā returned, as beloved daughter, to her original home where she can relax for a while and enjoy life? Bengalis often compare the Durgā Pūjā in spirit to the Christians' Christmas.

The most important days are the last five. Well before, however, preparations have been in hand. Let us concentrate on the festival in Calcutta, the capital of the state, where the festivities are the grandest and act as the model for Bengalis everywhere else. Orders to make the images of the Goddess and her attendants have been placed with the artisans of Kumartuli (see Chapter 7) weeks if not months earlier. The sponsors are of two kinds: (i) committees from various *ad hoc* or traditional localities of the city (their celebrations are called community or *bāro(y)āri* pūjās and do not necessarily follow municipality zones: a single street may have two to three community pūjās); and (ii) private individuals. Generally, the community pūjās are the most elaborate: they have the financial advantage of money raised from (almost compulsory) subscriptions in their catchment areas. Some Bengali families, however, can mount impressive individual displays. The images for Durgā Pūjā, as for the festival worship of other deities in Bengal, are traditionally of unbaked clay – traditionally, that is, on a large scale for over two hundred years, and to a lesser extent, perhaps for centuries earlier.[3] Some images may be made of the white pith (*śolā*) of the water reed *aeschynomere aspera*, and faddists today also use various kinds of unconventional materials: paper, foil, wicker, etc. But the overwhelming majority of images are of unbaked clay: they must be disposed of by immersion at the end of the Pūjā, and for this clay is suitable. Shelters or 'pandals' with platforms are constructed on sidewalks, cul-de-sacs, street corners, etc. before the proceedings to house the images; some are simply tarpaulin lean-tos, others can be extraordinarily elaborate, to resemble a temple, perhaps, or Parliament House in New Delhi, or a fort. Often intricate designs of flashing and coloured lights line the access to and silhouette the pandal. The interior can also be exquisitely decorated.

Such shelters are in fact 'sets' used not only to house the deity, but also to stage the cultural programmes which often follow the immersion. But none of the pandals are permanent; they will all be dismantled after the festivities. Within the traditional pattern of five figures, namely, Durgā in the centre, flanked by smaller images of Sarasvatī and Kārttikeya on her left and Lakṣmī and Gaṇeśa on her right, great care is taken to ensure that each tableau is distinctively designed and apparelled. Intense rivalry between various groups can develop in this respect, and soon after the major festivities have begun (by the sixth day) well-publicised commercially sponsored prizes, judged by leading artistic and other figures, are awarded to the four or five most artistically impressive tableaux and pandals. This encourages people to visit as many pandals as is practicable during the celebrations. During Durgā Pūjā in 1990, there were approximately 2,000 community tableaux in the city of Calcutta (not to mention the private ones). Because interaction between Calcutta and rural areas is increasing, there is a growing tendency for village pūjā celebrations to ape those of the cultural capital.

In the city's major pandals the central image can be huge, often reaching to a height of 15 ft. or more on its pedestal. Durgā, wearing a gorgeous sari, is invariably eight-armed, with a benign face and mounted on a snarling lion. With a lance or trident in one right hand she is despatching the buffalo demon, usually depicted as a dark muscular man in a loincloth, emerging from or standing next to a gory buffalo in its death throes. In other hands she carries a spoked disc, a bell, scimitar, bow, arrow, mace, shell, etc. (these objects, each with its symbolic value, may vary slightly from image to image and hand to hand). Sarasvatī and Lakṣmī are recognisable by their distinctive features – their *vāhana*s (the swan and here the owl, respectively), Sarasvatī's lute, etc. – as are Gaṇeśa and Kārttikeya, who is accompanied by his peacock mount.

Although Vālmīki's *Rāmāyaṇa* makes no mention of it, later Puranic texts record how Rāma successfully importuned Durgā to help him overcome Rāvaṇa. So on *ṣaṣṭhī* (the sixth day), the deity is unseasonably awoken (for most naturally her rite would be observed in spring) to use her power in the battle against life's evils. It is the custom for those who can afford it to wear items of new clothing. On *saptamī* (the seventh day), the icon is consecrated and 'animated'. This includes ritually bathing it (by symbolically bathing its reflection in a small mirror). From now on, the *ḍhāki*s or drummers, usually in groups of two or three, who, with sticks beat special drums suspended from the shoulders, and the accompanying beaters of the *kāṅgsa* (a small brass disc struck with a hand-stick), will keep up a thunderous rhythm during certain periods, especially at evening worship. The beat can vary intricately and reaches a frenzied pitch at its climax.

The daily pattern of worship, with one or two exceptions, now unfolds. As in the temple, standard rites such as waking the deities in the morning, putting them to bed, etc. are observed. There is also *añjali* or flower offerings in the morning. Worshippers, under the direction of the priest, gather in front of the dais, and at intervals thrice throw a flower or two towards the tableau. In the process they may offer a silent prayer. Towards midday large quantities of food are cooked; after this has been ritually offered to the deity, it is distributed as *prasāda* to those present. The most impressive period of worship is during the evening *ārati*. Huge crowds gather, standing rapt before the dais, mesmerised by the roll of the drums as the priest, dancing a slow jig, his bare torso sporting the sacred thread and gleaming with sweat in the glare of the arc lights, solemnly waves an oil-lamp, incense, etc. in the prescribed fashion before Durgā and her companions. The atmosphere is highly charged. One is reminded of Swami Vivekananda's Bengali rhyme: 'The Hindu doesn't worship dolls made from wood and clay. S/he sees the Spirit in the mud, and her soul just melts away'.[4] One can almost feel Durgā's awesome magnetism absorbing her votaries' souls. On leaving the presence the spell is broken; the flashing illuminations and the joyousness of the occasion take over and the votary moves on to visit another pandal.

On *aṣṭamī* (the eighth day), Devī's victory over evil is complete and the daily routine includes a fast till midday by the more pious, and fire offerings (*homa*) by the priests in the deity's presence. *Daśamī* is the tenth and last day of Durgā's sojourn. In the morning, (usually) married women, after bathing, visit the icon for a blessing with small containers of vermilion. Bengali women generally dab some of the red powder on the tip of the forehead (at the parting of the hair) to indicate that they are married. The blessed vermilion will be used for this purpose in the coming year. The *ārati* of the day is particularly solemn, for it is a kind of farewell. Late in the evening the images are placed in trucks and other transport and amid processions noisy with drums and music are carried to the Hooghly's banks. These (mostly male) processions are occasions for revelry, and it is common to see young men dancing and gyrating in various stages of alcoholic and/or narcotic intoxication. The mood is mixed; a good time is had by all, but the immersing of the images and their slipping away into oblivion mark the end of an extended, exhilarating celebration and a return to the rigours of life – until the following year.

Let us now consider the paths to spiritual fulfilment. Most educated Hindus regard these paths as a kind of *yoga*. This is a generic term, meaning an integrative discipline.[5] In this sense, the term must be distinguished from its specialised use in the classical system of Patañjali where it refers to a specific theory-cum-practice intended to co-ordinate mind and body for the attainment of liberative self-mastery. One can achieve this state while still in the body. The system is called *aṣṭāṅga* or 'eight-limbed' Yoga (or Pātañjala or Rāja, i.e. Royal, Yoga).[6] In the non-technical sense one might speak of many, more or less assimilative, forms of *yoga*: Haṭha *yoga* (the perfecting of various physical postures and techniques, to some extent the Yoga of the TV screen), Kuṇḍalinī *yoga* (the discipline of a number of Tantric and other schools), Bhakti *yoga* (the path of devotion), Karma *yoga* (the way of works), Christian *yoga* (which may incorporate features of Haṭha or other forms of Hindu *yoga*), and so on.[7] Sometimes in the Sanskritic tradition, and often in modern works on Hinduism, three basic forms of religious path or *yoga* are distinguished: Jñāna-*yoga*, Karma-*yoga*, and Bhakti-*yoga*, namely, the disciplines of knowledge, works and devotion respectively. This can be a highly misleading distinction for the simple reason that virtually every *yoga* followed as a path to spiritual fulfilment is some kind of blend of all three – knowledge, action or works, and devotion. The distinction is acceptable only from the point of view of emphasis, although one must keep in mind that in some cases the emphases are hard to disentangle, or vary according to the stage of the discipline.

At various points in this book we have commented upon knowledge, works and devotion as means to ultimate fulfilment. So here we can be brief, with the exception of *bhakti* since the overwhelming majority of Hindus are predominantly some kind of religious *bhakta* (votary or supplicant).[8] An example of a theologian who emphasised *jñāna* or knowledge as the means to liberation very much at the expense of *karman* and *bhakti* is Śaṃkara. This makes perfect sense, for Śaṃkara was an Advaitin, that is, he maintained that there was only one ultimate Reality – the utterly pure, homogeneous, undivided, ineffable Spirit called *Brahman* which is identical with the core of our being. The pluriform reality of this world, in which we are included as individuals, is provisional, and illusory to the extent that we think it self-sustaining and permanent. Salvation consists of dissolving the individual ego, the basis of rebirth and suffering, and realising that in spirit we are *identical* with Brahman. The path to this realisation is study and recitation of the Scriptures under the guidance of the guru, understanding with the help of reason what the Scriptures teach, relentless contemplation of their teaching, and interiorising it by a life of rigorous purity and (at least inward) withdrawal from the world.

In this conception, there is no real scope for devotion to God. This does not mean that Advaita Vedānta makes no room for God; it does. But God's existence is viewed religiously as a concession to our inveterate, and philosophically unenlightened, tendencies to worship a supreme Being, and theologically and psychologically as a stepping-stone to the final Advaitic vision. In this vision, which is *jñāna* proper, all dualistic distinctions, including the finite–infinite divide, dissolve into an all-consuming monistic experience. Then there is nothing to show *bhakti* to. One is *Brahman*, and *Brahman* is all there is. Period. Committed Hindu *bhakta*s, for whom the distinction between God and the finite world is inviolate, never cease to say that Advaitic *bhakti* is a sham. In Rāmānuja's words, the true *bhakta* wants only to glide away (*sarpati*) from the Advaitic goal.

So for Advaita all those mental and physical actions (*karmāṇi*) which shore up dualistic religion, contemplating, supplicating and worshipping the deity – temple worship, domestic worship, hymn-singing, icon-caring, theologising – and the life of service and support of one's *bhakti* associates, at best have only provisional validity and at worst are entirely misguided. Works are not on a par with knowledge in leading to enlightenment; at best they should be subordinately integrated into the Advaitic vision. Ideally one should withdraw physically from the world and act as little as possible; in any case, one should renounce the dualistic mentality and strive to act accordingly.

At the other extreme within the Vedic fold, Śaṃkara's great opponents were the Karma-Mīmāṃsakas. As their name implies, these emphasised the role of action in attaining ultimate fulfilment. The action *par excellence* was the Vedic ritual and its constituent and intricate web of physical and mental acts. Such action – and not some speculative monistic or theistic religious experience – leads to well-being in this life and the next. Knowledge of and supplication to the Vedic 'gods' were subject to the regular performance of the ritual. It was what was to be done (*kārya*) – supremely the solemn ritual – that was the consuming concern. We come now to the third and most popular religious path, that of *bhakti* or devotion to God.

I do not believe that the Sanskritic tradition has ever advocated polytheism proper, either in the religion of the Saṃhitās which refers largely to 'gods' as we have seen, or elsewhere. Early western Indologists glimpsed this where Saṃhitā religion was concerned. Max Müller, a leading pioneer among Indologists, in spite of being perhaps unduly influenced in his interpretation of this religion by his understanding of its classical European counterpart, nevertheless coined a new term (inevitably Greek-derived) to reflect his unease: *henotheism*, namely, belief in as-if-only-one God. The world view of Saṃhitā religion is not easy to analyse, yet some constants come through. One of these is a belief in a single nebulous underlying reality principle, the immortal source on the one hand of the unspoken Word (*Vāc*) which manifests itself in the sacrifice, and on the other of the various 'gods' and their wives and such unifying figures as Aditi, the somewhat mysterious divine mother matrix.[9] Through the sacrifice we can share in this immortality. In a late verse of the *Ṛg* Veda (I.164.46), this unitive idea is expressed as follows: 'They say Indra, Mitra, Varuṇa, Agni; and he is the celestial lovely-rayed Garutmat (the sun). What is one the sages utter variously; they call it Agni, Yama, Mātariśvan'. Thus the 'gods' (and 'goddesses') here are focuses of the transcendent. Their personal features remain nebulous; individual names have different roles to play, but as lacking in separate personality cults. Often a hymn to a particular 'god' contains 'absolutist epithets' (in respect of such qualities as sustaining power, efficacious might, overall greatness) which are in essence transferred to some other *deva* in another hymn (hence 'Henotheism').[10] The powers of the *devas* tend to converge in their underlying source. This is not polytheism in any conventional sense.

In time, however, as the performance of the sacrificial ritual became a mechanistic if all-absorbing norm and focus, the status of the 'gods' underwent change. No longer awe-inspiring, tenuous visages of the transcendent, to be supplicated, sometimes with touching ardour,[11] they became a sort of anonymous celestial super-human band, subject nevertheless to the all-powerful hold of the ritual. When this was performed properly for this or that objective, the *devas must* obey: Indra, Vāyu, Agni and the rest would gratify their supplicant. This was an unsatisfactory state of affairs for religion of the heart. Enter the *bhakti*-movement as intimated by the *Bhagavadgītā*. As the numerous cults of this approach developed they had one thing in common; theologically they all acknowledged in their various ways one supreme Being, the infinite personal source and mainstay of all finite reality, the dweller within, the ruler and bestower of all, and the object of a saving love. All other gods (Vedic and otherwise) are not suppressed; they live on mythologically, while in theology their role is either to express different aspects of the underlying One, or to function as creaturely departmental heads of the Godhead's all-encompassing causality. On this there is no compromise.

I am not suggesting that all Hindu religious supplicants are uncompromising monotheists. I noted earlier that 'for many worshippers of Manasā [the 'folk-goddess'] she is a manifestation of Devī, the source Goddess' (Chapter 5, p. 145). True. I have often heard Hindus, urban or rustic, speak this way. But this is not the whole story. Studies indicate that many votaries of folk goddesses and gods relate to their deities on a feudal basis, without apparently any clear idea of some single, underlying divine source. In Bengal for instance, Manasā may protect specifically from snakes, Śītalā from smallpox, Dakṣiṇ Rāy from tigers, and so on (some of these figures have counterparts, usually with different names and characteristics, in other regions). If Manasā or any of the others are not duly acknowledged they can be quite vengeful. If they *are* given their due they had better live up to their responsibilities, or their votaries will want to know the reason why. So far as polytheism is concerned, this seems very much like the real thing, unless some mode of Socratic interrogation, hitherto untried, will reveal an implicit monotheism. So in some cases, while folk gods and goddesses may be related to functionally as a kind of league of super-heroes, in other instances a folk goddess or god may be attributed with universal or relatively universal power. In the world of folk religion the picture is still confused.

> Because of what can seem very well defined functions, folk gods have sometimes been called 'departmental': god A performs function A, as Śītalā's function is, for example, to cure smallpox. Such neat classifications . . . have a limited validity. It is not at all certain that god A, who apparently has a very definite function in village A would be readily identified by the villagers themselves with a god with the same function in village B. Śītalā, neatly catalogued as a smallpox goddess, also serves as the chief deity of the Bengali Lodhas. Mariamman, the South Indian smallpox goddess not only protects against smallpox, cholera or any other disease but can also grant practically anything a worshipper may desire from her. Villagers themselves do not seem able to make such identifications easily. W. Crooke notes . . . that 'the jurisdiction of these gods is purely local, and when . . . (the

villager) leaves his village he finds himself in the land of new gods, whose hostility he knows not how to appease.[12]

In the religions of the 'high' tradition, generally monotheistic though they be,[13] different focuses of *bhakti* exist. We shall return to this point. Further, two levels of *bhakti* are usually distinguished theologically, in terms such as *aparā* ('lower') and *parā* ('higher'), or *gauṇī* ('indirect') and *mukhyā* ('direct'). The first kind of *bhakti* is imperfect. Here one loves the deity with mixed motives which invariably entails a self-centred element, e.g. to recover health, avoid danger, pass an examination, have a child or obtain a job, sometimes even to defeat a rival. We may include much of the worship of folk deities under this heading, though some purists may balk at describing what is essentially supplicatory-propitiatory religion as a form of genuine *bhakti*. I have no such qualms, for the simple reason that all but the purest *bhakti*, that is, even the so-called genuine, first-order *bhakti*, inevitably contains a supplicatory and therefore 'selfish' element. This may be present to a greater or lesser degree, but it *is* generally present.[14] The theologians call those who resort to such *bhakti 'arthins'*, i.e. devotees with personal ends in view. In theological discourse both the theologians and the deity are in general very tolerant of the *arthin*, for they realise that such devotion is perfectly human, the stuff of vows, fasts, pilgrimages, everyday worship, and so on. But the treatises are adamant that it is an inferior form of the love of God; it may be commendable – it is far better than an ungodly existence – but it is also egoistic and generates karma. As such it leads inevitably to rebirth. The devotee must be weaned away to the *parā* or higher form of *bhakti*. By its selflessness, this transforms the devotee's life and consciousness, consumes past karma, and bestows salvation. It is the easy way to ultimate fulfilment – far easier than the path of knowledge or works – delighting the deity, it is often said, more than the devotee.

II

Bhakti *is one but manifold. Some forms of selfless* bhakti *discussed, including various ideas (e.g.* avatāra, *evil, visualisation). An extra-ordinary form:* dveṣa-bhakti. Mokṣa *as enstasy, as identity, as communion. A final word.*

With the passage of time the various Hindu sects and traditions have evolved numerous understandings of the path of selfless devotion.

Some are meant to be implemented separately, others in combination. We cannot list them all. But a good idea of the range can be given by quoting from a well-known masterpiece on *bhakti*, the *Nārada Bhakti* Sūtras.[15] It is not very long, consisting of eighty-four sūtras. As its name implies, this treatise is ascribed to the Sage Nārada, who is supposed to have lived in pre-epic times. However, it is the work of more than one unknown hand, and can be dated to about the tenth to twelfth centuries. Sūtra 82 may be translated as follows:

> Though [*bhakti*] is one it becomes elevenfold – of the form of (1) the Attachment to the Greatness of the (divine) Qualities; (2) the Attachment to the (divine) Form(s); (3) the Attachment to the (divine) Worship; (4) the Attachment to Remembering (the deity); (5) the Attachment to (divine) Service; (6) the Attachment to the (divine) Companionship; (7) the Attachment of Parental Affection; (8) the Attachment of the Beloved; (9) the Attachment of Self-Offering; (10) the Attachment of being Suffused; (11) the Attachment of the deepest Separation.[16]

Each form of *bhakti* listed here has been followed either as a separate way of devotion or in combination with others. Further, it is not clear if the above is intended to be only a list or also a hierarchy, culminating in No. 11. This text has a Vaiṣṇava bias which we will have to respect, but the range of *bhakti* it describes overlaps more or less with the scope of devotion to Śiva and the Goddess, so we can use it as a convenient basis for a general discussion of *bhakti*.

The term *bhakti* is generally derived – not without dissension – from the root *bhaj*, meaning 'to share, to share in, to share with'. So, in this meaning, in the context of a personal relationship, it has a strong connotation of mutuality, of mingling, even on occasion to the point of a kind of compenetration; the whole person, not least the emotional side, is involved in this communicative relationship.[17] Sūtra 2 describes (religious) *bhakti* as of the nature of supreme *affection (parama-prema-rūpā)*, bringing out the affective dimension. These senses inform the religious *bhakti* ideal which will be the context of the ensuing discussion.

The prime object of *bhakti* is the deity. In Vaiṣṇava theology the generic term for God as the object of *bhakti* is *Bhagavān*, the Adorable One.[18] *Bhagavān* has been variously explained, e.g. as 'the One who possesses and shares *bhaga* or bliss, well-being' or 'the One who possesses the six *bhaga*s or attributes' (see below). The selfless devotee is the *bhāgavata* (or sometimes, *bhakta*; the Śākta devotee may be called the *bhakta* or *sādhaka*).

In this book we have followed the common practice of using the term *bhakti* generically and of then qualifying it further to refer to different 'species', or forms of *bhakti*. This is quite in order; note that the text supports this usage. It states clearly that *bhakti* is one but it becomes manifold.[19] Let us now comment briefly on each kind of *bhakti* mentioned, without necessarily following the line that commentators have taken under each heading.

Attachment to the greatness of the divine qualities

For the *bhakta* the deity is one, supreme, all-powerful, all-knowing, compassionate, etc. Vaiṣṇava theology speaks of *Bhagavān* being characterised by the six 'bhagas' or attributes, namely, majesty or sovereignty (*aiśvarya*), power (*vīrya*), glory (*yaśas*), beauty (*śrī*), wisdom (*jñāna*) and freedom (*vairāgya*).[20] One could even make a case for describing the deity as 'creative' in the strong sense of this term, for he or she is the universal originative, sustaining and terminating cause. The periodic production and dissolution of the world, the interim suspension of some of its constituents, and all secondary causes, depend existentially on the will of the deity.[21] The devotee delights in chanting and pondering the endless divine attributes, and the use of the various *sahasra-nāma*s, etc. exemplify this kind of *bhakti*.

Let us now examine a statement quoted from Zaehner earlier, namely 'Hindus postulate wrong at the very heart of Truth' (Chapter 8, p. 213). An easy response would be that Zaehner is being provocative again (true anyway), for no term for 'wrong' occurs in the standard theological lists of divine attributes. But Zaehner may be groping towards some truth. This concerns the divine causality. Hindus in general are almost blinded by their stress on the universality of the divine causality. Everything, but everything, comes from God. Nothing can exist or occur outside his or her omnipotence and omniscience. Then how to explain evil? Hindus respond to this question in various ways. One answer has been:

> God is not evil at all, God is good. But evil and good are relative terms. What is good, even morally good in one situation, may be evil in another. Often good and evil are what appear good and evil to us in the situation. So sometimes God or his or her saint

> may appear to do something evil but we must try to see or accept it as good, for it comes from a higher source and we cannot always see the whole picture

This is a dense and not entirely satisfactory answer, espousing a kind of 'situation ethics' often even to the point of the end justifying the means. Various assumptions are being made here which require a great deal of unpacking, e.g. about the relativity of evil, the divine 'exemption' to do something which we would regard as wrong, and so on. But these are the kinds of things that are often said. Another answer may be:

> Some things are always wrong and God neither sanctions nor does them. But myths sometimes cast the deity as perpetrating or inciting wrongdoing. A myth is a myth: understand its rationale. It may be teaching us about the sovereignty of God, or that the divine ways are not our ways, or something like that. It is not meant to be taken literally.

Yet a third response may be:

> God is good, yet he or she has made us free. So he or she permits us to exercise this freedom, even to do wrong. This may seem in some contexts as if God is not good. But it is a mark of weak religious insight and faith. Anyway, God can bring good out of evil. Exactly how or when we may not be able to understand.

Again:

> Myths speak of God giving *sva-dharma* or own-nature and mode of acting to all things, even to demons.[22] So demons behave demonically. But these are stories; they must be interpreted correctly. These stories may teach about the way evil can take a deep hold of one, or about the divine power or compassion in overcoming demonic evil. In any case, the demons in a number of these stories eventually turn to God and win his grace. So here the demons are not forced to commit evil; to say that their *sva-dharma* is to be demonic is to say that they have acquired or built up strong dispositions to do evil. Many of us are demonic in this way, but God triumphs over all.

Finally: 'Evil and good are what God says are evil and good. So it makes no sense to say that evil exists in the heart of God'.

These, and combinations of these responses, are all answers that I have come across. This does not mean, of course, that some

Hindus may not believe that God is evil or cannot do evil in some obvious sense of evil for us. There have been what the majority of Hindus regard as perverse religious cults, e.g. the Thugs, who lulled travellers into a false sense of security and then treacherously strangled and robbed them – in the name of Kālī.[23] They believed that their victims were acceptable offerings to Kālī who sanctioned their way of life. But neither Kālī nor Hinduism has a monopoly on perversity.[24] And there is no ground for saying generally that 'Hindus postulate wrong' as such 'at the very heart of Truth'.

Attachment to the divine form(s)

These are various. They include the personal celestial anthropomorphic form which, in many theologies, the deity displays to the liberated in heaven. Anticipating its presence, trying to capture it in the imagination by the divine favour, is a delight. Also included are various manifestations and avataric and iconic forms of the deity. Some of these may be terrible in appearance, but in different ways they all inspire devotion – Kālī no less than Durgā, Śiva as Bhairava the Frightful no less than Śiva the Gracious, Viṣṇu as the fearsome Narasiṃha, the man-lion tearing apart the reprobate Hiraṇyakaśipu on his lap with his claws no less than Viṣṇu-Nārāyaṇa, the sweetly smiling one. The devotee knows that in essence the Godhead is lovable and gracious; the terrible forms, in the psychology of devotion, just serve to accentuate this fact. The focus of *bhakti* may be a composite form, e.g. Śaiva-Śākta, or Ardhanārīśvara (Śiva as half male and half female), or Śaiva-Vaiṣṇava, or a conjoint one, e.g. Rādhā-Kṛṣṇa, or an 'associate' or manifestation of one of the major names, e.g. Pārvatī (Śiva's consort), Sītā or Lakṣmaṇa or Hanumān, or Gaṇeśa, or Caitanya.[25] In each case, this *iṣṭadevatā* represents the Godhead and is expected to lead to its heart.

Here we may comment briefly on the concepts of *vyūha* and *avatāra*. *Vyūha* or 'manifestation' derives from Pañcarātra, in some aspects a Tantric Vaiṣṇava tradition which rose to prominence from about the seventh century. In this conception the supreme Person manifests in four primary, graded forms. In 'descending' order these are called Vāsudeva (not to be confused with Kṛṣṇa Vāsudeva), Saṃkarṣaṇa, Pradyumna and Aniruddha. Each of these *vyūhas* has distinctive ontological and devotional attributes; some give rise to secondary manifestations or *vyūhas*. There are various views in this regard, but the underlying idea stresses the divine immanence in creation and the will to manifest specifically for particular reasons – another example of the *svarūpa–bahurūpa* relationship.

From the *vyūha* there also arises the *avatāra* or 'descent' of the deity, though in some avataric theologies there may be no significant mention of the *vyūha*-idea. This is distinctively a Vaiṣṇava concept, not because there is no talk of *avatāra* in Śaiva or Śākta religion (on occasion there is), but because it is only in Vaiṣhṇavism that there is a developed (i) mythology, (ii) theology, and (iii) cult of *avatāra*. *Avatāra* is derived from *ava-tṝ*, meaning to come down, descend. The *avatāra* then is a descent – not some spatial coming-down, for the deity is omnipresent – from the transcendent to the empirical level. The reason for this descent can be manifold; it is invariably to save, protect or punish, or to reveal or attest something (or perhaps some combination of these). It can be general or particular. In the *Gītā*, Kṛṣṇa says that he descends repeatedly 'for the protection of the good and the destruction of evil-doers, and for the establishing of right (*dharma*)' (4.8). No doubt the meaning of 'good', 'evil-doers' and *dharma* has been variously interpreted, but the purpose is a general one. The Narasiṃha *avatāra* on the other hand occurred specifically to save Viṣṇu's devotee, Prahlāda, from his demonic father, Hiraṇyakaśipu.

The being which descends is the *avatārin* (masculine) or *avatāriṇī* (feminine); *avatāra* means both the form of the descent and the individual that the *avatārin/iṇī* has descended *as*. The personality of the *avatāra* then may not be identical with the personality of the one who descends. The Kṛṣṇa who utters the *Gītā* clearly seems to be the *avatārin* himself, but in the later devotionalism of some cults Kṛṣṇa is just one *avatāra* of Viṣṇu the *avatārin*, revealing certain features of the Godhead. Other *avatāras* add to this revelation. Thus there can be more or less full *avatāras*, namely, part-*avatāras* (*aṃśa-avatāras*) of the deity. Similarly, in the worship of some sects, Rādhā and Kṛṣṇa seem to be, not simply *avatāras* of some Godhead, but even in their human forms, the *avatāriṇī* and *avatārin* themselves (whereas Caitanya may be only the *avatāra* of *both* Rādhā and Kṛṣṇa). It is the language of the devotion and theology concerned that will make this clear, but it is important to bear the distinctions in mind and to realise that these distinctions obtain among the various cults.

Again, it is not only the deity itself who can descend. Hindus believe that a divine manifestation or associate, e.g. Sītā, Lakṣmaṇa, Hanumān, or a liberated soul such as Nārada, can become an *avatāra*. The descent need not be only in human form, of course; thus Narasiṃha was half-man half-lion, the Matsya *avatāra* was a fish, and the Varāha *avatāra* a boar (all being *avatāras* of Viṣṇu). Many Hindus regard especially the non-human *avatāra*s as symbolic of the deity's immanent presence in and power to manifest through all forms of life. They sometimes refer to the classical list of Viṣṇu's ten *avatāra*s (*daśa-avatāra*) as intimating this. These ten *avatāra*s are: the fish (*matsya*), the tortoise (*kūrma*), the boar (*varāha*), the man-lion (*narasiṃha*), the dwarf (*vāmana*), Paraśu-Rāma (Rāma of the Axe), Rāma Dāśarathi (King Rāma of the *Rāmāyaṇa*), the Buddha, and Kalki (who will come on his white charger and bring the world to an end). In this transition, they say, of developing forms of life – from the aquatic and animal to increasingly developed forms of human existence (though Kalki is not easy to fit into this picture) – we see the providence of the deity at work, affirming, indwelling, sustaining and directing the harmony and development of creation. Some have used the *daśāvatāra* conception as a central plank of an ecological statement or stance. Whatever one may make of this, one should note that most Hindu tradition makes no ecological or 'evolutionary' claim for the list (current from about the sixth to seventh centuries), and that there are many other more numerous lists of divine *avatāra*s in the tradition.[26] Further, in cultic practice it is not at all usual to grade the *daśāvatāra*s devotionally according to some evolutionary scale.

Indeed, Hindus can see *avatāra*s everywhere. For some followers of the Āḷvār tradition, Nāmmāḷvār was a partial *avatāra* of Viṣṇu, while the tamarind tree under which he received enlightening knowledge was the *avatāra* of Śeṣa, Viṣṇu's serpent *vāhana*.[27] And it is not uncommon for modern and not-so-modern saintly figures across cultural divides, e.g. Ramakrishna, Gandhi, Socrates and Jesus, to be hailed as *avatāra*s today. It is important to note that whatever empirical form it assumes, the *avatāra* theologically (though not necessarily devotionally) is not regarded as constituted from real 'matter', that is, from *prakṛti*, in the way, say, ordinary empirical beings are. This is because, unlike ordinary empirical beings, the *avatāra* is not in any way the consequence or expression of past karma. The *avatāra* is entirely free of the grip of karma and displays the sovereignty of the liberated spirit. We can now understand why the *Bhāgavata* Purāṇa approvingly refers to Kṛṣṇa as a 'counterfeit-man' (*kapaṭa-mānuṣa*; 1.1.20). Kṛṣṇa only appears as a human; he is not really or fully human in the way we are, for *our* human (prakritic) embodiment is the consequence of karma. From the Hindu point of view this frees him from all natural and human constraints; he is thus able to display his lordship and grace and be a fitting object of devotion and worship.

The icon is sometimes spoken of as an *avatāra* (called the *arcā-avatāra*). In our description of icon worship we have already indicated what this might imply. So in this form of *bhakti*, the devotee attaches him or herself to some form(s) of the deity and in this way purifies devotion.

But besides 'form', *rūpa* also means 'beauty', so this kind of devotion can be an attachment to the divine beauty, in its terrible or gracious forms, or indeed even as paradoxically formless (*nir-ākāra*, sometimes *nir-guṇa*, i.e. 'without form-attributes'). Mahadevi again:

> I love the Handsome One:
> he has no death, decay nor form
> no place or side
> no end nor birthmarks.
> I love him O mother. Listen.
> I love the Beautiful One
> with no bond nor fear, no clan no land
> no landmarks for his beauty.
> So my Lord, white as jasmine, is my husband.
> Take these husbands who die, decay, and
> feed them to your kitchen fires![28]

Attachment to the divine worship

In this form of *bhakti* one delights in cultic worship (*pūjā*), in the various practices of admiring the icon, attending to it by bathing it, dressing it, singing and dancing before it, praising it, etc., and in the building and beautifying of temples, and so on.

Attachment to 'remembering' the deity

Here contemplation (*dhyāna*) of the deity is cultivated, especially mental visualisation. By constant practice one or more forms of the deity, pictured in accordance with the guidelines of one's tradition, are impressed on or evoked by the imagination. For example, here is how Rāmānuja, guided by the Upaniṣads and in particular the *Viṣṇu* Purāṇa, portrays the divine heavenly form:

> [Vishṇu's] splendour is like that of a colossal mountain of molten gold and His brilliance that of the rays of hundreds of thousands of suns. His long eyes are spotless like the petals of a lotus which, sprouting forth from deep water on a soft stalk, blossoms in the rays of the sun. His eyes and His forehead and His nose are

> beautiful, His coral-like lips smile graciously, and His soft cheeks are beaming. His neck is as delicately shaped as a conch-shell and His bud-like divine ears, beautifully formed, hang down on His stalwart shoulders. His arms are thick, round and long and He is adorned with fingers that are reddened by nails of a most becoming reddish tinge. His body, with its slender waist and broad chest, is well-proportioned in all parts, and His shape is of an unutterably divine form. His colour is pleasing. His feet are as beautiful as budding lotuses. He wears a yellow robe that suits Him and He is adorned with immeasurable, marvellous, endless and divine ornaments – a spotless diadem, earrings, necklaces, the Kaustubha gem, bracelets, anklets, belt etc. – and with Conch, Disc, Club, Sword, the Bow Śārṅga, the curl Śrīvatsa [on the breast] and the garland Vanamālā. He attracts eye and thought alike of all by the measureless and boundless beauty that is His. He overflows the entire creation of animate and inanimate beings with the nectar of His comeliness. His youth is exceedingly wonderful, unimaginable and eternal. He is as delicately tender as blossoming flowers. He perfumes the infinite space between the cardinal points with the odour of holiness. His profound majesty is forever encompassing the entire universe. He looks upon the hosts of His devotees with loving eyes, filled with compassion and affection. His sport is to evolve, sustain and dissolve all the worlds. All evil is foreign to Him – He is the treasury of all beautiful qualities and He is essentially different from all other entities. He is the Supreme Spirit, the Supreme Brahman, Nārāyaṇa.[29]

The aim is to make this remembrance as vivid as possible and as constant as required – 'like a steady flow of oil' – so that remembrance (*smaraṇa*) becomes living in the imaginative presence of the deity (*anu-smṛti*).[30] At its best it is like seeing God. In a broader sense, remembrance can also mean recalling over and over again, and thus renewing, either privately or publicly, the various exploits and great deeds of the deity as recorded in the tradition. For the *bhakta* this is a delightful activity, and is all that he or she wishes to talk about.

Attachment to service (*dāsya, kaiṃkarya*) of the deity

Relating to the deity as a familiar servant is a well-known path of *bhakti*. Rāmānuja may be regarded as a thinker who has provided a theological rationale for this way. For Rāmānuja, the whole world, ourselves included, is the 'body' of the Lord in the sense that he is our complete support and master and that we exist to praise him and do his bidding. Sometimes, *bhakta*s who are conscious of their obligation to serve the deity single-mindedly, add the suffix *dāsa* (masculine) or *dāsī* (feminine), namely, servant, to their name. This is a practice among the Hare Krishnas.

Attachment to the divine companionship (*sakhya*)

Here, the devotee relates to the deity in the role of an intimate friend (masculine *sakhā*, feminine *sakhī*) which can lead to expressions of great familiarity. The main Indian languages generally have three forms of 'you': the first is used to a superior or a stranger, or an acquaintance, etc. to whom one wishes to show respect. The second is used to address equals or even one's seniors (e.g. one's parents) as familiars. The third form is an expression of studied, even contemptuous, superiority, or alternatively of great intimacy (e.g. a mother will use it to her child; intimate friends, generally of the same sex, will use it to each other). Hindus *never* use the first form to the deity. It is just too formal and aloof. They tend to use the second form, sometimes even the third.

Of interest here is a kind of *bhakti* which is so familiar that it can even extend to insulting, belittling or scolding the deity in its expression of intimacy.[31] We get an indication of this in a song by Ramprasad Sen, an eighteenth-century Bengali Śākta devotee of Kālī who is still popular among his compatriots. Ramprasad would address the Goddess familiarly as 'mother', a standard practice in Bengal even today.

> Kali, why are you naked again? Come on, where is your modesty? You wear no splendid apparel, Ma, yet you boast of being a king's daughter. And Ma, is this standing on your husband a demonstration of your aristocracy?
> You are naked, and your husband is naked. You wander about the cremation grounds.
> Ma, we are dying of shame. Put your clothes back on.
> You have cast aside your necklace of jewels, Ma. A garland of human skulls glistens at your throat.
> Prasad says: Even the Naked Lord (Shiva) fears you in this form, Ma.[32]

But not Ramprasad! Or consider to what Basavanna, the South Indian Vīraśaiva twelfth-century saint, compares the Lord with his exclusive claims:

I drink the water we wash your feet with
I eat the food of worship,
and I say it's yours, everything:
goods, life, honour.
He's really the whore who takes every last bit of her night's wages,
and will take no words for payment,
he, my Lord of the meeting rivers![33]

Here we must mention another kind of *bhakti*, the extraordinary *dveṣa-bhakti* or hate *bhakti*. Surely here no devotion is involved, yet it is called *bhakti*. There are a number of instances of its occurrence in Hindu literature. Here '*bhakti*' is just attachment, having in common with the selfless kind its absorbing, single-minded commitment. But in *dveṣa-bhakti* it is unrelenting animosity towards the deity that saves. God's enemy hates God so much that they can think of nothing else; God absorbs their thoughts constantly. But even this is a form of passionate union which will save the 'devotee'. Exactly how is not made clear theologically; perhaps this will occur by a conversion experience before or after death. For to turn such all-consuming hatred to love can be the work of a gracious moment.[34] Or is *dveṣa-bhakti* part of Hindu hype, a way of saying that the divine name, which the hater thinks upon constantly, or the divine grace is so powerful that it can save anyone in any circumstance, leave alone God's friend?

The attachment of parental affection (*vātsalya*)

This is a very popular form of *bhakti*. Note that *vātsalya* can be expressed both ways, i.e. as if God is one's child or as if one is God's child. Devotees love to place themselves in the role of Kṛṣṇa's (foster)-mother (Yaśodā) or (foster-)father (Nanda) and imagine how they would treat him in different circumstances – scold him when he was naughty, play with him, teach him things, cuddle him. Or they live vicariously through Kṛṣṇa's parents. Sūrdās, a fifteenth-century Sant composing in Hindi, is noted for such sentiments.

Watching Krishna walk gives joy to Mother Yashoda. [*refrain*]
On all fours now, close to the floor, Krishna flounders;/his mother sees the scene and points it out to all./He makes it to the doorway then/comes back the other way again./He trips and he falls, doesn't manage to cross –/which makes the sages wonder: / Ten millions of worlds he creates in a flash/and can destroy them just as fast;/But he's picked up by Nanda's wife, who sets him

down, plays games with him,/then with her hand supports him while he steps outside the door./When they see Sūr's Lord, gods, men, and sages/lose track of their minds.[35]

Conversely, the devotee considers himself or herself as God's infant and delights in the divine protective love. We saw how Ramprasad was wont to refer to Kālī as 'mother'. Basavanna says:

As a mother runs
close behind her child
with his hand on a cobra
or a fire,
the Lord of the meeting rivers
stays with me
every step of the way
and looks after me.

(TSSH, p. 71)

And Parāśara Bhaṭṭar, a twelfth-century Śrī-Vaiṣṇava theologian, says when interpreting *vatsala* in his commentary on the divine names of Viṣṇu,

> Though God has been acquainted with [those who have taken refuge with Him] for a long time, for some reason He wanders about (seeking to do some favour for His devotees) like a cow that has just delivered a calf, bellowing because her teats are irritated by the fullness of her udders and perplexed as to what she should do. This state of God is known even in the case of Rāvaṇa [the ogre-king of Laṅkā].[36]

The attachment of the beloved

Here the relationship is one of lovers, and the love affair can be conducted with great, even wanton, realism, and in terms of explicit erotic imagery. The beloved may be related to as husband or wife, or paramour. This uninhibitedness, even indecorousness, in the *bhakti* relationship generally surfaces in one form or another again and again.

Her cloud of hair eclipses the luster of her face,
like Rāhu greedy for the moon.
The garland glitters in her unbound hair, a wave of the
Ganges [light] in the waters of the Yamunā [dark].
How beautiful the deliberate, sensuous union of the two; the
girl [Rādhā] playing this time the active role

riding her lover's [Kṛṣṇa's] outstretched body in delight.
Her smiling lips shine with drops of sweat: the god of love
offering pearls to the moon.
She of beautiful face hotly kisses the mouth of her beloved:
the moon, with face bent down, drinks of the lotus.
The garland hanging on her heavy breasts seems like a stream
of milk from golden jars,
the tinkling bells which decorate her hips sound the triumphal
music of the god of love.

So says Vidyāpati (*c.* fifteenth century), vicariously evoking the passion of union between Rādhā and Kṛṣṇa.[37]

The attachment of self-offering

This form of *bhakti* can also be understood in two ways: either as the deity's self-offering to the devotee or vice versa. Śrī Vaiṣṇavas speak of *prapatti*, complete self-surrender in love, to Viṣṇu.[38] What does *prapatti* entail? Either standing helpless before God, unable or thinking it unnecessary to practise arduous expiatory rites for one's sins, submissive like a baby kitten which will be picked up by its mother and carried to safety (the view of the 'cat-school'), or responding by works in love to the Lord and so finding deliverance, like the baby monkey clinging on to its mother for refuge (the view of the 'monkey school'). Leading *bhaktas* are wont to say that no one is more eager to offer their self in love than God.

The attachment of being suffused

Thus *tan-maya*, i.e. 'consisting of *tan*' or the deity. This is the *bhakti* of merging, of dissolving into the deity, of identification. It may take different forms: one can identify with the deity as having form, or with the divine, formless Spirit. Some devotees scorn conventional worship as inhibiting, others resort to it as enabling.

The Vīraśaiva Dasimayya (*c.* tenth century) says:

To the utterly at-one with Siva,
there's no dawn, no new moon,
no noonday, nor equinoxes,
nor sunsets, nor full moons.
His front yard is the true Benares,
O Ramanatha.[39]

And again:

I'm the one who has the body,
You're the one who holds the breath.
You know the secret of my body,
I know the secret of your breath.
That's why your body is in mine.
You know and I know, Ramanatha,
The miracle of your breath in my body.

(Ramanujan 1973: 106)

Now hear Kabīr:

No more separate am I.
All is submerged in Thee!
Now, O Brother, like molten iron
He and I are fused together.
There are no distinctions to be made.[40]

Bhakti is the religion of divine immanence; divine immanence characterises much of Hindu theology. As we have seen, the divine transcendence is no doubt acknowledged. One has but to read Rāmānuja's description of the supernal divine form to appreciate that (see above). But it is the divine immanence in every aspect of creation, barely latent to the eyes of faith and waiting to burst through, that catches the attention of most Hindu theologians and *bhakta*s. This gives rise to the tendency to view the divine causality as an 'emanation' or 'projection' of the Godhead, and a reluctance to sever the existential 'umbilical' cord between infinite and finite being. To the uninformed or untrained, this smacks of 'pantheism', but it is not really so. Rather, the deity is in everything and everything is in the deity. Or if Hindus say glibly that God is everything, a little probing will discover that they will qualify this by attributing 'transcendent' qualities to the deity – perfection, sinlessness, omnipotence, all-knowingness – and by expressing 'transcendent' aspirations: the desire to unite upwards with the deity, to rise above oneself in the love of God. There is a world of difference between the level of karma and/or other limitations on which humans live and the level of the sovereign Spirit. Nevertheless the ideal is to be suffused with the deity, for the deity is one's *antar-ātmā*, one's inner self.

The attachment of the deepest separation

Here we encounter another paradox. This is the *bhakti* of identity-in-difference, of immanence-in-transcendence. In the intensity of feeling the pain of separation from the beloved, of never having enough of the beloved, the devotee experiences the greatest love. Extraordinary descriptions are given of the emotional frenzy of this experience of separation: sweating, swooning, choking, gasping, heart-break, the anticipated ecstasy of union, the agony of parting.

When they had made love
                    she lay in his arms in the *kunja* grove,
Suddenly she called his name
and wept – as if she burned in the fire of separation.
The gold was in her *anchal* [end-knot of her sari]
but she looked afar for it!
– Where has he gone? Where has my love gone?
O why has he left me alone?
And she writhed on the ground in despair.
Only her pain kept her from fainting.
Krishna was astonished and could not speak.[41]

Yet Rādhā lay in his arms. The love of union carries the seed of separation and vice versa.

All the *bhakta*s mentioned here (and many more) have large followings among Hindus today, and the works of an increasing number are being immortalised through the performances – on stage, radio, television and cassette – of well-known virtuosi. Needless to say, it will not do to press the distinctions of the headings in the various poems quoted, since a particular poem may express the sentiments of more than one kind of *bhakti*; nor are rigid divisions intended, I believe, by the Nārada Sūtra itself. There are other divisions of *bhakti*, but enough has been said, I hope, to give a glimpse of the variety and styles of approach. It is also useful to bear in mind that devotees, and not only of the selfless variety, relish the satsang or company of kindred spirits, for all derive encouragement and support from each other. It is often said that for the true *bhakta* the distinctions of caste, sex and status dissolve, for God is in all and all is in God. But *para-bhakti* or selfless devotion is hard to find, and human nature being what it is *apara-bhakti* is commonplace. Nevertheless *para-bhakti* is the passive or active ideal of many.

We may conclude by considering briefly Hindu ideas of *mokṣa* (also called *mukti*). Some commentators limit this term to the final emancipation described by the monists. But this is unwarranted; in any case by *mokṣa* we mean 'salvation' or ultimate religious fulfilment. Typologically, there are three kinds of *mokṣa* in the Hindu tradition.

'Enstasy' or kaivalya

This is the goal of the Pātañjala Yogin or of the Sāṃkhya. If the path to kaivalya is successfully followed – this entails cultivating certain virtues such as non-injury and benevolence to all, truthfulness, non-acquisitiveness, celibacy, sense-restraint, and mastering certain meditative techniques by which mind and body are harmonised and brought under control – then the state of kaivalya can be attained while the Yogin is still living. In this condition the Yogin lives in the body, in the realm of *prakṛti*, but the spirit has mastered the body, namely, the sensual and other enslaving propensities of *prakṛti*. The Yogin is 'in', but not 'of' the world. The qualities of spirit (*puruṣa*), wisdom, kindness, serenity, forbearance, unassumingness, economy of action and thought etc., radiate outwards. According to this ideal it is not a good thing to have 'really lived' in the sense of being caught up in the passions of worldly relationships. Such 'living' perpetuates itself through the ignorance and misery attendant on karma and rebirth. For the Yogin, at death, all karma having been consumed, the link between his spirit and its prakritic complement is finally severed, and kaivalya is attained. No personality as we understand it survives to experience it. Apparently it is a state of never-ending, perfectly blissful, self-aware, ineffable, self-contained, relationless isolation. Hence 'kaivalya', which literally means 'aloneness'.[42]

Identity or ekatva

This is the monistic ideal. It can have either a theistic or a non-theistic complexion. In Advaita Vedānta *mokṣa* is the experience of absolute identity with the ultimate, qualityless, relationless, distinctionless, ineffable, spiritual *Brahman*. This is how Upanishadic statements like 'I am *Brahman*' (*ahaṃ brahma asmi, BĀUp* I.4.10) are interpreted. Again, 'I' here does not refer to some liberated personality; there is no room for a distinguishable personality in this ultimate experience. 'I' refers to the spirit at the core of one's being, seemingly embodied empirically and stamped by one's personality. All along, however, this spirit *is Brahman*, only we don't realise it. We live generally at the level of the ego-personality. Again, by a *sādhana* or spiritual discipline similar in many respects to that of the Yogin, but one which 'passes through' a provisional idea or projection or dualistic framework of a God/creature, infinite/finite divide, we are to strip away the prakritic 'I' and liberate the underlying spiritual 'I', the *Ātman*. Ultimately, *Ātman* is *Brahman*. In this tradition too 'jīvan mukti', liberation in the body, is possible, the mukta or liberated soul living and behaving analogously to the enlightened Yogin (see above).

In some schools of Tantra, however, it seems that the ultimate objective is to experience one's existing but unrealised identity with the supreme Being viewed and related to during the *sādhana* stage as the union of God and the Goddess (e.g. Śiva and Devī). This seems to be the view of Abhinavagupta. There are different stages in this ascent, characterisable as passing from a communion to difference-in-identity to identity-in-difference to absolute identity. At this point a distinguishable 'I' of the *sādhaka* or adept ceases to exist. The *sādhana* varies, but in general it consists of unalloyed service and devotion to the supreme Being (e.g. the Goddess) according to the ethical precepts, rituals and theory of one's particular tradition.[43] There seems to be a stronger theistic complexion here, not only to the *sādhana* but also to the description of the ultimate state, but one may be forcing this distinction. These Tantric religions and that of Advaita Vedānta are religions of the 'high' tradition in Hinduism. There is a marked reluctance in these 'theologies' to describe the liberated state, for it is essentially ineffable.

Communion with the deity

This is the passive or active ideal of the majority of religious Hindus, but it has been variously described. Theologically, it is generally a never-ending state of intimate and personal blissful and loving communion with the deity in the company of the heavenly court which comprises divine associates who have never been prakritically embodied (e.g. a divine consort or two, 'angelic beings' (*sūris*), etc.), and liberated souls. Here *mokṣa* consists of one's experience in the deity's dwelling-place.[44] In some (usually Vaiṣṇava) *bhakti* traditions, however, different kinds of communion are envisaged. These seem to be communions of degree in sharing the divine life. In this connection we may mention the states of *sālokya* (sharing the divine ambience), *sāmīpya* (sharing the divine presence), *sārūpya* (becoming an aspect of God or sharing his lustre or looking like him in some way), and *sāyujya* (becoming conjoined to or totally absorbed in God). These can be variously interpreted.[45] In general, *bhakti*-theologians are markedly less reluctant than their colleagues in the first two categories to describe the liberated state; these descriptions are invariably edited from texts like the Purāṇas. Devotees look forward to celestial bodies on which the earthly versions are modelled, but that are not susceptible to earthly laws and limitations. The heavenly court and regions are models of idyllic earthly scenes, e.g. jewelled and imposing palaces filled with never-ageing, happy inhabitants, with sparkling fountains and beautiful gardens in which animals naturally at odds with each other in this world roam amicably. Indeed, in some conceptions there are different levels of heaven, each with its own name and distinctive attributes, in which the supreme Being exists in a different form. Such models are current even today: I was assured recently by a Vaiṣṇava guru of a large cult that an accurate description of heaven could be drawn from the *Bhāgavata* Purāṇa. However, it would appear that an increasing number of people are seeking to demythologise such descriptions.

Mythologically, heaven is not always a never-ending state of happiness, both in the high and low traditions.[46] There are stories in the Purāṇas of celestial inhabitants quarrelling and cursing one another to incarnate on earth; this is quite different from the *avatāra* doctrine. Once the curse is expended return to heaven is possible. In the Manasā *maṅgal* too, Behulā, Lakhāi's wife and one of the main characters (see Chapter 5), is the human embodiment of Ūṣā, a dancer in Indra's heaven, who was cursed to be reborn on earth. Her earthly husband is the incarnate version of Aniruddha, Ūṣā's heavenly spouse. Other examples can be cited. Again, the theologians may attempt to demythologise these ideas, but for many ordinary religious Hindus, myth supplants theology or lives in uneasy juxtaposition with it.

In fact, it seems that a great many Hindus do not actively expect or even seek some post-mortem 'salvation' or liberation. If at all, this is a distant ideal. Religiously, they are more concerned just to stay afloat as they continue life's journey over the hazardous waters of *saṃsāra*. Health, recovery from illness, contentment, economic security, consolation in distress, offspring, success in various ventures, protection from various dangers, possibly a happy rebirth – these are the things that occupy their religious attention. This is not to say that many do not look to *mokṣa* in one form or another as a desirable goal. But the fact is that we cannot generalise. Life's ideal for the religious Hindu varies from context to context, from the sublime to the mundane. The Great and Ancient Banyan harbours birds of every feather in its labyrinthine worlds.

Notes

PREFACE

1 This expression can be contentious. It is not intended in the sense of a 'great' tradition neatly separable in form and content from various 'little' traditions, but rather in the sense of what is itself a plural phenomenon deriving more or less directly from Sanskritic paradigms of theory and practice incarnating variously in localised situations – the 'little' traditions. See further Fuller 1992: 24ff. This title came to hand when the typescript of the present book was with the publisher.

1 ABOUT 'HINDU', HINDUISM AND THIS BOOK

1 *The World Christian Encyclopedia* (Barrett 1982) records that at present there are over 650 million Hindus in about 69 countries of the world (the overwhelming majority being in India, of course).
2 Zaehner 1966: 1–3.
3 SH, p. 16.
4 H. von Stietencron in Küng *et al.* 1987: 138–43.
5 ST, pp. 4–6.
6 Farquhar 1913: 214–16.
7 Chaudhuri 1979: 1–10.
8 Radhakrishnan 1980: 18.
9 Al-Biruni, from *Alberuni's India*, English edn. Sachau 1888: 17–50.
10 Brahmabandhab Upadhyay (1861–1907); see Upadhyay 1981.
11 This must be so. In 1803 the second Earl of Valentia (George A. Mountnorris), writes of a visit to the (Calcutta) 'Botanic Garden', 'The finest object in the garden is a noble specimen of the Ficus Bengalensis'. See Nair 1989: 5.
12 On the history and formation of such abstractions see Smith 1978, esp. Chs. 3 and 5.
13 In modern scholarship, 'aryan' is used strictly as a linguistic rather than as an ethnic term. But less strictly, in the Indian context 'aryan' is commonly used to refer to the people who introduced Sanskrit to the subcontinent. Besides, in their sacred texts these people referred to themselves as '*āryas*' to distinguish themselves from the indigenous non-Sanskrit

speaking folk (about whom more later). For a recent discussion on this and related issues see IAA, pp. 13–24.

14 The word *sindhu* (for mystic river?) is used in the Avesta, an ancient (Iranian) Zoroastrian scripture which has cultural origins in common with those of the Vedas.

15 *Alberuni's India* (Sachau 1888: 39, n. 9). This work has been hailed as a landmark and likened to 'a magic island of quiet, impartial research in the midst of a world of clashing swords, burning towns, and plundered temples' (Sachau's Preface, 1888: xxiii). More soberly but equally positively, a modern scholar has summed up the work as exemplifying 'scholarly distance and objectivity' (see Halbfass 1988: 28). Phenomenologically Biruni's work is no doubt important, and on the whole a creditable attempt to write temperately in a world of prejudiced Hindu–Muslim relationships, but it is also full of (sometimes nonsensical) misrepresentation. The tendency of foreign observers to assimilate Hinduism to Brahminic religion is persistent. It is the basis on which another well-known pioneering record was written – see Dubois 1862. On the title page Dubois is described as 'Missionary in the Mysore'. As this description indicates, Dubois' record is South-centred; it was first translated into English from a French manuscript, apparently completed in 1806.

16 See e.g. Srinivas, 'The social system of a Mysore village' in Marriott 1955.

17 In the context of Hinduism this word (and its derivatives) may mislead since, as we shall see, Hindus are often at least as concerned with what may be called 'orthopraxy' (doing the acceptable thing) as with orthodoxy (in the restricted sense of believing the right thing). 'Orthodox' will generally be used in the popular if somewhat loose sense of 'conventional', 'standard', 'traditional'.

18 This distinction is discussed in Smith 1967, Ch. 4.

19 ST, p. 5.

20 The story is summarised in BCL, pp. 147ff.

21 The city is referred to variously as Benares, Banaras, Varanasi, Kashi, etc.

22 BCL, pp. 154–5. For a history of the Divodāsa myth in its Puranic context and its variants see OEHM, pp. 189ff.

23 The survey has been made by O'Connell 1973: 340ff.

24 i.e. 'Ionian', first applied to Greeks and then by extension to any foreigner.

25 Foreign barbarian.

26 In this style of poetry, the versifier often mentions himself or herself by name.

27 Quoted from Kumar 1984: 21. The distinction drawn between the Gorakhnāth Yogī and the Hindu is interesting; in today's reckoning the Gorakhnāth Yogī would clearly be a Hindu.

28 Members of this movement are debating as to whether they should call themselves Hindus. They should note that everybody else regards them as Hindus.

2 THE VOICE OF SCRIPTURE AS VEDA

1 There have been other challenges to Vedic authority, of course, from both inside and outside Hinduism, e.g. those of the *bhakti* and Tantric

traditions and of Islam respectively. But from the point of view of the steady growth of the Ancient Banyan, the former were coped with by assimilation or accommodation, while the latter were in large measure ignored.

2 On this see Keith 1970, Ch. 4. This is a valuable work which at times betrays its colonial origins.

3 For details on the Proto-Indo-Aryans and their migrations, see Mallory 1989, esp. Ch. 2. See also IAA.

4 For a dated but still useful account of Harappan culture, see Wheeler 1968. For a more recent and wide-ranging treatment see Allchin and Allchin 1982.

5 For the time being we shall have to be content with this description, or with 'god(s)' (*sic*). I shall comment on the theological status of the *devas* and the *devīs* in early Vedic religion in Chapter 12 of this book.

6 A scholarly account of the style and content of the earlier sections of the Vedas is given in J. Gonda 1975, vol. 1.1 in HIL. This extensive series is a valuable resource for Indological studies.

7 Keith 1970: 3.

8 See Chaudhuri 1979: 68–72.

9 Even today, in some circles Brahmins belonging to the first three Vedas tend to deprecate the ritual standing of the Brahmins of the *Atharva* Veda.

10 On its identity, see Falk 1989; but cf. Flattery and Schwartz 1989.

11 An elaborate Vedic ritual of the *soma* variety (called the *Atirātra-Agnicayana*) is recorded for posterity, with photographs of each step, cassettes and analyses of different aspects of the performance, in two volumes entitled *Agni: the Vedic Ritual of the Fire Altar* (Staal 1983). The sacrifice was performed by Nambudiri Brahmins of south India in twelve days over the period 12–25 April 1975.

12 The recension of the Mādhyaṃdina school has been translated into English by Julius Eggeling in SBE (Vols. 12, 26, 41, 43, 44; 1882ff.), and reprinted by Motilal Banarsidass, Delhi, 1963–72.

13 Called *vāc* in so far as it is sacrificial utterance, and *śabda* inasmuch as it is sacred speech or language.

14 A useful edition of these Upaniṣads, with an English translation and the transliterated Sanskrit, is that by Radhakrishnan 1953 (and subsequent impressions). References in this book to the classical Upaniṣads follow this text (though the translations are my own). Note that in his lengthy Introduction Radhakrishnan favours an Advaitic, i.e. monistic, interpretation of Upanishadic teaching. This represents only one important traditional systematic approach to the Upaniṣads, and by no means the dominant one. Recently a new anthology, entitled *Upaniṣads*, has appeared in paperback, edited by P. Olivelle, Oxford University Press, Oxford, 1996.

15 However, occasional, even widespread performance of the Vedic *yajña* is, as we shall note elsewhere, by no means a thing of the past.

16 There was also a concept of earthly immortality or longevity, probably envisaged ideally for males, namely, surviving with vigour for 'a hundred autumns'.

17 Note we speak of Brahm*ā*, with a long *a* at the end of the name and declined as masculine in Sanskrit, and not of Brahm*an*, sometimes written Brahma, with no long *a*, and declined as neuter.

18 'You are Brahmā, full of sacrificial wealth, O lord of the *brahman*!': *tvaṃ brahmā rayivid brahmaṇas pate*.

19 There may be other occurrences of *brahmā* which can be given a similar interpretation, e.g. RV 8.16.7; 10.141.3.

20 The Sanskrit text followed is that of the *Brahmāṇḍa Purāṇa* (Shastri 1973). See verses 50–6, p. 13 of text.

21 *ṛiṣi* is usually translated as 'seer', but as will become clear, the *ṛṣi* hears rather than sees the sacred word.

22 A good account of these ideas is given in SSV (NCW).

23 *Brahman* as pure spirit is sexless.

24 See Śaṃkara's commentary on Brahma Sūtra 1.1.3 (Abhyankar 1914).

25 For Śaṃkara, the existence of the Vedas is not strict proof for the existence of God, i.e. *Brahman*. We start by accepting the authority of the Vedas as scripture. The right understanding of their scope gives us a proper idea of the natuıe of their provenance and ultimate concern, namely *Brahman*; from this we can begin to appreciate what *Brahman's* omniscience is. It was another tradition acknowledging the authority of the Vedas, namely the Nyāya-Vaiśeshika (which relied on the processes of reasoning to arrive at fundamental truths), that sought to develop, from about the eleventh century CE, 'proofs' for the existence of God on the basis of the infallibility and cognitive scope of the Vedas (see Chapter 7). For Nyāya-Vaiśeshika, the Vedas are *pauruṣeya*, i.e. actually authored by God. This was not the dominant view about the production of the Vedas.

26 Translated from the Sanskrit in *Śrī-Bhāṣya by Rāmānujāchārya* (SBR) (Abhyankar 1914); commentary on Brahma Sūtra 1.3.29, p. 318.

27 See SBR, 1.3.28, p. 317.

28 From Raghavachar 1971: 5 v. 21.

29 For the Sanskrit see VS, p. 83, para 21, 'Are applied as before' etc.: *vaidikāḥ sarve śabdāḥ . . . pareṇaiva brahmaṇā sarvapadārthān pūrvavat sṛṣṭvā teṣu paramātmaparyanteṣu pūrvavan nāmatayā prayuktāḥ*.

30 Most of these normative scriptures are in Sanskrit. On the meaning and scope of the term *tantra*, see HT, pp. 7–9. There is also Buddhist and Jain Tantra.

31 Speaking simplistically, in Vaisnavism the divine focus is Viṣṇu in some form, or some (mythologically) related figure, while Saivism and Saktism analogously stress the divine supremacy of Śiva and the Goddess, or Devī, respectively. These distinctions will become clearer in the course of this book.

32 Padoux 1990: 50–1.

33 It has been suggested with plausibility that the tendency to develop eternalist theories about the nature of Sanskrit and the Vedas by the traditionalists was at least reinforced by a reaction to the rise of the anti-Vedic movements of Buddhism and Jainism in the centuries immediately preceding the beginning of the Common Era.

34 In the event my friend declined the request (and the makings of what seemed to be a new profession). This story also illustrates the desperate measures to which immigrants may be reduced in the absence of traditional religious resources, in this case a suitable local Hindu priest.

35 For details see Alper 1989.

36 In fact the art of Vedic sacrificial utterance and recitation makes considerable 'non-sense' of the mantric syllables and sounds. This art is still practised. For examples see Howard 1977.
37 Its early history is discussed in SSV.
38 The three realms of Vedic cosmology.
39 'Inspirer': *savitṛ*, the sun-*deva*.
40 Traditionally only twice-born males could utter the *Gāyatrī*.
41 The distinctions 'high' and 'low', 'great' and 'small' in this context are problematic but still useful for want of suitable alternatives.

3 THE VOICE OF SCRIPTURE AS VEDA AND 'VEDA'

1 Dhavamony 1971.
2 'These writings are at present scattered all over South India in manuscript form' (Dhavamony 1971: 117).
3 Timm 1990. Timm quotes v. 26 of K. N. Misra's edition of the TADN.
4 TADN v. 38.
5 *gītāyāṃ bhagavadvākyāni eva śāstram ity arthaḥ, vedānām api tadukta-prakāreṇaiva arthanirṇayaḥ*: TADN v. 17. '*śāstra*' here means interpretive criterion, teaching instrument.
6 Timm 1990.
7 See TVSS, in Krishna 1979: 29–87.
8 'A whole range of works, in Tamil and Sanskrit, popular and learned, and spanning the centuries up to the present day, illustrates the attraction and power of the *śūdra* and his Tamil Veda as a religious symbol' (Hardy in Krishna 1979: 70).
9 See Williams 1984: 158ff.
10 On these Bāuls and their anti-Vedic stance, see Openshaw 1994 and forthcoming.
11 Thapar 1966: 101.
12 Thapar 1966: 174.
13 From 'William Jones, "On the Hindus"', in Marshall 1970: 251.
14 Within a few years there was occasion for this intransigence to be overcome. See Crawford 1987: 86–92.
15 Even in his personal life, Ram Mohan was careful not to flout caste observances. Thus, as a Brahmin, he wore the sacred thread and even took a Brahmin cook with him to England.
16 'Swami' here means an ascetic teacher; 'Vivekananda' means 'the bliss of discerning knowledge'. It is usual for Hindu ascetics to assume a descriptive title to mark their resolve to renounce worldly ties.
17 Such interpretation had begun however, not least in Ram Mohan's pioneering analyses of Hindu and Christian scriptures.
18 See for example Bissoondoyal 1979: 16, n. 20; here, a publication, the *Organiser* (6 October 1952), is quoted to the effect that 'Vedic references to aeroplanes described eight kinds of machines in aeroplanes, all of which were electrically controlled'. It was on the basis of such ancient wisdom that an inhabitant of Bombay (with some collaborators) allegedly constructed an aeroplane in 1895 which 'rose to a height of 1500 feet

and automatically landed safely'. Later, the machine was sold 'to an English commercial concern'.

19 See Upadhyaya 1956; on Dayananda see Jordens 1978.

20 A good account of the controversy and its context is given in Young 1981. See also Lipner 1987.

21 *yadi granthe'sti viśvāso veda evāvalambyatām, yato'sau sṛṣṭikālādicalito'sti mahītale.* Young 1981: 99, fn. 95; my translation.

22 See Young 1981: 131 (fn. 146) for the Sanskrit.

23 For the Sanskrit see Young 1981: 107–8 (fn. 103).

24 Radhakrishnan 1961: 29–30.

25 Radhakrishnan 1980: 18.

26 See Radhakrishnan 1980: 24, where this is given in quotes but with obvious approval.

27 See Lipner 1989: 123–37.

28 See, for example, 'The changing status of a depressed caste', a study by Bernard S. Cohn, of the 'untouchable' Camars of Madhopur village in eastern UP, in Marriott 1955: 53–77.

4 THE VOICE OF TRADITION: VARṆĀŚRAMA DHARMA

1 The relationship between the Veda and *dharma* as perceived in (high) Hindu tradition is stated in the opening words of the Dharma Sūtras of Guatama, an ancient text: 'The Veda is the root of *dharma*': vedo dharmamūlam. Exactly how this is so in specific contexts is often not clear. As in the case of claiming Vedic sanction for apparently non-Vedic scripture, in many instances the supposed Vedic legitimation for what is said to be *dharma* is simply declared or assumed, and not shown.

2 This is the translation preferred by the *nirukta-* scholar Eivind Kahrs. For a clearer indication of what he means, see Kahrs 1984: 139ff.

3 Kahrs 1984: 139.

4 *Smārta* is a derivative of *smṛti.*

5 They allude to Saṃhitā texts by quoting only the first few words of the relevant text.

6 Like the Prātiśākhyas and Mantra-Saṃhitās, other kinds of auxiliary texts exist which were intended to further the understanding and implementation of the sacrificial cult of the Vedas. We do not need to examine these texts, since we already have a fair idea of the material available.

7 Haradatta Miśra, in the *Ujjvalā* (*c.* sixteenth century CE), his commentary on the Dharma Sūtras of Āpastamba, quotes a verse to the effect that *vyākaraṇa* is the mouth of the Veda, *jyotiṣa* the eyes, *nirukta* the ears, *śikṣā* the nose, *chandas* the feet, and *kalpa* the hands. It is thus that these disciplines serve the Veda as its limbs (*aṅgas*), he says: 2.4.8.11.

8 A good example of the sense of 'threading' or 'stringing' that 'sūtra' conveys occurs in *Bhagavadgītā* 7.7, where Kṛṣṇa, the supreme Being, says: 'There is nothing higher than I, Arjuna. All this (universe) is strung on me like multitudes of pearls on *a thread*' (*sūtre maṇigaṇā iva*)'. The English word 'suture' has a cognate meaning.

9 *alpākṣaram asandigdhaṃ sāravad viśvatomukham; astobham anavadyaṃ*

ca sūtraṃ sūtravido viduḥ. There are a number of variants of this definition.

10 For a survey under various headings see Gonda 1980. For detailed technical information see also his *The Ritual Sūtras*, vol. 1.2 of HIL, which deals largely with the Śrauta and Gṛhya Sūtras (Gonda 1975).

11 As we shall see later, it can also function as a descriptive concept.

12 See Kane 1930–62 (1st edn); a revised edn of Vol. 1 and a reprint of the rest was published from 1968 on. See revised edn, Vol. 1, Part I, p. 306ff.

13 The SBE contains translations of several important Gṛhya Sūtras, Dharma Sūtras and Śāstras. For Manu see O'Flaherty 1991.

14 In Sanskrit, the word is sometimes used in the plural, namely *dharmāṇi* (the older form) or *dharmāḥ*, to mean 'laws', 'rules', 'norms', '(approved) practices', etc.

15 'To protect (*guptyartham*) this whole creation (*sarga*) the resplendent One determined separate works (*karmāṇi*) for those produced from his mouth, arms, thighs and feet'.

16 In analysing these concepts I have derived leading insights from VC in Killingley *et al.* 1991.

17 2.2.2.6, 4.3.4.4., etc. (these references follow J. Eggeling's translation of the text in the SBE).

18 On 1.1.1.15 the *Ujjvalā* comments: 'Like a father out of a mother' (*yathā pitā mātuḥ*). Manu 2.146 notes: 'Of the two (i.e. who give birth) one's progenitor and the giver of the Veda, the "father" who gives the Veda is the superior, for the Vedic birth of one who knows the Veda (brings) eternal (reward) in this life and after death'.

19 Even then there were lines one could not cross. One could not, for example, live by occupations beyond the pale of ritual purity, such as that of corpse-carrier.

20 The Codes prescribe different material for the loop, depending on the *varṇa* of the initiate (e.g. see Manu 2.44). Nowadays cotton is often widely used for wearers of all castes.

21 Perhaps this is meant to symbolise the umbilical cord of the second birth.

22 'The ears of (the Śūdra) who listens to the Veda are to be filled with (molten) tin and lac. If he utters (a Vedic text, *udāharaṇe*) his tongue should be cut out. If he practises (Vedic utterance, *dhāraṇe*), his body should be broken (śarīrabheda)'; *Gautama* Dharma Sūtra, 12. 4–6 (SBE edn, Vol. 2).

23 *Baudhāyana* Dharma Sūtra, 1.10.18.5–6 (SBE edn, Vol. 14).

24 '(A Śūdra) who is always pure (*śuci*), attentive to his betters (*utkṛṣṭ-aśuśrūṣu*), soft-spoken, humble (*anahaṃkṛta*), and dependent on the Brahmin and (other twice-born *varṇas*) attains a higher birth (*utkṛṣṭaṃ jātim*) (in the next life)' (Manu 9.335).

25 Śūdras were dubbed 'non-Aryan' in the *dharma* codes; this gives some credence to the view that originally the majority came from the indigenous peoples of the subcontinent.

26 See further Olivelle 1974: 27ff.

27 In times of duress he could be initiated by and study under a Kṣatriya or Vaiśya teacher.

28 AV 11.5.3. It seems clear that by this time initiation was a formal ceremony and that '*upanayamāna*' is being used technically in this context.

29 The teacher was usually married and could have more than one wife: usually co-wives were not to be of the same *varṇa* (see Chapter 5).
30 Even today, to say that someone is a *brahmacārin*, or in the case of a woman, a *brahmacāriṇī*, is to imply that they follow a celibate way of life.
31 Cf. *Vāsiṣṭha* Dharma Sūtra 8.14–16.
32 Members of certain sects, e.g. within the Tantric tradition, not orthodox according to traditional standards, either permitted or revelled in meat-eating.
33 On abortion, see Lipner 1989.
34 This idea had much earlier roots however. See the Dharma Sūtra of *Baudhāyana*, 2.6.11.33.
35 Supposedly from a treatise, apparently not extant, on ascetics composed by the Sage Vikhānas, himself an ascetic. The relatively late *Vaikhānasa* Dharma Sūtras give the most elaborate description of the various kinds of ascetics and their practices.
36 According to Manu, 'Only when a householder sees that he has wrinkles and grey hair and a grandchild (or grandchildren?), may he resort to the forest' (6.2).
37 Cf. The *Maitrī* Upaniṣad I. 2.
38 On this see e.g. Altekar 1959, esp. Chs. 1 and 7; F. M. Smith, 'Indra's curse, Varuṇa's noose, and the suppression of the woman in the Vedic *Śrauta* Ritual' in Leslie 1991.
39 *ayajnīyo vā eṣa yo'patnīkaḥ*; quoted as 2.2.2.6 by Altekar 1959: 31; see also p. 197.
40 *BĀUp* IV.5.1.
41 Gārgī was not easily silenced. She seems to have made two attempts; it is her second attempt that we are interested in.
42 The same Upaniṣad informs us (IV.5.1, IV.5.5) that Yājñavalkya's favourite wife, Maitreyī, was a *brahmavādinī*. He knew how to deal with *brahmavādinīs*.
43 'It is the nature (*svābhava*) of women to be the bane (*dūṣaṇa*) of men here (in this life); for this reason wise men are never unguarded in the presence of women. In this world women are able to lead not only the fool but even the learned man astray, making him bounden to lust and anger': thus Manu 2. 213–14.
44 See also 5.147–9.
45 'The husband obtains his wife as a gift of the gods (*devadattāṃ patir bhāryāṃ vindate*; 9.95). . . . Let there be lifelong fidelity (*avyabhicāra . . . āmaraṇāntika*) between them' (9.101).
46 'Though devoid of virtue, debauched or completely bereft of good qualities, the husband must always be revered by a good wife as a god' (5.154).
47 The English word 'suttee' comes from this mark of the faithful wife or *satī*.
48 Thus the *Mitākṣara* on *Yājñavalkya Smṛti* 1.86 recommends suttee (*anvārohaṇa*, namely mounting (the pyre)) as righteous practice for all wives, even for the Caṇḍāla (a despised mixed caste), *except* for those who were pregnant or who had young children. Note that even Caṇḍālas were within the scope of *dharma*.
49 Suttee was traditionally more common in the Gangetic basin and in parts

of the west of the country. By the late eighteenth century, if we are to believe the Abbé Dubois, suttee was relatively rare and confined mainly to princely and aristocratic families. See Dubois 1862, Ch. xxi.

50 See Book 1.109–10 and 116 for the full story.

51 This story is probably apocryphal, but it typifies the horror of what is likely to have often happened. Here is a condensed account of what the Abbé Dubois himself witnessed on one occasion.

> The first instance that fell under my observation was in the year 1794, in a village of Tanjore . . . . A man of some note there, of the tribe of *Komati* or *Merchants*, having died, his wife, then about thirty years of age, resolved to accompany him to the pile, to be consumed together. The news having quickly spread around, a large concourse of people collected . . . to witness this extraordinary spectacle . . . . The body of the deceased was placed upon a sort of triumphal car, highly ornamented with costly stuffs, garlands of flowers, and the like. There he was seated, like a living man, elegantly set out with all his jewels, and clothed in rich attire.
>
> The corpse taking precedence, the wife immediately followed, borne on a rich palanquin. She was covered over with ornaments . . . . During the whole procession, which was very long, [the wife receiving the adulation of the accompanying crowd and offering advice and blessings to individual women who came up to consult her] she preserved a steady aspect. Her countenance was serene and even cheerful, until they came to the fatal pile, on which she was soon to yield up her life . . . . Her features were altered . . . she trembled with fear, and seemed ready to faint away . . . . They made her quit the palanquin, and her nearest relations supported her to a pond that was near the pile, and having there washed her, without taking off her clothes or ornaments, they soon reconducted her to the pyramid on which the body of her husband was already laid. It was surrounded by the Brahmans, each with a lighted torch in one hand and a bowl of melted butter in the other, all ready. . . . The relatives, all armed with muskets, sabres and other weapons, stood closely round, in a double line . . . . At length, the auspicious moment for firing the pile being announced by the Purohita Brahman [i.e. the priest-in-charge], the young woman was instantly divested of all her jewels, and led on, more dead than alive, to the fatal pyramid. She was then commanded, according to the universal practice, to walk round it three times, two of her nearest relations supporting her by the arms. The first round she accomplished with tottering steps; but in the second, her strength wholly forsook her and she fainted away in the arms of her conductors, who were obliged to complete the ceremony by dragging her between them for the third round. Then . . . unconscious, she was cast upon the carcase of her husband. At that instant the multitude making the air resound with acclamations and shouts of gladness, retired a short space, while the Brahmans, pouring the butter on the dry wood, applied their torches, and instantly the whole pile was in a blaze.
>
> Dubois 1862: 175–7.

52 For an account of Ram Mohan's role in the campaign, see S. Cromwell Crawford 1987, esp. p. 101ff.

53 For an account of the incident see *India Today*, 15 October 1987, p. 58ff.
54 It is interesting that Vaiśyas are included in the list, a sign that the norms of the Codes were not being followed by many traders in pursuit of their livelihood.
55 A religious movement deriving inspiration from the life of Caitanya (sixteenth century; see Chapter 10). Caitanya was regarded by his followers as an embodiment of both the Lord Kṛṣṇa and his divine lover, Rādhā.
56 On this, and on the domestic *dharma* of women generally, see Leslie 1989.
57 Often, on festive occasions, e.g. a wedding, they are ritually marginalised.
58 See *Gautama* Dharma Sūtra, SBE edn, 21.1–9.
59 *dvijātikarmabhyo hāniḥ patanam, tathā paratra cāsiddhiḥ.*
60 From *Story of a Widow Remarriage*, by Madhowdas Rugnathdas, p. 54. Further bibliographical details wanting.

5 THE VOICE OF TRADITION: 'CASTE' AND NARRATIVE

1 One cannot say 'varṇa status' because as we shall see, there could be intermarriage between *varṇa*s, and this generated mixed castes, members of which were usually recommended to marry endogamously.
2 Conveniently, the twice-born could take sustenance from their hands in cases of dire emergency.
3 e.g. 'From a Kṣatriya (who mates) with a daughter of a Śūdra is born being called an "Ugra" (*jantur ugro nāma prajāyate*); he resembles both a Kṣatriya and a Śūdra, delighting in savage behaviour' (Manu 10.9).
4 Thus, according to Manu 10.49, the Ugra (see previous note) was to subsist by catching and killing creatures that lived in holes.
5 As always in Hinduism, there are exceptions. Thus, among some communities in Kerala, caste status is matrilineal. But these are only exceptions.
6 'The seed is to be valued' (bījaṃ praśasyate) (Manu 10.72).
7 Manu itself implies as much. If appearance does not reveal one's caste status, says Manu, appealing to the naturalistic conception of *dharma*, then one's behaviour will. *Dharma*, or rather *adharma* (in this sense) will out. 'A stranger who claimed a (twice-born) varṇa but who arose from some impure source, would be shown up as non-Aryan by his deeds even though he looked Aryan. In daily life, non-Aryan behaviour, cruelty, uncouthness and neglect of religious duties reveal someone as arising from an impure source . . . bad origin (*duryoni*) can never conceal its nature (*svāṃ prakṛtim*)' (10.57–9).
8 Note that about 70 per cent of the Indian population live in villages.
9 1.5.10.27 in SBE translation.
10 Killingley (VC) quotes two verses: 'Truth, generosity, patience, good conduct, harmlessness, tapas [asceticism], compassion: where this is found, that man is said to be a brahmin' (3.180.21), and 'Not birth, not initiation, not Veda-knowledge, not even lineage cause a person to be twice-born; the only cause is behaviour' (13.143.50).

11 The hugely popular Hindi film *Maine Pyar Kiya* (1989) gives an example. Both the arch-villain and the rich young hero are upper caste, while the heroine is poor and of lower-caste status. The arch-villain wants to marry his daughter off to the hero only to discover that the latter is in love with the heroine. So he (arch-villain) throws the heroine's low '*jāt*' (i.e. *jāti*) in her face, with mortifying results for hero, heroine and heroine's father. After convolutions in the story which only modern Hindi films seem to manage, arch-villain seeks the heroine's father's help in ruining the hero's father. The heroine's father replies with dignity that it is below his *jāt* to resort to such underhand tactics. Stung, arch-villain mutters that he will show him his (arch-villain's) true *jāt* now, and lives up to his role by indulging in the most dastardly behaviour. *Jāt* is being used here with various nuances – of birth, breeding, moral behaviour, economic status, exogamy and endogamy and so on, all of which the audience would understand perfectly.

12 These rules can dictate the kind of food (e.g. food cooked in water rather than in oil) one Brahmin *jāti* can give to or take from another, and the marital relationships between them (e.g. which *jāti* is to be the wife-receiver and which the wife-giver).

13 *Jāti* (or its variants) is the word most in use in Indian vernaculars in talk about caste matters and the social relationships between groups, not *varṇa*.

14 Thus, 'In general, the paṇḍās [or family priests of Hardwar] fit the different castes and sub-castes into the varṇa scheme and then into an order which they consider determined from antiquity by criteria of purity. In interactional terms, they distinguish Brāhmans from Kṣatriya and Vaiśya, the twice-born from Śūdra and Śūdra from Untouchables' (Jameson 1976:25); the lower down the scale one goes, the greater the tendency to contest their classification.

15 See Manu 10. 51–6.

16 The *Vaikhānasa* Dharma Sūtra allows all four *varṇa*s to live off agriculture. The village situation seems to have been the same then as it is now, at least in southern India, where the Sūtra is thought to have been compiled.

17 See e.g. *India Today*, 31 July 1991, p. 84.

18 Although the same economic equations do not obtain in urban contexts, and there is greater scope for breaking the mould of the caste system here, similar psychological, social and religious pressures conspire to constrain aspirations of the low castes for betterment.

19 See Jameson 1976, Ch. 1.

20 B. S. Cohn in Marriot 1955, esp. p. 61.

21 'Dalit' is derived from *dalita* which is the passive past participle of the Sanskrit verb *dal*, to crush, break, split. It is ironic that Dalits refer to themselves by a name derived from a language which they generally regard has been traditionally used to oppress them.

22 For an ideological treatment see Ayrookuzhiel 1989.

23 By Harish Barisode. Quoted in Hiro 1982: 14.

24 By Waman Nimbalkar in Hiro 1982: 14.

25 For more detailed information about the untouchables and their experiences, see Joshi 1986.

26 See the *Satyārth Prakāś* (Upadhyaya 1956, Chs. 4 and 11).
27 For Dayananda, *dharma* means right morality or true faith or religion, or what is perceived as such. One's own religious faith is *dharma*, another's is his/her *mat*, i.e. view. For this usage, see e.g. the Preface to Ch. 13 of the *Satyārth Prakāś* (Upadhyaya 1956).
28 In general, the Sants have been called 'non-sectarian Vaiṣṇavas', but even in this context 'Vaiṣṇava' is too strong a description for some Sants. As to names straddling religious divides on occasion, remember that Islam had become a power in the land.
29 For a good account of the tradition and some of its chief figures, see SSDT. See also Hawley and Juergensmeyer 1988.
30 SSDT, pp. 155–6, from Linda Hess' article 'Kabīr's rough rhetoric'. The reference to the clay vessels probably takes in the popular belief that it was only after many births as an animal that one attained human birth from which alone salvation was possible. If this is the case, asks Kabīr, how can untouchability, from which there is supposed to be no access to salvation, be justified?
31 See David Lorenzen's article, 'The Kabīr-Panth and Social Protest' in SSDT, p. 281ff.
32 Judith M. Brown discusses some of these in the first three chapters of *Gandhi: Prisoner of Hope* (1989).
33 The articles are translated in Iyer (vol. 1), 1986: 66–72. But Gandhi also says that the varnashramic ideal 'is *dharma*, unalterable, universal and in harmony with Nature, as also a social arrangement; it is a pure outward form of Hinduism' (p. 71). Thus Gandhi implies, without expatiating, that there is no conflict between *varnāśrama dharma* and the *dharma* for which untouchability is an evil.
34 As Brown (1989) makes clear.
35 What was new here was not the name – Kabīr uses the term 'Harijan' to refer to enlightened souls – but its application.
36 See n. 17 – not to mention discrimination among Hindus outside India, including Britain; see e.g. *The Times*, 6 July 1990, an article entitled 'Apart, and hated?' (p. 14).
37 If one travels by train from the suburb of Chembur, say, to the Victoria terminus in Bombay, one may well marvel at the number of television aerials on the hovels in the slums along the way.
38 It is *possible* to translate *itihāsa* differently by dividing the compound thus: *iti-hāsa*, which can be rendered 'So? Derision!', i.e. So it could never have been! This is nearer in sense to the 'Once upon a time', but it won't catch on.
39 An artificial concept. Can there be a 'critical edition' of the kind of oral transmission that itihāsa represents? Similarly, it is futile to seek out 'the original text' of either epic. Critical editions of oral epics are the constructs of scholars; with variant readings and addenda as footnotes they give us an idea of the main story-line as it has developed over time in style and content. This has its uses as we shall see, but on a level which sacred narrative often transcends. For further details see Shastri 1976 and van Buitenen 1973.
40 As the *Rāmāyaṇa* says of itself, it is the best dharmic narrative (*dharmyam ākhyānam uttamam*; 1.4.11), though the epics do claim to foster

(traditional) ritual purity usually by a variant of the standard formula '*dharma-artha-kāma*'.

41 'This meter presents a very free pattern well suited to narratives', writes van Buitenen, going on to explain its versatility in the Introduction to his translation of the *Mahābhārata*, 1973, vol. 1, p. xxxviii.

42 The Poona critical edition consists of about 75,000 verses.

43 In a suggestive article comparing the origin, style and content of the two epics, Dr John Smith writes that while both works 'represent the end-products of processes of textual inflation' of oral songs about heroes, with Brahmins as their literary editors, 'the *Rāmāyaṇa* had been composed *in the manner of* an epic, rather than having evolved [like the *Mahābhārata*] as an epic'. In other words, the *Mahābhārata* is an epic proper, growing from the diffuse nucleus of an orally transmitted tradition via Brahminic literary redaction; the *Rāmāyaṇa*, on the other hand, may well have started out as a literary oral composition in epic style before it was subjected to Brahminic editing. This would explain the more sophisticated style of Vālmīki's poem, and the tendency in Hindu tradition to refer to the *Rāmāyaṇa* as '*kāvya*', i.e. 'poetry', whereas the *Mahābhārata* 'is most commonly referred to as *itihāsa*'. See John D. Smith, 'The two Sanskrit epics' in Hatto 1980 (vol. 1).

44 Hindu aristocracy traditionally traced its ancestry to either the solar or lunar lines of succession. The former was derived from Manu Vaivasvat, son of Vivasvat, the solar god. Ikṣvāku was the first king of this dynasty to rule at Ayodhyā. The lunar dynasty descended from Soma, the moon god, forbear of Puru and Yadu from whom sprang the two lineages of the lunar line.

45 The modern city of Ayodhya lies in the north-east of the main sub-continental land-mass on the bank of the Ghagara river which joins the Ganges north of Patna. This is where Hindus and Muslims have recently clashed over the location of their respective places of worship in connection with Rāma's supposed birthplace.

46 On the horse sacrifice and its implications for fertility, see O'Flaherty 1988: 7ff and 14ff.

47 One may recall that it was he who sponsored the great sacrifice with its holy quizz at which Yājñavalkya and Gārgī competed (see Chapter 4).

48 Generally, but not on incontrovertible evidence, believed to be the island south of India, formerly known as Ceylon but now called Sri Lanka.

49 Hanumān, as may be imagined, has become a favourite character in devotional Hindu traditions, both great and small, to the present day. He is regarded as a model of sometimes impetuous devotion to God in a Vaiṣṇava context, and is often worshipped himself as a luminous focus of the divine presence. For characteristics of devotion to Hanumān as bestower of strength, virility, etc. in popular Hinduism in a Śaiva context, see Wolcott 1978. For information on Hanumān and devotion to him, see also Lutgendorf (forthcoming).

50 There is a more detailed and analytic summary of the story in Whaling 1980, Ch. 2. See also Brockington 1984, Ch. 1. Whaling's book is useful for an understanding of the religious and theological implications of the Rāma story and its subsequent development in Hindu tradition; Brockington provides a good scholarly analysis of the language and

content of Vālmīki's *Rāmāyaṇa*. A major new English translation of the Rāmāyaṇa is being prepared under the general editorship of R. P. Goldman (1984 on). The story is also summarised in vol. 1.

51 According to the mythic conception of time in Hinduism (see Chapter 10), the main events of the *Rāmāyaṇa* are supposed to have occurred in the Dvāpara, or second of four world ages, when *dharma* is generally more respected than at the conjunction of the Dvāpara and the Kali or most degenerate age, when the story of the *Mahābhārata* is believed to have happened.

52 This will be somewhat expanded in Chapter 8.

53 A derivative of 'Kuru'; Kuru was a descendent of Bharata and a forbear of Śaṃtanu.

54 The episode of the dicing match presents a fine opportunity for a discussion of *dharma* (see Chapter 8).

55 van Buitenen 1973: p. xxiii.

56 A number of interpretive keys to the inner meaning of the Mbh have been offered by scholars. For a plausible example see Fitzgerald 1983.

57 For a translation of the *Gītā* see Deutsch 1968 and Johnson 1994.

58 For an anlaysis comparing a monistic and a dualistic interpretation in a Vedantic context, see the author's article in NCW.

59 Themes which are repeated in a key text of devotional Vaiṣṇavism, the *Bhāgavata* Purāṇa (see Chapter 6).

60 Thus Varāhamihira in his *Bṛhatsaṃhitā* (*c.* sixth century) refers to the height of Rāma images in an iconometric context (as does the *Matsya* Purāṇa, another quite early source). Reliefs exist from the late Gupta period (fifth to sixth century) illustrating incidents from the *Rāmāyaṇa* (e.g. in the famous *Daśāvātara* stone temple at Deogarh in Jhansi district). Among others, the Aḻvārs of south India (second half of the first millennium) are recorded as expressing religious devotion to Rāma.

61 Whaling 1980: 181.

62 Translated under the title *The Holy Lake of the Acts of Rāma* (Hill 1952); see alo *The Rāmāyaṇa of Tulasīdāsa* (Growse 1987). Other translations exist in English.

63 For a mainly literary analysis of Tulsīdās' works, see McGregor 1984, esp. pp. 109 (vol. VIII.6 of HIL); for a theological analysis see Whaling 1980, Part E.

64 Ghosh 1948: 76.

65 Sen 1920: 170; see Ch. 3 for a comparison between Vālmīki's *Rāmāyaṇa* and Krittivās' version.

66 Private communication.

67 Cf. the Sikh custom of prolonged recitation of the *Granth Sahib*, the main Sikh scripture. More on *pāṭha* elsewhere.

68 See *India Today*, 31 August 1988, p. 81ff.

69 For an authoritative treatment, see Smith 1991.

70 Pābūjī is also worshipped 'though to a statistically lesser extent, in Panjab, Sindh, Kacch, Malwa and Saurashtra' (Smith 1991: 5–6).

71 See Blackburn *et al.* 1989.

72 Smith 1976: 2.

6 THE VOICE OF TRADITION: FOLKLORE AND THE INTELLECTUAL HERITAGE

1 This follows the list given by Wendy O'Flaherty (TSSH, p. 5) about which she says quite properly: 'The unruly Puranas can be corralled into rough groups which can be ranged in chronological relationship to one another. All these dates . . . are based upon the often misguided conjectures of scholars; I have arranged them alphabetically to augment the false semblance of scientific efficiency'. Strictly speaking the *Harivaṃśa*, which we have encountered already, is not reckoned a Purāṇa, though it is Puranic in nature. There is not much point in trying to list the Upa-Purāṇas separately. For technical and other information on the Purāṇas, and a comprehensive list, see Rocher, *The Purāṇas*, 1986, vol. II.3 of HIL. For more on the misguided, or at least one-sided, conjectures of Purāṇa scholars see Bailey 1987: 106ff. It is Bailey's plausible contention that Purāṇa scholarship has hitherto been vitiated by a preoccupation with what may be called a diachronic approach, namely, taking a specific topic in a Purāṇa, e.g. a particular myth or didactic theme, and analysing the way it is treated both in that Purāṇa and other texts (including other Purāṇas) with a view to isolating the 'paradigm' myth and its 'edited' developments. Bailey rightly points out that this approach is usually based on unsupported assumptions, e.g. that the Purāṇas have no intrinsic cohesiveness as a rule, that they are a confused mass of material, and indeed that there is such a thing as a paradigm form of the myth or theme under consideration. We have seen from our discussion on the epics that this last assumption at least is very suspect indeed. Bailey argues for the addition of the 'synchronic' approach in Purāṇa studies whereby the Purāṇas are studied as a genre in their own right and on their own terms. We await the outcome of Bailey's continuing research with interest.

2 Brockington (abbr. PPP) 1987.

3 This is of particular interest to royal houses claiming Kṣatriya ancestry, and is one indication that the Purāṇas originated in a Kṣatriya context.

4 No doubt epic oral tradition also contains much folklore, but its main purpose is narrative. The Purāṇas as we have them, *par excellence* represent and store (Sanskritic) folkloric tradition.

5 Indeed, it is sometimes said that the Purāṇas collectively are the 'fifth Veda', especially for women and Śūdras.

6 For the Sanskrit text see VS, pp. 129–30.

7 On this movement, see e.g. Gelberg 1983, and Rochford 1985.

8 Original name, Abhaycaran De (1896–1977). ISKCON was established in New York in 1966.

9 O'Flaherty (TSSH, pp. 74–5) gives a translation of the story. This is a summary.

10 O'Flaherty, TSSH, p. 75.

11 Rameswaram is a holy place situated near the tip of the slim finger of land pointing towards Sri Lanka in south-east India.

12 For example, also in 1990, the following *pāṭhas* were held: the *Śiva* Purāṇa in London, the *Rāmāyaṇa* in Bolton. In 1989 the *Rāmāyaṇa* was read in Preston and Leicester. In 1988, the *Bhāgavata* Purāṇa was read

in Leicester and the *Rāmāyaṇa* in London. Though there were no caste or other barriers at these occasions, they seem to have been intended mainly for a particular linguistic group. Thus they were both religious and social occasions. For the information recorded here I am indebted to Mr J. Buhecha and Dr J. Hirst, of Cambridge and Manchester respectively.

13 Brockington, PPP, p. 130.

14 Rocher 1986: 70.

15 S. N. Dasgupta's monumental but somewhat dated treatment, *History of Indian Philosophy* (5 vols., 1922–55), may be consulted for details of the *ṣaḍ-darśanas* and other systems. More succinct is Hiriyanna 1932 (and later printings).

16 See Jha 1911; Keith 1921/1978; and D'Sa 1980.

17 They are also known as the *Bādarāyaṇa* Sūtras, the *Vedānta* Sūtras and the *Śārīraka* Sūtras. *Śarīra* means 'body'; the idea here is that these Sūtras teach about Brahman as being the goal of spiritual endeavour in its relationship to the world, i.e. as embodied by finite reality and indwelling the person.

18 A good comparative introduction to three major schools of classical Vedantic theology is given in Lott 1980.

19 Thus the well-known adage that the Vedantic tradition rests on a threefold textual support (called the *prasthāna-traya*), namely the Upaniṣads, the *Bhagavadgītā* and the *Brahma* Sūtras is inaccurate.

20 Hence *Vaiśeṣika* from *viśeṣa*, meaning particular, individual.

21 The writings of D. H. H. Ingalls, B. K. Matilal, Arindam Chakrabarti and J. Vattanky may be consulted as some of the best examples of these bridge-building attempts.

22 See Larson 1979.

23 On classical Yoga see Koelman 1970; Feuerstein 1979; and Whicher 1992.

24 For more information on this see Sharma 1982.

25 This could be an expensive affair if a number of priests were to be given handsome fees, animals procured for the sacrifice, etc.

26 Hence *kāma* can mean (unprincipled) passion, or lust, and is often used in this sense in Hindu tradition. In its generic sense it refers simply to desire which may be acceptable or unacceptable.

27 The traditional view is forcefully and comprehensively defended by R. P. Kangle in Part III of his *The Kauṭilīya Arthaśāstra*. The proponent of the other view is Thomas R. Trautmann; see his *Kauṭilya and the Arthaśāstra: A Statistical Investigation of the Authorship and Evolution of the Text* (1971).

28 I have modified Kangle's translation.

29 From the *Kāmasūtram* (with Jayamaṅgala's Commentary), Kashi Sanskrit Series No. 29, ed. G. D. Shastri, Benares, 1929, 1.2.11; see also 1.2.12.

30 The work of the great poet Kālidāsa (*c.* fourth to fifth century CE), for example, seems to have been so influenced, or at least draws on the same tradition.

7 THE VOICE OF EXPERIENCE

1 Quoted and translated from the *Dīghanikāya* 1.55 by Basham 1967: 299.

2 In the text this quotation is attributed to Bṛhaspati who is reputed to have

lived *c.* 600 BCE. In Purāṇic mythology Bṛhaspati is regarded as the Sage who taught the heresy of materialism to the antigods, and via them to humans, particularly the Buddhists and Jains. See O'Flaherty, OEHM, p. 124ff.

3 Clarified butter, i.e. rich food.

4 For the Sanskrit see Abhyankar 1924: 13–14 (with an original commentary in Sanskrit by the editor). Some of the remarks in this diatribe are thought to derive from Buddhist and Jain critiques.

5 See Ramanujan 1973: 116.

6 From the Bengali in *Sañcayitā*, the collected poems of Rabindranath Tagore, Visvabharati 6th edn, 1963, p. 510.

7 For a scholarly introduction and a translation, see Miller 1977.

8 In distinction from but analogous to the traditional Christian doctrine of the Trinity according to which there are three persons in one divine nature. On Rādhā's religious history see Miller 1977: 26ff.

9 Established traditions of commentary and manuscripts exist in every part of India. Its songs are an important part of the devotional music and literature of Orissa, Bengal, and South India. The songs were introduced into Kerala in the sixteenth century and are still sung in temples there. Portions of the poem represent one of the major subjects in medieval Rājput painting. . . . Because of the role of the songs in the nightly worship of the deity in Jagannātha Temple at Puri, they are venerated and sung throughout Orissa. Their performance is an essential aspect of Orissi dance, which has developed through the religious art of temple dancers called Maharis who still dance *Gītagovinda* songs before Jagannātha. . . . In Bengal, the singing of *Gītagovinda* is especially prominent at an annual spring fair in the village of Kenduli in Birbhum district, which is identified as the birthplace of Jayadeva in Bengali tradition. . . . In Nepal, the *Gītagovinda* is sung during the spring celebration in honor of the goddess Sarasvatī, in which worship is offered to the god of love, Kāmadeva, and his consort. . . . In much of South India the poem is sung according to the classical Karnatic system of music. . . . *Gītagovinda* songs . . . are sung by members of a drummer caste in the courtyard of Guruvayur and other temples of Kerala while certain rituals are being performed by brahman priests within the sanctuary.

(Miller 1977: ix–xii)

This is by no means an exhaustive survey.

10 See Vatsyayan 1968.

11 This helps explain, and perhaps to some extent justifies, the rationale of the popular Hindi movie. The Hindu aesthetic rationale lives on in these movies. Their underlying aim is not to be 'realistic' but to activate various sensibilities of the psyche and evoke different *rasa*s in the audience. Unfortunately this is often done in poor taste.

12 For a survey of Śiva mythology see EA, 2nd edn, 1981.

13 The Liṅgarāj Mahāprabhu temple in Bhubaneswar, Orissa, is a famous example of a 'mighty temple' dedicated to the *liṅga* (see Chapter 11). As is well known, the temple authorities generally deny access to western visitors, which is not a good advertisement of 'Hindu religious tolerance'. But westerners are welcome at many Śiva shrines in Benares, for example

(see Eck, BCL, passim), and at the Dakshineshwar temple on the east bank of the Hooghly, in the northern outskirts of Calcutta city. Here there is a row of twelve similar *liṅga* shrines.

14 This is '*māyā*'s' oldest meaning. The sense of 'illusion' is a derived one, especially in monistic traditions.

15 This is one of the main points of the story about Śaṃkara, one of the founding fathers of Advaita Vedānta.

16 For an idea of Roy's use of argument see Killingley 1982 (pamphlet, 48 pp.). For a more wide-ranging treatment of the way in which nineteenth-century Hindu 'conservatives' sought to defend their faith, see Young 1981. See also Lipner, 'A modern Indian Christian response' (Ch: 13) in Coward 1987.

17 I am aware that such terms as 'faith' and 'reason' have western connotations alien to their putative Hindu counterparts. But I submit that they carry core meanings which justify their bridging-use in this context.

18 Then why, we may ask, did the Naiyāyikas, Vedāntins, Buddhists, etc. engage in religious debate with each other? The answer seems to be (i) to clarify and justify their own positions with regard to their own clientele; (ii) to show that the opponent's view was inconsistent; and (iii) in the light of (i) and (ii) to make use of whatever common ground was available to win over the opponent.

19 By the time this book first went to press the mosque had been unilaterally destroyed by a mob of so-called Hindu *kar sevaks*, or workers in the divine service.

20 From the *Śrī Bhāṣya*, 1.1.1. For the full Sanskrit text, see SBR: 27–8.

21 *Satya/sat* also means 'steadfastness, order' (see Chapter 4); sometimes these different senses shade into one another.

22 Here various nuances of *satya* come into play, namely, order, truth-telling, unchanged, i.e. steadfast, reality.

23 *asato mā sad gamaya, tamaso mā jyotir gamaya, mṛtyor māmṛtaṃ gamaya.*

24 See Gispert-Sauch 1988.

25 It is also popular with Christians.

26 See n. 12.

27 EA, Ch. VI, provides a review.

28 Keshab Chandra Sen (1838–84), one of the best known socio-religious reformers from the westernised Bengali élite of the nineteenth century, sought to bolster the religion he founded (the New Dispensation) by this approach. He failed. For details see Damen 1983.

29 Hindu myths have always supplied a variety of functions, e.g. psychological (catharsis, vicarious participation, etc.), social (status-preserving, identity-forming and changing, conflict-resolving), moral (legitimating or condemning certain kinds of behaviour), religious (reinforcing, eroding, assimilating various patterns of orientation, salvation, etc.), as well as 'veridical', namely instructing in truth and about truth, as analysed and stressed here.

30 Most Hindu philosophical theories of error can be explained in these terms.

31 For a complementary analysis of Gandhi's understanding of truth, with attention given to its social and political dimensions, see Ambler 1989: 90ff. For an anthology of Gandhi's writings see Iyer 1986–7.

32 Gandhi had a maddening capacity to suit the action to the word, sometimes seemingly to the point of obstinacy. On one occasion he refused to allow his seriously ill but acquiescent son to be treated in a way that would violate his (Gandhi's) naturalistic beliefs. God would be pleased, he said, to see that he was treating his son exactly as he would treat himself in similar circumstances. The son recovered. Or consider Gandhi's adamant (and sometimes only theoretical) opposition to aspects of modern (western) technology and practice, e.g. modes of travel and production, and the teaching, legal and medical professions.

33 Thus it is officially in terms of the Advaitic vision that the Ramakrishna Order seeks to make sense of religious experience.

34 For an analysis of Ramakrishna's religious views see Neevel 1976: 53ff.

35 See the *Śrī Bhāṣya* 2.2.42 (in Thibaut's translation under 2.2.43).

36 For a discussion of Radhakrishnan's religious stance see Lipner 1989.

37 One continues to hear of agitations, expulsions and concessions in this regard. See e.g. *India Today*, 31 July 1987, p. 78ff.

38 The title of P. Mitter's book, subtitled 'History of European Reactions to Indian Art' (1977).

39 1.1.20–2.

40 The everyday word for child in the Sanskrit-based languages, namely *bāccā*, appears to have derived from this term.

41 Various editions and translations exist: e.g. *Upadeśa Sāhasrí: A Thousand Teachings*, translated into English with explanatory notes by Swami Jagadānanda (1970); Mayeda, *Śaṅkara's Upadeśasāhasrī* (critically edited text) 1973, and *A Thousand Teachings* (annotated English translation with Introduction) 1979; see also Alston 1990 (transliterated text, English translation and comment).

42 In fact, the prose section seems to contain conversations between a guru and two different disciples, the role of reasoning being emphasised more in the second dialogue.

43 On Ramana Maharshi see the writings of Arthur Osborne, and *Talks with Sri Ramana Maharshi (in 3 vols.)*, n.d., published by T. N. Venkaṭaraman. See also Godman 1985. For a good atmospheric account of the role of the guru, see Abhishiktananda (Henri le Saux) 1974, esp. the part entitled 'A Sage from the East'.

44 Thus in various denominations of the Swaminarayan religion, the spiritual leader, who also functions as a spiritual guide, is appointed by fixed, in some instances hereditary, procedures. But it is also possible for individuals in the movement to choose a personal guru from among a body of ascetics. See Williams 1984, esp. Chs 2–4.

45 Some Indian Christians are beginning to speak this way about Christ.

46 See e.g. Hirst 1983.

47 See Ambler 1989: 99.

48 In this discussion we have focused on the religious guru or spiritual preceptor. But Hindus also speak of gurus in other disciplines, e.g. in learning various skills, including the musical arts. We have noted that in the Mbh Droṇa was the Pāṇḍavas' guru in archery. It is common today for Indian musicians, for example, to have or acknowledge gurus in their specialisations. Here too there may be lines of succession, and the guru–disciple relationship often crosses sectarian divides. For an insight as to

how this may be so in the context of a contemporary classical singer, see *India Today*, 30 September 1988, p. 80ff.

8 A STORY WITH A TAIL

1 References follow the Sanskrit text of the Poona Edition. The translations here are my own. A continuous English translation exists in van Buitenen, vol. 2, book 2, of *The Mahābhārata* (1975).

2 At least, the 'critical edition' of the *Sabhā Parvan*.

3 Thus van Buitenen is pleading a special case when he contends that it makes no sense to appeal to Dhṛtarāṣṭra unless Vidura considers Yudhiṣṭhira bound to play by the rules of the *rājasūya* sacrifice. For this was a formal obligation to play a token game. The game in the story has gone well beyond this. In fact, the text makes use of this formal requirement to articulate the dharmic tension we are considering.

4 As the text indicates later, the blind king was sitting in a section of the assembly hall a little apart from where the match was being played; but close enough to be part of the overall scene.

5 For specialised knowledge on this see Hara 1986.

6 2.60.31; 'by abandoning what's proper to me', thus *svaguṇān visṛjya* (literally, 'by abandoning my qualities'). The expression '*svaguṇān*' indicates that *dharma* in both its moral and naturalistic senses is intended here. Draupadī does not wish to abandon virtuous behaviour, nor 'her qualities', namely, the role of Kṣatriya wife and mother to which she has been born. She does not wish to transgress by promiscuity or infidelity (to virtue or her natural calling) in any way. This is *strī-dharma*, the *dharma* of a woman/wife.

7 The text is more subtle than van Buitenen's rendering, namely 'Given that wives are the husband's chattels'. The text says rather that the wife is to be ruled by her husband, implying: but what if the husband does not rule himself?

8 This is where 'critical editions' fall short. They can fail to do justice to traditions of popular imagination and piety. In such tellings of the dicing episode Kṛṣṇa is already the supreme Lord.

9 See 2.62.22.

10 There was a further reason for this: when his legal father, Pāṇḍu, was prevented by a curse from producing offspring, Yudhiṣṭhira was fathered by the god Dharma, according to the law of levirate (see Chapter 5). This patrimony and the title to which it gave rise, namely 'King Dharma', remains an added background, somewhat ironical, twist to the story.

11 A subtle way of putting it, especially for Bhīma. *Vijita* can mean 'lost (by dicing)' and 'defeated'.

12 In this context the left thigh stands for the phallus. On this see OEHM, pp. 321ff. Note especially 'the Ṛg Veda calls the phallus a "boneless thigh" [RV.8.4.1]' (p. 334). In support, the Mbh compares Duryodhana's bared thigh to the soft stem of a plantain tree (*kadalīdaṇḍa*), which has no hard bark ('bone') like other trees. Duryodhana's insult is plain.

13 The sequel is recapitulative and structurally forced in places. It seems that it resulted from one incident being embroidered into two. The

original story may well have been as follows: Duryodhana and Yudhiṣṭhira gamble as described until the nineteenth throw, when Yudhiṣṭhira loses himself (and debatably, Draupadī). Draupadī is humiliated. Dhṛtarāṣṭra intervenes and restores the Pāṇḍavas' freedom. The final throw remains. This is played with exile for the losers as stake. Śakuni cheats as before, wins on Duryodhana's behalf, and the Pāṇḍavas retreat into exile.

14 See e.g. Smith 1991: 69–70.

15 'Sin' is strictly a theological term in Christian usage. It must be used with great caution when interpreting traditional Hindu religious thought. Our indebtedness to O'Flaherty's scholarship in OEHM notwithstanding, her indiscriminate use of 'sin' (see p. 7) and one or two other methodological flaws, e.g. the unwarranted slide from 'gods' (pl., lower case) to 'God' (sing., higher case) in discussion, can significantly mar the analyses.

16 See Bandyopadhyay and Mignon 1984. For *pāpī*, see Luke 5.8; *pāp*, Romans 6.2ff, 7.7ff; for the contrast between *dharmik* and *pāpī*, Luke 5.32; for that between *dharma* and *adharma*, Romans 12.21. For *pāpa* and *puṇya* as used by religious Hindus in Malayalam today, see Ayrookuzhiel 1983, esp. p. 139ff.

17 The balance between *pravṛtti* and *nivṛtti* varies.

18 Śaṃkara is here using the word 'Veda' in a restricted sense, to refer to the religion of sacrificial ritual.

19 See Sastry's translation, first published in 1897.

20 In the third book of the epic, the *Forest Book*, there is an incident where Bhīma accuses Yudhiṣṭhira of being powerless to control his addiction and Yudhiṣṭhira agrees. How this is to be interpreted or how it relates to the episode of the dicing match is a separate question, in view of the accretive nature of the story. In any case, the point is that though Yudhiṣṭhira's addiction to gambling may be regarded as a 'grand passion', the indulging of which has injected a dose of real tragedy into the overall narrative, it is certainly not intended to be pathological. If it were, we would be confronted with a very different story.

21 In later strata of the epic it seems that fate or deterministic forces are given a stronger hand.

22 We speak here of a 'vision', not necessarily of a particular historical form of Advaita. Radhakrishnan's view of Advaita is essentialist, not historicist. Glyn Richards makes this point in his essay 'Radhakrishnan's essentialist view of the nature of religion' in Parthasarathi and Chattopadhyaya 1989.

23 For more on this see the article cited in Ch. 3, n. 27.

24 Commentary on *Gītā* 9.25. This ethic of intention applied even to the performance of the traditional sacrificial ritual. The Vedāntins (Śaṃkara included) objected not to the general performance of the ritual, but to the '*yajña*-mentality' which implemented the ritual for selfish ends. The disinterested performance of the ritual continued to be vital, for this is how the maintenance of the universe and the stability of natural laws and society, the necessary condition for attaining liberation, could be ensured. Even the monistic Śaṃkara was a realist in this respect.

9 MORALITY AND THE PERSON

1 In Biderman and Scharfstein 1989.
2 10.30. See Manu 6.91–2. Cf. *Āpastamba* 1.8.6.
3 The *Mahānirvāṇa* Tantra, a late (eighteenth-century) Sanskrit text, says: 'Except for a divine purpose (*devoddeṣam*), injury must always be avoided. But if a man commits injury in accordance with precept, he is not tainted by evil (*pāpair na lipyate*)' (11.143).
4 For accounts of animal sacrifice and its extent, see Fuller 1992, esp. Chs 4 and 6.
5 See Tahtinen 1976.
6 Tahtinen 1976 makes this point: 'Non-violence did not come to be generally recognised so much as a reaction against injury done to men (e.g. in war), rather than as a profound opposition to the institutionalised killing of animals' (1976: 38).
7 By Tahtinen.
8 See under 'Prasthāna-vākyas' (Chapter 6).
9 For more on the Kānphaṭās, but especially for information on similar (Tantric) sects see Lorenzen 1972.
10 From Orr 1940: 16–17.
11 The hymn was sung at the 1896 session of the Indian National Congress.
12 On this see Hara 1973. Cf. e.g. *Śatapatha Brāhmaṇa* 2.2.1.21 (SBE edn): 'This (earth) is like a cow; she yields all desires for humans. The cow is a mother; this earth is like a mother – she supports human beings'.
13 BCL, pp. 38–9.
14 It is therefore perhaps ironic, as some have pointed out, that while India is the 'motherland' for Hindus, Sanskrit has acted as their 'father-tongue'. Traditionally Sanskrit has been the language used by twice-born males to assert orthodoxy and dominance.
15 'The entire Veda is the root of *dharma* as are the traditional wisdom and practice of those who know (the Veda), the conduct of the good, and the satisfaction of one's own (mind)'; *vedo 'khilo dharmamūlaṃ smṛtiśīle ca tadvidām, ācāraś caiva sādhūnām ātmanas tuṣṭir eva ca*. 2.6.
16 E.g. 12.110: 'A council of not less than ten, or at least of three, consisting of persons in good standing, should deliberate the *dharma* in question, and that decision should not be rejected'. In the next verse the text goes on to specify members of a council, taking care to mention experts in various kinds of reasoning; these comprise a logician (*hetuka*), a dialectician (*tarkī*) and a semanticist (*nairukta*). It seems that ideally all these members were to be Brahmins. Note also, e.g. 12.106: 'Only that person and no other knows *dharma* who studies the seers (i.e. the Veda) and the tradition on *dharma* (*dharmopadeśa*) by reasoning not opposed to Vedic teaching.'
17 Some scholars detect such reference; see e.g. Werner 1978. However, the texts cited seem more plausibly to be explained as making reference to post-mortem existences in eschatological worlds.
18 This is the burden, as I understand it, of Y. Krishan's article, 'The Vedic origins of the doctrine of karma' (1988: 51ff). Krishan argues plausibly for the view that in Saṃhitā religion the concept of *iṣṭāpūrta* refers to accumulated sacrificial merit carried over to the hereafter, and as such

'provided the core and the framework from which the classical concept of Karma developed'. According to Krishan, Saṃhitā religion entailed belief in rebirth in heaven in a glorious body (see p. 52). This is rebirth in an eschatological context, however. Further, I do not go along with the tenor of Krishan's remarks on the difference between Saṃhitā and Upaniṣadic teaching about the ethical concept of good and evil. We have broached this topic in Chapter 8.

19 See e.g. RV 5.4.10, 8.27.16.

20 For an apologia of the doctrine of karma as 'the solution offered by Hinduism to the great riddle of the origin of suffering and the inequalities which exist among men in this world' see R. N. Dandekar's article in Morgan 1953.

21 In this connection, there is talk sometimes of karmic recompense occurring in two ways: as *dṛṣṭa-phala* or 'visible fruit' and as *adṛṣṭa-phala* or 'invisible fruit', the precise time and manner of the maturation (*vipāka*) of such fruit being a matter of opinion.

22 See Canto 4, Ch. 26ff.

23 For a review of modern religious accounts of different aspects of the karma doctrine see K. Klostermaier, 'Contemporary conceptions of karma and rebirth among North Indian Vaiṣṇavas' in Neufeldt 1986. Note that in essence the article consists of a summary of the views of upper-caste Vaiṣṇava leaders and thinkers, namely interpreters of a normative orthodoxy, writing for a special number of the Hindi devotional monthly Kalyāṇa (which has a circulation of over 150,000 copies per month), entitled 'The Beyond and Rebirth'; vol. 43 January 1969. This contains over 700 pages with 280 individual contributions, 'all in Hindi'. The author writes that

> Apparently the volume is the fruit of years of systematic effort. The (then) living leaders of all major *saṃpradāyas* and a great number of well-known scholars contributed essays on all aspects of the topic. . . . [The volume] is designed to demonstrate that the belief in karma and rebirth is not only an integral part of Hindu devotionalism, but an organic part of a world view, intrinsically meaningful and plausible . . . quite often [the contributors] state that belief in rebirth is the central article of faith in the Vedas, Upaniṣads, Smṛtis, Purāṇas, and Śāstras. (p. 85)

The author has summarised the data under ten headings: death, the next world, rebirth, time, karma, the devotee and liberation, devotional practices designed to reach the other world, rites for the dead, Yama and his realm, and birth as a ghost.

24 *The Complete Works of Sri Aurobindo* (Centenary edition), Pondicherry, vol. 16, p. 131.

25 To cite Dandekar, see n. 19. For two surveys see Ayrookuzhiel 1983, Ch. 6, and Gosling 1974.

26 *Aurobindo*, op. cit., vol. 16, p. 86. This is in keeping with Aurobindo's religious vision of the one underlying Spirit hierarchically 'involving' in all grades of being and progressively 'evolving' towards a collective supermind.

27 In terms of the doctrine, the growing human population of the world can be conveniently explained by positing traffic (in the direction of increasing

numbers of human beings) between human and non-human forms of life not only in this world but also between this and other worlds. On a famous nineteenth-century Hindu intellectual's understanding of evolution, see Killingley 1990: 151–79. For accounts of Aurobindo's, Radhakrishnan's and Vivekananda's views on karma and rebirth see Neufeldt 1986, Chs 1–3.

28 In some traditional orthodox accounts only 'twice-born' men in good dharmic standing are eligible for salvation, but in many *bhakti* traditions this crippling criterion is not endorsed: salvation is open to all who take recourse to the deity.

29 This is sometimes expressed by calling human existence the *karma bhūmi* (field of action) as opposed to other forms of life as *bhoga-bhūmi* (field of experiencing). However, the belief in *krama mukti* also exists. According to this ancient belief one can pass on to liberation from a heavenly world once one's good karma has been expended. This is the exceptional variant to the general traditional teaching mentioned earlier. As already noted, the basic belief in karma and rebirth is open-ended in complex ways, and contains many elements which may or may not be regarded as essential, according to differing views of individuals.

30 So the *Aitareya* Āraṇyaka says:

> The spirit is most manifest in the human being (*puruṣe tvevavistarām ātmā*), for he is best endowed with intelligence. He speaks . . . he recognises . . . he knows the future, he knows the visible and the invisible; being mortal he desires the immortal. But these others, the animals, they know only hunger and thirst. They don't speak what they have known . . . they don't know the future . . . they exist only within the scope of their [empirical-] knowledge (*ta etāvanto bhavanti yathāprajñāṃ hi saṃbhavāḥ*; II.3.2).

31 See *KauUp* 1.4; 2.15. See also the story of King Yayāti in the Mbh 1.76ff.

32 See *KaṭhUp* I.1.8, BĀUp VI.4.12.

33 A Sanderson, 'Śaivism and the tantric traditions' in Sutherland *et al.* 1988: 664–5.

34 Sanderson (1988: 691) mentions how with respect to the Kashmiri Śaiva Siddhānta.

35 Quoted from Weiss, '*Caraka Saṃhitā* on the doctrine of karma' in O'Flaherty 1980: 95.

36 See e.g. RV 7.104.3.

37 The three *guṇas* are used to characterise almost every aspect of life. Thus it is still not uncommon among certain sections of society to describe foodstuffs as either sattvic (e.g. nuts, some fruits and vegetables, boiled rice, perhaps milk), rajasic (e.g. spices, onions, garlic, all or most kinds of meat), or tamasic (e.g. liquor and beef).

38 For this reason R. C. Zaehner's rendering of *buddhi* by 'soul' in his much-used translation of the *Bhagavadgītā* is quite misleading. The soul in the western religious understanding is essentially spiritual whereas *buddhi* as prakritic is essentially non-spiritual.

39 For an analysis of this idea see FOT, esp. Ch. 7; see also Carman 1976.

40 An old idea. 'Just as a person gets rid of old clothes and puts on new

ones, so the embodied self gets rid of old bodies and takes on new ones' (*Gītā* 2.22).

41 For careful treatments of the belief in rebirth and/or karma at the levels of (i) experience and (ii) theory, see Stevenson 1974 and Reichenbach 1990.

10 MODES OF RECKONING TIME AND 'PROGRESS'

1 There is an account of different traditional views about time in Balslev 1983.

2 The Sanskrit word for one who experiences, *bhoktṛ*, can also be translated as 'eater'.

3 For a more detailed account see Zimmer 1962, Ch. 1, esp. pp. 13ff.

4 The bulk of which Kane (1930–62) assigns to a period between the seventh to tenth centuries CE; see vol. 5, Part II, 1962, p. 876ff., and p. 910.

5 The view of the *Viṣṇudharmottara* is quoted in Banerjea 1956: 229.

6 Quoted from Zimmer 1962:15.

7 Further, in Sanskrit, the verbs in the deliberative statement are in the optative mood (*vidhi liṅ*) which presupposes freedom to act. See FOT, Ch. 5.

8 See Puthiadam 1973.

9 For an eloquent but non-theological treatment of this idea in Vaiṣṇava context, see Kinsley 1979.

10 See also our comments on *līlā* in Ch. 5.

11 Also called Kṛṣṇa-Caitanya, Caitanya Mahāprabhu, and Gaurāṅga ('Fair-limbed'). These are religious names; his given name was Viśvambhara Miśra.

12 See e.g. the *Āpastamba* Dharma Sūtra, I.5.17.30: *dhenvanaḍuhor bhakṣyam*.

13 In a joint family parents have traditionally lived in the home of a son (preferably the eldest).

14 The reality of monastic practice can be very different. For a readable account of contemporary monastic practice and the life-histories of several ascetics in a holy Indian city, see HML.

15 The notion that *tapas* is a kind of physical resource which may be built up and then used for transformative purposes seems to have been derived from early Vedic ideas about the transformative properties of the sacrificial fire. See Vesci 1985.

16 Chs. 277ff.

17 Her story, often idealised and textually distorted to suit modern prejudices, appears in popular forms, from children's comics to magazine articles.

18 See Smith 1976: 4ff.

19 Cf.

> 'What is the test of a true *sadhu* [holy man]?' [the interviewer asked Kamakara Brahmacharin]. Kamakara answered, 'When you are not excited when you see a nude woman . . . . Then you will see the deity; then you will become a true *sadhu*. If you spend semen by lady or hand, then you will not get concentration.' This 'test of a true *sadhu*'

represents an ancient folk tradition still popular among the less sophisticated ascetics.

(HML, p. 58)

We may add that it applies no less to sophisticated ascetics.

20 In this context, sexual intercourse by virtue of its churning motion is regarded as a prime means of generating spiritual energy or heat, i.e. *tapas*.

21 Thus *saṃskṛta* (of which 'Sanskrit' is the anglicised form) refers to language at its most refined.

22 The number dealt with by Pandey (1969).

23 At the same time, the practice of giving meaningless or diminutive nicknames is widespread among the middle and upper classes. Not surprisingly, Śūdras do not fare well in the prescriptions of the ancient authorities; they are to be given names consonant with their low status. Even today one comes across such names/euphemisms as 'Bhūtnāth' (which may be translated as 'Lord of the Ghosts' or perhaps, more acceptably, 'Lord of the Elements') and 'Maṅgal' ('Auspicious') among the low castes.

24 It is interesting to note, however, that the ears of some Brahmin groups are still pierced as a ritual requirement for priestly ministry.

25 For traditional rulings on inter-caste marriage see Chapter 5.

26 Many ancient texts also recognise the *svayaṃvara* form of marriage; here the woman, with her parents' permission, freely chose her husband-to-be, whom she then duly married. In the story, Sāvitrī chooses to marry Satyavat in this way. *Svayaṃvara* was usually followed by royalty and the aristocracy.

27 This rite was generally regarded as canonically completing the marriage, and is usually performed by circling the fire.

28 For a discussion on the historicity of Puranic dynastic accounts see Rocher 1986:115–27, namely 'The Purāṇas as Historical documents'.

11 THE SACRED AND ITS FORMS

1 Hooker 1989. There are many useful comments and observations about religious Hinduism in this book.

2 On the Ganges, see e.g. Eck, 'Gaṅgā: The goddess in Hindu sacred geography' in Hawley and Wulff 1984.

3 There is a fine description of the scene in Zimmer 1962: 112ff.

4 For reasons stated in Chapter 2, there is only conjectural evidence for cultic worship, including religious structures, in the Indus civilisation.

5

> The temple at Tanjore . . . [at about the turn of the first millennium CE] had an income of 500 lb. troy of gold, 250 lb. troy of precious stones, and 600 lb. troy of silver, which was acquired through donations and contributions and in addition to the revenue from hundreds of villages. As temple staff, it maintained in considerable comfort 400 women . . . (*devadasis* or 'female servants of the deity'), 212 attendants, 57 musicians and readers of the texts, quite apart . . . from the many hundreds of priests who also lived off the temple.
>
> (Thapar 1966: 210–11)

Even today some temples are very wealthy. As to temple functionaries, it was estimated about a decade ago that there were approximately 1,500 people with ritual duties in the great temple complex of Jagannātha at Puri; see Marglin 1985.

6 See Michell 1977, esp. Chs 3ff.

7 Temple finials are called *śikhara*s or crests, and temple roofs can be contoured to look like a mountain range.

8 We have seen that low castes often have their own priests.

9 BCL, p. 21; see also Jameson 1976, e.g. Ch. 3.

10 Traditionally, the *purohita* was the personal priest and adviser of the king and a person of great influence. Today the term refers to the family priest.

11 Not to be understood in the sense used by orthodox Christianity. Hindus themselves, alas, often blithely use the word 'idol' to refer to their sacred images. But they should realise that the term is so fraught with tendentious western associations as to be quite unsuitable in this context.

12 These terms may be nuanced differently but their underlying meaning is the same.

13 For a fairly detailed description of icon ritual at a large temple, namely, the Jagannāth temple at Puri, see Marglin 1985, Appendix 1 to Ch. 6. Fuller (1992, Ch. 5) shows how the idea of kingship, without its political trappings, is still so much a part of the Hindu religious mentality.

14

> In older temples, one quite often finds so-called *svayamvyaktā mūrtis*, images not fashioned by human hands but miraculously sent by God himself: washed up on the seashore, carried to a place by a river, or found by someone instructed in a dream. Local tradition often tells that a *ṛṣi* [sage] received the image of the temple directly from the deity.
>
> (SH, p. 295)

Images, like volcanoes, may be extinct, dormant or active; that is, some are perceived as no longer harbouring the presence of the deity, others are viewed as not very effective sources of divine power, while yet others – which may not be much to look at – are related to as powerhouses of divine activity and largesse.

15

> *Prasada* is the material symbol of the deities' power and grace. During *puja*, different substances – ash, water, flowers, food, or other items – have been transferred to the deity, so that they have been in contact with the images or, as with food, have been symbolically consumed by the deity in its image form. As a result, these substances have been ritually transmuted to become *prasada* imbued with divine power and grace, which are absorbed or internalized when the *prasada* is placed on the devotee's body or swallowed. Whenever *puja* is concluded by waving a camphor flame, taking in the *prasada* is a process that replicates and consolidates the transfer of divine power and grace through the immaterial medium of the flame. Hence the flame and *prasada* together divinize the human actor to achieve the identify between deity and worshipper (including nonparticipatory devotees), which completes the transformation initiated by the offerings and services made during *puja*.
>
> Fuller 1992: 74

Of course this identification is temporary, which is one reason for the repetitiveness of *pūjā*. Fuller goes on to describe how the priest distributes *prasāda* hierarchically in temple-worship (79ff).

16 BCL, p. 20.

17 See AEV 1954; Bhandarkar 1929; Jaiswal 1967.

18 On Śiva's origins see Chapter 2 and EA.

19 For information on Gaṇeśa, see Courtright 1985.

20 Gaṇeśa is also called Gaṇapati (same meaning) especially in western India, and Piḷḷaiyār in the South.

21 Courtright (1985) gives a description.

22 See Courtright 1985: 4 and elsewhere.

23 For these various Tantric techniques see the works cited of Gupta *et al.* 1979.

24 Even early Vedic religion seems exceptionally to have sanctioned human sacrifice (the *puruṣa-medha*).

25 Brown 1974: 185–6. On the Goddess see e.g. Hawley and Wulff 1984; Kinsley 1987. Part II of SF is on Kālī.

26 Thus Openshaw (n. 10 of article cited), has pointed out that

> In some parts of Bengal, for example the Santiniketan area, the word 'bāul' has largely positive connotations. Here the right to proclaim one's identity as 'bāul' is at times a matter of acrimonious dispute, often associated with the perceived economic gain to be derived from this identity. [This is because Santiniketan is a centre of Bāul studies; it was Rabindranath Tagore's rural retreat and is the site of the University he founded. Tagore romanticised the Bāuls.] However, in many other parts of Bengal, for example in parts of Nadia and Mushidabad districts, the word 'bāul' is most usually a term of abuse, and is owned to, if at all, in only certain limited contexts.

27 Miller and Wertz 1976: 7–8. Or consider

> the Cave of Amarnath, the Eternal Lord. The cave lies thirteen thousand feet up the eighteen-thousand-foot Amarnath Mountain, some ninety miles northeast of Srinagar, and is made holy by the five-foot ice *lingam* . . . which forms there during the summer months [the mountain is impassable in winter]. The *lingam*, it is believed, waxes and wanes with the moon and reaches its greatest height on the day of the August full moon: on this day the pilgrimage arrives.
>
> (Naipaul 1964: 163)

28 AEV, pp. 94–5. Predominantly purple *śālagrāmas* are often reckoned to be inauspicious.

29 See AEV, pp. 54ff. Nor must it be thought that veneration for the Ganges is universal among religious Hindus. The same survey maintains that only 25 out of 187 believers questioned from among the five caste groups – they were mostly Nairs – acknowledged that 'the Ganges is a *puṇya nadī* [sacred river], that bathing in it removes *pāpam* [sin, guilt, impurity], and that for their dead it is a means of getting *moksha*' (p. 49). This is surprising, but can hardly be taken as representative of Hindu belief. Note the urbanised context of the survey (a minority context in India), and the fact that the course of the Ganges is far from Chirakkal. Jameson's account (1976) paints a very different picture.

30 For an account of the range and types of spirit-possession in popular Hinduism, see Fuller 1992.
31 For an evocative description of one kind of *kīrtan* in a rural setting see Dimock and Levertov 1967: xiff. For an analysis of how devotional singing can reinforce traditional socio-religious inequalities in an urban context see Fuller 1992: 158–63.
32 *The Vishnu Sahasranama* (with various commentaries) (Sastry 1927: viii–ix).

12 MEANS, WAYS AND ENDS

1 Some Hindus, not least in some countries of the West, also tend to stress another, lesser motif: Rāma's return with Sītā to Ayodhyā, after defeating Rāvaṇa.
2 After deaths occurred in a stampede during an earlier Kumbha Melā, elephants are no longer allowed where crowds gather as the climax approaches.
3 See Robinson 1983.
4 *putul pūjo kare nā hindu, kāṭh māṭi diye gaḍā; mṛnmay mājhe cinmay dekhe, haye jāy ātmahārā.*
5 The word is derived from the root *yuj* (to bond, yoke) which has an ancient Sanskrit pedigree. It is found in this context in RV, e.g. 5.81.1: 'The wise integrate the mind, integrate spiritual insight . . . (*yuñjate mana uta yuñjate dhiyo viprāḥ*)'; in the Upaniṣads, e.g. *BĀUP* IV.3.10: 'There are no chariots there, no (animals) harnessed to chariots . . . (*na tatra rathāḥ na rathayogāḥ . . . bhavanti*)'. Whicher (1992, Ch. 1) shows how the semantic emphasis of this term develops from signifying the yoking of external things like hymns, the 'gods' and the *yajña*, animals and carts, etc. to an internal joining (e.g. the union between the senses), to a method or way of union or integration. A development only of semantic emphasis has been traced here; in some instances all three nuances may be present simultaneously.
6 The eight limbs are as follows: (i) *yama*, restraining oneself by the practice of various virtues, e.g. abstaining from injury to living beings, from lying, theft, etc.; (ii) *niyama* or practising such observances as cleanliness, contentment with one's lot, and mindfulness of the Lord; (iii) *āsana* or physical posture(s) conducive to concentration; (iv) *prāṇāyāma*, i.e. 'breath control' to focus concentration; (v) *pratyāhāra* or sense withdrawal, both physically (so that the senses are not excited by their usual stimuli) and mentally (to the point of being detached from sense-gratification); (vi) *dhāraṇā* or focusing the concentration; (vii) *dhyāna* or mentally assimilating the object of concentration; and (viii) *samādhi*, identifying with the object of concentration to the point of perfect mind control, and subordinating the mind to the purposes of spirit or *puruṣa* within. The aspirant is then a perfect yogī, in full self-mastery, and empowered to radiate the *puruṣa* as a beneficent influence to all and sundry. As one progresses in this discipline, the various 'limbs' function together, so much so that the adept is perfectly co-ordinated in mind and body.
7 For an introduction to different kinds of Hindu *yoga*, see Feuerstein 1975.

8 This does not mean that the religion of the traditional sacrificial ritual is dead.

> In February 1962, Indian newspapers carried numerous articles describing measures to meet a predicted *aṣṭāgraha*, an astronomical conjunction of earth, sun, moon, and five planets. The astrologers were unanimous in considering it an extremely evil omen, possibly the harbinger of the end of the world. . . . Despite the fact that, astronomically speaking, the *aṣṭāgraha* was not quite accurate, millions of Hindus were frankly worried, expecting a ghastly catastrophe. Many sold all their belongings and went to Prayāga, Kāśī, or some other holy place, from which one goes directly to heaven at the time of death or one can attain *mokṣa*. The rich engaged thousands of pandits and Brahmins to organize Vedic *yajñas* that would go on for weeks, reciting millions of Vedic *mantras*. The dreaded event passed without a major disaster.
>
> (SH, p. 148)

What happened? The *yajña*s worked, of course.

9 Some of these ideas are expressed in SSV, and in Werner 1978. See also Panikkar 1977.

10 Thus in RV 1.19.2 Agni's unexcelled splendour is lauded while in 1.52.13 it is Indra who is said to have pervasive greatness. In 1.67.3 and 6.1.5 Agni sustains all; in 2.13.6 and 2.17.5, for example, it is Indra to whom this power is attributed, while in 2.33.9 Rudra is the mighty one. In 10.168.2 Vāyu is sovereign, whereas in 10.170.4 Sūrya is the overlord. And so on. For a suggestive treatment, among other things, of theological conflict among the makers of Vedic religion, see Matas 1991.

11 For example, RV 6.28.5: 'I long for Indra with heart and mind'.

12 Smith 1976: 68.

13 Theologically yes, but in popular piety the force of this monotheism may be blunted by the compulsion to relate to the underlying One 'departmentally'; thus the devotee might believe that protection from obstacles can be gained only by worship of Gaṇeśa.

14 Perhaps the problem lies in translating *bhakti* as 'devotion' which connotes affection. A more acceptable translation might be 'attachment' (see later); one can be attached to the deity in various ways (not necessarily by affection) and for various reasons. But who is to say that propitiation notwithstanding, there is no element of genuine affection in folk religion generally, especially when it is based on a feudal, familiar relationship? So I have followed the convention and translated *bhakti* as 'devotion', for the norm and ideal of *bhakti* entail affection. And the popular practice of *pāṭha*s etc. with their regular glosses, inculcates this. But I am prepared to concede that there have been (and perhaps are) in Hinduism, as in other great religions, cults of a personal deity in which all sorts of attitudes and emotions ('affection' in the technical sense) dominate, notably greed and fear, but in which genuine affection (in the conventional sense) is conspicuous by its absence. Further, 'devotion' is an attitudinal term no less than an 'affective' one, as is *bhakti*.

15 There is a nearly complete translation in *Sources of Indian Tradition*,

vol. I, (de Bary 1958: 327–30). For an elaborate treatment from a Hindu point of view see Tyagisananda 1972.

16 *guṇa.māhātmya.āsakti-rūpa.āsakti-pūjā.āsakti-smaraṇa.āsakti-dāsya.āsakti-sakhya.āsakti-vātsalya.āsakti-kāntā.āsakti-ātma.nivedana.āsakti-tan-maya.āsakti-parama. viraha.āsakti-rūpā+ekadhā+api+ekādaśadhā bhavati*. Note that *bhakti* is here described as 'attachment' (*āsakti*) of various kinds, but as sūtra 2 makes clear (see below), it is an attachment based on devotion.

17 Thus the root has a sexual use, as in *bhaja mām*, 'share in/with me', i.e. make love to me.

18 It is not clear if there are corresponding Śaiva and Śākta terms; perhaps *Maheśvara/Maheśa* (Great Lord) and *(Mahā-)Devī* (Great Goddess).

19 I am not happy then with the way that Hardy has deployed his distinction between 'intellectual bhakti' and 'emotional bhakti' (Hardy 1983). According to this distinction there is little if any emotion involved in 'intellectual' *bhakti*. Hardy speaks of a '"basic distinction" between an intellectual and an emotional variety of bhakti' (p. 38), the *Gītā, Viṣṇu* Purāṇa and Rāmānuja representing the former and the *Bhāgavata Purāṇa* 'mysteriously' heralding the latter. Hardy has a point, but it has been forced. The *bhakti* of the *Gītā* for example (which Hardy admits is genuine devotion) is hardly unemotional. It is difficult to see how in a number of places Arjuna's words may be understood as lacking in emotion: e.g. 'Explain again, in detail, Kṛṣṇa, your manifest power (*vibhūti*) . . . for listening to the nectar (of your words) I just cannot have enough' (10.18), or (during the revelation of the Universal Form in Ch. 11) 'Bowing humbly, prostrating my body, I beg of you, the Lord to be adored, to bear with me as a father his son, a friend his friend, a lover his beloved, O God' (11.44; surprisingly this chapter doesn't figure in Hardy's discussion). There are different kinds of emotion involved here, especially awe and wonder, but to call this 'intellectual' *bhakti* seems a misnomer. Even the intellectual Rāmānuja describes the *bhakti* he advocates as 'thrilling at being an appendage of the plenary Lord' (*aśeṣaśeṣataikarati*). In terms of Hardy's distinction, perhaps a fuller discussion of what is meant by 'emotional' and indeed by 'intellectual' is called for. Certainly the effusive *bhakti* Hardy deals with (the *bhakti* of Separation) is quite distinctive, though this does not mean that other forms of *bhakti* are not emotional, even characteristically so. At this point a well-known scholastic distinction may be helpful. In order to do justice to the variegated phenomenon of *bhakti qua devotional* (the reason for this emphasis will soon become clear), it may be appropriate to regard the concept, not as univocal, but as *analogical*. In other words, there are various degrees and kinds of *bhakti* but in such a way as to allow the term to cover all in a core-sense, as suggested above. In Hardy's discussion the term *bhakti* tends to become *equivocal*: this has the effect of throwing the distinctiveness of his subject matter into great relief. But I do not think that my methodological objection affects the substance of Hardy's monumental work.

20 There are minor variants of this list.

21 For some idea of the argument see Lipner 1978. See also Chapter 10.

22 Sometimes myths speak of *asuras* as enemies of the *deva*s; neither camp

is irrevocably good or evil. This is why we have generally translated *deva* by 'god' and *asura* by 'anti-god'.

23 An account of their practices, based on sound knowledge, is given in John Master's novel, *The Deceivers* (1955).

24 Though, for obvious reasons, Kālī does seem to attract such votaries. Here is a modern example mentioned by Naipaul in *India: A Million Mutinies Now* (Naipaul 1990). Naipaul interviewed a band of gangsters who were not averse to murder. They realised that they were outcasts in Hindu society. 'Though outcasts, they were religious. They felt protected by the deity of the temple, Santoshi Mata. She was a version of Durga or Kali, the goddess of power. The leader said with perfect seriousness, "She's the goddess of the victory of good over bad"' (p. 74).

25 On the evidence available there seems to have been a *bhakti* cult of Brahmā, and of Sūrya who manifests as the sun.

26 In 1.3 the *Bhāgavata* Purāṇa lists twenty-two *avatāras*.

27 See TVSS.

28 From Ramanujan 1973: 134.

29 From VS, p. 289–90; van Buitenen's translation.

30 Visualisation can play a very important part in Tantric ritual too. Whether one can call this an expression of *bhakti* is debatable; it seems to have a different rationale in Tantra. But in the context of ritual and worship, visualisation is a distinctive Hindu technique. From his point of view Abhinavagupta comments on it as follows:

> [The officiant] should [mentally] install [=*nyāsa*] the three Bhairavas [consorts] and the three goddesses as follows: Bhairavasadbhāva on the central [lotus], Ratiśekhara on the [lotus to his] right, and Navātman on the [lotus to his] left; then Parā [white] as the full moon on the central [lotus], Parāparā on [her] right, red and somewhat ferocious but not terrifying, and Aparā on the [lotus of the] cuspid on her left, terrifying and red-black. He should then subject them to the same double six-fold *mantra*-installation to which he has already subjected his body. Thereafter he may contemplate [the goddesses in detail, visualizing] whichever of their desiderative forms may be appropriate, i.e. with two, four, six or more arms, according to which of the various goals of worship he is pursuing; and [in that case] he should variously dispose in their left and right hands such attributes as the skull-bowl, the trident, the skull-staff, the gestures of generosity and protection, and the jar [of nectar].
>
> In reality these goddesses are consciousness itself. They are therefore embodied as everything that exists [rather than in any single form]. Consequently, if they are to bestow liberation [through their worship] they must be [contemplated as being] essentially this same, unlimited, uninflected consciousness.
>
> (Sanderson 1990: 64, 67)

I have omitted the Sanskrit insertions. Some examples in this essay indicate how vivid the visualisation can be. The Goddess in her various forms is mentally 'installed' in the initiate's body, with the intention of identifying with her ultimately. Thus the initiate passes from being a living temple to a living icon. We can also mention here another Tantric device called the *yantra*. The *yantra* is a symmetrical diagram, usually consisting of an outer square perimeter with 'entrances' bounding a design of concentric circles and triangles (some inverted) and arcs resembling the petals of a lotus. Everything converges on the centre point.

For the *sādhaka* the *yantra* is a ritual instrument for identification with the Goddess. Different features of the *yantra* represent corresponding aspects and associates of the Goddess. By entering through one of the perimeter doors, the *sādhaka* projects himself, ritually purified, into sacred space and time. Progressively he mentally installs, by the use of certain *mantras*, aspects of the Goddess in his person, with the help of various objects (e.g. wine, leaves, gram), with or without recourse to a *śakti*, i.e. a non-menstruating female, in attendance. The idea is to unite his person, the Goddess and the *yantra* in its various aspects, in an experience of identity culminating in the centre point of the *yantra* which represents the essence of the Goddess. Different *yantras* are resorted to for different purposes, whether temporal or liberative. The *yantra* is a device for dissolving time and controlling its effects. For a description of *yantra*-implementation in recent times see F. A. Marglin 1985, Ch. 8.

31 This is not to be confused with the berating that folk gods and goddesses are sometimes subjected to when they fail to deliver the goods, though occasionally the dividing line is blurred.

32 Translation taken from TSSH, p. 167.

33 A. K. Ramanujan 1973: 81.

34 An example of such a hater is King Śiśupāla whose death at the hands of Kṛṣṇa is recounted in the MBh 2.37ff. Śiśupāla reviles Kṛṣṇa mercilessly and, the text suggests, inexorably, as if he wanted to be slain by Kṛṣṇa so that his spirit could unite with its divine source. Kṛṣṇa duly cuts off his head, and a marvellous radiance issues from Śiśupāla's body. 'Then it saluted the lovely-eyed Kṛṣṇa, revered by the worlds, and entered him' (2.42.23). The theologians can have a field-day with 'saluted' (*vavande*) in that context.

35 TSSH, p. 143.

36 Quoted from J. B. Carman 1976: 196.

37 The lyric is taken from Dimock and Levertov 1967: 56.

38 For a discussion see Carman 1976: 214ff.

39 Ramanujan 1973: 105. Dasimayya mentions the traditional focuses for auspicious or efficacious worship.

40 Kumar 1984: 134.

41 A poem by Govinda-dāsa (Dimock and Levertov 1967: 23). The pandits divide the *bhakti* of separation into two broad phases: *vipralambha* or separation and *saṃbhoga* or union.

> *Vipralambha* is in its turn divided into four main subsections: (a) *pūrva-rāga*, in which condition desire is aroused in each of the lovers by sight and by listening to descriptions of each other; (b) *māna* . . . in which the girl feels that . . . her pride has been injured, especially because her lover has been paying attention to other women; (c) *premavaicittya* . . . in which simultaneous satisfaction and pain of longing are present; (d) *pravāsa*, the pain of separation aroused in the girl because of her lover's departure. . . . These categories are further subdivided.

By this time no doubt real devotion is well and truly lost. (Quotation taken from Dimock and Levertov 1967: xix; see also Hardy 1983.)

42 But some interpret even disembodied kaivalya not as a relationless state, but as final separation from *prakṛti* and rebirth. In this view liberated *puruṣas* may interrelate.

43 See Sanderson's mapping of Śaiva Tantra in Sutherland *et al.* 1988.

44 This must still be distinguished from experience in lesser heavens in which one may reside for a time as a reward for good karma.

45 For a list of six kinds of *mukti*, see Brown 1974: 109ff.

46 And uniquely, so far as I am aware, for the Arya Samaj in a theological context (see Chapter 3). According to Swami Dayananda, the founder of the Samaj, there is no permanent liberation from *saṃsāra*. One may reach the heavenly company of God as a reward for one's good deeds, but when this is expended, there is a return to the cycle of rebirth.

Select glossary

ahiṃsā:	non-injury.
amāvāsyā:	day of the new moon.
ānanda:	bliss; often contrasted with *sukha*.
artha:	object; meaning; something of substance, property; one of the *puruṣārtha*s.
āśrama:	stage of life: traditionally four for the twice-born (*dvija*) – brahmacarya, vānaprasthya, gārhasthya, saṃnyāsa.
asura:	anti-god; cf. *deva*.
ātman:	self; spirit.
avatāra:	literally 'descent': in corporeal form of a/the deity or a superhuman being.
bhajan:	devotional hymn.
bhakti (bhakta):	devotion, attachment; (devotee).
Brahmā:	a particular *deva* to whom is ascribed, in folklore, the fashioning of the world.
Brahman (Brahma):	literally, 'the Great One': the supreme spiritual being.
darśana:	intellectual perspective or orientation; a 'viewing' of the deity or some other great personage in his or her presence.
deva (devī):	celestial; god; a persona or personification of the transcendent; sometimes the supreme Being (devī=feminine of deva).
dharma:	order; code of practice; religion; virtue; characteristic.
duḥkha:	suffering; grief; usually paired with *sukha*.
dvija:	twice-born.
guṇa:	constituent of *prakṛti*: quality.
guru:	spiritual preceptor, teacher to whom one defers.

iṣṭadevatā:	one's chosen (form of the) deity.
jāti:	birth; class, kind; socio-religious status, position: in this sense cf. with *varṇa*.
kāma:	desire: concupiscence; lust.
karma:	ritual action; action; acquired merit or demerit.
līlā:	an unnecessitated or spontaneous display.
liṅga:	distinctive mark; phallus.
mantra:	empowering or transformative religious utterance/formula.
māyā:	wondrous power; deceptiveness.
mokṣa:	spiritual liberation from worldliness.
nivṛtti:	withdrawal from the world; cf. *pravṛtti*.
Om:	mantric syllable or utterance.
paddhati:	authoritative manual.
pāṭha (pāṭhaka):	(religious) recitation; (reciter).
prakṛti:	non-spiritual cosmogonic principle comprised of the three *guṇa*s: sattva, rajas and tamas.
pravṛtti:	engagement with the world; cf. *nivṛtti*.
pūjā:	(image) worship.
puruṣa:	(male) person; spirit.
puruṣārtha:	accredited goal in life.
ṛṣi:	(usually ancient) seer, sage.
śabda:	word; speech, language; testimony.
sādhaka:	follower of a *sādhana*; religious devotee.
sādhana:	spiritual discipline.
śakti:	literally 'power, energy'; power as or of the Goddess (Devī).
saṃpradāya:	teaching or hermeneutic tradition/ denomination.
saṃsāra:	cycle of existence; flow of life.
saṃskāra:	a perfecting ritual in various events, phases or stages of life; (mental) impression.
sanātana (sanatanist):	eternal; (follower of sanātana *dharma*).
śāstra:	authoritative text.
satya:	being; reality; truth.
smārta:	pertaining to or derived from *smṛti*.
smṛti:	tradition; remembrance.
śraddhā:	trust, confidence, faith.
śrāddha:	death rites.
śrauta:	pertaining to or derived from *śruti*.
śruti:	canonical scripture, usually equated with the Veda.

sukha: pleasure, happiness; see *duḥka* and *ānanda*.
sūtra: (authoritative) aphorism or text of aphorisms.
tantra: esoteric ritual/ritual path; text concerning such a ritual or path.
tapas: ascetic energy or power.
tīrtha: religious crossing or ford.
vāc: sacred utterance; speech.
vāhana: deity's animal-mount/associate.
varṇa: literally, 'appearance, colour, form'; one of the four basic socio-religious orders or 'castes', i.e. Brāhmaṇa (Brahmin), Kṣatriya, Vaiśya, Śūdra.
varṇa-saṃkara: caste-miscegenation.
yajña: sacrificial rite.
yoga (yogī): integrative discipline/path; union; (practitioner of yoga).
yoni: source; womb; female sexual organ.

Select bibliography

Some titles are included which are not mentioned in the book.

Abhishiktananda, S. *Guru and Disciple*, SPCK, London, 1974.

Abhyankar, V. S. (ed.) *Srī-Bhāṣya of Rāmānujāchārya*, Government Central Press, Bombay, 1914.

—— (ed.) *Sarva-Darśana-Saṃgraha of Sāyaṇa-Mādhava*, The Bhandarkar Oriental Research Institute, Poona, 1924.

Allchin, B. and Allchin, R. *The Rise of Civilisation in Indian and Pakistan*, Cambridge University Press, Cambridge, 1982.

Allchin, F. R. 'Indo-Aryan and Aryan' in *Ancient Ceylon* (Journal of the Archaeological Survey Department of Sri Lanka), No. 10, 1990, Vol. 4.

Alper, H. P. (ed.) *Understanding Mantras*, State University of New York Press, Albany, 1989.

Alston, A. J. *The Thousand Teachings of Śaṃkara* (transliterated text, English translation and comment), Shanti Sadan, London, 1990.

Altekar, A. S. *The Position of Women in Hindu Civilization*, Motilal Banarsidass, Delhi, 1959 (2nd edn).

Ambler, R. 'Gandhi's concept of truth' in *Gandhi's Significance for Today: The Elusive Legacy*, J. Hick and L. C. Hempel (eds), Macmillan, London, 1989.

Ayrookuzhiel, A. *The Sacred in Popular Hinduism: An Empirical Study in Chirakkal, North Malabar*, The Christian Literature Society, Madras, 1983.

—— 'Dalit theology: A movement of counter-culture' in *Towards a Dalit Theology*, ed. M. E. Prabhakar, Indian Society for the Propagation of Christian Knowledge, Delhi, 1989.

Bailey, G. 'On the object of study in Puranic research: Three recent books on the Puranas', in *Asian Studies Association of Australia Review*, April 1987.

Balslev, A. N. *A Study of Time in Indian Philosophy*, Otto Harrassowitz, Wiesbaden, 1983.

Bandyopadhyay, S. and Mignon, C. *Maṅgalbārtā*, a translation, Xavier Press, Calcutta, 1984.

Banerjea, J. N. *The Development of Hindu Iconography*, University of Calcutta, Calcutta, 1956.

Barrett, D. B. *The World Christian Encyclopedia*, Oxford University Press, Oxford, 1982.

Basham, A. L. *The Wonder that was India*, 3d rev edn, Sidgwick & Jackson, London, 1967.

Bhandarkar, R. G. *Vaiṣṇavism, Śaivism and Minor Religious Systems* in Collected Works, Vol IV, eds N. B. Utgikar and V. J. Paranjpe, Poona, 1929.

Biderman, S. and Scharfstein, B-A. (eds) *Rationality in Question: On Eastern and Western Views of Rationality*, Brill, Leiden, 1989.

Bissoondoyal, B. *Hindu Scriptures*, G. Gangaram, Port Louis, Mauritius, 1979.

Blackburn, S. H., Claus, P. J., Flueckiger, J. B. and Wadley, S. S. (eds) *Oral Epics in India*, University of California Press, Berkeley, 1989.

Brockington, J. L. *The Sacred Thread: Hinduism in its Continuity and Diversity*, Edinburgh University Press, 1981.

—— *Righteous Rama: The Evolution of an Epic*, Oxford University Press, Delhi, 1984.

—— 'The Purāṇas – priestly or popular', in *Haryana Sahitya Academy Journal of Indological Studies*, 2, 1987.

Brown, C. M. *God as Mother: An Historical and Theological Study of the Brahmavaivarta Purāṇa*, Claude Stark & Co., Hartford, Vermont, 1974.

Brown, J. M. *Gandhi: Prisoner of Hope*, Yale University Prss, London and New Haven, 1989.

Carman, J. B. *The Theology of Rāmānuja: An Essay in Interreligious Understanding*, Yale University Press, London and New Haven, 1976.

Chatterjee, M. *Gandhi's Religious Thought*, Macmillan, London, 1983.

Chaudhuri, N. C. *Hinduism: A Religion to Live By*, Chatto & Windus, London, 1979.

Clooney, F. X. *Thinking Ritually (Rediscovering the Pūrva Mīmāṃsā of Jaimini)*, Publications of the de Nobili Research Library, Vienna, and Motilal Banarsidass, Delhi, 1990.

Courtright, P. B. *Gaṇeśa: Lord of Obstacles, Lord of Beginnings*, Oxford University Press, Oxford, 1985.

Coward, H. G. *Sphoṭa Theory of Language*, Motilal Banarsidass, Delhi, 1980.

—— (ed.) *Modern Indian Responses to Religious Pluralism*, State University of New York Press, Albany, 1987.

Coward, H. G., Lipner, J. J. and Young, K. K. *Hindu Ethics: Purity, Abortion, and Euthanasia*, State University of New York Press, Albany, 1989.

Crawford, C. *Ram Mohan Roy: Social, Political, and Religious Reform in 19th Century India*, Paragon House Publishers, New York, 1987.

Damen, F. L. *Crisis and Religious Renewal in the Brahmo Samaj (1860–1884): A Documentary Study of the Emergence of the 'New Dispensation' under Keshab Chandra Sen*, Katholieke Universiteit, Leuven, 1983.

Dasgupta, S. N. *History of Indian Philosophy*, 5 vols., Cambridge University Press, Cambridge, 1922–55.

Dayananda Sarasvati, S. *See under* Upadhyay, Ganga Prasad, and Jordens.

de Bary, W. T. (ed.) *Sources of Indian Tradition*, 2 vols., Columbia University Press, New York, 1958.

Deutsch, E. *The Bhagavad Gītā: Translated, With Introduction and Critical Essays*, Holt, Rinehart & Winston, New York, 1968.

Dhavamony, M. *Love of God According to Śaiva Siddhānta*, Oxford University Press, Oxford, 1971.

Dimock, E. and Levertov, D. *In Praise of Krishna: Songs from the Bengali*, Anchor Books, Doubleday & Co., New York, 1967.

Doniger, W. and Smith, B. K. *The Laws of Manu*, with Introduction and Notes, Harmondsworth, Penguin Classics, 1991.

D'Sa, F. X. *Śabdaprāmāṇyam in Śabara and Kumārila*, Vol. VII of publications of the de Nobili Research Library, ed. G. Oberhammer, Vienna, 1980.

Dubois, Abbé J. A. *A Description of the Character, Manners, and Customs of the People of India; And of their Institutions Religious and Civil*, ed. G. V. Pope, Alan & Co., London, 1862 (2nd edn).

Eck, D. *Banaras: City of Light*, Routledge & Kegan Paul, London, 1983.

Eggeling, J. *The Śatapatha Brāhmaṇa* (Mādhyaṃdina Recension), trans into English in 5 vols., in *The Sacred Books of the East*, general editor Max Müller, The Clarendon Press, Oxford, 1882.

Falk, H. Soma I and II, in *Bulletin of the School of Oriental and African Studies*, Lll, 1, 1989.

Farquhar, J. N. *The Crown of Hinduism*, Humphrey Milford, Oxford University Press, Oxford, 1913.

Feuerstein, G. *Textbook of Yoga*, Rider & Co., London, 1975.

—— *The Yoga-Sūtra of Patañjali: A New Translation and Commentary*, Dawson & Sons, Folkestone, 1979.

Fitzgerald, J. L. 'The great epic of India as religious rhetoric: A fresh look at the Mahābhārata' in *Journal of the American Academy of Religion*, vol. LI, 4, 1983.

Flattery, D. S. and Schwartz, M. *Haoma and Harmaline: The Botanical Identity of the Indo-Iranian Sacred Hallucinogen 'Soma' and its Legacy in Religion, Language and Middle Eastern Folklore*, University of California Press, Berkeley, 1989.

Fuller, C. J. *The Camphor Flame: Popular Hinduism and Society in India*, Princeton University Press, Princeton, 1992.

Gelberg, S. J. *Hare Krishna, Hare Krishna: Five Distinguished Scholars on the Krishna Movement in the West*, Grove Press Inc, New York, 1983.

Ghosh, J. C. *Bengali Literature*, Oxford University Press, London, 1948.

Gispert-Sauch, G. (ed.) *God's Word Among Men*, Vidyajyoti Institute of Religious Studies, Delhi, 1973.

—— 'An inquiry into the Upanishadic prayer: "From the Unreal Lead Me to the Real"', in Lars Thunberg, Moti Lal Pandit and Carl Vilh Fogh (eds), *Dialogue in Action: Essays in Honour of Johannes Aagarrd*, Prajna Publications, New Delhi, 1988.

Godman, D. (ed.) *Be As You Are: The Teachings of Sri Ramana Maharshi*, Arkana (Penguin), Harmondsworth, 1985.

Goldman, R. P. (ed.) *The Rāmāyaṇa of Vālmīki: An Epic of Ancient India*, Princeton University Press, Princeton, 1984 on.

Gonda, J. *Aspects of Early Viṣṇuism*, N. V. A. Oosthoek's Uitgevers Mij, Utrecht, 1954.

—— *Vedic Literature (Saṃhitās and Brāhmaṇas)*, vol. I.1 of *A History of Indian Literature*, Gonda, J. (ed.) Otto Harrassowitz, Wiesbaden, 1975.

—— *The Ritual Sūtras*, vol. I.2 of *A History of Indian Literature*, Gonda, J. (ed.), Otto Harrossowitz, Wiesbaden, 1975.

—— *Vedic Ritual: The Non-Solemn Rites*, E. J. Brill, Leiden-Koln, 1980.

Gosling, D. 'Scientific perspectives on rebirth' in *Religion*, 4, 1974.

Growse, F. S. *The Ramayana of Tulasidasa*, Motilal Banarsidass, Delhi, 1987, 2nd rev edn.

Gupta, S., Hoens, D. J. and Goudriaan, T. *Hindu Tantrism*, E. J. Brill, Leiden, 1979.

Halbfass, W. *India and Europe: An Essay in Understanding*, State University of New York Press, Albany, 1988.

Hara, M. 'The king as husband of the earth', in *Asiatische Studient Etudes Asiatiques*, xxvii.2, 1973.

—— 'The holding of the hair (*Keśa Grahaṇa*)', in *Acta Orientalia*, 47, 1986.

Hardy, F. 'The Tamil Veda of a *Śūdra* saint (The Śrīvaiṣṇava interpretation of Nammāḻvār)', in G. Krishna (ed.), *Contributions to South Asian Studies I*, Oxford University Press, Delhi, 1979.

—— *Viraha-Bhakti: The Early History of Kṛṣṇa Devotion in South India*, Oxford University Press, Oxford, 1983.

Hatto, A. T. (ed.) *Traditions of Heroic and Epic Poetry*, vol. 1, The Modern Humanities Research Association, London, 1980.

Hawley, J. S. and Juergensmeyer, M. *Songs of the Saints of India*, Oxford University Press, Oxford and New York, 1988.

Hawley, J. S. and Wulff, D. M. (eds) *The Divine Consort: Rādhā and the Goddesses of India*, Motilal Banarsidass edn, Delhi, 1984.

Hess, L. 'Kabīr's rough rhetoric' in K. Schomer and W. McLeod (eds), *The Sants: Studies in a Devotional Tradition of India*, Motilal Banarsidass, Delhi, 1987.

Hick, J. and Hempel, L. C. (eds) *Gandhi's Significance for Today: The Elusive Legacy*, Macmillan, London, 1989.

Hill, W. D. P. *The Holy Lake of the Acts of Rāma*, Oxford University Press, Oxford, 1952.

Hiltebeitel, A. (ed.) *Criminal Gods and Demon Devotees: Essays on the Guardians of Popular Hinduism*, State University of New York Press, Albany, 1989.

Hiriyanna, M. *Outlines of Indian Philosophy*, Allen & Unwin, London, 1932.

Hiro, D. *The Untouchables of India*, Minority Rights Group, Report No. 26, London, 1982.

Hirst, J. G. S. *The Teacher and the Avatāra: Mediators of Realisation in Śaṃkara's Advaitin Theology*, Cambridge University Ph.D. Thesis, 1983.

Hooker, R. *Themes in Hinduism and Christianity*, Verlag Peter Lang, New York, 1989.

Howard, W. *Sāmavedic Chant*, Yale University Press, London and New Haven, 1977.

Iyer, R. *The Moral and Political Writings of Mahatma Gandhi*, 3 vols., Clarendon Press, Oxford, 1986–7.

Jagadananda, S. *Upadeśa Sāhasrī: A Thousand Teachings*, Sri Ramakrishna Math, Mylapore, Madras, 1970 (4th edn).

Jaiswal, S. *The Origin and Development of Vaiṣṇavism*, Munshiram Manoharlal, Delhi, 1967.

Jameson, A. S. *Gangaguru: The Public and Private Life of a Brahman Community*, Oxford University D.Phil., 1976.

Jha, G. *The Prabhākara School of Pūrvamīmāṃsā*, University of Allahabad, 1911.

Johnson, W. J. *The Bhagavad Gita*, Oxford University Press, Oxford, 1994.

Jordens, J. T. F. *Dayānanda Sarasvatī: His Life and Ideas*, Oxford University Press, Delhi, 1978.

Joshi, B. R. *Untouchable: Voices of the Dalit Liberation Movement*, Zed Books and the Minority Rights Group, London, 1986.

Kahrs, E. 'Yāska's *nirukta*: The quest for a new interpretation' in *Indologica Taurinensia*, vol. XII, 1984.

Kane, P. V. *History of Dharmaśāstra*, 5 vols., Bhandarkar Oriental Research Institute, Poona, 1930–62 (1st edn).

Kangle, R. P. *The Kauṭilīya Arthaśāstra* in 3 Parts (Part I: the Sanskrit text 1960; Part II: Translation with notes, 1963; Part III: A Study, 1965), University of Bombay, Bombay, 1960–5.

Keith, A. B. *The Religion and Philosophy of the Veda and Upanishads*, vols. 31–2 of The Harvard Oriental Series ed. C. R. Lanman *et al.* 1925; reprinted by Motilal Banarsidass, Delhi, in 2 vols., 1970.

—— *The Karma-Mīmāṃsā*, 1921, republished, Oriental Books, Reprint Corporation, New Delhi, 1978.

Killingley, D. H. *Rammohun Roy's Interpretation of the Vedānta*, School of Oriental and African Studies, London, 1977 (Unpublished Ph.D. thesis).

—— *The Only True God: Works on Religion by Rammohun Roy* (selected and translated from Bengali and Sanskrit), Grevatt & Grevatt, Newcastle upon Tyne, 1982.

—— '*Oṃ*: The sacred syllable in the Veda' in J. Lipner, assisted by D. Killingley (eds), *A Net Cast Wide: Investigations into Indian Thought in Memory of David Friedman*, Grevatt & Grevatt, Newcastle upon Tyne, 1986.

—— 'Yoga Sūtra IV .2–3 and Vivekananda's interpretation of evolution' in *Journal of Indian Philosophy*, 18, 1990.

—— 'Varṇa and caste in Hindu apologetic' in *Hindu Ritual and Society*, by D. Killingley, W. Menski, and S. Firth, Grevatt & Grevatt, Newcastle upon Tyne, 1991.

Kinsley, D. *The Sword and the Flute*, University of California Press, 1977.

—— *The Divine Player: A Study of Kṛṣṇa Līlā*, Motilal Banarsidass, Delhi, 1979.

—— *Hindu Goddesses: Visions of the Divine Feminine in the Hindu Religious Tradition*, Motilal Banarsidass, Delhi, 1987.

Klostermaier, K. K. 'Contemporary conceptions of Karma and rebirth among North Indian Vaiṣṇavas', in R. W. Neufeldt (ed.), *Karma and Rebirth: Post Classical Developments*, State University of New York Press, Albany, 1986.

—— *A Survey of Hinduism*, State University of New York Press, Albany, 1989.

Koelman, G. M. *Patanjala Yoga: From Related Ego to Absolute Self*, Papal Athenaeum, Poona, 1970.

Kopf, D. *The Brahmo Samaj and the Shaping of the Modern Indian Mind*, Princeton University Press, 1979.

Kramrisch, S. *The Presence of Śiva*, Motilal Banarsidass, Delhi, 1988.

Krishna, G. (ed.) *Contributions to South Asian Studies I*, Oxford University Press, Delhi, 1979.

Krishan, Y. 'The Vedic origins of the doctrine of Karma', in *South Asian Studies*, vol. 4, 1988.

Kumar, S. *The Vision of Kabīr: Love Poems of a 15th Century Weaver-sage*, Alpha & Omega Books, Concord, Ontario, and Motilal Banarsidass, Delhi, 1984.

Küng, H., van Ess, H. and von Stietencron, H. (eds) *Christianity and the World Religions: Paths of Dialogue with Islam, Hinduism, and Buddhism*, Collins (Fount Paperbacks), London, 1987.

Larson, G. J. *Classical Sāṃkhya: An Interpretation of its History and Meaning*, Motilal Banarsidass, 2nd edn, Delhi, 1979.

Leslie, I. J. *The Perfect Wife: The Orthodox Hindu Woman According to the Strīdharmapaddhati of Tryambakayajvan*, Oxford University Press, Delhi, 1989.

—— *Roles and Rituals for Hindu Women*, Pinter Publishers, London, 1991.

Lipner, J. J. 'The Christian and Vedantic theories of originative causality: a study in transcendence and immanence', in *Philosophy East and West*, January 1978.

—— *The Face of Truth: A Study of Meaning and Metaphysics in the Vedāntic Theology of Rāmānuja*, Macmillan, London, and State University of New York Press, Albany, 1986.

—— 'A modern Indian Christian response' in H. G. Coward (ed.), *Modern Indian Responses to Religious Pluralism*, State University of New York Press, Albany, 1987.

—— 'Radhakrishnan on religion and religions' in G. Parthasarathi and D. P. Chattopadhyaya (eds), *Radhakrishnan Centenary Volume*, Oxford University Press, Delhi, 1989.

—— 'The classical Hindu view on abortion and the moral status of the unborn' in *Hindu Ethics: Purity, Abortion, and Euthanasia*, H. G. Coward, J. J. Lipner and K. K. Young, State University of New York Press, Albany, 1989.

Lipner, J. J. with Killingley, D. H. (eds) *A Net Cast Wide: Investigations into Indian Thoughts in Memory of David Friedman*, Grevatt & Grevatt, Newcastle upon Tyne, 1986.

Lorenzen, D. N. *The Kāpālikas and Kālāmukhas: Two Lost Śaivite Sects*, Thomson Press (India) Ltd, New Delhi, 1972.

—— 'The kabīr-panth and social protest' in K. Schomer and W. H. McLeod (eds) *The Sants: Studies in a Devotional Tradition of India*, Motilal Banarsidass, Delhi, 1987.

Lott, E. *Vedantic Approaches to God*, Macmillan Press, London, 1980.

Lutgendorf, P. 'My Hanuman is bigger than yours', in *History of Religions*, forthcoming.

McGregor, R. S. *Hindi Literature from its Beginnings to the Nineteenth Century*, vol. VIII.6 of Gonda, J., *A History of Indian Literature*, Otto Harrassowitz, Wiesbaden, 1984.

Mallory, J. P. *In Search of the Indo-Europeans: Language, Archaeology and Myth*, Thames & Hudson, London, 1989.

Marglin, F. A. *Wives of the God-King: The Rituals of the Devadāsīs of Puri*, Oxford University Press, Oxford, 1985.

Marriott, M. (ed.) *Village India: Studies in the Little Community*, University of Chicago Press, Chicago, 1955.
Marshall, P. J. *The British Discovery of Hinduism in the Eighteenth Century*, Cambridge University Press, Cambridge, 1970.
Masters, J. *The Deceivers*, Penguin, 1955.
Matas, E. A. *Rgvedic Society*, E. J. Brill, Leiden and New York, 1991.
Matilal, B. K. 'Dharma and rationality' in S. Biderman and B-A. Scharfstein (eds), *Rationality in Question: On Eastern and Western Views of Rationality*, E. J. Brill, Leiden, 1989.
Mayeda, S. *A Thousand Teachings*, annotated English translation of Śaṃkara's *Upadeśasāhasrī*, Tokyo, 1979.
Michell, G. *The Hindu Temple: An Introduction to its Meaning and Forms*, Elek Books Ltd, London, 1977.
Miller, B. S. *Love Song of the Dark Lord: Jayadeva's Gītagovinda*, Columbia University Press, New York, 1977.
Miller, D. M. and Wertz, D. C. *Hindu Monastic Life: the Monks and Monasteries of Bhubaneswar*, McGill-Queen's University Press, Montreal and London, 1976.
Mitter, P. *Much Maligned Monsters: History of European Reactions to Indian Art*, Clarendon Press, Oxford, 1977.
Morgan, K. W. *The Religion of the Hindus*, Ronald Press Co, Oxford, 1953.
Naipaul, V. S. *An Area of Darkness*, Andre Deutsch, London, 1964.
—— *India: A Million Mutinies Now*, Heinemann, London, 1990.
Nair, P. T. (ed.) *Calcutta in the Nineteenth Century (Company's Days)* Firma KLM Private Ltd, Calcutta, 1989.
Neeval, W. G. 'The transformation of Śrī Rāmakrishna' in B. L. Smith (ed.) *Hinduism: New Essays in the History of Religions*, E. J. Brill, Leiden, 1976.
Neufeldt, R. W. (ed.) *Karma and Rebirth: Post Classical Developments*, State University of New York Press, Albany, 1986.
O'Connell, J. T. 'The word "Hindu" in Gauḍīya Vaiṣṇava texts' in *Journal of the American Oriental Society*, 93.3, 1973.
O'Flaherty, W. D. *Hindu Myths: A Sourcebook translated from the Sanskrit*, Penguin, 1975.
—— *Karma and Rebirth in Classical Indian Traditions*, University of California Press, Berkeley, 1980.
—— *The Origins of Evil in Hindu Mythology*, University of California Press, 1976; Paperback edition 1980.
—— *Śiva: The Erotic Ascetic*, 2nd edn, Oxford University Press, Oxford, 1981.
—— (ed.) *Textual Sources for the Study of Hinduism*, Manchester University Press, Manchester, 1988.
Olivelle, P. 'The notion of Āśrama in the Dharmasūtras' in *Wiener Zeitschrift Für De Kunde Südasiens Und Archiv Für Indische Philosophie*, 18, 1974.
Openshaw, J. *'Bāuls' of West Bengal: with special reference to Rāj Khyāpā and his followers*, London University Ph.D. Thesis, 1994.
—— 'Rāj Kṛṣṇa: Perspectives on the worlds of a little-known Bengali guru' in R. K. Ray (ed.), forthcoming.
Orr, W. G. 'Armed religious ascetics in Northern India', *Bulletin of the John Rylands Library*, 24, 1, April 1940.
Padoux, A. *Vāc: The Concept of the Word in Selected Hindu Tantras*, trans. J. Gontier, State University of New York Press, Albany, 1990.
Pandey, R. B. *Hindu Saṃskāras: Socio-Religious Study of the Hindu Sacraments*, Motilal Banarsidass, Delhi, 2nd rev. edn, 1969.

Panikkar, R. *The Vedic Experience: Mantramañjarī (An Anthology of The Vedas for Modern Man and Contemporary Celebration)*, Darton, Longman & Todd, London, 1977.
Parthasarathi, G. and Chattopadhyaya, D. P. (eds) *Radhakrishnan Centenary Volume*, Oxford University Press, Delhi, 1989.
Prabhakar, M. E. (ed.) *Toward a Dalit Theology*, Indian Society for the Propagation of Christian Knowledge, Delhi, 1989.
Puthiadam, I. '"Svatantro Viṣṇuḥ" – an analysis of the Dvaita Vedānta concept of divine independence' in G. Gispert-Sauch (ed.), *God's Word Among Men*, Vidyajyoti Institute of Religious studies, Delhi, 1973.
Radhakrishnan, S. *The Hindu View of Life*, Allen & Unwin, London 1927; Unwin Paperbacks edn, 1980.
—— *The Principal Upaniṣads*, Allen & Unwin Ltd, London, 1953.
—— *An Idealist View of Life*, Unwin Books edn, 1961.
Raghavachar, S. S. *Śrimad Viṣṇu-Tattva-Vinirṇaya of Śrī Madhvācārya*, Sri Ramakrishna Ashrama, Mangalore, 2nd edn, 1971 (contains English translation).
Ramana Maharshi, S. *Talks with Sri Ramana Maharshi*, 3 vols, T. N. Venkataraman, Sri Ramanasram, Tiruvannamalai, n.d.
Ramanujan, A. K. *Speaking of Śiva*, Penguin Books, 1973.
Ray, R. K. *Mind, Body and Society; Life and Mentality in Colonial Bengal*, Oxford University Press, forthcoming.
Reichenbach, B. R. *The Law of Karma: A Philosophical Study*, Macmillan, London, 1990.
Robinson, J. D. *The Worship of Clay Images in Bengal*, Oxford University D.Phil., 1983.
Rocher, L. *The Purāṇas*, vol. II.3 of Gonda, J. (ed.) *A History of Indian Literature*, Otto Harrassowitz, Wiesbaden, 1986.
Rochford, E. B. jr. *Hare Krishna in America*, Rutgers University Press, New Brunswick, NJ, 1985.
Sachau, E. C. *Alberuni's India: An Account of the Religious Philosophy, Literature, Geography, Chronology, Astronomy, Customs, Laws and Astrology of India about AD 1030* (2 vols), English edn, Trubner & Co, London, 1888.
Sanderson, A. 'Saivism and the tantric traditions' in *The World's Religions*, ed. S. Sutherland *et al.*, Routledge & Kegan Paul, London, 1988.
—— 'The visualizations of the deities of the Trika', in A. Padoux (ed.), *L'Image Divine: Culte et Méditation dans L'Hindouisme*, Centre national de la Recherche Scientifique, Paris, 1990.
Sastry, A. A. *The Vishnu Sahasranama*, translation, Theosophical Publishing House, Adyar, Madras, 1927, 2nd edn.
Schomer, K. and McLeod, W. H. (eds) *The Sants: Studies in a Devotional Tradition of India*, Motilal Banarsidass, Delhi, 1987.
Sen, D. *The Bengali Rāmāyaṇas*, University of Calcutta, Calcutta, 1920.
Sharma, A. *The Puruṣārthas – A Study in Hindu Axiology*, Asian Studies Center, Michigan State University, East Lansing, 1982.
Shastri, H. P. *The Ramayana of Valmiki*, 3 vols, trans. from Sanskrit, Shantisadan, London, 1976 (3rd edn).
Shastri, J. L. (ed.) *Brahmāṇḍa Purāṇa*, Motilal Banarsidass, Delhi, 1973.

Singer, M. (ed.) *Krishna: Myths, Rites, and Attitudes*, University of Chicago Press, Chicago, 1968.
Smith, B. L. (ed.) *Hinduism: New Essays in the History of Religions*, E. J. Brill, Leiden, 1976.
Smith, J. D. 'The two Sanskrit epics' in *Traditions of Heroic and Epic Poetry*, ed. A. T. Hatto, The Modern Humanities Research Association, London, 1980.
—— *The Epic of Pābūjī: A Study, Transcription and Translation*, Cambridge University Press, Cambridge, 1991.
Smith, W. C. *Questions of Religious Truth*, Victor Gollancz Ltd, London, 1967.
—— *The Meaning and End of Religion*, SPCK, London, 1978.
Smith, W.L. *The Myth of Manasā: A Study in the Popular Hinduism of Medieval Bengal*, Published by the author, Stockholm, 1976.
Srinivas, M. N. 'The social system of a Mysore village' in *Village India: Studies in the Little Community*, ed. M. Marriott, University of Chicago Press, Chicago, 1955.
Staal, F. *Agni: The Vedic Ritual of the Fire Altar*, 2 vols, Asian Humanities Press, Berkeley, 1983.
Stevenson, I. *Twenty Cases Suggestive of Reincarnation*, University Press of Virginia, Virginia 1974 (2nd edn, revised and enlarged).
Stutley, M. and Stutley, J. *A Dictionary of Hinduism: Its Mythology, Folklore and Development 1500 BC–AD 1500*, Routledge & Kegan Paul, London, 1977.
Sutherland, S., Houlden, L., Clarke, P. and Hardy, F. *The World's Religions*, Routledge & Kegan Paul, 1988.
Tahtinen, U. *Ahiṃsā: Non-violence in Indian Tradition*, Rider & Co., London, 1976.
Thapar, R. *A History of India*, vol. 1, Penguin Books, Harmondsworth, 1966.
Thunberg, L. *et al.* (eds) *Dialogue in Action: Essays in Honour of Johannes Aagarrd*, Prajna Publications, New Delhi, 1988.
Timm, J. 'Vallabha's Commentary (?) on the Bhagavad Gītā', unpublished paper, 1990.
Trautmann, T. R. *Kauṭilya and the Arthaśāstra: A Statistical Investigation of the Authorship and Evolution of the Text*, Leiden, E. J. Brill, 1971.
Tyagisananda, S. *Aphorisms on the Gospel of Divine Love or Nārada Bhaktisūtras*, Ramakrishna Math, Madras, 1972, 2nd edn.
Upadhyay, B. 'The one-centredness of the Hindu race', trans. from the Bengali by J. Lipner, in *Vidyajyoti (Journal of Theological Reflection)*, Delhi, October 1981.
Upadhyay, G. P. *The Light of Truth, English Translation of Swami Dayananda's Satyarth Prakasha*, The Kala Press, Allahabad, 1956.
van Buitenen, J. A. B. *Rāmānuja's Vedārthasaṃgraha*, Deccan College Postgraduate and Research Institute, Poona, 1956 (contains English translation).
—— *The Mahābhārata*, English translation (incomplete), The University of Chicago Press, Chicago, 1973.
Vatsyayan, K. *Classical Indian Dance in Literature and the Arts*, Sangeet Natak Akademi, New Delhi, 1968.

Vattanky, J. *Gaṅgeśa's Philosophy of God*, The Adyar Library and Research Centre, Madras, 1984.

Vesci, U. M. *Heat and Sacrifice in the Vedas*, Motilal Banarsidass, Delhi, 1985.

von Stietencron, H. 'Hindu perspectives' in H. Kung, J. van Ess and H. von Stietencron (eds), *Christianity and the World Religions: Paths of Dialogue with Islam, Hinduism, and Buddhism*, Collins (Fount Paperbacks), London, 1987.

Weiss, M. G. '*Caraka Saṃhitā* on the doctrine of karma' in *Karma and Rebirth in Classical Indian Traditions*, ed. W. D. O'Flaherty, University of California Press, Berkeley, 1980.

Werner, K. 'The Vedic concept of human personality and its destiny' in *Journal of Indian Philosophy*, 5, 1978.

Whaling, F. *The Rise of the Religious Significance of Rāma*, Motilal Banarsidass, Delhi, 1980.

Wheeler, M. *The Indus Civilisation*, Cambridge University Press, 3rd edn, 1968.

Whicher, I. *A Study of Patañjali's Definition of Yoga: Uniting Theory and Practice in the Yoga-Sūtras*, Cambridge University Ph.D., 1992.

Williams, R. B. *A New Face of Hinduism: The Swaminarayan Religion*, Cambridge University Press, Cambridge, 1984.

Wolcott, L. T. 'Hanumān: The power-dispensing monkey in North Indian folk religion' in *Journal of Asian Studies*, xxxvii, 4, August 1978.

Young, R. F. *Resistant Hinduism: Sanskrit Sources on Anti-Christian Apologetics in Early Nineteenth-Century India*, Publications of the de Nobili Research Library, Vienna, 1981.

Zaehner, R. C. *Hinduism*, Oxford University Press, Oxford, 1966.

—— *The Bhagavadgītā*, Oxford University Press, Oxford, 1969.

—— *Our Savage God*, Collins, London, 1974.

Zimmer, H. *Myths and Symbols in Indian Art and Civilization*, edited for publication by J. Campbell, Harper Torchbook edn, New York, 1962.

Index